T0337410

The New Frontier

The New Frontier

Merit vs. Caste in the Indian IT Sector

Marilyn Fernandez

OXFORD
UNIVERSITY PRESS

OXFORD
UNIVERSITY PRESS

Oxford University Press is a department of the University of Oxford.
It furthers the University's objective of excellence in research, scholarship,
and education by publishing worldwide. Oxford is a registered trademark of
Oxford University Press in the UK and in certain other countries.

Published in India by
Oxford University Press
2/11 Ground Floor, Ansari Road, Daryaganj, New Delhi 110 002, India

© Oxford University Press 2018

ISBN-13 (print edition): 978-0-19-947949-8
ISBN-10 (print edition): 0-19-947949-6

ISBN-13 (eBook): 978-0-19-909171-3
ISBN-10 (eBook): 0-19-909171-4

Typeset in Adobe Jenson Pro 10.5/13
by The Graphics Solution, New Delhi 110 092
Printed in India by Rakmo Press, New Delhi 110 020

To
Peter D'Souza (my husband)
and
Sr. Crystal Fernandez, FMA (my sister)
Thank you for opening up your networks
in the Indian IT world to me.

Contents

Tables

Abbreviations

AIEEE	All India Engineering Entrance Examination
AIIMS	All India Institute of Medical Sciences
AMU	Aligarh Muslim University
ANI	Ancestral North Indians
ASI	Ancestral South Indians
BITS	Birla Institute of Technology & Science
BPO	Business Process Outsourcing
CET	Common Entrance Tests
DBA	data base applications
DTE	Directorate of Technical Education
E-Cities	Electronic Cities
EE	economic empowerment
EEO	Equal Employment Opportunity
EO	equal opportunity
FC	Forward Caste
HR	Human Resource

ICT	Information and Communication Technology
IGNOU	Indira Gandhi National Open University
IHDS	India Human Development Survey
IIIT	Indian Institute of Information Technology
IIM	Indian Institute of Management
IISER	Indian Institute of Science Education and Research
IIT	Indian Institute of Technology
BTech	bachelor's degree in technology
INI	Institute of National Importance
IT	Information Technology
ITES	Information Technology Enabled Services
ITT	Information Technology and Telecom
JEE	Joint Entrance Examination
JNU	Jawaharlal Nehru University
K4D	knowledge for development
KPO	Knowledge Process Outsourcing
MCA	masters in computer applications
MHRD	Ministry of Human Resource Development
MIT	Manipal Institute of Technology
NAAC	National Assessment and Accreditation Council
NCDHR	National Campaign on Dalit Human Rights
NFHS	National Family Health Survey
NIT	National Institute of Technology
OBC	Other Backward Classes
R&D	Research and Development
SC	Scheduled Castes
PPP	Public-Private Partnerships
ST	Scheduled Tribes
UGC	University Grants Commission
VIT	Vellore Institute of Technology
VOCAD	vocation institutes or Vocational Academy

Acknowledgements

My first introduction to social science research was in India. My parents (now deceased), were the first to teach me, through their lived examples, how to observe and make sense of reality around me. As an economics undergraduate at St. Teresa's College in Ernakulum, Kerala, and as a student of master's in sociology at Loyola College of Social Sciences, Trivandrum, Kerala, I learnt the foundations of survey research and theoretically grounded data analyses. Since moving to the USA, those early lessons have stood me well in graduate school at Loyola University of Chicago as well as in my teaching career at Santa Clara University.

As a sociologist, my research has focused on inequalities faced by race/ethnic minorities and women in the USA. Nevertheless, I always wanted to return to India to do a major piece of research about a contemporary issue in the country that got me started on my research journey. This manuscript is a tribute to all my teachers in India and in the USA.

This book has been long in the making. Even though I left India about 40 years ago, I thought I knew India. It was not until I started to talk to people on the Information Technology (IT) ground, that I realized that while there has been a lot of change, much has stayed the same. The first round of key industry informants and knowledge leaders I contacted in the field, pointedly reminded me of the limits to open discussion about topics like caste. During my fieldwork and through the fielding of the web surveys, I was asked, 'Why does an American want to know about how caste operates in India and for that matter in IT?' They preferred that I study work-life balance in family life or women's progress in IT than caste. Caste was too much of a third rail, they indicated. On the other hand, the social activists were excited about the project and were even concerned that I will 'academically' water down the caste tensions that I will uncover in IT. Nevertheless, through it all I learnt valuable lessons, both substantive and methodological, that have shaped this work. I am grateful to all my sources, web survey respondents, key industry informants, knowledge leaders, and social activists for sharing their experiences and perspectives with me. I have tried to use my research judgement to sift through the conflicting and combative arguments, to portray as objectively as possible, how the caste-based inequalities and their deep interplay with class and gender, as seen in the broader society have influenced, and are manifested, in the IT sector in India.

I also owe a debt of gratitude to Santa Clara University, my academic home, for the resources they have made available to me through my academic career and during this project. My husband, Peter D'Souza, and other family members have been generous to say the least, in making ample space for me to work on a project that has been seven years in the making. Thank you for your patience. Last, but not the least, are the manuscript reviewers and the editorial team at Oxford University Press, New Delhi. The reviewers prodded me to sharpen the theoretical arguments and to tell more clearly, the story of how caste dynamics have found their way into a sector that was once heralded to be a model pathway to extricate India from the vestiges of caste inequalities. The editorial team shepherded this book through its publication. Their interest and faith in this work and guidance through the review process kept me going. My gratitude to all.

1 The Indian Information Technology Sector

The New Caste Inequality Frontier

My conversations with IT professionals, and Indians I met in social settings, about the current state of 'caste' in India and in Indian IT sector often went like this:[1] 'Why are we talking about caste in this modern age? Aren't we perpetuating caste distinctions by continuing to talk about it? Isn't it time to get rid of reservations as IT has done? Look at the progress the IT sector has brought to the country! It is "merit, pure merit" that matters, and not caste or any other background'. Such were the assessments, often angry and even dismissive, of many Indians and professionals who work in the IT sector.

These vociferous denials notwithstanding, the Indian IT occupational sector has become a new vector of caste inequality. A singular focus on

---

[1] Responses represent compilations of typical comments by several respondents. In the interest of authentic reporting, the written linguistic style of respondents has been largely left intact, including any grammatical errors, except for minimal changes presented within '[]' to improve readability.

'Merit, Pure Merit', assiduously honed in ideology and in practice, has ironically become responsible for reproducing caste structures in IT. How is this merit constructed and practiced in the IT sector? And how does caste factor into, even if implicitly, the merit constructions? Theoretically guided empirical answers to this set of questions are offered to clarify the broad assertion that Indian IT is the new caste inequality vector.

Pure merit in the Indian IT world, simply put, refers to technical skills and qualifications that are earned through a much heralded Horatio Alger model of personal aspiration, initiative, and hard work. It is the opposite of caste-reservation or caste-earmarked[2] merit—merit acquired through the constitutionally mandated caste-based social redress and justice programs, popularly referred to as reservation and affirmative action.[3] These programs were designed to reduce, and even to eliminate, the vestiges of centuries-long caste-based inequalities. But, how pure is 'pure merit' after all? Because, often left unspoken and not examined in the valorized abstract IT merit discourse is, the 'symbolic[4] merit'—the fact that the cultivation and practice of pure-merit is deeply embedded in, supported by, and 'hidden' behind the social and material privileges of the dominant castes and middle classes. In this sense, symbolically embedded merit is, ironically, not that different after all from reservation merit. But, unlike symbolic merit, reservation or earmarked-merit is foregrounded on minority caste status and authorized by the government, but not culturally accepted in the broader societal context.

---

[2] 'Reservation' and 'earmarked merit' are used interchangeably in the manuscript.

[3] Dalits, the lowest 'scheduled caste' in the caste hierarchy, and other backward classes (OBCs) are eligible for earmarked reservation benefits in public sector education, including IT higher education institutions. See Chapter 1 Appendix for a brief note about the caste system, definitions of caste groups, and state sponsored reservation programs. While the terms Scheduled Castes (SCs) and Scheduled Tribes (STs) are often used in combination as SC/ST, much of the political, social, and academic foci have been on Scheduled Castes (SCs) as is the case in this research. Despite attempts to repeal caste-based reservation, particularly in higher education, a recent Supreme Court judgement of 10 April 2008, has upheld reservation for SC, ST, and OBC students in higher educational institutions (NCDHR 20 July 2008).

[4] Adapted from Bourdieu's culturally authorized symbolic capital (1990; 1995).

It is also quite clear, that to many in the IT sector, *caste* means *caste reservations* and not the caste privileges in which pure merit is embedded. Pure merit advocates are quick to point out that caste, meaning caste reservations, is not part of their organizational landscape. To them, *Reservation or Earmarked Merit*, because of its relaxed entry and promotion criteria, does not quite pass muster on the venerated pure IT merit yardstick; ergo, merit-worthy lower caste Dalits and their counterparts do not qualify as per the pure-merit requirements. The caste-free or caste-neutral claims of the IT organizational social space, hinge on this singular perspective which equates caste with reservation. It is these particular understandings of caste and merit that intermingle to create a 'caste-free IT' occupational space.

On closer scrutiny, there are spaces that open up in the IT merit construction processes for hidden caste privileges to filter through, and colour pure merit with caste undertones. For one, neither admitted nor recognized in the process, is the caste and class privileged embeddedness of pure IT merit dynamics in IT employment and in related educational preparation. Such 'misrecognized' dominance, as per Bourdieu (1990), leaves the construction of valorized 'pure' IT merit to be fiercely defended in a delicate and yet passionately contested balance between *pure IT merit* and *reservation merit*. The competition for scarce, open, or non-reserved[5] seats in elite public sector technical education institutions, along with the steep costs of private technology education and highly sought after IT jobs, has turned into a combative, competitive *blood sport* in which merit is pitted against caste rhetorically and sometimes even physically.

In short, more than half a century after the country gained independence in 1947, caste continues to be an ambivalent issue at best and vehemently combative in its worst moments. In the new private sector, Indian IT, questions about caste are either not raised or become very antagonistic and derisive when raised even in casual conversations. Besides, Indian IT, with its emphasis on the ideology of merit, associated technical skills, and education, is seen by many as the new equalizer and societal savior from a variety of caste inequalities and injustices. But, is it, really? To what extent has the new IT sector transformed India into a 'post-caste' society?

---

[5] As it currently stands, the 'reserved' or earmarked seats for Dalits and OBCs in elite publicly funded educational institutions are not to exceed 50 per cent, leaving only the rest open to dominant castes.

Despite the passionate caste deniers, Indian IT offers an excellent test case for proponents of 'post-caste' India. The caste system in India,[6] with its traditional occupational foundations, is as old as the IT occupational sector is new. Besides, the new Indian IT sector, in contrast to the traditional caste occupations, does not have a traditional caste basis (D'Cruz and Noronha 2013). Does the IT revolution in India represent a new bend in the historical arc of caste inequality? Or has the IT sector become another new site of inequality in India? Even though caste discrimination is officially outlawed in India for over 50 years, caste and associated intersectional privileges continue to permeate the Indian social fabric. Privileges are valued and vociferously defended by members and allies of the upper (or forward)[7] castes, particularly in the face of continued reservation programs in public sector education and employment. Adding fuel to the privilege furor is the fact, that despite equal employment and opportunity initiatives extended by the state, the lowest caste members or the Dalits continue to face deficits in education, employment, or in other life options.

Given this contested caste history, raising and answering caste-related questions are of scholarly, and even economic, significance. Empirical questions about whether caste is relevant to Indian IT, the kind of roles it plays, at what levels, and how it is manifested, are important in the scholarship of inequalities in developing societies. Such research might also offer insights into how the country can begin to more effectively move beyond the existing state sponsored programs to realize the vision of the country's founding fathers. After all, egregious and longstanding inequalities, particularly those based on caste and other ascribed characteristics, are not productive for any society.

In the interest of full disclosure, the original purpose of this research, perhaps naively, was to explore caste diversity, inclusivity, and possible discrimination in the private IT sector, implicit in the prevalence and incorporation rates of different caste groups. But, as preparations for fieldwork were being made, it soon became clear that the Indian IT sector neither maintained data on nor was interested in, and even resisted talking about,

---

[6] More detailed analyses are offered in the section titled 'Merit-Caste Contestations in Historical and Contemporary India', Appendix 1A.1.

[7] Forward Castes (FCs) or Upper Castes (UCs) are used interchangeably throughout the manuscript.

employee caste status. Consequently, the research purpose was altered. It was not possible to test overt/explicit discrimination against SCs, STs, and even OBCs in the private Indian IT sector. Rather, research attention was shifted to an examination of the 'disguised animus'[8] or implicit caste filtering bias in the avowed 'caste neutral' policies and their potential disparate caste impact.

As my conversations with IT professionals and their sector leaders proceeded, it became clear that the *pure IT merit* construction process has become an ironic vehicle for reproduction of caste hierarchies in the IT occupational world. The seemingly caste-neutral merit construction project has turned discriminatory of the lowest castes while privileging the dominant castes and classes. How is this pure merit culture constructed? What are the contours of the merit-caste debate in the IT merit culture production? How do IT professionals articulate caste neutrality of IT merit? How do they make sense of the caste/class laden, symbolic privileges that undergird IT merit? How does the merit construction process limit access to Dalits/the SCs, the 'other', even when the 'others' are qualified on the requisite IT merit markers? And how do Dalits or, for that matter, other less privileged groups, experience the caste stratified IT occupational sector? What lessons can be gleaned about caste inequality from IT women's experiences—another traditionally disadvantaged group? This research monograph is devoted to examining these questions to shed light on whether, and how, the Indian IT sector has become the new vector of inequality.

A Globalization Paradox: Case of Indian Information Technology

Caste and other inequalities in the new IT vector illustrate a globalization paradox. While proponents of globalized information revolution in India have touted the unprecedented prosperity that IT has brought to the society, detractors have been quick to point out its checkered presence. Prosperity, and the idealized Horatio Alger model of IT merit associated with globalization, has not only been over-hyped but has not been shared equally in the IT sector or for that matter in the broader society.

---

[8] SCOTUS Justice Anthony Kennedy in the Fair Housing Act decision of 25 June 2015.

Even the telling of the early history of the Indian IT sector belies the idealized global model of personal and private sector initiatives. The IT sector in India is in reality a product of the joint efforts between the government, individual firms, and industry associations, with the government being a central catalyst in the initial stages of the IT sector at the national and regional levels. India was 'one of the pioneering developing countries to make deliberate policy measures and institutional interventions, as early in the mid-1960s, towards developing an electronic production base in the country' (Joseph 2009: 4). Following a strategy for self-reliant growth, with limited foreign direct investment, public sector units were set up to meet local electronic hardware production needs. It was not until the 1980s and even the 1990s, with hardware trade lagging,[9] that the government liberalized foreign investment and its import-export policies. These economic reforms of 1991 are credited with facilitating the country's transformation into a global hub for Information and Communication Technology (ICT) services. There have been corresponding shifts in ownership profiles of the IT industry, from government to private and foreign firms, and from hardware production to software development (Joseph 2009).

Proponents of Globalization

Proponents of globalization, like Friedman (2005), have argued that information technologies and economic globalization, that these new technologies have made possible, have 'flattened' the global landscape. Globalization has levelled, they posit, the playing field for, and reduced the gap between, developed and developing countries. Globalization is expected to bring unprecedented prosperity to all. On key, the growth in the size and diversity of the Indian IT sector has kept pace with the globalization frenzy of the 2000s.

The Indian IT sector is currently segmented into a broad spectrum of industry groups: Information and Communication Technology (ICT); Information Technology and Telecom (ITT); Information Technology Enabled Services and Solutions (ITES) for banking, insurance, and

---

[9] According to many industry experts, lack of foresight as well as political and social will to invest in the assembly oriented electronic industry has contributed to the decline in Indian hardware production and exports. Looming threats to the Indian software segments include limits placed by USA on outsourcing.

e-commerce; Business Process Outsourcing (BPO); and more recently the Knowledge Process Outsourcing (KPO) units in market research, engineering design, biotech, or pharmaceutical research (Remesh 2009; Sahoo and Patnaik 2009).

The contribution of the IT sector—hardware, software, and services—to the Indian GDP has also steadily grown from 1.2 per cent or US$ 4.8 billion in 1997 to 7.5 per cent in 2012.[10] According to Dubey and Garg (2014), quoting data from NASSCOM, a major trade body and the chamber of commerce of the IT-BPO industry in India, the primary contributors to this growth have been software services, followed by BPOs, and thirdly by software products and engineering services. Revenues from the export and domestic IT-BPO sectors increased six-fold from US$ 16.1 billion in 2003 to 100.8 billion in 2012. About two-thirds of this increase was from exports; the percent export share of revenues went up 8 percentage points from 61 per cent to 69 per cent. In 2015, the IT sector's aggregated revenues were US$ 147 billion—export revenue stood at US$ 99 billion, domestic at US$48 billion—a growth of over 13 per cent.

It is such growth in productivity, associated mushrooming of employment opportunities, and diversification in the Indian IT sector that are touted by proponents of globalization. Highly skilled engineering jobs in the IT software sub-sector, and more broad-based work in ITES, which is open to non-engineering graduates, have grown while employment opportunities in electronic manufacturing have shrunk. Between 2003 and 2012, there was a fourfold increase in employment numbers—from 670,000 to 2,770,000—with the growth focused primarily in the export sector.[11] Tata Consulting Services or TCS is reported to have hired 20,000 fresh graduates from all over India in 2013; other organizations like Wipro, Infosys, IBM, and Dell, among others, also added to the employment numbers.[12] Capitalizing on advancements in ICT technologies, major corporations in industrialized countries like the USA, have

---

[10] See Dubey and Garg (2014).

[11] Revenue and employment data from Dr. Anupam Khanna (2013), Chief Economist, 14 February 2013. 'India's IT/ITeS Industry: The Next Phase Non-Linear Growth & Broad-Based Innovation.' Knowledge-Based Capital Conference, OECD, Paris. Retrieved on 24 July 2015.

[12] Available at: http://info.shine.com/industry/it-ites-bpo/11.html. Retrieved on 24 July 2015.

offshored and/or outsourced many business services to India and other developing countries. At the same time, India has been successful in creating and attracting high-skill jobs in the IT[13] and in the BPO sectors[14] (Bhatt and Illiyan 2009; NASSCOM 2008; Sahoo and Patnaik 2009). These new occupational sectors, IT and BPO, include jobs that are outsourced through Indian companies like Infosys Technologies or Wipro and/or offshored by American companies like Oracle, HP, Microsoft, or IBM who have set up shop in India.[15] Recently, Indian corporations, like TCS, Wipro, Infosys offering software solutions, and Hindustan Computers Limited (HCL Technologies) with their hardware products and solutions, have developed and successfully exported software packages for banking, finance, accounting, and health care. Other industry developments have included a shift from on-site IT work at the site of the foreign company to offshore work done at the many software technology parks, say in Bangalore, Hyderabad, and Chennai. Multi-national western corporations like Oracle, Texas Instruments, HP, Microsoft, and IBM have also set up software development bases in India. Even though western multinational exports represent a small portion of Indian sales and exports, they are important clients of Indian software companies.

Such unprecedented growth in IT employment has been made possible in the sector by capitalizing on the information technology related skill sets, particularly of its educated segments. When additional language skills (such as English accents) are needed to serve the Western customer better, accent neutralization centres teach workers Western accents, popular culture, and even names to adopt in order to 'pass' as a Westerner (Nadeem 2009). It is also important to note that the IT-BPO sector jobs are the most sought after because of their monetary and associated benefits, including better than the typical Indian working environments and access to western culture.

Amidst this growth, pure or caste-neutral IT educational credentials and skills—a critical yardstick for IT work qualification—has become

---

[13] The IT sector includes computer or information technology programming, IT infrastructure management, research and development services, E-commerce & web services, and engineering services.

[14] The ITES/BPO sector covers customer service, financial service, and back office services for multinational companies.

[15] Loosing such work, previously done in the USA and Europe, has caused a lot of worry in the USA and in other advanced nations.

an article of faith in the community's social habitus. IT employment is purely merit-, and not caste-based, say the industry leaders. IT-BPO occupations, in principle, do not have a caste basis. Besides, the current surplus of Indian engineering graduates allows IT firms to be highly selective in choosing the most 'qualified' candidates. The ideal IT candidate is expected to have a certain blend of technical, social, and cultural skills. In fact, a pilot qualitative interview study by Jodhka and Newman (2010)[16] found employers who consistently spoke of 'merit'-based talent. These employers contrasted merit-based hiring in IT to the nepotism of old industries, where personal ties came first, family second, and caste third.

Detractors of Globalization

Yet, say the detractors, because of the exclusionary mechanisms at work in the Indian social and educational institutions, the most 'meritorious' IT professionals tend to come from upper caste, middle class, educated, urban, and male backgrounds. The globalization detractors also point to the continued and even deepening global and national inequalities, amidst the unprecedented prosperity. Economists Joseph Stiglitz (2007, 2003) and others (Appadurai 1996; Sassen 2000) have contrasted the dramatic changes in the global economy with various countries being more connected than ever before to the world of widening gaps both among and within societies. They cite cases, Africa for example, being disconnected from the globalizing world and of segments like the poor, even within the connected countries like India, for whom the world is certainly not flat. More realistically, globalized IT has brought prosperity only to some of the local economies. The lack of skills and resources needed to compete in the global economy is one important factor perpetuating the economic divide both among and within countries. But the problem according to Stiglitz, is not with globalization per se, but the way it has been managed. Stiglitz posited that the very global trade and financial practices, as well as the politics of international economic institutions, like IMF, World Bank, and WTO, which give advanced industrialized nations a definite advantage, have come at the expense of the poor countries and their poorer segments. The Dalits or 'Scheduled

---

[16] Their study had a convenience sample of 25 HR managers of large multinational and Indian firms based in New Delhi and their Indian satellite offices.

Castes', the focus of this research monograph, is one such marginalized segment in globalizing India.

India is a textbook case of globalized inequalities. The Indian IT success markers stand in stark contrast to a nation still characterized by high rates of illiteracy, US$2 per day median income, and a predominantly rural and agricultural economy. Poverty rates in the country continue to be high; poverty headcount ratio at US$1.25 a day (adjusted for inflation) has certainly declined from 55.5 per cent in 1983 to 32.7 per cent in 2010. But, these rates are still rather high when compared to Asian rates of 50.1 per cent in 1983 and down to 13.1 per cent in 2010.[17]

Scholars have documented social inequalities even within the new IT sector. At an intra-sectoral level, researchers have characterized the Indian IT world as one-third hardware/software IT and two-thirds softer BPO (Mohanty 2003). The privileges of IT professionals or symbolic analysts (Reich 1991) are contrasted with the repetitive work in routine production in the BPO sector.[18] Body shopping practices (Biao 2007) and associated contingent work conditions, under which many on site (working abroad) IT workers toil, are yet another illustration of the inequalities in the new IT sector. Nadeem (2009) documented the social hierarchy that has developed between the IT programmers vs. the transnational call centre workers in BPO. The night work shifts needed to synchronize with the rhythms of the global economy, along with the social parties and other non-monetary incentives (alcohol and cigarettes) provided to recruit and retain workers in these non-traditional working conditions, have lowered the social standing of transnational call centre workers in contrast to IT programmers. 'Depersonalized bullying' (to borrow a term from D'Cruz and Noronha 2013) that accompanies the 'othering', as per Michel Foucault, of call centre and soft-skilled workers, marks the perceived

[17] Available at http://humanprogress.org/story/2439. Retrieved on 23 July 2015.

[18] Chandra Mohanty's (2003) depiction of 'one-third world' versus the 'two-thirds world' is an appropriate IT privilege metaphor. The one-third world is represented by IT hardware and software producers while BPO is the two-thirds world. As per Reich (2001), symbolic analysts were ranked above the BPO or repetitive workers. Of course, given the economic benefits accruing to IT workers, irrespective of type of work, IT employment in general is more desired than non-IT work.

social weakness and low standing of BPO workers in the IT hierarchy. No doubt, BPO workers along with other marginalized groups like women, lower castes, lower class, and rural residents, if and when they make it into the IT world, make sense of and learn to live with their 'otherized' status.

These IT related inequalities have, according to scholars,[19] exacerbated, rather than diminished, the potency of other inequality vectors of gender, caste, and urbanicity. Specific examples of such multilayered inequalities abound. IT recruitment practices that favour a certain mix of technical, social, and cultural skills, when layered on to educational inequalities extant in the Indian society,[20] have fortified the multidimensional stratification in the Indian social fabric (Upadhya 2007a, 2007b). The gendered and cultural (English fluency) dynamics of the transnational class of IT workers (Radhakrishnan 2011) are other cases in point. Top IT positions are held by men while women are often relegated to lower entry level jobs. Individuals from upper/middle caste and class backgrounds dominate the IT industry (D'Costa 2011; Raghunath 2010). Because of the global industry's functional need for those with technical engineering education (bachelor's or even master's degrees), there is an inherent class bias in favour of the urban (often a proxy for English proficiency) educated middle class; those who have access to such education typically hail from upper and middle classes/caste urban backgrounds. Granted, the origins of educational disparities start early on in one's life course. While government technical institutes are well resourced, only limited resources are devoted to basic primary/secondary education. These early disparities create a narrowing funnel up the ladder to higher education. On balance, while merit in the IT industry is judged by educational credentials, access to these credentials continues to be influenced by early academic performance that is contingent on caste and class status, and urban location.

Such accumulated research evidence has begun to undermine the idea that the Indian IT sector, in contrast to the more traditional professional/white collar sectors, has opened up employment opportunities to a wider cross section of society. The highly selective IT hiring and promotion

---

[19] Annapoorna and Bagalkoti (2011) and Suriya and Nagarajan (2004) among others.

[20] More details on endemic educational inequalities are outlined later in Appendix 1A.1 and Chapter 4.

processes have created interesting social dynamics around the nexus of 'merit' and upper caste, urban, and gender identities, among others. In the judgement of the forward or higher castes, they do not explicitly discriminate or exclude SCs. Rather, they contend, educated SCs (because of the reservation system) simply do not have the appropriate 'merit' or requisite skill sets for the IT job, particularly in a market where impeccable technical credentials are critical. There is general agreement that the stringent academic environment in publicly funded engineering higher education often disadvantages the SCs who were granted admission based on quotas or reservation policies and/or poor socio-economic background. No doubt, many reservation (SC) students do not perform at a high level because of their prior weak educational preparation or limited English proficiency. Academic problems, however, are not unique to SC students; they are also faced by many from poor and rural communities. In a similar vein, for employers that doubt the legitimacy of the reservation system, the merit of SC's training and qualifications for hiring and advancement, become questionable. Yet, the quality of private technical credentials, sought after by many dominant caste and class students who did not get into the elite public institutions, is often left unquestioned. There has been a mushrooming of private and expensive technical education in response to the limited open seats available to forward castes (FC) and classes in publicly funded technical institutions.

Against this complicated background continue the raging debates about the effects of caste and casteism in India. There is growing political and public backlash against quotas or set aside privileges for SC/ST/OBC in government educational institutions, occupations, and political elections. Many upper castes, including some academicians, have claimed that caste discrimination is a thing of the past and it is time that the decades long privileges enjoyed by the SCs and OBCs are ended (Haub 2011). To others, reservation policies have met their goals and therefore should be discontinued. There are those who blame the constitutional redress provisions for caste dynamics continuing to permeate everyday life and politics in modern India. Some even argue that the reservation policies should never have been implemented in the first place because they have undermined the chances of poor Brahmins and other upper castes, even if the costs of exclusion for the poor FC members may not be as high as it would be for the lowest castes. Some FC members are taking actions to rectify their apparent disadvantages. A case in point is a Brahmin Trust

Fund which seeks to assist 'ONLY poor Brahmins' to pursue their education.[21] Debates also continue about caste enumeration in the decennial Census and other government sponsored surveys; should the government of India continue enumerating castes, asked Haub in 2011?

Unfortunately, while untouchability (against SCs) practices are illegal and waning a bit in urban India, casteism has an enduring and insidious presence.[22] At the dawn of the twenty-first century, the caste system remains a unique social organizing framework in the nation, leaving its unequal imprint on education, labour practices, electoral politics, and even health outcomes. As long as the intricate connections between caste-based inequalities and the nation's economic development are unsettled, politicians, community activists, and their lobbyists will continue to manipulate the government's reservation policies. At the national level, research questions need to be raised and answered about how restricted better-paying jobs are to the SC segment in the national talent pool and whether such restrictions severely shrink the prospects for national growth and individual achievement. Other questions that need to be publicly debated are whether information scarcity and mobility traps, based on caste and other ascribed characteristics, can be resolved through more effective institutional means. More importantly, correcting these disparities will require organizational and cultural changes not only in the public governmental sector, but also in the private sector, including IT sector where caste baste reservations do not apply.

Theoretically Disentangling Contradictions in the Caste-Merit Constructions

Returning to my conversations with IT professionals, managers, technical staff, and the general Indian public, it was clear that many vehemently denied the contemporary relevance of caste in IT—either of the caste earmarked or of the symbolically privileged kind. They touted an idealized work social habitus marked by individualized merit ideology, skills, and worldviews that are authorized globally and nationally. However, as

---

[21] As per personal communication with author.

[22] See Atul Sethi and Divya A. 'A Gene Called Caste' in *Times of India*, 16 May 2010.

postulated in this research, it is the very ideology and practice of merit that has led to caste reproductions in the Indian IT workplace. There is evidence, in the lived experiences of IT professionals and industry informants, that the Indian IT *social habitus* (Bourdieu 1990), the occupational sector and its workplace structures[23] have become *a new site of caste inequality* through transference and replication of broader social caste hierarchies into the work structures in the IT occupational sector. Bourdieu's notions of *symbolic and hidden capital* (1990, 1995) are useful in unpacking the contradictory connections between merit capital and other inequalities reproduced in the IT sector. Unequal caste, gender, community, and even religious structures and processes operative in the larger Indian society have found their way into the IT sector. But, not all inequalities are equal; IT sector leaders seem more open to addressing gender than caste inequalities, as evidenced in NASSCOM's recent gender inclusive initiatives. These contradictions can be viewed as byproducts of the gender, family, and caste intersections (Fernandez 1997).[24] In the final analyses, search for ways to disrupt caste hierarchies will have to be located in the 'symbolic struggles' in the context of 'social domination' (Pratto et al. 1994; Whitley Jr. 1999).

How can the IT sector go from being the new inequalities saviour to becoming another vector of caste reproduction? Theoretically speaking, *pure merit* and the associated skill sets, the golden currency in the IT workplace and in the broader society, operate as central mediating mechanisms through which caste hierarchies can enter and take root in Indian IT. *Pure merit* is used to articulate 'appropriate differences'[25] at multiple

---

[23] Following a noted organizational theorist, Dr. Charles Powers (2016 personal communication), a workplace can be treated as a setting in which to see the meaning of social structure. A social structure is a set of recurrent and patterned ways in which people are allocated to different roles that are defined relative to one another and linked by regular communication links between the occupants of different roles, with rules and role expectations are enforced, and role performance monitored. The work structure has both, formal (aspects of role behaviour, organized communication, and officially proscribed rule enforcement) and informal (aspects of role behaviour, communication, and rule enforcement which unofficially emerge but take place alongside of officially prescribed behaviour) dimensions.

[24] Discussed further in Chapter 5; also see Shenoy-Packer (2014).

[25] This is an adaptation of Radhakrishnan's (2011) appropriate difference in which she distinguishes between traditional and respectable middle-class

levels of structures and discourse. It sets apart the globalized IT structure from the non-IT work sectors. It is also posited to be the opposite of merit gained through state sponsored social redress programs in education and workplace hiring and promotion. To reiterate, a clear distinction is drawn between the ideology and practice of *pure/sheer/caste neutral merit* and *earmarked* or *reservation* merit. Pure merit is ostensibly unsullied by the traditional vectors of caste or class while reservation merit is weak because reservation beneficiaries do not face the same stringent qualifications as dominant castes and classes. The pure merit argument is bolstered by the reality that Dalits/SCs continue to face deficits in economic, social, and cultural capital resources, despite more than half century long reserved quotas. But, as scholars have noted, the practice of 'pure' merit is deeply *embedded in the social and economic privileges* of the dominant castes and classes.[26] By virtue of how merit is defined and acquired, the socially constructed IT 'merit' culture favours the higher castes (HCs) and other privileged segments. If this is the case, can IT merit be caste neutral?

How do symbolic and hidden capital resources and processes fade to the background in the caste-merit debate? To be sure, the functional need for efficiency and productivity in the globalized IT industry has prompted the sector and its professionals to 'streamline'[27] and to anchor the ideology and practice of pure merit, the educational preparations for and cultivation of associated skills and work habits, in the individual and not in the family or other social groupings. The new streamlined IT merit ostensibly is tightly honed and stripped off of the particularistic inequality vectors of caste, gender, and religion, among others, which allegedly dominate the public sector and non-IT family owned private sector. Anathema in the Indian IT workplace, as per IT professionals and key informants/knowledge leaders, is the caste-based public sector reservations as well

---

femininity embodied by the female IT professional, between the Indian and global, and between IT ideology and practices versus reservations in jobs and education.

[26] For example, see Annapoorna and Bagalkoti (2011); Bourdieu (1977, 1990, 1995); Radhakrishnan (2011); Suriya and Nagarajan (2004); Upadhya (2006, 2007a, 2007b).

[27] Another adaptation of Radhakrishnan's cultural streamlining (2011: 21) which she defined as 'the process of simplifying a dizzying diversity of cultural practices into a stable, transferable, modular set of norms and beliefs that can move quickly and easily through space'.

as the weight of community-caste-religious ties, and resultant *homosocial reproduction*[28] of dominant community employees and management that is rampant in the non-IT private sector, they posit.

Concurrently, a perfect storm of events has turned the acquisition of merit skills into a fiercely contested competition to the point of becoming a *blood sport*. As streamlined pure merit collides with the reservation merit, particularly in the preparation for merit skills needed in the IT workplace, caste contestations get to the forefront. Distinctions are drawn between open, or 'pure merit', and earmarked or 'caste reservation merit' seats in education. The vehemence in the merit competition is fuelled by the restricted open seats for dominant castes in elite publicly funded educational institutions; there is a 50 per cent upper limit on earmarked or 'reserved' seats for Dalits and OBCs.[29] In response to this perceived crunch, private technical education institutions, where redress earmarks do not apply, have mushroomed in recent years. But, the prohibitive cost of private technical education, affordable primarily by the wealthier castes and classes, has fuelled the bitterness of the competition. For its part, the private IT employment sector has vigorously and fiercely sought to keep out 'reservation merit' because of its purported weak quality. In a highly coveted, but limited employment market, the ideology and practice of pure merit is upheld in opposition to social redress policies, injecting fierceness, and a metaphorical bloodiness, into the debate.

Yet, the *unacknowledged embeddedness* of the Indian IT sector and its professionals in multiple, intersectionally intertwining, and traditional inequality vectors renders the streamlining of meritorious symbolic capital to be hidden, and loosely woven, leaving enough room for caste and other traditional inequality vectors to seep through and layer 'pure' IT merit with caste inequalities. For example, if 'pure' merit is primarily accessible to the dominant castes and classes, it stands to reason that caste privileges are reproduced in the new IT sector. Caste privileges, percolated into the preparation of 'pure' merit and in its application in the recruitment and promotion structures in the IT workplace, set the stage for diffusion and replication of caste hierarchies in the IT workplace structure and

---

[28] From Chapter 3 of Kanter's (1977a) homosocial social reproduction of management.

[29] More details on the history and specifics of reservation policies are available in Appendix 1A.1.

practices. Rather than being the expected social saviour from the deep rooted ravages of caste inequalities, the new Indian IT sector has itself turned into a new vector of inequality.

Following these theoretical strands, a *broad definition of Merit* is proposed for the analyses of caste reproduction in the Indian IT workplace. For one, merit refers to the skill sets validated by a streamlined 'pure' merit ideology. Merit, to the *Merit Camp*, refers to the efforts and successes of the individual in acquiring the skills sets, work habits as well as orientations imbued with a thirst for learning, tireless work ethic, flexibility, and willingness to adapt to new technologies and shifting work conditions. This set of pure merit ideology and practices, deemed a functional prerequisite for success in global IT, is authorized and privileged by the global IT world and the larger Indian society. *Pure merit*, to many Indians from dominant caste and class backgrounds, is also the opposite of reservation merit. In fact, to the privileged dominant castes and classes in the *Pure Merit Camp*, who are embedded in normalized caste privileges, equating caste privileges with merit is oxymoronic. Caste, to them, stands for SC (Dalits) and for reservation merit gained by Dalits and other minorities through the social justice programs. If there is a 'Dalit deficit' in Indian IT, it is because Dalits' IT qualifications, acquired through less stringent admission requirements, are weaker than pure merit.

But, merit is also the caste and class embedded kind, deeply rooted, and unacknowledged, in the economic and cultural privileges of dominant castes and classes. It is this caste embedded merit, hidden and normalized, that offers clues into the caste diffusion and replicating potential in Indian IT. To the *Caste Camp*, 'pure' merit is just a 'code' word for caste advantages fiercely defended by the historically privileged, to the point of turning the competition into a 'blood sport'. It is ironic that many in the IT professional circles do not recognize the hidden caste undertones of the pure merit yardstick that they so ardently bandy about. Many seem unaware of their middle class background and resources (hidden capital) that have privileged them in the acquisition of merit, be it in elite educational human capital or in other social/cultural capital. Even though hidden symbolic merit is not that different from reservation merit, it is caste privileged merit of the dominant castes that offers the key to understanding how IT has become the new vector of caste inequality. Ironically, reservation merit, contrary to its maligned portrayal as weak and reinforcing caste distinctions, has the potential for disrupting caste inequality reproduction, provided the necessary supportive structures are in place in the educational and workplace systems. It is also in the unpacking of these conflicting strands in the merit-caste debates—caste neutrality, reservation caste merit, and caste privilege embeddedness—that the keys to understanding the caste privileges in a sector that was expected to dismantle the historic caste-based inequalities lie.

How are these conflicting Merit-Caste strands experienced on the ground? On the one hand, the ideology of IT based skill or caste neutral 'merit' has become preeminent dogma in the IT community. Skill based merit is essential for Indian IT companies to function successfully in a globalized industry, they say. On the other, contrary to these pronouncements, minorities from SCs and rural backgrounds, and even women, have experienced the culture and practices of the new Indian IT sector as discriminatory. To these groups, the centuries old caste traditions and inequalities have not simply disappeared even in the purportedly caste-less new occupational sector. It is in this context that the broad set of questions that guided this research was located: How is the 'merit' IT culture project constructed in the Indian IT sector? How does the merit project become discriminatory in ways that even a new occupational sector undergoes caste-based (and other minority statuses) transformation? And, if caste-inequalities have been imported into the IT culture, how can it get disrupted?

Merit Culture Making in the IT Social Habitus

On the face of it, *pure IT 'skills'* appear to have replaced caste, religion, and/or communities as social vectors in the IT sector, and by extension, in the IT imbued contemporary Indian society. Merit, another term for IT skills, is often valorized in the daily social discourse on IT campuses and on the street. As Parthasarathy noted, 'The valorization of particularistic notions of merit dominates much of the public and even academic debate on the issue of caste-based reservations in higher education in India ...' (2012: 256). Even in the social habitus of a globalized IT workplace, merit and its underlying ideology has become the unquestioned refrain. A frequently offered rationale is that merit signals 'quality' to western customers (Krishna and Brihmadesam 2006; Upadhya 2007a). This merit-based culture has come to represent a 'paracosm' of structured mental attributes that helps map, organize, and shed light on the particular unique new world of Indian IT.

How has this paracosm been developed and maintained in IT? One credible theoretical answer can be offered by adapting Radhakrishnan's (2011) idea of '*streamlining*' to create '*appropriate differences*' between IT merit and merit created by reservation policies.[30] To appropriately differentiate, the Indian IT sector has identified and assiduously honed 'a generic, transferable set of "Indian" (Radhakrishnan 2011: 5) cultural norms that are palatable to their Western clients; "merit" has become the key/overt marker of transferable norms.' In Radhakrishnan's analysis, the resulting 'transnational class' (2011: 3), an exemplar of appropriate difference, is simultaneously Indian, but different from the India-Indian. The ideal IT professional is someone with skills, communication styles, and processes (adaptability and flexibility) that are pragmatic and transferable anywhere globally. In fact, the framers of modern India set up elite technical institutions (like the IITs)[31] to offer broad based science and technology based resources to spur industrial modernity and development. Products of these elite technical institutions, the privileged transnational knowledge class, espouse a particular worldview, of beliefs, ethos, and knowledge that could be employed globally.

The IT sector and those connected with that world streamline multiple identities (class, caste, urbanism, religion, and gender) and create 'appropriate differences' to highlight and privilege those skills that have cache and symbolic capital in the new global IT sector. Merit, and associated IT skills, has become the basis for appropriate difference between IT on the one hand and the public sector on the other. Streamlining is used to draw sharp contrasts between the private Indian IT and the government sectors. The IT sector with its caste neutral merit ideology and practices is set apart from the public sector with its caste-based reservations or quotas and ostensibly merit neutral principles. While reservation merit has cache in the government sector, streamlined merit is a pre-requisite for success in the IT knowledge sector. Merit terminology, with its singular focus on

---

[30] Radhakrishnan (2011) conceptualized the merit ideology in opposition to quota policies that reinforces caste. In this sense, merit was not necessarily a marker of appropriate difference between IT and non-IT occupational sectors.

[31] IITs, deemed 'Institutes of National Importance' were approved by the Indian Parliament between 1951 and 1961. Initially, five IITs were set up; since 1994, 11 more were added (more details in Chapter 4).

merit/skill, also offers a way to streamline hiring and advancement expectations in the IT workplace.

It is in this streamlining process that *pure merit* can become delinked from caste, rendering merit *caste neutral*. It is also in this process that the 'merit-based IT culture' can become discriminatory implicitly, or even in reality, on the basis of caste (or class and community) status. Valorized merit, because of its hidden symbolic nature, has become a tool for transferring and perpetuating caste and its hierarchies in Indian IT. In addition to the distinctions drawn between the IT and non-IT government sector occupations, sub-sectors in IT, like BPO, are also stratified using appropriately different skill sets. In the final analyses, it is the appropriate differentiation based on merit valorization that has the potential for reproducing centuries-old caste hierarchical practices in hiring and promotions in the new IT occupational sector.

The Merit vs. Caste Debate in the IT Culture Making Project

It is also in this 'caste-neutral merit culture' context that the *Merit-Caste* debate is waged. To the *Merit Camp*, streamlining has become the basis for moulding a global IT professional for a global workplace. There is a general assumption that the cultural and work norms/skills of the traditional Indian occupational sectors are not compatible with the demands of the global IT industry. Therefore, a transnational IT class, that is appropriately different from the 'reservation-class' in other occupational sectors, had to be created and cultivated. The IT elite and non-elite alike rationalize the appropriately different IT professional on the grounds that a globally transferable skill set is critical to appeal to the Western cosmopolitan culture of multinational clients. For another, streamlined merit is an imperative in the (avowed) interests of efficiency and productivity. In a culturally streamlined Indian IT sector, *pure merit* is viewed as normal (naturalized á la Bourdieu), universal, and respected. An IT value set, that includes adaptability, flexibility, drive, and performance, required and valorized in the knowledge economy, reinforces the ideology of merit and fits well with merit construction in the IT sector; if you have merit and work hard you will be rewarded. Once again, pure merit in the IT sector is claimed to be free from the restrictions of traditional social vectors such as caste, community, or religion.

But, the implications of streamlining go beyond just being a functional management tool. Merit streamlining, says the *Caste Camp*, is not so much an efficient merit-based management tool, but rather is used to manage the matrix of privileges associated with symbolic and material capital that intertwine and reinforce each other to create and sustain the merit IT culture. Besides, if 'pattern recognition',[32] is used as a hiring and promotion tool in the IT job sectors, with resultant 'homosocial reproduction' (Kanter 1977a), it stands to reason that the matrix of caste privileges in the broader society are replicated in the Indian IT sector. For sure, homosocial reproduction is not a simple byproduct of sexism or racism or casteism; rather it often is an insidious byproduct of organizational uncertainty, organizational efficiency, and manager discretions in hiring.

In the final analyses, the passionately argued reasoning on either side of the merit-caste debate continues, with each side getting more entrenched in their respective *Blood Sport* competitive camp corners. In a global environment with its merit imperatives, the obscured privileges of the dominant castes combined with historical distressed social/cultural capital assets of SCs, have added fuel to the ongoing debate.

Obscured/Hidden Privileges as IT Symbolic Capital

It should be clear by now that the globalized Indian IT sector can be rife with inequality contradictions. It has rendered invisible the privileged backgrounds of the transnational class. Interestingly, the obscured privileges play out at both the macro-state and meso-IT sectoral levels. At the macro state level, the knowledge for development (K4D) model (Radhakrishnan 2007: 2011) was used by the government as a tool for leapfrogging traditional modernization/development pathways. Ironically, the broad-based K4D models were 'not to be restricted' to elites. Because the framers of modern India firmly believed that science and technology would offer the best nationwide resources to spur industrial modernity

---

[32] Pattern recognition perspective in entrepreneurship (Baron 2006) is typically applied to separate the successful from the less successful entrepreneurs. Successful entrepreneurs, using their prior knowledge of the industry, are able to connect the dots among emerging technologies, changing demographics, markets, and government policies, to identify opportunities for new products, services, and ventures. Applied to hiring and promotion in the IT industry, pattern identification would include using personal success markers in evaluating potential candidates.

and development, the Indian Parliament established IITs, the elite technical institutions, with reservation quotas mandates. But the very principle
of elite education, at one level, has obscured the caste/class privilege of
the knowledge class. For example, the IITs currently serve as pipelines
for many knowledge professionals recruited into the Indian IT sector.
Besides, IT professionals, erroneously but ardently, believe that the IT
industry ahistorically emerged and succeeded without state intervention.
Even today it is the extensive government policies and programs, such as
setting up technology parks in IT hubs, which continue to invigorate and
cultivate the IT sector.

At the meso IT sector level, privileges associated with social and cultural locations of individuals, and even companies, make higher technical
education possible for, or even available only to, those from certain backgrounds, including upper caste, education, family ties, and other obscure
privileges.[33] For one, as noted earlier, IT educated professionals, who have
received rigorous training in hardware and software, come from an overwhelmingly homogenous social-economic-urban location background.
Although IT professionals and the IT sector claim universality in the
knowledge class's resource access, it is, in historic reality, restricted to a
relatively few, namely the educated professional class who are sons and
daughters of the previous generations of middle class government workers, bank staff, and petit bourgeoisie. Education and higher education in
particular, has continued to be the vehicle through which class inequality
in the technology sector is perpetuated. For sure, the BPO sub-sector, and
its non- or semi-technical skilled employees in call centres, data entry and
management, and printing shops, is more open to a broader social range
of society and less elitist in the IT hierarchy.

Bourdieu's theoretical treatment of *symbolic capital* nicely captures the
obscured privileges underlying merit-caste nexus in IT. In Bourdieu's rendering of the symbolic nature of capital, indicated by education, income,
urban location, language, or culture, those who own capital resources 'exert
power from a dominant position; but this dominance is "*misrecognized*" as
natural and permanent, thus making it appear as if the dominant group is
not exerting power at all' (Radhakrishnan 2009: 200). Privileged Indians
(by class, caste, urban residence) take pride in their ability to speak fluent,

---

[33] Drawn from Fernandes and Heller (2006); Krishna and Brihmadesam
(2006); Radhakrishnan (2011); Rai (2002); Upadhya (2007a).

even if British accented, English. English language facility is a critical cultural capital in a globalized workplace and groups like the Dalits are found lacking in this resource (Upadhya and Vasavi 2006). Even Call Centre workplaces of the BPO sector, where employees are trained in accent modification for their 24/7 working shifts, are not quite open to Dalits and other minority groups. To recast the rampant hidden privileges in Bourdieuian terms, *pure merit* is valorized to the extent that the privileges and exclusion at work in Indian IT are concealed, even before the IT professional enters the workplace. The Indian self, embedded in the family-caste-class-gender-religion-community nexus, privileges some while disadvantaging others, often only because of the social location of their birth.

Another mechanism through which privileges are obscured lies in the *agency*, more specifically lack thereof, associated with the disadvantaged. Symbolic and material privileges accrued by knowledge professionals are authorized by the nation;[34] national authorization implies that 'merit is available to everyone who desires it'. Those who do not access these valued resources, as in the case of lower castes, either do not want them (remember they are dependent on government subsidies) or could not get them because they were not qualified enough (as in lower entrance scores for the SCs). In this privilege discourse, educational and professional credentials are equated with personal 'merit'. To the new professional class and their particular types of work, ethos, and lifestyles, the IT occupational system is open or accessible to anyone who desires it. Paradoxically, such misplaced agency further masks or obscures the perpetuated inequalities in merit acquisition. The cultural dominance of the old middle class and castes is continued, while contributing to the limited presence of Dalits, a Dalit Deficit, in the IT sector.

Dalit Deficits in Indian IT: Distressed Capital or Caste Filtering?

Considering the historical discrimination faced by SCs (Dalits), one might argue that the younger generations of Dalits face an *insecure or distressed*

---

[34] National authorization is part of the reason why IT professionals are considered the most privileged workers in the global economy as per Reich (1991).

social habitus that offers them limited access to the kinds of social and cultural capital needed in the globalized IT world. *Social capital resources* (Coleman 1988), embedded in family and community networks, are necessary for successful educational outcomes in the USA, be they school retention or low drop-out rates (Dika and Singh 2002). Extant research on US job search processes and occupational attainment has tied individual mobilization of resources to successful entry into and retention in a job. Other multiple dimensions of the resource mobilization needed for life success in education and in the job market include: cultural habitus or lifestyles characterized by aesthetic preferences, value commitments, and associated consumption patterns (Bourdieu 1977, 1984); *'resources-in-networks'* and information flows (Lin 1999, 2001); *'strength of weak ties'* (Granovetter 1973), and *'bridging-bonding'* social capital (Fernandez and Nichols 2002). In social capital terms, the successful FCs in IT have access to the required socially and culturally approved capital as well as the broad networks of acquaintances (weak ties) with deep resource networks that connect them to the educational and labour market. On the contrary, disadvantages in resource mobilization contribute to the Dalit deficit in IT. Even when Dalits have the requisite qualifications for the IT-BPO occupational sector, the fact that they are associated with the quota systems in education and occupations renders their merit questionable. In short, despite the official outlawing of caste-based discrimination, caste continues to be a potent, even if hidden, bridge that channels one's access to resources in modern India.

A counter explanation for the Dalit deficit in IT lies in the *'caste positionality'* and *implicit 'caste position filtering'* bias embedded in the hiring management's pattern recognition strategies. Applied to caste, symbolic capital can operate via the lens of 'Caste Positionality' through which a person's success experiences are filtered. Positionality can also work through class, community, urban location, and other ascribed boundaries. Because caste and community are ascribed characteristics that are near immutable, the power of 'Particularity'[35] becomes salient in people's lived experiences. If one's identity is framed by hard, ascribed boundaries, that is, if you come from a particular social/caste position and even urban or rural location, you might have more depth and definition to your identity that is harder to change than if you grew up in an eclectic, multi-cultural/ caste/class/geographical environment. And if caste filtering undergirds

[35] See Brooks (2012).

the recognition of patterns of behaviours/skills/values predicted to lead to success, new hires can be quite similar to those already in the industry, namely the forward castes and cultural elites. In other words, through a homo-social reproduction process, caste hierarchy and related norms can be diffused and reproduced in the IT sector structures.

Against these theoretical contexts, it is possible to ask: to what extent do IT professionals, embedded in gendered, religious, national, and class histories, engage in hidden 'implicit caste filtering' as part of their pattern recognition processes. IT professionals represent quite a homogenous elite and are almost always drawn from certain (class, caste, and urban) backgrounds. Caste and privilege filtering in IT, when it exists, lead to reproduction of privileges. Stated differently, the worker profile required in IT and the outsourcing business makes it more difficult for people from lower caste/class and non-urban backgrounds to break into IT, because they are deemed to lack the social and cultural attributes deemed necessary to work in a '"global" environment' (Channa 1993; Upadhya 2007a). SC skills are not authorized as fitting into the patterns known to succeed in the IT world. Given the potency of the 'appropriately different' IT persona, there is no reason to expect drastically different filtering processes in the BPO sector either, even though it is lower on the IT stratification hierarchy.

A Gendered Lens

A gendered lens offers another tool in clarifying the embedded nature of caste privileges in the IT sector. Highlighting the extent to which women are included in a national narrative of pure IT merit and the ways gender based inequalities and gender-caste privilege interactions are factored into the constructions of IT merit are instructive in clarifying the boundaries of caste reproduction in IT.

To their credit, Indian IT companies have been making concerted efforts in recent years to not only include but also to empower women in their workforce. An illustrative case in point is NASSCOM's gender inclusivity awards.[36] To NASSCOM's credit, the award recognizes best

---

[36] Available at: https://www.infosys.com/about/awards/Pages/nasscom-gender-inclusivity-award.aspx. Perhaps in response to pressures from their global parent companies and partners, there are also initiatives for the PWDs (people with disability), LGBT communities, multiple generations, and nationalities.

practices in IT companies that promote gender empowerment and leadership development. Infosys won the award in the 'IT services and product companies' category for the second consecutive year. Gender initiatives are driven partly by the growing number of women graduating with engineering and information technology degrees, notwithstanding the leaky gender pipelines in engineering education. But, if meritorious IT women are also products of caste and class privileges,[37] caste inequality reproduction in Indian IT can only deepen. Besides, the IT sector remains silent on caste diversity/inclusivity initiatives.

Like their male counterparts, Indian women in IT also culturally streamline their work lives. Upadhya (2007b) and Radhakrishnan (2011) demonstrated some ways in which Indian women knowledge professionals maintain an Indian core while adopting a global persona in the interest of their own productivity and advancement. There was a time when government bank jobs, the jobs that their parents held, were considered appropriate for Indian women; but, not anymore. IT women, unlike their parents, want to attain financial independence before getting married. But marriage is still heavily desired, indicating a gendered adaptation to appropriate difference. The new Indian IT woman creates a respectable femininity that is 'marked simultaneously through her potential for professionalism in the workplace and through her adherence to an essentialized notion of Indianness' (Radhakrishnan 2011: 49). Even when faced with the proverbial glass ceiling, the women 'naturalized [it] in gendered terms' (Radhakrishnan 2011: 105). Radhakrishnan's women were more likely to do the softer and natural jobs of communication, writing, quality control, and maintenance but not ones with the harder, as in coding, content. Many technically degreed Indian women, and families on their behalf, desired to work in IT divisions that offered palpable insulation from non-related-outsider males. Computer work in cubicles located in fancy air conditioned buildings that did not involve much face-to-face interactions with outsiders, particularly men, was attractive to IT women. IT jobs with flexible relationship to work choices and hours compatible with family-work balance, were also more appealing than those considered

---

[37] See also Shenoy-Packer (2014) for a discussion of the multi-dimensional lives of Indian women; they simultaneously benefit from their caste-class privileges while living within a patriarchal society that disadvantages them in the public and private spheres.

inappropriate and 'unsafe' because of the required travel. For sure, these women were 'penalized' in their professional advancement and often hit the glass ceiling, perhaps because of their limited weak network ties (Granovetter 1973), resources-in-IT *networks* (Coleman 1988; Lin 1999, 2001), and *gendered pattern recognition* (Kanter 1977b) by management with their *symbolic, hidden sources* (Bourdieu 1977, 1984) *of gendered merit.*

Notwithstanding women's pigeon-holing and advancement penalties in IT, not all women are so blessed with the options of crafting their appropriate difference. Indian women of dominant groups tend to have the edge over other women or for that matter even lower caste men. Because of the *interlocking or intersectional matrix* (Fernandez 1997) of compounding privileges of gender and caste,[38] only the merit/skills of dominant caste/class women and their *strong family ties* (Granovetter 1973) to IT men are culturally authorized. They are also authorized by the society to create married roles that are appropriately different. It is also interesting that, in the IT habitus, privileged gender equality, or inequality, as the case might be, is more readily accessible and amenable for discussion, analyses, and redress than caste (in)equality. While women of dominant castes have increasingly been recognized and authorized as national symbols, the same recognition does not seem to be afforded to lower caste women and their men.

Here again, isomorphic pressures offer clues. Normative, coercive, and mimetic isomorphic[39] pressures from international partners might encourage, or even coerce, Indian IT companies to mimic the gender inclusive

---

[38] In a patriarchal society like India, an additive hierarchical ranking of caste and gender might look like this: men from the upper castes will be at the top of the pyramid, followed by men from the less dominant castes. Women, albeit similarly caste stratified as their male counterparts, will follow below men in the hierarchy. In an interactional ranking, upper caste women follow their caste men; lower caste men and women remain at the bottom.

[39] Isomorphism in its traditional institutional sense, as defined by DiMaggio and Powell (1983), captured an organizational reality where the less powerful companies followed the models for organizational structures and norms offered by more powerful companies. While there is no systematic evidence, in this manuscript, for caste isomorphism in the Indian IT workplace, it can be argued that the recent attention to gender diversity in the IT occupational sector is perhaps due to isomorphic pressures.

social habitus of their parent or client companies (Parthasarathy 2012; Currie 2012). Gender equality is a global issue and Indian IT companies operating in a globalized environment are strongly encouraged to craft gender inclusive workplaces. But, caste inequalities, localized to the Indian context, escape the inequality radar of international parent companies. Absent external pressures, caste hierarchies, and dynamics in the broader Indian society are more likely, than not, to filter into IT corporations.

Resistance to Caste Diversity Revisited

To recap the resistance to caste diversity in Indian IT: The main driver of the dissonance in the gender and caste discourse is, once again, the perceived disconnects, be they putative or real, between the practice of quotas (reservation) in government educational institutions and IT *pure merit*. The reservation castes do not have to meet the same stringent entrance criteria as the dominant castes in admission to government technical institutions. Consequently, in the 'merit' discourse of the IT sector and in the public arena, SC IT professionals are not judged to be as meritorious as those who do not have the benefits of reservations. Arguments against reservations in the public discourse have ranged widely. One common narrative is that unearned privileges awarded to the (inherently) less qualified, less talented, and unmotivated (aka backward castes and classes) has itself created a new system of inequality. That only the 'creamy layer' (the rich) in the lower caste groups have been beneficiaries of reservation programs is another accusation. Reservations in electoral offices being used as a vote getting tool by caste politicians adds more fuel to the already heated caste-merit contests.

The deep resistance to caste reservations evoked in the private sector, including IT, is because in the words of Radhakrishnan (2011: 93), ' ... the introduction of caste-based quotas appears to threaten not only the talent base of the company, as the leaders in the industry claim, but more fundamentally the abstract language of merit ... '. In the contentious and visceral caste reservations vs merit debates, the government/public sector educational and work institutions are dubbed 'backward'. The projections are so gloomy that the IT sector views the government, and the reserved groups, as standing in the way of India and Indian IT industry's rosy future trajectory. In fact, discussions about caste diversity and inclusivity have become non-negotiable.

On balance, pitting merit against caste in the organization of the Indian IT social habitus and its 'merit' culture making project has led to reproduction of caste-based inequalities in Indian IT. Even the progress women have made in Indian IT, unlike the strong resistance to disrupting caste domination, has caste undertones.[40] It is then axiomatic that these embedded processes, left to their natural evolution, will lead to deepening of inequalities in the Indian IT sector. The ostensibly non-caste IT occupational sector, mimics by replicating the hierarchies of the broader Indian society in which it is embedded. Applied to IT organizations, caste inequalities can be theorized to be a consequence, even if unintended, of institutions trying to achieve rationality in uncertain and constraining globalized environments. These pressures, and associated emphasis on 'merit', may also explain some of the resistance to opening the IT world of work to SCs.

Disrupting Caste Reproduction: Theoretical Possibilities

Other sources of resistance to disrupting caste reproduction lie in historical incidents and philosophical understandings of the workings of social dominance and related discrimination in India. The equal opportunity and quota/reservation policies were formulated by the founders of modern India without the benefit of empirical research on market and non-market caste discrimination (Annapoorna and Bagalkoti 2011; Biao 2007; Rai 2002; Upadhya 2007a). Besides, the social and economic benefits that the quota system make available to the disadvantaged SCs is viewed by dominant castes from a 'zero-sum' perspective.

While history cannot be changed, and perceptions are difficult to alter, Social Dominance Theory (Pratto et al. 1994; Whitley 1999) and Bourdieu's (1995) *Symbolic Struggles* open up some realistic possibilities for reducing the role caste plays in Indian IT. Starting from the assumption that individuals tend to form and maintain group-based hierarchies, social dominance theorists have examined both structural and individual psychological factors that lead to group dominance and oppression. Group-based hierarchies and oppression are conceptualized to be functions of the complex and mutually reinforcing mix of individual

---

[40] For example, Shenoy-Parker's upper-caste/class women felt the limiting burden of caste quotas as they tried to advance their professional career.

orientation, discriminatory behaviours, legitimizing ideologies, and social allocation practices of institutions. For an individual, a social dominance orientation is the product of in-group desires to dominate over and to be superior to out-groups (Pratto et al. 1994: 742; Whitley 1999). Groups perpetuate dominant ideologies by institutionalizing practices and beliefs about their dominance. Individuals who share these beliefs and ideologies tend to support institutions that reinforce these ideals and practices. As a result, desired resources, including the rewards of power, status, and privileges, are funnelled towards dominant and powerful groups while less desirable goods are allocated to the powerless. Under this scenario, it stands to reason that dominant groups will have little incentive to challenge the status quo and enact real change. Restructuring caste hierarchies to be more equal, even in the new globalized IT occupational settings, is bound to be perceived by the dominant castes to be a personal loss, an outcome to be avoided at all costs. In fact, they can be expected to justify and legitimize ideologies that place the onus for unequal caste standing on the individuals' lack of merit qualifications for the job.

However, there are conditions under which we could expect the dominant castes to be open to structural changes in institutions. Again, Bourdieu's symbolic struggles and the limits of symbolic capital in preserving the status quo offer promise (Appelrouth and Edles 2011). To Bourdieu, while symbolic capital embodied in prestige, honour, reputation, or charisma offers individuals the options to mould the social world according to their 'self-interested' economic and political desires, there are limits to the powers of symbolic capital (2011: 454). To successfully utilize symbolic capital so that one's interests are preserved and promoted, Bourdieu argues, such capital must be perceived by subordinate groups as legitimate and authoritative, or at least 'disinterested' or unaffected by self-interest. Also, as interpreted by Radhakrishnan (2009: 200), in Bourdieu's 'treatment of symbolic capital', those with symbolic capital implicitly exert power from a dominant position, implicit because their dominance is 'misrecognized' as being natural and permanent, making it appear as if they are not exerting their power at all.

By extension, a scenario can be hypothesized where the dominant caste group supports realignment of caste hierarchies, at least in the new IT occupational sectors. They can legitimize caste inequalities as products of historical legacies and consequently absolve themselves of personal responsibility for the same. Recast in Bourdieu's (particularly 1990 and in other publications as well) language, dominant castes desirous of participating in realigning caste hierarchies in Indian IT need to become more aware of the structural sources of inequalities and legitimate stakeholders in caste equality, as well as become disinterested in zero-sum outcomes. It is then reasonable to predict that dominant castes, in response to global economic imperatives, might become more open to structural caste realignments. However, such caste realignments will not be complete without a concomitant fostering of positive caste consciousness (following Rajashekar's (2002) 'caste identity theory'), a call to lower castes to become conscious of and affirm their own caste identity just as the dominant castes do.

Of course, these changes will require active public (government)-private partnerships. Thorat and Newman (2010a: 24) and some of their colleagues have offered evidence that casts doubt on whether market or individual/private corporate initiatives by themselves can correct inefficiencies of caste-based labour market allocation. Public economic empowerment along with equal opportunity policies might be needed in the IT sector, if the sector is to disrupt its march towards deepening caste inequalities and if India is to begin shedding its caste foundations. Realistically, such disruptions might initially be localized to the cutting edge IT sub-sectors.

Caste Reproduction Potential in Indian IT: A Recapitulation

In the caste-imbued Indian social atmosphere, the ICT based occupational revolution in India has the untapped potential of being an ideal site for disrupting the traditional caste-occupation link. Unfortunately, much scholarly research signals the introduction of caste inequalities in the IT industry. The IT-BPO occupational sector has turned into a new domain of the privileged castes, they say. Educational credentials in the IT sector, while seemingly modern and non-nepotistic in terminology, rather than equalizing opportunities, often act as a double edged sword (D'Costa 2011; Jodhka and Newman 2010; Raghunath 2010; Upadhya 2006). IT professionals, almost uniformly, tend to hail from well-resourced backgrounds. Merit-based elites are, more often than not, urban and upper castes.[41]

---

[41] Specific examples can be found in Banerjee, Bertrand, Datta, and Mullainathan (2008); Krishna and Brihmadesam (2006); Raghunath (2010); and Upadhya (2007a).

Distinctions within the intra-IT occupational sector, and between inter-occupational sectors of IT and non-IT, have been attributed to the filtering through inter-sectioning privileges based on caste, class, gender, religion, community, and urban location. In the final analyses, even though the IT occupational sector, unlike the traditional Indian occupations, does not have a caste foundation, the *inter-sectioning privileged processes* have led to the re-creation and fostering of caste-based cultural hierarchies in the new IT habitus. Since the constitutional protections accorded to Dalits and OBCs in the public sector do not have a standing in the private IT industry, they face hurdles in entry, retention, and advancement. Given more than half a century of educational quotas for SCs, including in the prestigious public institutions of higher education like the IITs and other technical institutions, one may expect to find qualified Dalits in the IT-BOP occupational sector in proportions approximately similar to their graduation rates from technical institutions. Unfortunately data to test this expectation are not maintained in the private sector.

Nonetheless, unpacking the IT Merit Construction Project offers a window into caste reproduction in the IT social habitus. The fervent contrasts that are drawn between a streamlined *pure IT merit* and *reservation merit* obscure the symbolic privileges of forward castes in the industry. The Merit Camp equates caste with caste reservations; reservations, they say, undermine the attentively crafted and practiced pure merit credentials, an efficient management tool for success in a globalized industry. To the Merit Camp, caste hierarchy and associated symbolic capital, and hidden privileges are not constituent elements of caste. But, as the Caste Camp has countered, streamlined pure merit is but a symbolic tool to manage the matrix of symbolic and material caste privileges that intertwine and reinforce each other to create and sustain the unique merit IT culture. The merit construction project makes it possible for caste to be factored into pure merit constructions and become discriminatory of lower castes.

It is the passionately vocal, sometimes strident, arguments on either side of the debate that take on the shades of a 'blood sport'. The growing popularity of technology jobs, along with structural constraints in access to technical education, further fuels the 'blood sport'. Yet, the caste dimensions in the competitive sport of technical education favour the dominant castes and even IT qualified women. Disrupting caste reproduction in Indian IT will require corporate social responsibility that leverages the strategic business values of caste diversity and inclusiveness.

Settling the Caste-Merit Debates: Using Mixed Methodologies

Sorting out the volatile contestations about the nature of the merit-caste debates in Indian IT and claims about the new inequality vector require a multilayered set of perspectives. Multiple voices, expressed through different media, were tapped to provide a more robust empirical foundation for the Merit Culture Making project and its potential for reproducing caste inequalities in the Indian IT sector.

An online web survey, fielded with rank-and-file Indian IT professionals about their IT work experiences, offered a ground level view of their merit culture making experiences. Supplementing the individual employee experiences, were interviews with IT key informants or knowledge leaders who provided a broader organizational perspective. National secondary data on Human Capital, and other capital resources set the national context for the merit-caste debates. Rounding out this multilayered portrayal was content analyses of scholarly writing on Indian IT and newspaper reports of caste tensions and successes. Informed consent, voluntary participation, and relevant anonymity/confidentiality guarantees marked the ethical protocol for the primary data collection process, both through the web surveys and narrative interviews.

Web Survey

The web survey, administered during January–August 2010, was completed by 514 professionals who worked in Indian IT companies. Survey respondents answered questions about their employment history in IT, their views on the relative weights of 'merit' versus 'caste' in their portrayal of an ideal IT employee, and general thoughts on caste and the role of women in IT.

Planning to field the survey offered the first valuable lesson about the contentious nature of caste in contemporary India. The original plan was to distribute the surveys through the Human Resource (HR) divisions of Indian IT companies. However, in initial conversations with a few HR staff in India, it quickly became clear that they would not (and could not, according to them) officially distribute a survey on caste to their employees because of their companies' equal employment opportunity policies. Consequently, IT professionals in India, identified through snowball sampling, were invited to complete the survey. The goal was to get a large enough sample (at least 500) to counter at least two sets of potential limitations in snowball sampling: the first of generalizability that comes with a non-random snow-ball sampling technique; the second of authentic reporting problems potentially associated with a confidential web survey.

As of 15 August 2010, 514 IT professionals completed the survey. The initial 'full' survey, which included detailed caste questions, was completed by 149 individuals. However, due to the intense resistance to completing a survey that included multiple questions about caste, a more streamlined survey with only 1 caste question[42] was distributed, through HR managers and other knowledge leaders; this version was completed by 365 IT professionals. In the following chapters, these respondents will be referred to, alternatively, as rank-and-file IT professionals, or IT professionals, or survey respondents. Copies of the email invitation with anonymity assurances and informed consent procedures, as well as the long and streamlined forms of the surveys are available in Appendix 1A.2 and 1A.3.

Qualitative Interviews with Key Informants

To flesh out an organizational perspective on the IT merit construction process, caste reproduction and other related dynamics, in-person qualitative narrative interviews were conducted with sources knowledgeable about the Indian IT industry. Conversations were held with 30 key informants, including HR managers, senior staff, consultants, educators, and social commentators. These leaders were located in Bangalore, Hyderabad, Chennai, and Trivandrum; these are Tier I IT cities in the four southern Indian states that either have IT hubs or emerging IT hubs.[43] A wide range of topics were explored; these included the hiring process, such as what they look for in a potential employee and what qualifies and disqualifies an applicant, as well as important elements in their retention success. Discussions about reservation and quota system were gingerly approached. There was general consensus in the IT

---

[42] More details of the specific caste questions are available in Chapters 2 and 3.

[43] Most multinational technology firms have operations in these hub cities and have significantly transformed the landscapes of these cities. IT hubs are expanding to Tier II cities also (John and Phadnis 2014).

knowledge community that Dalits often gravitate towards public sector jobs (Deshpande and Newman 2010).

Unlike the guaranteed reserved quotas for entrance into and job security in the public sector, private companies including IT/BPOs are not required to adhere to the SC/ST/OBC quota system. Recent demands in certain political circles to require private companies to hire employees according to the public sector reservation/quota system were resisted by most key informants. However, a few BPO companies like Infosys Technologies, have instituted pilot programs to recruit and retain qualified Dalits in their workforce; sources knowledgeable about these programs were also interviewed to ascertain their experiences with the caste diversity initiatives. All interview respondents were guaranteed confidentiality in reports of their responses.

National Secondary Data

To provide a national empirical basis for the caste-merit debates, data from two national human and economic capital surveys were accessed. The 2005–6 NFHS-3 National Family Health Survey[44] and the 2005 India Human Development Survey (IHDS)[45] included valuable information on caste and regional distribution of wealth, education, and other socioeconomic resources per individuals and households. This data offered a national assessment of the Dalit deficit thesis and related issues.

Scholarly and Newspaper Sources

Content analyses of scholarly literature, case studies, and other empirical writings, on the Indian IT companies offered additional glimpses into the workings of IT companies. Also used were newspaper sources that regularly publish reports on caste, caste induced tensions, and commentaries on the current national discussions on caste. Some examples of newspapers accessed were: *The Indian Express* (indianexpress.com) *Times of India* (timesofindia.com), *Deccan Herald* (deccanherald.com), and

---

[44] See Desai, Vanneman, and National Council of Applied Economic Research (2005). India Human Development Survey (IHDS) New Delhi.

[45] International Institute for Population Sciences (IIPS) and Macro International (2007).

electronic sources like The National Campaign on Dalit Human Rights (NCDHR)'s *Dalits in News* (ncdhr.org.in).

Data Analyses Strategies

Both quantitative statistical and qualitative analytic tools were utilized in an iterative, dialectic, and convergent fashion to capitalize on the complementary data sources. Survey data, interview comments, and scholarly and newspaper writings were merged and interspersed throughout the manuscript to critically validate the main themes. For example, to develop a portrait of the Indian IT occupational structure, the employment and educational histories of web survey respondents and national sample demographics were analyzed using descriptive statistical techniques. Factor analyses captured the IT merit and other metrics in the 'merit-culture making' project. The comments in the survey and in the qualitative interviews offered rich narratives on the IT merit-making project and the caste-merit debates. Van Manen's (1997) hermeneutic phenomenology,[46] emerging out of people's lived experiences, was another analytic strategy used. On the one hand, the main tropes or themes in the study participants' (both surveys and interviews) narrative comments about caste in the IT sector were guided by the objectives of the research. At the same time, enough room was allowed for new tropes to emerge in the study participants' verbal and written responses about additional dimensions they thought were relevant for a study on caste in the Indian IT sector.

A Road Map to the Upcoming Chapters

The story of how the Indian IT has the potential to become *a new vector of caste inequality is rooted in the IT merit construction project* and the contradictions in the *Merit-Caste debates* in the Indian IT social habitus (Chapter 2). What does the profile of the IT occupational structure look like in the lived experiences of rank-and-file IT professionals? What is a typical occupational trajectory of IT professionals in the new occupational sector? As IT professionals engaged in their merit culture making project in their work habitus, they *valorized merit as pure* while *caste and other traditional symbolic privileges stayed obscured.* Yet, merit, to them, *was*

---

[46]   Also see Laverty (2003).

also holistic, with subjective markers of English fluency, habits of the mind, intellect, spirit, and of 'soft' skills of communication, that offered entry points through which traditional social vectors of caste, community, and religion make their way into the IT occupational habitat.

It was when rank-and-file IT professionals and key informants were pointedly invited to talk about their views of and experiences with caste in the merit construction process, that the conversations became passionately vocal, sometimes strident, and other times palpably silent (Chapter 3). Sifting through the vehement and nuanced voices of IT professionals, shades of a competitive 'blood sport' were revealed. Those on the '''Merit' side of the rink characterized the IT social space as '*caste neutral*'; Indian IT companies, they say, are guided by ideals of meritocracy and equality. Private IT companies did not abide by the government's reservation policies. Reservations, with their diluted or reduced standards, were equated with merit deficits. On the other hand, the opposing '*Caste Camp*' emphasized the *obscured forward caste privileges*, the *implicit caste filtering* based on perceived and/or real upper caste merit, *the Dalit social capital deficit*, and *resultant discriminatory outcomes*. Using caste hermeneutical lenses to articulate their case, the Caste Camp asserted with equal vehemence that casteism has not disappeared. *Societal caste hierarchies* have been reproduced in the IT sector either in its original or modified forms through *caste networks and caste-tinged filtered pattern recognitions*. In the original representation of caste in Indian society, SCs are at the bottom of the hierarchy. In the modified form, SCs are still at the lowest rung, but the top caste tier has been expanded to make room for other dominant class/ castes, 'communities', in the top tier of a resource intensive IT sector. In the absence of hard caste evidence to test the competing contentions and their respective outcomes, the only tenable conclusion to be deductively drawn was that the IT sector, rather than being the caste neutral bastion many claim it to be, has in fact become the new frontier for caste. The much *valorized 'merit'* criteria, by virtue of *embedded-privilege exclusion of SCs and other disadvantaged groups*, has opened the doors for *diffusion of caste norms and reproduction* in Indian IT, and the rise of a new caste inequality vector.

The arguments and counter arguments about caste in the merit culture making project are also played out in the arena of Indian higher technical education (Chapter 4). The intensity of the debate is fuelled partly by the growing popularity of technology jobs but in equal part by the caste underpinnings in access to education. The elite public funded Indian technical education system stands in sharp contrast to the weaker, but pricier, private technical institutions. Even so, the *caste dimensions in the competitive sport of technical education still favour the dominant castes*. To the SC and poor OBC youth, who are priced out of the private market, the relatively less expensive seats reserved for them in public institutions are the only realistic choice. Ironically, the public nature of prestigious technical institutions has made them a primary site where the Merit-Caste blood sport is overtly waged. Yet, private technical institutions are where the solid foundations for caste inequalities in the IT occupational sector are silently laid. Just as both public and private institutions of technical higher education have become the sites where merit is culturally constructed, they can also be ideal locations for deconstructing the merit culture making project and revealing the project's caste foundations.

Gender initiatives in the IT sector (Chapter 5) offered a useful contrast to the resistance to caste diversity in Indian IT. The singular tool for gender parity, the current diversity hallmark in the IT work habitus, has been *gender neutral IT merit*. However, gender diversity in the IT workplace is a work in progress; the gender-neutral IT merit values, the *glass ceiling faced by women*, and a *singular gender perspective* were indicative of the persistent challenges faced by women and by the IT sector in transforming the IT work habitat into a more gender inclusive space. While *gender inclusiveness* was not quite on the radar of the rank-and-file IT professionals, gender discussion—analyses and redress options—were more accessible and amenable in the IT sector than caste inequalities. At this time in the nation's history, caste, perhaps, is a bridge too high or far to cross.

What would it take for the IT sector to live up to its predicted role as the new equalizer and societal savior from the vestiges of casteism and other inequalities (Chapter 6)? Taking cues from the gender diversity models that the leaders in the IT sector, like NASSCOM, have celebrated and encouraged, a call is made for corporate social responsibility *to adopt caste inclusive human resource techniques* to potentially disrupt caste transference and reproduction in IT. If Indian IT is to deliver on its promise to bend the arc of inequality in India, sector *sub-units, like their cutting-edge knowledge production divisions*, will need to take leadership in leveraging the strategic business values of caste diversity and inclusiveness.

Appendix 1A.1: Merit-Caste Contestations in Historical and Contemporary India

Because the Merit-Caste debates, and their potential for existing caste-based inequalities to be reinforced in the Indian IT sector, are rooted in the historicity of the caste system, a brief review of historical and contemporary caste dynamics in India is pertinent. The caste system continues to permeate, even if subtly, major life course events in the lives of Indians. Whether hidden in caste privileges or explicit in caste social redress programs, caste identity is an important marker for many Indians, in deciding who is merit worthy in access to education, jobs, the legal and political systems as well as in marriage and in community relationships.

The Caste System and Inequalities in Historical Perspective

The roots of the caste system have been associated, in recent genetic studies (Engelhardt and Stephens 2010; Moorjani et al. 2013), with the practice of endogamy that originated about 4,000 years ago. Genetic information collected from 73 Indian and Pakistani groups showed that, around that period, mixing through marriage stopped and the endogamous caste system started.

Prior to the start of admixture, there was free genetic mixture between two broad homogenous groups, Ancestral North Indians (ANI) and Ancestral South Indians (ASI).[47] Later, socio-economic imperatives, such as protection of wealth, were predicted to have contributed to the rise of caste endogamy.

At an elementary historical level, the caste system comprises an endogamous set of groups with religiously prescribed set of practices that define some as hierarchically 'purer' than others. Stated in broad terms, the caste hierarchy or the Varna system in India has five strata: Brahmin, Kshatriya, Vaisya, Shudra, and SCs (also referred to as Dalits). However, within each of these ranks are the scores of ground-level 'castes' or jatis into which people are born, marry, and die. To add to complexity, the caste system is simultaneously an all India phenomenon as well as highly localized.

---

[47] ANIs are related to Central Asians, middle easterners, Caucasians, and Europeans while the ASIs were primarily from the sub-continent (Engelhardt and Stephens 2010; Moorjani et al. 2013).

Caste names, for example, vary from place to place. But, irrespective of the local variability, caste privileges have traditionally been translated into educational and economic privileges afforded to some and denied to others. And, far from being a historical anachronism, caste continues to be socially relevant in modern India.

While the caste system is a social and economic classification supported by religious ideologies and unique customary rules and norms, the core governing principle of the system is not simply of distinctions among different caste groups, but also about inequality, social exclusion and discrimination. The graded caste inequality implies hierarchically unequal entitlement; every caste, except the forward or higher castes, has suffered and continues to do so, a degree of exclusion and denial. As one moves down the caste hierarchy, the rights and privileges get reduced even more. Dalits or SCs suffer the most from untouchability, residential, and social exclusion. The OBCs have also faced exclusion in education and employment, but not as much as the SCs.

Who are the Scheduled Castes (SCs), Scheduled Tribes (STs), and Other Backward Classes (OBCs)?

In contemporary India, SCs, STs, and OBCs are three historically marginalized groups in India that are constitutionally recognized. 'Scheduled Castes', which includes the former 'untouchables', are called so because their caste names are listed in the Constitution (Scheduled Castes) Order, 1950, a schedule of the Indian constitution. Currently, the term Dalits, meaning downtrodden or oppressed, has gained currency because it is a non-pejorative term. The list of schedules castes are periodically updated (caste names are deleted or added) by each state in the Union to account for changing social and economic circumstances (see Government of India 1978 and 2014). The term 'Scheduled Tribes' refers to specific indigenous peoples of India whose status is acknowledged, to some formal degree, by national legislation (Government of India, Constitution, Scheduled Tribes Order, 1950); the list has been amended in 1976 and later.

When the Indian Constitution listed SCs/Dalits in a separate schedule, only those who professed Hinduism, Sikhism, and Buddhism were included; Christian or Muslims were entirely omitted (Paragraph 3 of the Constitution, Scheduled Caste Order of 1950). However, because there were many marginalized groups in the Christian and Muslim communities, there was a growing clamour for making reservation provisions for them too. The Mandal Commission, which was set up in response, denoted a third category, 'Other Backward Classes' (OBCs) in its report issued in 1980; OBCs included the socially and economically exploited groups of Christians and Muslims (Rai 2002). Other Backward Classes, a third collective term used by the Indian government classifies castes and classes, irrespective of religion, which are socially and educationally disadvantaged.

As of the 2011 Census of India, SCs represented 16.6 percent and STs 8.6 percent of the population. The OBC count was at 41.0 per cent of the population in 2006. A third (30.8 per cent) belonged to the FCs (Sachar 2006). Like the SC and ST listing, the OBC list is also periodically updated (as recently as 2014) through constitutional amendments, to account for changing social and economic circumstances. For example, OBCs comprised 52 per cent of the country's population (across all religions) in the Mandal Commission report of 1980; by 2006, when the National Sample Survey Organization was conducted, the OBC numbers shrunk to 41 per cent. Downward or upward shifts in the OBC numbers and OBC group lists (which are maintained both by the Central and State governments to account for local variations) are the result of communities being added or removed depending on their social, educational, and economic conditions.

How is the OBC Classification Distributed Across Different Religious Communities?

As seen in the Table 1A.1, OBCs were more likely to be Hindus (42.8 per cent), followed by Muslims (39.2 per cent) and Christians (24.8 per cent). The Hindu, Christian, and Sikh communities had the most caste diversity. Aside from the plurality of Hindu OBCs (42.8 per cent), the rest were primarily from either forward communities (26 per cent) or SCs (22.2 per cent). Christians were more likely to be part of the forward groups (33.3 per cent) or Scheduled Tribes (32.8 per cent) than OBC (24.8 per cent). In contrast, Muslims were either forward (59.5 per cent) or OBC (39.2 per cent). The Sikh community was similar, yet slightly different, to their Hindu counterparts in their caste diversity: a plurality of Sikhs were from forward communities (46.1 per cent), followed by the

Appendix: Table 1A.1   Distribution of Population of Each Religion by Caste Categories

Religion/Caste	SCs	STs	OBCs	Forward Castes/Others	(n per 1,000)
Hinduism	22.2%	9.0	42.8	26.0	1,598 (80.0%)
Islam	0.8%	0.5	39.2	59.5	283 (14.1%)
Christianity	9.0%	32.8	24.8	33.3	46 (2.3%)
Sikhism	30.7%	0.9	22.4	46.1	39 (1.9%)
Jainism	0.0%	2.6	3.0	94.3	8 (0.4%)
Buddhism	89.5%	7.4	0.4	2.7	16 (0.8%)
Zoroastrianism	0.0%	15.9	13.7	70.4	7 (0.4%)
Others	2.6%	82.5	6.25	8.7	2 (0.1%)
Total	**19.7%**	**8.5%**	**41.1%**	**30.8%**	**1,997**

Source: Merged sample of Schedule 1 and Schedule 10 of available data from the NSSO 55th (1999-2000) and NSSO 61st Rounds (2004–05) Round Survey. Available at: http://mospi.gov.in/national_data_bank/pdf/NSS%2061st%20 Round-521.pdf. Retrieved on 28 April 2015.

30.7 per cent of SCs and 22.4 per cent of OBCs. Finally, the Jain (94.3 per cent) and Zoroastrian (70.4 per cent) communities were primarily FCs.

Why Do SCs, STs, and OBCs Receive Special Privileges?

The historical occupational foundation of castes is one mechanism through which the caste-economic nexus has been enacted and inequalities perpetuated. Each caste group has a traditional association with one or two occupations (Srinivas 1976). The Brahmins who occupy the top strata of the caste hierarchy are priests and educators; Kshatriyas, on the second rung, are the warriors/landowners and are followed by Vaisyas, the merchants/farmers. The Shudras, the fourth and lower caste, are the artisans, agriculturalists, dhobis (clothes washers). The Scheduled Castes, also known as Dalits or Harijans, the former untouchables, are outside the caste hierarchy, relegated to jobs that are considered ritually polluting to the upper caste members; street cleaning, barbering, and working with animal products such as leather and meat, and with human and animal waste and the dead are some examples of polluting occupations.

It was to address the centuries old exclusion and discrimination of SCs and STs that the founders and writers of the Constitution of the republic of independent India (1950) established economic empowerment or EE (pro-poor) policies, supplemented with equal opportunity (EO) policies for SC and STs (Thorat and Newman 2010b). While the EE policies were expected to improve the capital assets of the poor, irrespective of caste status, the founders made a prescient assumption that in the absence of EO policies, SCs will continue to be discriminated against. Moved by the manifest, visible social and economic disparities between the upper and lower castes (particularly 'scheduled' castes), the framers of the Indian constitution did not wait for academic research to demonstrate said inequalities before implementing equal opportunity policies or reservations in government sponsored education, employment, and in the political process.

The quotas and earmarked seats (not to exceed 50 per cent) in government institutions of education, occupations, and elected bodies are part of the EO social redress programs. For example, all central government-funded educational institutions, including higher education institutions, reserve 15 per cent of the seats for students of SCs or Dalit groups. Later in 1980 (based on the Mandal Commission Report) the reservation group was expanded to include a broader range of excluded groups, under the title 'Other Backward Classes' (OBCs). The total percentage of reservations (for SCs, STs, and OBCs) was also increased up to 49.5 per cent in higher education, jobs, and in elected political offices; 15 per cent for SCs; 7.5 per cent for STs; 27 per cent for OBC.

Special Privileges and Caste Tensions

The reservation and quota system has been a simple, but administratively robust program to redress centuries old inequalities in access to higher education (but not with what happens once they are admitted (Parthasarathy 2012)). Under the existing social justice program, community identity (not class within the community) is the sole marker of entitlement to social justice redress programs. But, questions have been raised about whether everybody in the SC and OBC communities qualifies for reservation. Scheduled caste and OBC based reservations have been litigated periodically[48] but have withstood legal scrutiny. For

---

[48] Few salient examples: (*a*) M R Balaji v Mysore AIR 1963 SC 649: put 50 per cent cap on reservations; (*b*) Supreme Court in Indira Sawhney &

example, the exclusion of the 'creamy layer' in OBC communities from the scope of reservation policies is one issue about OBC reservation quotas that has been litigated and sustained in the country's Supreme Court, first in 2007 (in Ashok Kumar vs. Union of India). The 'creamy layer' was defined by economic (family income above 600,000 rupees a year) or social capital; this group includes, children of doctors, engineers, chartered accountants, actors, consultants, media professionals, writers, bureaucrats, defense officers of colonel and equivalent rank or higher, high court and Supreme Court judges, all central and state government Class A and B officials, and MPs and MLAs. But the 'creamy layer' issue in higher education has been litigated in favour of OBC and SC caste status, and not class, identities. The primary reasoning has been two-fold: excluding the creamy layer of SCs and OBCs from the reservation program will shut out the very group (creamy layer) that is most likely to go to college and make reservations in education available only to the economically marginalized groups that are the least likely to use it. Besides, with creamy layer exclusions, where caste is replaced by class, discount caste discrimination or disadvantage (Deshpande 2012). Indian courts have been very clear that the 'Creamy Layer' principle, cannot be applied to STs and SCs. SCs and STs are legally deemed to be separate classes by themselves. In addition, the quota provisions were extended to what some call, the last bastion of upper caste privilege, the elite central government educational institutes like IITs, IIMs (Indian Institute of Management), and central universities. 'With social justice legislation now covering two-thirds of the population, the upper castes were exposed for the minority they have always been' (Deshpande 2012: 229). However, the redress programs did not address what happens once SCs are admitted to these institutions (see Parthasarathy 2012).

Ors vs. Union of India. AIR 1993 SC 477, 1992 Supp (3) SCC 217: upheld implementation of separate reservation for other backward classes in central government jobs; ordered exclusion of 'creamy layer' of OBCs from enjoying reservation facilities; reinforced restrictions of reservations within 50 per cent limit; declared separate reservations for economically poor among forward castes as invalid; and declared separate reservations for economically poor among forward castes as invalid; (c) A variety of court judgements about reservations as they apply, or do not, to promotions within jobs. See http://en.wikipedia.org/wiki/Court_Cases_Related_to_Reservation_in_India.

Complaints against the reservation system have come from both sides. Those against the system point to reserved seats being left unfilled; only 7 per cent of 27 per cent quota filled mainly because of limited numbers of OBC students in the primary school pipelines. A political party using these communities as vote banks is another complaint. But, say the pro-reservation group, these reservations do not apply to private sector industries. It is not a coincidence that the Indian IT sector, which is mostly private, has become the new vector of caste inequality.

Caste Exclusion and Discrimination: Research Evidence[49]

The contemporary societal caste literature and discussions are replete with caste terminology. A review of simple definitions of these terms showed that discrimination against SCs is multidimensional in nature. *Casteism* refers to the complete or partial exclusion of certain castes from participation in social and institutional processes on the basis of group identities. These exclusionary social relations have outcomes that deprive some caste groups, say SCs, from full participation in social and economic opportunities (Thorat 2008). *Caste Discrimination (Active Exclusion)* is the practice of casteism which manifests in a variety of insidious forms of exclusions. The following examples offered by Thorat (2008) are instructive: (*a*) Complete exclusion of SCs and OBCs by members of the Forward Castes (FCs) from the sale/purchase of factors of production and hiring, housing and other consumer goods; (*b*) Selective inclusion and privileges for FCs in the pricing mechanisms; FCs are charged or receive preferred prices breaching market rates, even in public institutions; (*c*) Unfavourable inclusion, often by force, of SCs who are bound by caste obligations and duties resulting in overwork, loss of freedom, bondage and differential treatment at work; and (*d*) Exclusion of SC/STs, that traditionally worked in 'unclean jobs', from certain categories of 'clean' jobs. While the discriminatory examples outlined above represent active acts of exclusion, scholars and activists have also identified instances of *passive exclusion* of SCs from social and economic opportunities. Often social processes (requiring English fluency and other cultural markers of dress and appearance) are set up and operate in ways that, even in the absence

---

[49] The analyses in this section were drawn from Buvinic (2004), Sen (2000), and other researchers noted in the text.

of active exclusion, result in exclusion of SCs from many competitive positions (Sen 2000).

More specifically, the caste system works to enhance, or limit as the case might be, the life options of the average Indian. These inequalities are reflected in limited education, employment, and overall reduced life options for SCs. An individual's caste identity is hereditarily predetermined or 'ascribed' at birth and is accompanied by unequal and hierarchical entitlement to economic and social rights. The caste system does not recognize the individual or family. Rather, the caste group is the primary unit of Indian society with individuals' rights and privileges (or lack thereof) derived from the caste to which they belong. As one goes down the graded caste hierarchy, rights and privileges become narrower. Also one's caste group does not exist singularly in isolation, but as an interlinking graded hierarchy with unequal measures of rights and privileges in all walks of life. To reiterate, forward or high upper castes have more rights than OBCs; and SCs have the fewest rights and suffer the most exclusion from full participation in the Indian society.

In addition to the rights and privileges that caste groups offer their members, the system also provides a community regulatory mechanism of social ostracism to enforce exclusion and discrimination. These regulatory mechanisms are, in some circles, justified using selective philosophical elements of the Hindu religious code. The fixed and predetermined social and economic rights associated with each caste and their members imply 'forced exclusion', a necessary outcome of its governing principles. For example, SCs are prevented from participating fully in socio-economic-political opportunities primarily because of restrictions imposed by upper castes on the lower castes. Contrary to true free market principles, the restrictions embedded in caste-based social-economic-political relations, are imposed and suffered by culturally delineated, ascribed groups rather than because of individual agency and responsibility.

It is not surprising that despite the legal redress provisions caste remains an important troubling undercurrent in the Indian social fabric. Caste-based conflict persist in education, employment, and in social relations. The National Campaign on Dalit Human Rights (NCDHR), which monitors newspaper accounts of daily human rights violations, has reported a variety of incidents of caste-based conflict. There are incidents of public humiliation, rape, murder, accusations of caste slurs in academic institutions, and Dalit student expulsion from the premier IITs on grounds of 'poor performance'. There have also been reports of legal challenges and policy intervention in caste conflicts. Amidst these continuing struggles, are the few high profile successes, such as a Dalit who was the chief economist of the Reserve Bank of India and then vice-chancellor of Pune University ('Dalit Dreams' in *Times Of India*, 16 January 2004). Even the purportedly a-political Indian bureaucracy is heavily politicized with caste undertones. For example, a state chief minister from one of the SC castes is more likely to appoint and promote bureaucrats from the same caste, superseding equally qualified candidates of other castes. The same is true of the dominant castes as well (Iyer and Mani 2012). Such politicized bureaucrats help politicians during elections.

Inequality and Casteism in the (Non-IT) Private Job Sector

In this caste imbued social milieu, it should be no surprise if discrimination and exclusion of SCs along with simultaneous passive inclusion of FCs continues in the private sector of contemporary India. Starting at the job application stage, earnings, and overall limited options for life, SCs remain marginalized because they are deemed less merit worthy. Thorat and Attewell (2010: 48) found caste favouritism and social exclusion of Dalits and Muslims to occur in private Indian companies at the job application stage. Urban FCs (in Madheswaran and Attewell's 2010 study) fared better than SCs in employment and earnings; discrimination, defined as inequalities in access to certain occupations and some wage discrimination, accounted for the gross earning differentials between SCs and non-SCs in the regular salaried urban labour market.

Deficits in education and other capital endowments of SCs added to the earning inequalities. Caste-based disparities are blatantly stronger in rural than in urban areas. Only a fifth of urban Dalits that Thorat, Mahamallik, and Sadana (2010) surveyed were self-employed and property owners; besides, the market for the purchase and sales of Dalit products were often restricted to members of their community. There were other poignant reminders of the pervasiveness of the caste hierarchies in rural communities: SCs were not hired for household work in FC households; they were paid lower wages (for similar work); their payments were delayed due to social restrictions like avoidance of physical touch; and were not sold land in proximity to upper castes to avoid 'pollution', a practice akin to 'red lining' in the US real estate market. These inequalities also transferred into realms of food insecurities (Thorat and Lee 2010) and unequal health outcomes for Dalits (Acharya 2010; Borooah 2010).

Researchers have found that such caste-based exclusion and economic discrimination practices have significant negative consequences for the nation and for SCs. Whatever the original functions of the caste system, the foundation of the current/classic form of casteism is not so much economic efficiency but rather the economic motive of income maximization through coercion (Thorat and Newman 2010a: 12). Unequal access of SCs to economic rights directly translates into deprivations of opportunities in educational and economic spheres and high poverty rates. Unfortunately, despite the insidious nature of casteism, powerful deterrents against changing the system are posed by practices of social ostracism, the economic costs of breaking caste rules, and FC monopolies.

SC Educational Deficits Start Early and Continue into Adulthood

While no more than 4–7 per cent of all Indians are college educated, SCs are even less so. On average, older SC men and women (36 and older in the 2015 IHDS) have completed only 4 and 1 years of education respectively. The comparable rates for men and women of the forward castes were 7 and 4 in completed years of education. In fact, SC educational disadvantages start at the *elementary and secondary school levels* (Hasan and Nussbaum 2012). Even though primary/elementary and secondary education, provided through the public and private sectors, is quasi mandatory in India, there are many caste and class based obstacles to entering and completing elementary and secondary schools (Ghosh 2012). For one, SC/ST caste members are typically first generation school goers, if they even make it into the educational system. Also, the almost 'essential' reliance on private out-of-the classroom tutoring for basic elementary education (consequences of the heavy ambitious curriculum combined with poor teacher performance) put SC/STs without the necessary family resources at a competitive disadvantage. Subtle forms of discouragement and ostracism in grade schools (Nambissan 2010) and net inequalities in the mastery of reading and arithmetic (Desai, Adams, and Dubey 2010) add to the educational deficits of SC students.

These early mechanisms continue their disparate impacts into the SC youth's *later educational careers* (Deshpande 2012).[50] Compounding the limited higher education access of SCs, nearly half the institutions of higher learning are concentrated in urban areas of mainly five southern Indian states; professional courses are located primarily in another five states (Government of India 2009). Cumulatively, these factors, contribute to the low education rates in the SC/ST communities (Amartya Sen's Op-Ed in *The Hindu*, 19 December, 2009). The ubiquitous practice of using expensive *'coaching centres'*, to prepare candidates for entrance exams and ultimate admissions into the elite IT related higher education institutions, is often beyond the means of poor SC families.[51] Even when SC/ST students secure admission to the prestigious IITs,[52] say based on caste reservations, the academic and social structures and climate in these institutions are often not conducive to the success of minority students. Parthasarathy's (2012) analyses of key informant opinions, emails, and fora comments found traditional educational practices to not help, and even hindered the success of minority students. IIT faculty in his study were more interested in research than in teaching, in using traditional standardized tests for evaluation rather

[50] Of the Indian youth who finish their higher secondary education, only about 12 per cent enrol in higher education.

[51] Stringent entrance criteria for the limited and coveted seats in the 16 Indian Institutes of Technology (the premier technology institutions in the country with only 9,000 seats per year) and other professional and technical institutions, has given rise to private, expensive coaching centres. For example, there has been a proliferation of coaching centres for the competitive entrance tests administered by the Joint Admission Board (JAB) for admission to the IITs, the premier technology institutions which are feeders for IT occupations. Other top engineering colleges, like the BITS-Pilani, have their own separate test requirements; two examples are AIEEE and CET. Because the syllabi for these entrance examinations are much tougher than the regular Class XII curriculum (final year of high school), parents who can afford the extra tuition shell out anywhere between 40,000 rupees and 1.2 lakh rupees to get their children prepared for the tests (Sangeetha 2009).

[52] Dalit alums of IIT have an alumni association, named IIT Dalits, which aims to 'to bring together Dalits educated at IITs to contribute to the Dalit cause by helping Dalit students to avail scholarships to pursue higher education'. Available at: http://iit.org/alumni-groups/iit-dalits/?searchterm=dalit. As of 18 July 2008, the organization had 76 members.

than projects or essays, and allowing exams only in English (and not also in Hindi or a regional language); these alternative educational practices, Parthasarathy argued, could benefit minority students.

Even after graduation from IT institutions, there are profound differences in life course expectations between equally qualified Dalit and non-reservation students (Deshpande and Newman 2010).[53] Dalit/SC students expected to work more in the public sector than in the private sector, confirming the critical importance of reservations in the public sector job market. In contrast, family connections were the catch-phrase for non-SC students; they were likely to rely on family connections and expected to find jobs much sooner, about five months after graduation rather than the ten months predicted by SC students.

Multiple Pathways to Caste Reproduction in Indian IT

There is some empirical evidence for a variety of intervening mechanisms through which IT Merit construction operates to limit opportunities, or enhance them as the case may be. To quote Jodhka and Newman (2010: 57), ' ... the production of merit itself is a highly unequal business, and hence the linkage ... of merit with cultural capital, effectively eliminates Dalits, for example, from the competition'. Individuals from urban areas, high/middle castes and classes, and men, who were privileged in the merit construction process, have dominated the IT industry. In intersecting fashion, these ascribed statuses, associated capital resources, and cosmopolitan outlooks, inherited from educated parents, have recreated inequalities by limiting IT Merit opportunities for some while boosting them for others. The distribution of 'merit' or credentials along the ascribed axes renders questionable whether 'merit' is solely a function of individual talent. In other words, to minorities, say SCs, those from rural backgrounds, and even women in these groups, the centuries old caste traditions and inequalities have not simply disappeared even in the purportedly casteless IT occupational sector.

Some specific examples of the intersecting exclusionary mechanism at work in the inequality processes are illustrative here. The credential or

---

[53] Of the 173 students who were completing their post-graduate degrees from prestigious universities in India, a third of the students were from reserved caste groups.

'degree' requirement for employment in the IT industry excludes a larger percentage of the population without access to college (secondary or tertiary) education, thereby skewing employment opportunities in favour of *educated middle classes*. Without the foundation of a quality basic education,[54] those at the bottom of the social hierarchies, have little chance of reaching higher levels of education, effectively excluding them from the IT sector. Indian IT has been described as a class 'enclave' (D'Costa 2011), with an inherent upper class bias working within the sector. In Raghunath's (2010) ethnographic study,[55] while 'merit' was judged by educational credentials, access to higher education was dictated by caste status and prior academic performance. Family background, denoted by parent's occupation, education, and family surname, were used to ratify 'merit' in another survey of three software firms in Bangalore by Krishna and Brihmadesam (2006).[56] Having two educated parents, and not so much the place of origin or family economic background, most commonly characterized newly recruited software professionals. In an environment where career-related information is hard to come by, because no counselling centres or career guidance were available either in high schools or in most undergraduate colleges, having two educated parents was a distinct advantage and asset. Educated parents networked with other educated and well-informed people about IT job options for their children.

Recruitment practices in IT companies add yet another stratifying mechanism in the IT industry (Upadhya and Vasavi 2006). Carol Upadhya's (2007a) software engineers[57] came from high/middle caste, middle class, well educated, and urban families despite industry leaders' claims of diversity in hiring. Rather than being based solely on 'merit', employers tended to be biased towards skills possessed mainly by the privileged in society, adding another layer to the existing social hierarchies. These social and

[54] As noted earlier, resources for primary education are limited in contrast to the well-funded, highly regarded government technical institutes (where quotas for SCs apply).

[55] The ethnography included three workplaces in Bangalore, India, from 2002 to 2006. Ascribed parental status still plays a more dominant role than 'just' or 'pure' merit.

[56] Fathers of all new recruits in their sample had at least a high school degree or better (75 per cent were college graduates). More than 80 per cent of all mothers also had at least a high school education.

[57] They were in a survey of 132 software engineers working in Bangalore.

economic hierarchies that produce 'meritorious candidates' exclude the marginalized SCs.

A *soft skills* component of merit, a less than objective measure, is yet another mechanism through which inequality is reproduced in the Indian IT sector. Apart from the required education credentials, the language of meritocracy also includes a requisite set of cultural capital resources or sophistication or know-how. These cultural resources are denoted by English fluency, urban location of education, 'professional' appearance, and parent/family background. Soft skills become code words or corroborating evidence for 'merit', particularly for promotion into managerial positions. Evidence from a field experiment reported by Banerjee, Bertrand, Datta, and Mullainathan (2008) found that formal educational qualifications were not sufficient; companies added soft skills in hiring the 'ideal' worker, in addition to hard technical skills. In this hiring scenario, candidates from OBCs, ST, or SC were ranked lower than higher caste candidates. Employment practices that emphasized soft skills, by definition reduced, if not eliminated, the chances of SCs and even OBCs of entering and succeeding in IT. In the absence of quantifiable measures for soft skills, proxy measures of family background, educational location, and caste offered corroborating evidence for 'merit', and rendered culturally reproduced 'merit' to be meritorious.

Soft skills that vary by *urban-rural location* add to the SC deficits. Jodhka and Newman's HR managers (2010: 64–71), in charge of hiring decisions in large urban location firms, were likely to prefer candidates from cosmopolitan cities; the assumption was that non-cosmopolitan candidates would not have or be weak in the cultural capital, worldviews, verbal and behavioural styles, all required to succeed in the IT sector. The urban preference, ostensibly, was to reduce workplace tensions that might be created by placing workers with different lifestyles on the same project. Stereotypical preferences, whether by caste, region, religion, were particularly pronounced in family owned and operated companies. Even when caste was not an explicit factor, regional ethnicities or religion[58] were invoked as selection criteria, all in the name of suitability for a given occupation, like nursing, that the upper caste find unsuitable. In the final analyses, SCs were thought not to have the requisite skills or the mind-set for the IT job and therefore excluded.

---

[58] The preponderance of Christian nurses from Kerala is rationalized by the state's long tradition of women with nursing degrees.

SCs who break through the caste ceiling in prestigious educational institutions or into the IT workplace have complained about being made to feel guilty for stealing slots from 'qualified' non-SC candidates (Parthasarathy 2012). Others internalize the extant hierarchies or find ways to make sense (almost rationalize) of the apparent contradictions. Mahalingam's (2003) quasi-experimental design or thought experiment, with a hypothetical brain transplant or transfer paradigm is illustrative; a Brahmin's brain was hypothesized to have been transferred to a poor man and vice versa. He concluded that, unlike subordinate groups, Brahmins tended to essentialize social identities; they believed in the inalterable nature of privileged social class identity. Some Dalits half-heartedly essentialized the privilege that potential mobility options offered through reservation programs. Faced with depersonalized bullying, subtle devaluation based on group membership, in the workplace, D'Cruz and Noronha's sample of SCs made sense of their dissatisfaction by focusing on the economic, 'bounded benefits' (2013: 6) they accrued.

It is also not surprising that *women in the Indian IT sector* are targets of cumulative disparities. Top IT positions were held by men, with women relegated to the lower entry level jobs (Annapoorna and Bagalkoti 2011). More specifically, women piled up in low end IT jobs such as coding and programming than in high end areas of development (Suriya and Nagarajan 2004). While women have made inroads in the IT industry, they have yet to assume significant roles and status in IT. The unequal distribution of men and women in IT often is attributed to the unbalanced gender ratio in the Indian educational system as well as the social family-work pressures that women face.

Appendix 1A.2:　Survey of Indian Information Technology Professionals

Web Survey invitation:

RE: SEEKING YOUR THOUGHTS ON THE ROLE OF CASTE IN THE INDIAN INFORMATION TECHNOLOGY SECTOR

Dear colleague,

Hello. My name is Dr. Marilyn Fernandez, Professor of Sociology at Santa Clara University in California, USA. I am conducting a study of professionals who work in Indian information technology companies. I would very much appreciate it if you would answer all, or as many, of the following questions below. Please remember that there is neither a right nor wrong answer to these questions. Please respond based on your experiences. Your honest and complete responses would be greatly appreciated.

This data will become the basis for a book that I'm writing. Your responses will be reported anonymously with no names attached and will be presented only in the aggregate when appropriate. If you chose to complete (in part or in full) the survey it will represent informed consent to use your responses in my research. Thank you for your help in this project. If you have any questions or comments, I can be reached at mfernandez@scu.edu.

Please go to www.scu.edu/survey/?s=260 where you will find the survey. Your **password** is **ITSURVEY** (in CAPS). It will take you approximately 10 minutes to complete the survey. Thank you, again, for sharing your work experiences with me.

Sincerely,

Marilyn Fernandez, Ph.D.
Professor
Department of Sociology
O'Connor 331
Santa Clara University
Santa Clara, CA 95053
408-554-4432 (Telephone)
408-554-4189 (Fax)
www.scu.edu/cas/sociology/

1. **What type of Information Technology company do you work for? Check all that apply to you**

   a. Computer or information technology programming   _____

   b. IT Infrastructure Management   _____

   c. R&D services   _____

   d. E-commerce & web services   _____

   e. Engineering services

   f. Business Process Outsourcing (Customer service for multinational companies)   _____

   g. Business Process Outsourcing (Financial and back office services for multinational Companies   _____

   h. Other; please specify   _____

2. **Approximately how many employees does your company have?**   _____

3. **How long have you worked for this company?**   _____

4. **What is your current position in this company?**   _____

5. **How long have you held this current position?**   _____

6. **If you have changed positions within this company, please list the previous positions:**

   _____

7. **What is the highest degree you have completed?**   _____

8. **From which institution (name and country) did you receive your highest degree?**

   _____

9. **Where (state, city, village) did you finish your high school?**

   _____

10. What is your sex: Are you?

   Male _____   Female _____

11. Your age?   _____

12. Are you currently married?

   Yes _____   No _____

13. If you have children, how many do you have?   _____

14. Listed below are some characteristics of an excellent IT worker.
   Please check (X) how important each characteristic is on the scale
   provided.

	Not at all Important	Not Important	Not Relevant	Important	Very Important
a). Technical skills (specific to the job)					
b). Ability to work well in a team					
c). Willing to put in the extra effort (hours, days) to get the job done					
d). Someone who shows individual initiative					
e). Someone who is meticulous (complete the work correctly)					
f). Ability to communicate in English (Written)					
g). Ability to communicate in English (Verbal)					

	Not at all Important	Not Important	Not Relevant	Important	Very Important
h). Where he/she went to college					
i). Which college she/he went to					
j). Whether he/she grew up in a city or urban area					
k). Someone from a non-scheduled caste background					
l). Someone you would feel comfortable socializing with after work					
m). Someone your family would be comfortable meeting					
n). Someone your family would be comfortable having a meal with					

15. What other skills do you think are important for an excellent IT professional? And why do you think so? _____

_____

16. There are many who claim that the new information technology jobs are open ONLY to those who are qualified (they have the right education and skills) for the job. What do you think?

_____

_____

17. Of all the different colleges that offer technical degrees and diplomas, name three colleges that you think are good. Why do you think so?

_____

_____

18. Name three colleges that you think are not that good? Why do you think so?

_____

_____

_____

19. How open are employment opportunities in Information Technology to women? Why do you think that?

_____

_____

20. Do you think the women who work in Information Technology jobs these days are as qualified as the men? Please explain why you think so.

_____

_____

21. There are many who claim that caste/community is no longer a barrier to work in the information technology sector in India. What do you think?

_____

_____

22. There are many who claim that too many jobs in high-tech companies are offered to scheduled caste members. What do you think?

Yes, there are too many (Go to Question 23) No, there are not many (Skip to Question 24)

23. If yes, why do you think that is the case?

_____

_____

24. If not, why do you think so?

_____

_____

25. There are many who think that hiring managers will hire mainly people from their own caste/community. What do you think?

_____

_____

26. Based on your experience, to which caste/community do hiring managers belong?

_____

_____

27. And finally, what would you say is your caste/community background?

_____

_____

28. Date completed _____

Appendix 1A.3: Survey of Indian Information Technology Professionals

Web Survey invitation:

RE. SEEKING YOUR THOUGHTS ON THE ROLE OF CASTE IN THE INDIAN INFORMATION TECHNOLOGY SECTOR

Dear colleague,

Hello. My name is Dr. Marilyn Fernandez, Professor of Sociology at Santa Clara University in California, USA. I am conducting a study of professionals who work in Indian information technology companies. I would very much appreciate it if you would answer all, or as many, of the following questions below. Please remember that there is neither a right nor wrong answer to these questions. Please respond based on your experiences. Your honest and complete responses would be greatly appreciated.

This data will become the basis for a book that I'm writing. Your responses will be reported anonymously with no names attached and will be presented only in the aggregate when appropriate. If you chose to complete (in part or in full) the survey, it will represent informed consent to use your responses in my research. Thank you for your help in this project. If you have any questions or comments, I can be reached at mfernandez@scu.edu.

Please go to www.scu.edu/survey/?s=260 where you will find the survey. Your **password** is **ITSURVEY** (in CAPS). It will take you approximately 10 minutes to complete the survey. Thank you, again, for sharing your work experiences with me.

Sincerely,

Marilyn Fernandez, Ph.D.
Professor
Department of Sociology
O'Connor 331
Santa Clara University
Santa Clara, CA 95053
408-554-4432 (Telephone)
408-554-4189 (Fax)
www.scu.edu/cas/sociology/

1. **What type of Information Technology company do you work for? Check all that apply to you**

   a. Computer or information technology programming   _____

   b. IT Infrastructure Management   _____

   c. R&D services   _____

   d. E-commerce & web services   _____

   e. Engineering services   _____

   f. Business Process Outsourcing (Customer service for multinational companies)   _____

   g. Business Process Outsourcing (Financial and back office services for multinational Companies   _____

   h. Other; please specify   _____

2. **Approximately how many employees does your company have?**   _____

3. **How long have you worked for this company?**   _____

4. **What is your current position in this company?**   _____

5. **How long have you held this current position?**   _____

6. **If you have changed positions within this company, please list the previous positions:**

   _____

7. **What is the highest degree you have completed?**   _____

8. **From which institution (name and country) did you receive your highest degree?**

   _____

9. **Where (state, city, village) did you finish your high school?**

   _____

10. **What is your sex: Are you?**

   Male _____   Female _____

11. **Your age?**   _____

12. **Are you currently married?**

   Yes _____   No _____

13. **If you have children, how many do you have?**   _____

14. **Listed below are some characteristics of an excellent IT worker. Please check (X) how important each characteristic is on the scale provided.**

	Not at all Important	Not Important	Not Relevant	Important	Very Important
a). Technical skills (specific to the job)					
b). Ability to work well in a team					
c). Willing to put in the extra effort (hours, days) to get the job done					
d). Someone who shows individual initiative					
e). Someone who is meticulous (complete the work correctly)					
f). Ability to communicate in English (Written)					
g). Ability to communicate in English (Verbal)					

	Not at all Important	Not Important	Not Relevant	Important	Very Important
h). Where he/she went to college					
i). Which college she/he went to					
j). Whether he/she grew up in a city or urban area					
k). Someone you would feel comfortable socializing with after work					
l). Someone your family would be comfortable meeting					
m). Someone your family would be comfortable having a meal with					

15. What other skills do you think are important for an excellent IT professional? And why do you think so? _____

_____

16. There are many who claim that the new information technology jobs are open ONLY to those who are qualified (they have the right education and skills) for the job. What do you think?

_____

_____

17. Of all the different colleges that offer technical degrees and diplomas, name three colleges that you think are good. Why do you think so?

_____

_____

18. Name three colleges that you think are not that good? Why do you think so?

_____

_____

_____

19. How open are employment opportunities in Information Technology to women? Why do you think that?

_____

_____

20. Do you think the women who work in Information Technology jobs these days are as qualified as the men? Please explain why you think so.

_____

_____

21. There are many who claim that caste/community is no longer a barrier to work in the information technology sector in India. What do you think?

_____

_____

22. Date completed _____

2 Merit Construction and Caste Loopholes in the Indian IT Social Habitus

Pure Merit. Right education and skills are basic requirements in information technology. IT professionals must be able to learn new technologies, and be proactive in doing so.

Soft skills like English fluency, presentation, communication, interpersonal, and ability to work independently or in a team with very less supervision [are also critical].

These were typical of the sentiments expressed by rank-and-file IT professionals when they reflected on the merit construction project in the IT workplace. At first glance, *Pure, 'Streamlined'*[1] *IT Skills* appeared central to merit culture making and seemed to overtly out-shadow traditional Indian social vectors of caste/religion/communities. However, closer scrutiny of the merit metrics in the Indian

---

[1] Adapted from Radhakrishnan's (2011) cultural streamlining.

Technology social habitus, the rink where the 'merit culture' is honed and practiced, raised questions about the caste-neutral potential of IT. While eloquently waxing about the new cutting-edge occupational sector, many professionals also pointed out, perhaps inadvertently, that while technical skills are necessary for success in a globalized industry, they simply are not sufficient. They developed *holistic IT merit metrics* that included not only technical skills but also *subjective markers* of merit, such as English fluency, habits of the mind-intellect-spirit, integration, and other 'soft' skills of communication. It is in this holistic profile that loopholes or spaces open up for introducing, sorting out, and stratifying IT employees by traditional social vectors of caste and even community, and religion. These subjective markers, and the related *'pattern recognition'*[2] in the hiring, retention, and promotion decision-making in the IT workplace have become the conduits through which caste dynamics can be reproduced and reinforced in the Indian IT, transforming it into the new vector of inequality.

History of the Indian Information Technology Sector and IT Merit

Unpacking the story of the IT merit culture making project, merit valorization, and caste reproduction is best contextualized in the historical development of the Indian IT revolution. IT history also demonstrates the development of internal hierarchies, of the one-third and two-third worlds (Mohanty 2003), in the globalized IT occupational structure.[3] As noted in Chapter 1, during the early years of post-independence India, there was a robust, mostly public, IT hardware industry and professionals that met local electronic production needs. It was not until when the country's hardware trade began lagging in the 1980s, and even the 1990s,

---

[2] Baron (2006) and Chapter 3 of Kanter (1977a).

[3] The composite history of Indian IT, developed and presented below, drew on detailed scholarly ethnographies presented by Biao (2007), Radhakrishnan (2011), Hamm (2007), and other scholarly resources. This composite was supplemented with interviews with 30 Indian IT knowledge sources or key informants; the key informants of HR managers, senior staff, consultants (who worked with Indian IT companies), and educators were located in Bangalore (Karnataka state), Hyderabad (Andhra Pradesh), Chennai (Tamil Nadu), and Trivandrum (Kerala).

that the government liberalized its investments and import-export policies, which in turn led to a shift in the IT industry ownership profile from the government to private and foreign firms (Joseph 2009). Starting in the early 1990s, offshoring and outsourcing business practices,[4] as well as the ITES segment emerged in India when American Express started using its India operations to provide book-keeping support to its subsidiaries in other Asian countries.[5] It was also in this period that the two-third world of softer BPO sub-sector of Indian IT was launched.

Then, in the late 1990s (more specifically 1993 onward), an interesting 'perfect storm' of events led to the mushrooming and segmentation of the Indian IT occupational sector, the valorization of IT jobs, and the high premium placed on IT merit. The Y2K hysteria to fix a computer glitch that needed massive overhaul of the world's existing software, 'financialization' of the IT industry making it susceptible to the ups and downs in the stock market, and the US economic downturn in the early 2000s that drove American companies to cut costs, collectively created the dot-com boom in India. For example, in anticipation of the potential Y2K debacle, American companies that needed programmers, *en masse*, to re-program their mission critical computer programs before the arrival of the year 2000, looked to other countries for skilled programmers available at low(er) costs than found in the USA. India was an excellent source; they not only had qualified and abundant 'cheap' skilled labour[6] but also offered the advantage of working around the clock, made possible by the 12 ½ to 13 ½ hour time difference between India and the USA; Hamm (2007) referred to this process as 'labour arbitrage'.

---

[4] Offshoring and outsourcing business models became popular buzzwords in business and management in the mid-1990s, as companies attempted to lower costs by focusing on competencies (Foster 2007).

[5] The initial impetus for the global technology boom came with the democratization of the internet when Marc Andreessen and his colleagues, an undergraduate student at University of Illinois at Urbana Champaign, in 1993, designed the first internet browser, Mosaic. Mosaic was an easy-to-use entry portal to the net (Hamm 2007). Until then, the internet was used mainly by academics and scientists for sharing scholarly papers and research data.

[6] The All India Council for Technical Education (AICTE) estimated that 1.5 million engineers graduate on an annual basis for many years (AICTE-india. org-dashboard).

These transnational searches by US companies for labour led to a variety of new labour management practices and stratified tiers in the IT industry. Offshoring and outsourcing business models, driven by the industry's search for lower labour costs gained steam, along with body shopping (a specific form of outsourcing), and combinations thereof. Offshoring involved relocation or transferring business processes, be they production, manufacturing or services, to another country, typically to the same company overseas with cheaper labour costs. Outsourcing often meant delegation of non-core operations of business functions and related internal production jobs within a business to an external entity, as a subcontractor, who specializes in that operation and offers the same services at lower costs. No doubt, outsourcing or contracting out within nations is a long standing business practice world-wide.[7] However, in the new dot-com environment and with internet technology flourishing, outsourcing as a labour management practice came into its own, either as part of offshoring or as a standalone practice. Indian IT companies, like Wipro, TCS, and Infosys, were early recipients of US outsourcing business practices. Over a short period of time, American companies like Oracle, HP, and Cisco, among others, decided to set up operations in India and in other developing countries by offshoring or relocating business processes, of production, manufacturing, or services, to their own companies but located in another country.

In the mix of the Indian IT boom was body shopping. Biao (2007: xv) defined body shopping as a labour management 'practice connecting IT corporations, placement agencies, small IT consultancies (body shops), and IT workers'. Body shopped IT employees engaged in highly labour intensive, monotonous, repetitive, and tedious work. This work included software development, particularly programming or writing software code, testing, and debugging, for western corporate customers who often wrote the specs or instructions which Indian body shops followed to the letter. In this sense, body shoppers, who were managed by head-hunters, were different from brain or knowledge shoppers. At the outset, body shopping work for US companies was done off-site, as in India. But, overtime, body shopping practices evolved to include Indian body shop

---

[7] Electronic Data Systems (EDS), the American company that invented and dominated the outsourcing business practice for many years, had a market cap of US$13 billion in 2000.

employees working on-site in client western companies located outside India and later into a combination of off-site, say in India, and on-site in the US operations. In India, body shopping practice was initiated by Tata Consulting Services (TCS), the first export oriented software services company (Biao 2007: 5).[8]

The rise of the body shopping business model was an ironic underside of globalization. As Biao (2007) noted, body shopping came into existence as a response to US labour regulations and immigration controls. Between 1998 and 2000, delegations from around 20 countries were going to India to recruit low-cost (compared to US wage standards) Indian IT workers. These recruitment trips were happening despite 2001 industry projections of 850,000 labour shortage, and concomitant layoffs of 350,000 high tech workers in the US IT sector. The financialization of the IT industry, reflecting the ups and downs of the stock market, meant that the IT workforce were hired and fired based on market supported needs. In other words, the IT industry needed only a sufficient number of IT workers, provided they were mobile. These labour ironies led to two primary forms of body shopping. One, US companies hired foreign IT workers through the limited H1B visas (three years with renewable terms up to 6 years). Second, IT workers were hired through body shopping agents who were able to hire, bring to the US, and deploy or bench IT workers depending on the need of hiring companies.

Mixed Local Implications: Economic and Social

How has this global IT transformation been experienced by Indian IT professionals and their families, in Indian cities, and in the broader

---

[8] Speaking to the internal stratification within IT, Biao, who offered a rich ethnography of the body shopping business model, made several observations about the historical rise of Indian body shopping. For one, the Y2K problem towards the end of the 1990s spurred the immense expansion of body shopping practices, a surge that continued with the dot-com boom. Additional impetus for the body shopping explosion came from the proliferation and wider customization of internet technology products to meet different needs of different companies. However, these developments meant that IT professionals had to move from one company to another in different parts of the world, exacerbating the contingency nature of their work.

society? For city dwellers, the growth of E-Cities or Electronic Cities has transformed their urban landscape. The casual, frequent visitors to Bangalore, for example, cannot help notice the IT flavour of the city. 'We are an IT family', meaning both partners work in the IT industry, was an oft heard refrain. Local newspapers hailed the IT boom with bylines like, 'Moolah [Money] Is Hauled In Through The IT Way' (R. Akhileshwari in *Deccan Herald*, 17 June 2000). The writer described the new middle class lifestyles as flush with money and all the associated perks; personal cars, home computers and Wifi access, massage and nail parlours, shopping centres with restaurants and food courts, and other amenities have proliferated. For the average citizen, even if they do not have a computer at their home, the proliferation of IT parlours, which charge approximately INR 30 per 30 minutes of usage, made the internet more accessible.

As for E-Cities, reporters described them as an 'Oasis in the chaos; Hyderabad heating up as the next IT destination' (Swati Sucharia in *Times of India*, 12 June 2000). Another byline, 'IT Parks in TN Soon' in the *Times of India*, 12 June 2000 , reported the Indian government lending financial support to establish Software Technology Parks (STP) in Tamil Nadu, another southern state with promising IT hubs. In Tamil Nadu, Tidel Software Park, and other parks, were being planned because the state government expected the state to emerge shortly as the largest IT state in India.

Amidst this rosy growth bubble, is it right to reflect on the future prospects of Indian IT and of the broader Indian society? One reads in the scholarly and journalistic writings, hints of impending concerns at different levels about the IT boom. At the IT sectoral level, despite the current growth, dark economic clouds are looming. For example, given growing offshoring estimates that by 2015, 3.4 million American jobs will be offshored with Americans losing jobs, scholars have hinted at possible external threats to Indian companies. Continued offshoring has raised concerns that US lawmakers could impose barriers to stem the tide of American job losses. On the other hand, as Hamm (2007) predicted, the globalization genie is out of the bottle and nothing might stop it, at least in short haul, unless Americans reinvent themselves with technical and other educational credentials.

At the local community levels, Indian IT cities have also become recipients of unintended negative consequences of the IT boom, as was evident in several journalistic reports.[9] Typical metropolitan problems have been exacerbated by unplanned urban growth, without concomitant infrastructure development. Office buildings that go up in bunches or the building of brand new campuses with multiple buildings in E-Cities, as in Bangalore, Delhi, Hyderabad, Chennai, and other smaller cities, have aggravated the congestion of urban spaces and roads. The ensuing lengthy daily commutes—two hour one-way rides to and from work because of being stuck in traffic jams have become quite common—must definitely cut into productivity. Unless the local IT growth is better planned, the boon might soon begin to lose some of its glow and dull its economic and social promise.

The IT boom has also been a mixed blessing for IT professionals and their families. While extolling the financial boom brought by the IT sector to India, reporters like R. Akhileshwari (in *Deccan Herald*, 17 June 2000) lamented that IT jobs brought 'Money yet no job security', partly due to the constant labour calibrations of Indian IT companies that are dependent on the fluctuating demands from outside companies. Scholars (like Nadeem 2009 and Radhakrishnan 2011: 43–4) have also noted the symbolic status hierarchies, but not necessarily economic or status distinctions, between the worlds of IT: between transnational knowledge workers like engineers and technical writers versus ITES/BPO call centre workers, data entry workers, or medical transcriptionists. The software/hardware industries in India are older and more established than BPO and ITES companies. Besides, the software and hardware sub-sectors require an engineering degree as opposed to BPO jobs that are open to most with a college degree and fluency in English. And as Nadeem (2009) and Reena Patel (as quoted in Radhakrishnan 2011) have documented in their ethnographic works with call centre workers, despite the English linguistic capital and substantial salaries available to BPO workers, most middle class Indians view BPO jobs to be less desirable than IT work. The night work shifts needed to synchronize with the rhythms of the global economy, along with social parties and other non-monetary incentives, of alcohol and cigarettes, provided to recruit and retain workers in these non-traditional working conditions, have lowered the social standing of transnational call centre workers vis-à-vis the IT programmers and engineers. On balance, despite the financial benefits of working in call

---

[9] *Deccan Herald* (Bangalore) and *Times of India* (New Delhi) have often carried such reports.

centres, the BPO sub-sector lacks the symbolic legitimacy conferred on the software and hardware sub-sectors.

Another Indian IT story byline, central to the analyses presented in this book, is the predicted and rosy disassociation of the IT social milieu from caste and other traditionally divisive social anchors. Two pathways, one idealized and the other materialized, were predicted. On the ideal front, just as globalization and virtual corporations freed labour markets from nation-states, expanded IT industry foci beyond national boundaries and broader work ties across specific companies was predicted by scholars to bring commensurate transformations in tangible social and inter-personal relations (for example, Biao 2007: 2). Applied to the Indian context, these disassociations, in principle, meant that unlike the age-old Indian non-IT occupational structures that had caste foundations, the brand new IT sector labour was theoretically disassociated from caste boundaries. The virtual world and the transnational workplace that the IT revolution introduced, arguably, meant that the IT world did not have to be anchored in, and was therefore freed from the traditional caste, regional, religious, community, and even gender obligations endemic to the Indian society. For one, the structural and functional connections of the Indian IT sector with the transnational western corporations might lead to the expectation that western labour practices like Equal Employment Opportunity (EEO) and pay parity might apply to their Indian counterparts as well.

On the ground, however, the shining bright hopes for a casteless Indian IT sector or at least an attenuation of the caste stranglehold appear to have dimmed because of the transnational, yet local, business practices and intransigent social expectations, among others. That the Indian society is still anchored in the age-old social ways of life restricts the potential social transformational impact of the new IT occupational sector. Most of the new IT new middle class have parents who were part of the 'old middle class' that was made up of government, financial, education, and other public sector employees.[10] And strong family ties

---

[10] Evidence from the 2005 IHDS (Table 2A.1) showed that FC respondents were twice as likely to work in a government job (15.2 per cent) than SC respondents (7.9 per cent), a potential byproduct, even if obscured, of what Radhakrishnan (2011: 42–3) called the 'old middle class' that made up of government, financial, education, and other public sector employees. That the average FC respondent in the web survey who was only 30 years old, most likely was

have meant that the old forms of social relations rooted in caste and religious traditions may not have been disrupted by the new economic relations. At the structural level, as Biao (2007: 4–6) noted, despite the symbiotic relations between the western and Indian IT labour management systems, western corporations are often freed from labour management obligations in their subsidiaries. Body shoppers, for example, manage the labour of their IT employees and are free to continue their traditional labour practices, even if they go against western EEO policies. In the final analyses, whether the IT sector appears to offer a new flatter social model for India, continues to be an open question and the issue explored in this monograph.

The Indian IT Work Structure: In the Lived Work Experiences of Indian IT Professionals

The story about whether Indian IT is transforming the social landscape, or perpetuating the historical caste and other inequalities, is played out on the ground in IT companies. What does the contemporary IT work structure look like? A portrait of the IT organization and work structures offers a valuable context for exploring the caste reproduction and reinforcement in the IT merit culture project.

The focus in this analyses were companies[11] in a select group of IT Hubs and the emerging IT hubs in the south Indian states of Karnataka, Kerala, Tamil Nadu, and Andhra Pradesh, which account for a majority of IT exports as per NASSCOM reports. They have been active in courting and working with international information technology corporations and provide the entire spectrum of IT related products. Their products include: hardware product engineering, such as, designing computer chips, circuit boards, and related machinery; software programming, such as, writing code; systems integration and management; and BPO services in managing business functions, be they accounting, medical claims, or

---

part of the generation that came after the 'old middle class', should give pause to the often heard non-nepotistic and caste neutral claims in the contemporary job market.

[11] As seen through the experiences of the 514 web survey respondents who answered questions about the IT companies in which they were employed.

customer service.[12] In short, these Indian IT companies participated in a 'global service delivery model', confirming Hamm (2007: 4).

As seen in Table 2.1, a plurality of 514 IT professionals[13] who responded to the web survey (45.3 per cent), reportedly worked in core IT companies that focused solely on computer/software programming, Infrastructure, and R&D; the newer softer IT sub-sectors were not part of their company mission. Another quarter (24.9 per cent) worked for companies that combined hard IT along with BPO and IT enabled services such as E-Commerce and Engineering Services (ITES). About 16 per cent of the companies represented by the respondents focused solely on either ITES such as E-Commerce or Engineering Services (10.9 per

Table 2.1 Distribution of Web-Survey Respondents by Current Company Focus in IT Sector (n = 514)*

	Percentage	Mean Size of Company (Standard Dev.)
1 = Sole BPO (MNC Customer Service and MNC Financial/Back Office)	5.1%	67,189 (213,292.3)
2 = Sole ITES (E-Commerce and Engineering Service)	10.9	8,469 (23,685.8)
3 = BPO AND ITES	9.9	22,459 (59,525.4)
4 = IT with other services	24.9	14,322 (43,410.4)
5 = Core IT (Programming, Infrastructure, and R&D)	45.3	23,689 (58,584.9)
6 = Other (non-IT organizations)	3.9	32, 139 (140,659.4)
Total:	100.0	23,121 (80,271.6)

Source: Author.
* Highlighted categories and numbers represent the modal responses.

[12] The products and services provided to transnational clients often represent their core functionalities. These core functions range from ICT, ITT, ITES and solutions for banking, insurance, and E-commerce, BPO, and more recently KPO in market research, engineering design, biotech, and pharmaceutical research.

[13] Web survey respondents will be referred to, alternatively, as rank-and-file IT professionals or IT professionals, or survey respondents.

cent) or BPO (5.1 per cent in MNC customer service or financial/back office). A small segment (3.9 per cent) of non-IT organizations, colleges, secondary, and elementary schools, included IT professionals, who had prior to the survey date, worked in the IT sector and/or had working knowledge of IT and caste dynamics in the Indian society.

It was clear that Indian IT companies, as seen through the work experience of IT professionals, were not monolithic in their core competencies (Table 2.2). There was a plurality (44.9 per cent of 514) of companies that restricted themselves to their core competencies of programming, Infrastructure, and R&D functions. On the other hand, ITES and BPO companies were more likely than not, to combine their competencies. For example, only 4.5 per cent (of 514) and 7.4 per cent (of 514) limited themselves to either BPO or ITES. It was more common for ITES companies to also have BPO sub-sectors (22.8 per cent) and for BPO companies to also include ITES sub-sectors (10.1 per cent).

Another interesting dimension of Indian IT companies was the scale of the companies in terms of their size (measured by reported number of employees). For example, companies that focused on BPO competencies,

Table 2.2 Number of Sub-Sectors by Company Type (Current)*

# of IT sub-sectors	Type of Company						Total
	1 = Other	2 = Sole BPO	3 = BPO with ITES	4 = Sole ITES	5 = IT with other sub-sectors	6 = Core IT	
0	73.6%	8.7%	0.0%	0.0%	0.0%	0.0%	8.0%
1	15.1	**91.3**	0.0	**100.0**	1.7	**100.0**	58.4
2	5.7	0.0	1.9	0.0	**43.6**	0.0	10.7
3	1.9	0.0	**23.1**	0.0	31.6	0.0	9.7
4	1.9	0.0	**21.2**	0.0	17.1	0.0	6.2
5	1.9	0.0	19.2	0.0	6.0	0.0	3.5
6	1.9	0.0	19.2	0.0	6.0	0.0	1.8
7	0.0	0.0	17.3	0.0	0.0	0.0	1.8
(n)	(53)	(23)	(52)	(38)	(117)	(231)	(514)

Source: Author.

*Highlighted categories and numbers represent the modal responses.

either by themselves ($\bar{x}$ = 67,189 employees) or combined BPO with ITES functionalities ($\bar{x}$ = 22,459 employees) had the largest number of employees. Core IT companies, in contrast, employed only an average of 23,689. These differences in scale between IT versus BPO companies are by-products of the differences in the nature of the work to which scholars, like Nadeem (2009) and Radhakrishnan (2011), have alluded. Engineering jobs in core IT companies require a specialized technical education. On the other hand, BPOs and call centres, for example, are more relaxed about the education requirements; a college degree and fluency in English often suffice and have opened opportunities to broader segments of the population. The more than average salaries (compared to work in the public sector) and the intensive accent modification and western cultural training that BPO workers receive add further appeal to BPO jobs.

Nascent IT Job Titles and Short Career Ladders

A nascent, but rapidly bourgeoning, IT industry was reflected in the specific job titles or positions held by web survey respondents. The youthful career of IT professionals was evident in the most common job titles in the career ladder (Table 2.3) as well as in their short IT career histories (Tables 2.4–2.9).

A majority (close to 50 per cent) of IT professionals was not in managerial positions and listed their specific job title as engineers or analysts. In other words, they were individual contributors. For example, 'Individual Contributors: Engineers', was the most common job title at 34.2 per cent (in Table 2.3). Another 15 per cent listed their job title as some form of 'Analysts', who are also 'Individual Contributors'.

As for managers with some level of supervisory and personnel responsibilities, only a fifth of the IT respondents held such positions. For example, of the 85 (16.5 per cent of the 514 respondents) who were managers, a third (Table 2.3) each were Mid-level Managers (32.9 per cent) or Product/Project Managers (30.6 per cent). Only 5.4 per cent listed their job title as 'Upper Level Management' or 'Executive'.

'Lead', as in leader of an IT project or group or a function (such as system analysis) or a module or QA, was the next common job title (11.1 per cent). Leads are responsible for delivery of project goals. They coordinate and organize the project work until it is complete. But, unlike

Table 2.3 Current Position in Company (n = 514)*

Category	Current Position	% within Category (n)	% within Total Sample (n = 514)
Upper Level Management (5.4%/ n = 28)	Upper Level Management (Survey code = 1):	**64.3%** (n = 18)	3.5%
	Executive - HR (Code = 1.01):	**25.0** (n = 7)	1.4
	General Manager (Code = 1.02):	7.1 (n = 2)	0.4
	Business Relations and Business Development (Code = 1.03):	3.6 (n = 1)	0.2
Managers: All Levels (16.5%/ n = 85)	Senior Manager or Executive (Code = 2.10):	11.8% (n = 10)	1.9
	Mid-Level Management (Code = 2):	**32.9** (n = 28)	5.4
	Manager, Not Specified (Code = 2.01):	11.8 (n = 10)	1.9
	Associate Manager-HR (Code = 2.02):	2.4 (n = 2)	0.4
	Assistant Manager-IT (Code = 2.03):	4.8 (n = 4)	0.8
	Product or Project Manager (Code = 2.04):	**30.6** (n = 26)	**5.1**
	Deputy Manager (Code = 2.05):	2.4 (n = 2)	0.4
	Junior Executive (Code = 2.07):	2.4 (n = 2)	0.4
	Junior HR Manager (Code = 2.09):	1.2 (n = 1)	0.2
Leads (But Not Managers) (11.1%/ n = 57)	Lead Positions, IT Related (Code = 3.00):	**86.0%** (n = 49)	**9.5**
	Module Leader or Process Head (Code = 3.02):	3.5 (n = 2)	0.4
	QA Lead (Code = 3.03):	3.5 (n = 2)	0.4

(Cont'd)

Table 2.3   (*Cont'd*)

Category	Current Position	% within Category (n)	% within Total Sample (n = 514)
Individual Contributors:Not Engineers (**15.4%/ n = 79**)	Professional Practice Trainer (Code = 3.04):	7.0 (n = 4)	0.8
	Analyst (Code = 4.01):	**26.6** (n = 21)	4.1
	Senior Analyst (Code = 4.10):	16.4 (n = 13)	2.5
	Engineer (Code = 5):	**76.7%** (n = 134)	26.2
	Associate Engineer (Code = 5.01):	2.3 (n = 4)	0.8
	Assistant Systems Engineer(Code = 5.02):	3.4 (n = 6)	1.2
	Engineer Trainee (Code = 5.04):	2.8 (n = 5)	1.0
Individual Contributors: Engineers (**34.1%/ n = 175**)	Support Programmer or Engineer (Code = 5.05):	1.1 (n = 2)	0.4
	Technology or Applications Support Engineer (Code = 5.06):	4.6 (n = 8)	1.6
	Test Engineer or Software (Code = 5.07):	5.1 (n = 9)	1.8
	Junior Software Engineer or Programmer (Code = 5.10): Network Administrator (Code = 5.13):	2.3 (n = 4) 1.7 (n = 3)	0.8 0.6
IT Support Positions (**16.7%/ n = 86**)	Other, IT Related (Code = 6.00):	**31.4%** (n = 27)	5.2
	Senior Consultant Positions (Code = 7.00):	**10.5** (n = 9)	1.8
	Consultant (Code = 8.0):	**10.5** (n = 9)	1.8
	Other (Non-IT) (Code = 10.00):	8.1 (n = 7)	1.4

(*Cont'd*)

Table 2.3 *(Cont'd)*

Category	Current Position	% within Category (n)	% within Total Sample (n = 514)
	Trainer HR Manager, Administrator, Resource Executive (Code = 6.02):	4.7 (n = 4)	0.8
	Process Associate (Code = 6.03)	2.3 (n = 2)	0.4
	Verifier (Code = 6.04)	1.2 (n = 1)	0.2
	Route Settlement (Code = 6.06)	1.2 (n = 1)	0.2
	Senior Business Development, Recruiter, or Resource Executive (Code = 6.10)	1.2 (n = 1)	0.2
	Trainee (Non-specialty Engineer) (Code = 9.00)	**13.9 (n = 12)**	2.3
	TOC 1 (Trainee on contract 1) (Code = 9.01)	**8.1** (n = 7)	1.4
	TOC 2 (Trainee on Contract 2) (Code = 9.02)	**5.8** (n = 5)	1.0
	Front Office Manager (Code = 6.01)	1.2 (n = 1)	0.2
Non-IT Key Sectors(0.8%/ n = 4)	Assistant Professor (Code = 10.02):	25.0 (n = 1)	0.2
	Assistant Professor (Code = 10.02):	25.0 (n = 1)	0.2
	Lecturer or Instructor (Code = 10.01):	25.0 (n = 1)	0.2

Source: Author.

* Highlighted categories and numbers represent modal responses.

managers, Leads do not have budgetary and/or personnel responsibilities. For example, they do not have a budget. As for personnel matters, they can locate and interview candidates, but do not have final approval prerogative. They can also provide input and feedback on evaluations but do not sign off on the final appraisal.

A variety of 'IT Support Positions' made up the rest of the career ladder (16.7 per cent in Table 2.3). This support group consisted of titles ranging from consultants or non-specified IT related positions. Another third (27.8 per cent) were 'Trainees' at different levels, including TOC 1 (Trainees on Contract Level 1) or TOC 2 (Trainees on Contract Level 2). In short, the typical Indian IT employees in the survey were in their early-to-mid career life courses.

Early but Upwardly Mobile IT Career Trajectories

What are the typical career trajectories of Indian IT respondents? IT professionals, unlike their 'old middle class' parents who worked in the government or banking sectors with limited upward mobility, had more mobility options in the core IT and high-end service sub-sectors. Using the IT career progression of the web survey respondents, it was possible to assess the mobility and career paths of IT employees. The web survey asked respondents to list as many as four job titles they had held.

Overall, most IT respondents were in their first jobs, or second jobs at best, perhaps a reflection of an industry in its young adulthood. Professionals with job titles such as Leads (not managers) or Engineers had the most career 'pasts'. For example, Engineers had multiple pathways to current positions, particularly if they were (at survey time) in leadership, even if mid-level positions. Yet, a disaggregated examination of career trajectories by the current position revealed varied and un-uniform career trajectories.

Upper Level Management Positions (Table 2.4). Top tier management positions (occupied by 28 respondents) included upper level management (n = 18), HR Executive (n = 7), General Manager (n = 2), and Business Development (n = 1). Of the 18 respondents who held upper level management positions, half (n = 10) were new to IT. The rest reported at least one prior title, such as HR Executive, or Deputy Manager, or some mid-level management. Before becoming the HR executive, this professional was an Assistant Manager. The Deputy

Table 2.4 IT Career Trajectories: Upper Level Management (Current Position; n = 28)

Current Position Minus 3	Current Position Minus 2	Current Position Minus 1	Current Position
Other, IT/6.0* (n = 1) →	Asst. Manager/2.03 (n = 1) →	Exec. HR/1.01 (n = 3)	Upper Level Management/1 (n = 18)
No Position†/11 (n = 17) →	Bus. Dev./2.08 (n = 1) →	Deputy Manager/2.05 (n = 1) →	
	No Position/11 (n = 16)² ↗	Mid Management/2.00 (n = 2); Other, IT /6.00 (n = 1); Asst. Prof./10.02 (n = 1); No Position/11 (n = 10) →	
No Position/11 (n = 7) →	No Position/11 (n = 7) →	Engineer/5.00 (n = 1); Management Trainee/9.04 (n = 2); No Position/11.00 (n = 4) →	Executive - HR /1.01 (n = 7)
No Position/11 (n = 2) →	No Position/11 (n = 2) →	Upper Management/1 (n = 1); Lead /3 (n = 1) →	General Manager/ 1.02 (n = 2)
No Position/11 (n = 1) →	No Position/11 (n = 1) →	Other, IT /6 (n = 1) →	Business Relations and Business Development/1.03 (n = 1)

Source: Author.

* Number after job title Other, IT/6.0, refers to the survey codes.

† No Position = did not have previous positions: either Minus 3 or Minus 2 or Minus 1.

Manager was in Business Development in his prior job. Of the seven HR Executives, one was an Engineer and two were management trainees; the rest of the HR Executives were in their first positions in IT. Overall, many survey respondents who held top tier positions did not have long and deep IT careers.

Managers, All Levels (Table 2.5). On the other hand, working up the IT career ladder was more typical of managers (n = 85). Only the top managerial hierarchy (10 Senior Managers) had one appointment prior to their current position; they were either managers, project managers, or in some mid-level management. In this sense, they were similar to their top tier management profiled above in Table 2.4.

The two most common manager positions at the time of the survey were Mid-Level Management (33 per cent or 28 respondents) and Product/Project Managers (26 respondents or 31 per cent). Those (10 out 18) in mid-level management had held at least one prior position in IT; they were Managers or Project Managers, or Leads, Senior Consultants, or Assistant Managers. Four of the Mid-Level Managers, at survey time, had even deeper IT career paths. Three specific examples of deep career paths looked as follows: (a) Of the two respondents who were Engineers in their first IT job, one became an Analyst (n = 1) while the other was a Senior Lead (n = 1) in their second positions. The 'Senior' title is a reflection of years of experience and often used for retention purposes. The analyst went on to become a Manager before being promoted to Mid-level Management. The Senior Lead became a Project Manager and then moved on to the Mid-Level Management ranks; (b) The HR Executive who became a Senior Executive, moved into a Business Development position, and finally into Mid-Level Management; and (c) A Senior IT professional was promoted to a Senior Analyst position and became a Lead before becoming a Mid-Level Manager.

Similarly, the 26 Product/Project Managers at the time of the web survey had been in one (n = 20), if not two (n = 8), or even three (n = 2) previous positions in IT. Prior to becoming Product/Project Managers, they held one of the following positions: Lead (n = 8), Associate Manager (n = 2), Senior IT (n = 2), Senior Lead (n = 2), Engineer (n = 2), or Consultant (n = 2). Of the 8 respondents who held even prior positions, they listed Lead, Senior IT, or Senior Consultant (2 cases) or Advisory Consultant positions. Four had started as Engineers (current position Minus 3), before becoming Leads (n = 2) or Senior IT (n = 2); the Leads

Table 2.5 Managers, All Levels (Current Position; n = 85)

Current Position Minus 3	Current Position Minus 2	Current Position Minus 1	Current Position
No Position*/11.00† (n = 10)	Asst Manager/2.03 (n = 1) Analyst/4.01 (n = 1) No Position/11 (n = 8)	Manager/2.01 (n = 2) Project Manager/2.04 (n = 1) Mid Management /2.00 (n = 1) IT/Tech/Engineer Manager/2.06 (n = 3) No Position/11 (n = 3)	Senior Manager /2.10 (n = 10)
Engineer/5.00 (n = 2) Exec. HR/1.01 (n = 1) Sr. IT./4.00 (n = 1) No Position/11.00 (n = 24)	Analyst/4.01 (n = 1) Sr. Lead./3.10 (n = 1) Sr. Exec./1.03 (n = 1) Sr. Analyst/Engineer/4.10 (n = 1) Test Engineer/Software 5.07 (n = 1) Engineer/5.00 (n = 1) No Position /11.00 (n = 22)	Manager /2.01 (n = 1) Project Manager/2.04 (n = 3) Business Dev /2.08 (n = 1) Lead/3.00 (n = 2) Sr. Consultant /7.00 (n = 1) Asst. Manager /2.03 (n = 1) IT/Tech/Engineer Manager/2.06 (n = 1) No Position /11 (n = 18)	Mid-Level Management/2 (n = 28)

(Cont'd)

Table 2.5 (Cont'd)

Current Position Minus 3		Current Position Minus 2		Current Position Minus 1		Current Position
Sr. Manager/ Executive /2.10 (n = 1) No Position (9)	→	Lead / 3.00 (n = 1)	→	IT/Tech/Engineer Manager/2.06 (n = 1)		Manager, NotSpecified/ 2.01 (n = 10)
		Asst. Manager /2.03 (n = 1)	↗	Deputy Manager /2.05 (n = 2)	→	
		Business Dev. /2.08 (n = 1)	↗	Sr. Business Dev./6.1 (n = 1)	→	
		Engineer/5.0 (n = 1)	→	Lead /3.00 (n = 2)	↗	
		No Position (n = 6)	→	Assist. Manager/ 2.03 (n = 1)		
				Engineer/5.00 (n = 1)		
				No Position /11 (n = 2)		
No Position/ 11 (n = 2)	→	Assoc. Engineer/5.01 (n = 1)	→	Sr. IT/4.00 (n = 1)	→	Associate Manager— HR/2.02 (n = 2)
	↗	No Position /11 (n = 1)	→	No Position / 11 (n = 1)		
No Position/11 (n = 4)	→	No Position/11 (n = 4)	→	No Position / 11 (n = 4)	→	Assistant Manager— IT/2.03 (n = 4)
Engineer/5.0 (n = 4) No Position /11 (n = 22)	→	Lead/3.00 (n = 2)	→	Associate Manager/2.02 (n = 2)	→	Product or Project Manager/2.04 (n = 26)
	↗	Sr. IT/4.00 (n = 2)	→	Sr. Lead/3.10 (n = 2)		
	↖	Sr. Consultant/7.00 (n = 2)	→	Lead/3.00 (n = 8)	↗	
	↗	Advisory Conslt./8.01 (n = 2)	→	Engineer/5.00 (n = 2)	↗	
	↘	No Position /11 (n = 18)		Consultant/8.00 (n = 2)		
				Sr. IT/4.00 (n = 4)		
				No Position /11 (n = 6)		

Current Position Minus 3		Current Position Minus 2		Current Position Minus 1		Current Position
No Position /11 (n = 4)	→	No Position /11 (n = 4)	→	No Position /11 (n = 4)	↘ ↗	Deputy Manager / 2.05 (n = 2) Junior Executive / 2.07 (n = 2)
No Position /11 (n = 1)	→	No Position/11 (n = 1)	→	Management Trainee /9.04 (n = 1)	→	Junior HR Manager /2.09 (n = 1)

Source: Author.

* No Position = did not have previous positions: either Minus 3 or Minus 2 or Minus 1.

† Number after job title, 'No Position/11.00' refers to the survey codes.

became Associate Manager, the Senior IT became a Senior Lead before going on to become Product/Project Managers.

Leads, But Not Managers (Table 2.6). Leads are those in charge of a deliverable project or a module in a project and coordinate the work of the team. Unlike managers who have a broader personnel portfolio, Leads are in charge of and organize team activities but do not have hiring and firing privileges or responsibilities. Often they move from project to project, before moving upward into a senior lead position (based on experience) or into managerial positions. Many of the Leads in the survey had moved up the IT career ladder; they typically held at least two prior IT positions as individual contributors (engineers or analysts) before being promoted to the Lead position.

Some specifics: Of the 36 IT professionals whose job title at the time of the survey was Lead, 26 (72 per cent) held a range of prior positions. More than a third were Engineers (n = 10). Other examples included Module Leader or Process Head (n = 3), Senior IT (n = 4), Senior Analyst (n = 2), and an assortment of other titles such as Trainee, Tech Apps engineer, and Management Trainee. Of these 26 Lead IT professionals, 10 had longer experiences in IT (Current job Minus 2). Four had the title of Engineer. One each held the positions of Analyst, Test/ Software or Junior Engineer, Trainee or Trainee on Contract.

There were 13 respondents whose job title at survey time was Project or Senior Lead. Five IT professionals, out of nine, were engineers in their previous positions. The remaining titles were: Lead, Senior IT, QA Lead, or a Trainee. All nine reported at least one other prior position (current Minus 2). The most common position was an Engineer (n = 5).

In short, a typical deep career path for a Lead was: Engineer → to Lead or Test Engineer; or Programmer or Trainee → Engineer → Lead; or Engineer → Senior IT → Project or Senior Lead. More specifically, as per an interviewee (a Lead Software Engineer), the typical career progression in the software field is: Associate Software Engineer → Software Engineer → Senior Software Engineer → Lead Engineer → Senior Lead Engineer Mid-Level Management → Upper Management.

Individual Contributors, but not Engineers (Table 2.7). Another job title in Indian IT was that of individual contributors (n = 79). They were neither managers nor leads in that they did not supervise, manage, or organize the activities of others. The most common specific job titles for an individual contributor were Senior IT (n = 45), Analyst (n = 21),

Table 2.6 IT Career Trajectories: Leads, but Not Managers (Current Position; n = 57)

Current Position Minus 3	Current Position Minus 2	Current Position Minus 1	Current Position
No Position*/11† (n = 13)	QA Lead/3.03 (n = 1) Trainee/5.04 (n = 1) Engineer/5.00 (n = 5)	Lead/3.00 (n = 1) Sr. IT/4.00 (n = 1) Engineer/5.00 (n = 5)	Project or Senior Lead/3.10 (n = 13)
	Lead /3.00 (n = 1) Sr. IT/4.00 (n = 1) No Position /11 (n = 4)	QA Lead/3.03 (n = 1) Trainee/5.04 (n = 1) No Position /11 (n = 4)	
Trainee/5.04 (n = 1) Tech./App. Engineer/5.06 (n = 1) TOC/9.00 (n = 1) No Position /11 (n = 33)	Engineer/5.00 (n = 4) Test/Software Engin./5.07 (n = 1) TOC 2/9.02 (n = 1) Analyst/ 4.01 (n = 1)	Mod. Leader//3.02 (n = 3); Analyst/4.01 (n = 1); Sr. Analyst/ 4.10 (n = 2) Lead/3.00 (n = 1) Sr. IT/4.00(n = 4)	Lead Positions, IT Related/ 3.00 (n = 36)

(Cont'd)

Table 2.6 (Cont'd)

Current Position Minus 3	Current Position Minus 2		Current Position Minus 1		Current Position
	Jr. SE/Prog/5.10 (n = 1) Trainee/ 5.04 (n = 2) No Position / 11.00 (n = 26)	↗	Engineer/5.0 (n = 10); Trainee (Eng, software, Developer/5.04 (n = 1); Tech Apps/Support Engr./5.06 (n = 1); Senr. Bus. Dev./Resource Exec./6.10 (n = 1); Trainee (non-specialty Engineer /9.00 (n = 1) Management Trainee/9.04 (n = 1) No Position /11 (n = 10)		
No Position /11 (n = 2)	No Position /11 (n = 2)	↑	Engineer/5.00 (n = 2)	↑	Module Leader or Process Head /3.02 (n = 2)
No Position /11 (n = 2)	No Position /11 (n = 2)	↑	Engineer/5.00 (n = 1) No Position /11 (n = 1)	↑	QA Lead/3.03 (n = 2)
No Position /11 (n = 4)	No Position /11 (n = 4)	↑	TOC/9.00 (n = 1) No Position/11 (n = 3)	↑	Professional Practice Trainer; 3.04 (n = 4)

Source: Author.

* No Position = did not have previous positions: either Minus 3 or Minus 2 or Minus 1.

† Number after job title, 'No Position/11/', refers to the survey codes.

Table 2.7 IT Career Trajectories: Individual Contributors (Current Position; n = 79)

Current Position Minus 3	Current Position Minus 2	Current Position Minus 1	Current Position
Project Manager/2.04* (n = 1) →	Test Sft./Eng./5.07 (n = 1)	Engineer/5.00 (n = 23)	
No Position† /11 (n = 44)	Analyst/4.01 (n = 1) Trainee/5.04 (n = 3) Engineer/5.00(n = 1)	Jr. SE/Prog./ 5.10 (n = 2) Assoc. Engineer/ 5.01\ (n = 1)	Senior IT Related/4.00 (n = 45)
	No Position /11 (n = 39)	No Position /11 (n = 19) →	
Engineer/5.00 (n = 1) →	Test Engineer/Sft./5.07 (n = 1)	Mid-level management (not Senior and not IT related/2 (n = 1);	
No Position /11 (n = 12)	Analyst/4.01 (n = 1) No Position /11 (n = 11)	Sr. IT/4.00 (n = 1); Engineer/5.0 (n = 5); Test Engin/Sft/5.07 (n = 1)	Senior Analyst /4/10 (n = 13)
		No Position /11 (n = 5) →	

(Cont'd)

Table 2.7 (Cont'd)

Current Position Minus 3	Current Position Minus 2	Current Position Minus 1		Current Position
No Position /11 (n = 21)	Engineer/5.00 (n = 3) ↗↘	Sr. IT/4.00 (n = 2); Lead /3.00 (n = 1);		
	No Position /11 (n = 18) ↗↗↗↗↗	Engineer/5.00 (n = 2); Asst Sys Engin/5.02 (n = 1); Test Engin/Sft/5.07 (n = 1); Trainee/5.04 (n = 1); Other, IT /6.00 (n = 1) No Position /11 (n = 12)	→	Analyst/4.01 (n = 21)

Source: Author.

* Number after job title, 'Project Manager/2.04' refers to the survey codes.

† No Position = did not have previous positions: either Minus 3 or Minus 2 or Minus 1.

and Senior Analyst (n = 13). Most Senior IT Professionals who were Individual Contributors held at least one prior IT positions. They were typically Engineers (n = 23) before becoming Senior IT.

Many engineers shifted (most likely horizontal moves) in their career ladder to become Individual Contributors as Analysts. Of the 45 professionals who were in Senior IT positions, 26 (more than half) were Engineers before becoming Individual Contributors. For the rest, it was their first appointment in IT. Engineers (n = 5) also moved into another type of Individual Contributor positions as Senior Analysts (n = 13). Two Senior Analysts were in some form of mid-level management in their prior positions. Becoming Individual Contributors as Analysts was another career move for Engineers (n = 21). For example, three engineers were in Senior IT (2) or Lead positions before becoming Individual Contributors. Another four engineers (in their Current Position Minus 1) moved into the Individual Contributor positions. In short, most Individual Contributors were Engineers in their former positions.

Engineers, Individual Contributors (Table 2.8). It is not surprising that 'Engineer' was the most common job title in the survey (175 or 34.2 per cent). Engineers, like Analysts, are also Individual Contributors. The vast majority (n = 135) listed their current title as Engineer. There was also an assortment of other levels of engineers. This included Associate or Assistant Engineer, Support Programmer, Technology or Application Support Engineer, Test and Junior Software Engineer, and Network Administrator. It was interesting to note that for most, this was their first IT position.

IT Support Positions (Table 2.9). The final set of job titles in the web survey were an assortment of IT support positions (86 or 17 per cent). They included Consultants (n = 18), Trainer (n = 4), two Process Associates, a Verifier, a Route Settler, a Recruiter, and a Front Office Manager. A few (n = 24) were hired as Trainees. Half of the Trainees were in their first IT job as Non-specialty Engineer Trainees (n = 12). The other half of the Trainees was hired on contract. At least three levels of Trainees on Contract (TOC) were reported (n = 12). The typical career progression for trainees on contract was as follows: TOC → TOC1 → TOC2.

Table 2.8 IT Career Trajectories of Engineers (Current Position; n = 175)

Current Position Minus 3		Current Position Minus 2	Current Position Minus 1		Current Position
TOC/9.00* (n = 4)	→ → →	TOC 1/9.01 (n = 2); TOC 2/9.02 (n = 1); Trainee/5.04 (n = 1)	TOC 2/9.02 (n = .2); TOC 3/9.02/ (n = 1); Engineer/5/ (n = 1)	→	Engineer/5 (n = 134)
No Position† /11.0 (n = 130)	→ →	Tech/App Engineer/5.06 (n = 1); No Position /11 (n = 129)	Sup. Prog./Engineer/5.05 (n = 1); Lead/3.00 (n = 1); Engineer/5.0 (n = 2); Assoc. Engineer/ 5.01 (n = 3); Trainee/5.04 (n = 18); Test Engineer/Sft/5.07 (n = 1); Jr. SE/Programmer/5.10 (n = 3); Trainee (non-specialty Engineer/9.00 (n = 3); No Position 11 (n = 98)		
		No Position /11 (n = 4)	Analyst/4.01 (n = 1) No Position /11 (n = 3)	→	Associate Engineer/5.01 (n = 4)
		No Position/11 (n = 6)	PP Trainer/3.04 (n = 1) Trainee/5.04 (n = 5)	→	Assistant Systems Engineer/5.02 (n = 6)

Earlier Position	Previous Position	Current Job Title
	No Position /11/ (n = 5)	→ Trainee/5.04 (n = 5)
	No Position /11 (n = 2)	→ Support Programmer/Engineer/5.05 (n = 2)
	Engineer/5.00 (n = 1) No Position /11 (n = 7)	→ Technology or Applications Support Engineer/5.06 (n = 8)
TOC /9.01 (n = 1) →	Engineer/5.00 (n = 1) →	
No Position /11 (n = 8) →		
TOC 2/9.02 (n = 1) →	Manager/2.01 (n = 1) →	→ Test Engineer or Software/5.07 (n = 9)
Engineer/5.00 (n = 1) Other/IT related/6.00 (n = 1) →	Trainee (Non-specialty Engineer)/9.00 (n = 1) →	
No Position /11.00 (n = 6)	Trainee/5.04 (n = 1) No Position /11 (n = 5)	
	Trainee/5.04 (n = 1) No Position/11 (n = 3)	→ Junior SoftwareEngineer/Programmer /5.10 (n = 4)
	Mid Management /2.0 (n = 1); No Position/11.00 (n = 2)	→ Network Administrator/ 5.13 (n = 3)

Source: Author.

* Number after job title, 'TOC/9.00' refers to the survey codes.

† No Position = did not have previous positions: either Minus 3 or Minus 2 or Minus 1.

Table 2.9 IT Support Positions (Current; n = 86)

Position Minus 3		Position Minus 2		Position Minus 1		Current Position
No Position*/11† (n = 27)	→	No Position/11 (n = 27)	⟋⟍	Trainer/6.02 (n = 1) Route Settlement/6.05 (n = 1) TOC/9.00 (n = 1) No Position/11 (n = 24)	→	Other, IT Related / 6.00 (n = 27)
No Position/11 (n = 9)	⟋⟍	Sr. Analyst/Engineer/4.10 n = 1 No Position /11 (n = 8)	⟋	Consultant/8.00 (n = 4)	→	Senior ConsultantPositions/7.00 (n = 9)
				Sr. Lead/3.10 (n = 1) No Position/11 (n = 4)	→	
No Position/11 (n = 9)	→	No Position /11 (n = 9)	⟋⟍	Sr. Analyst/Specialist/Engineer/4.10(n = 1) Tech/Applications Engineer/5.06 (n = 1) No Position /11 (n = 7)	→	Consultant/8.0 (n = 9)
Engineer/5.0 (n = 1)	→	Sr. IT/4.00 (n = 1)	→	Lead Positions (IT related but not Manager)/3 (n = 1)	→	Other (Non-IT')/10.00 (n = 7)
No Position /11 (n = 6)	→	No Position /11 (n = 6)	→	No Position /11 (n = 6)		
No Position /11 (n = 4)	→	No Position /11 (n = 4)	⟋⟍	Engineer/5.00 (n = 1) No Position /11 (n = 3)	→	Trainer HR Manager, Administrator, Resource Executive/6.02 (n = 4)

Current Position	Minus 1	Minus 2
Process Associate /6.03 (n = 2)		
Verifier/ 6.04 (n = 1) →	Other, IT/6.00 (n = 1)	
Route Settlement/6.06 (n = 1) →	Assistant Manager/2.03 (n = 1)	
Senior Business Development, Recruiter, or Resource Executive/6.10 (n = 1)		
Trainee (Non-specialty Engineer)/9.00 (n = 12) →	TOC (Non-specialty Engineer) /9.00 (n = 1); No Position /11 (n = 11)	
TOC 1 (Trainee on contract 1) /9.01 (n = 7) →	TOC (Non-specialty Engineer)/9.00 (n = 7)	
TOC 2 (Trainee on Contract 2)/9.02 (n = 5) →	TOC 1 (Trainee on contract 1)/9.01 (n=4); No Position /11 (n = 1) →	TOC/9.00 (n = 4); No Position/11 (n = 1)
Front Office Manager/6.01 (n = 1)		

Source: Author.

* No Position = did not have previous positions: either Minus 3 or Minus 2 or Minus 1.

† Number after job title, 'No Position/11', refers to the survey codes.

Why the Youthful Career Life Course Positions?

A review of the characteristics of the course of life of IT Survey respondents provided clues to their youthful or young-adulthood careers which were fitting to their early course of life. Irrespective of the specific IT sub-sector (BPO or ITES, or IT), the average IT employee was 27–28 years of age. And they were more likely to be single than married (28–44 per cent). And those who were married, were in the early stages of family building; they either had no children, or a maximum of 2 children (Table 2A.2).

The male-female distribution (63.5 per cent male versus 36.5 per cent female) of the survey respondents, while confirming the male presence in the Indian industry, also indicated the inroads that Indian women have made. Whether the sub-sector was BPO, ITES, IT, or any combination thereof, males outnumbered women; generally, there were twice as many men as women, albeit among those who completed the web survey. However, the IT sub-sector (that requires formal degrees in engineering or related technical fields) had the most women (39 per cent), followed by ITES (35.2 per cent) and BPO (32.0 per cent). The presence of IT women engineers is primarily attributed to the Indian 'knowledge for development paradigm'[14] and openness of and access to technical education available to talented Indian women. In addition, as Radhakrishnan (2011: 61, 64–5) detailed, the 'cultivated place-lessness' of Indian IT companies suits the desire of Indian women and their families for a safe and appropriate working environment for women. Indian IT companies, particularly the MNCs but also the home grown companies like Wipro and Infosys, not only look like their parent companies in the West on the outside but in their inside the office environment as well. The palpable safety that the IT work environments provide—as sitting in front of a computer in an air-conditioned office, with limited physical exertion, travel, and face to face interactions with the Indian and western public—make ITES and even some types of back office or financial BPO work more suitable for Indian women. Added to the appropriateness of some types of IT work for women, is the ability to earn money and financial independence before

---

[14] The knowledge for development (K4D) model (see Radhakrishnan 2007, 2011) was used by the Indian government as a tool for not only leapfrogging traditional modernization/development pathways but also for broad based development (so that development will not be restricted to elites, including men).

and after marriage, which also render them more desirable in the marriage market.

Project of IT Merit Culture Making

The lived work experiences of IT professionals in the web survey and other scholarly writings offered useful entry points into the merit culture making project and its potential for caste reproduction in Indian IT. Merit has become a valorized article of faith in the IT discourse and rationalized as 'quality' to western customers.[15] It dominates the daily social discourse in the IT workplaces, public spheres, and even academic circles. A *pure merit*-based culture and related structured mental attributes is the framework used to map, organize and understand the particular and unique new world fashioned by IT. For some, pure merit indicates *appropriate difference* between the IT and non-IT sectors of public government institutions which use caste quotas in addition to merit. And depending on one's *caste positionality*, the merit accumulated through state-sponsored reservation educational programs, also known as *earmarked* or *reservation merit*, either does or does not qualify as merit. However, it is in the *holistic approaches to merit*, adopted by many IT professionals, that gaps open up for caste considerations to be introduced into the seemingly tightly written script of the merit culture project. In fact, whether merit is deemed *pure* and/or *holistic*, the cultivation and practice of merit is deeply embedded in, supported by, and *symbolically hidden* (as per Bourdieu) behind the social and material privileges of the dominant castes and middle classes.

Wipro: A Case Study of Valorized Merit Construction in IT[16]

The story of an IT corporation like Wipro, detailed by journalistic ethnographer Hamm (2007), serves as a useful case example of the historical development and honing of the *streamlined* IT merit culture deemed a functional pre-requisite in a globalized world. Wipro, an Indian IT

---

[15] See Parthasarathy (2012: 256), Upadhya (2007a), and Krishna and Brihmadesam (2006).

[16] The account of merit valorization in Wipro is drawn from Hamm (2007).

powerhouse corporation has become known for its transformational 'global service delivery' business model using transnational and virtual cooperation labour practices. It is this transnational environment that has become the host for both streamlined and holistic IT merit culture making project.

Wipro Ltd., founded by Azim Premji and debuted on the NYSE on 18 October 2000, with annual revenues of about US$500 million, was considered a symbol of rising India at the start of the decade. That year Wipro had more than 800,000 engineers (the one-third world) writing software for Wall Street, Motor City in Detroit, and even for the American entertainment industry. They also designed computer chips, circuit boards, and other machinery producing hardware for consumer electronics, aerospace, and health care. And they engaged in software programming, tech systems integration, and systems management. In addition, another half a million worked in Wipro's BPO segment (the two-thirds world) handling accounting, medical claims processing, customer service, and other business functions for western clients. Wipro, in other words, pioneered the strategy of developing expertise in a wide range of different industries, from technology, banking, manufacturing, to retail. As Hamm (2007: 17) called it, 'Wipro is like Walmart. It's everywhere', offering to its Western clients a wide selection from a broad array of services based on multiple low-cost business models. These bold business forays allowed Wipro to stand out from the pack', even though Wipro was only a number 3 player in size, next to Tata Consulting Services and Infosys.[17]

Wipro is symbolic of the transnational, flexible, and creative IT professional. When the restrictive policies of the Indian government, in the late 1970s, forced Western tech companies (like IBM) to leave India, the founder, Aziz Premji, seized the opportunity to create a home grown Indian computer business in 1977. He made mini-computers with micro-processors aimed at the business market for a substantially less cost than the IBM mainframe and shipped the processors within one year. When the western tech giants re-entered India in the early 1990s,

---

[17] Tata Consultancy Services (TCS) founded in 1968 with almost US$3 billion in sales in 2006 was the pioneer of the 'body shopping' business model doing routine software updating and patching work for western corporations. Infosys, the second largest, started as a tech services company and added high-end consulting practice to its global delivery portfolio.

coinciding with the government relaxing its trade policies, Wipro shifted its business focus to offering for hire, to the western companies who had returned to India, an electronics R&D lab, software programming services, and electronic engineering expertise/services. Their rationale was that while the doors opened for others to come into India, it also gave Wipro the opportunities to go out. Software programming (designing embedded applications for telecommunication and computers), was their first target and was quickly followed up with hardware and chip design, taking the clue from Texas Instruments and Motorola who had opened their own software shops in India to access quality programmers on the cheap. When the Y2K debacle approached, Wipro was ready with its army of programmers.

It is not surprising that by 2003, Wipro and its employees had gone beyond routine software programming tasks. The company had a full array of IT outsourcing services, including testing of products, managing clients' computer data centres, and call centre outsourcing. They also broadened their expertise to transactional BPO services; for example, in accounting, travel and entertainment expensing, insurance claims, real estate mortgage processing, and even a small group of radiologists in India who evaluated X-rays of patients for American hospitals for a fraction of what it would cost them with in-house specialists. Wipro made its name as a key global services partner and an end-to-end supplier for companies like HP, all the while blending offshore labour with on-site client services.

In a globalizing environment, Wipro changed the ways of doing business. With its 'transnational model' for a 'global service delivery portfolio', enabled by global cooperation, it has become a 'virtual' corporation. The transnational nature of the business model, at Wipro's core, meant, 'A company's work is performed at the places in the world where talent can be tapped most efficiently' (Hamm 2007: 17). In the resulting Virtual Corporations,[18] companies identified parts of their practice that were crucial to their success and outsourced or offshored everything else. Dividing the work for a particular client, say HP, between employees at

---

[18] This is unlike the vertically integrated corporations of the twentieth century. Standard Oil, for example, did all its operations starting with extracting oil, transporting it in its own trucks, refined it in its own factories, shipped gas in its own trucks, and sold it in its own service stations (Hamm 2007: 18).

the client's office in India or in the home country, at Indian companies, or at other low-cost countries (a ratio of 30 per cent work near customer to 70 per cent offshore was typical) enabled Wipro to deliver its service portfolio globally. Of course, these new business models required new management techniques that would not have been possible without the ongoing advances in telecommunication technologies. Hamm illustrated Wipro's art and techniques of global collaboration and management as: thousands of software programmers worked in teams, whose members were scattered across continents and multiple time zones, while Wipro managers kept the business running smoothly through teleconferencing and other sophisticated tech tools.

In the final analyses, these business models and management techniques enabled transnational, virtual corporations, like Wipro, Infosys, and TCS, to offer efficiently up-to-date, quality, and operational excellence. They identified fundamental shifts in the business environment and then scrambled to create whole new businesses. When the tech industry was innovating (and producing) new technologies faster than corporations could absorb, the Indian tech giants shifted their focus to services integrating and distributing technologies, in the mode of Dell and Google. Hamm claimed that Wipro could quickly develop new electronic products by combining standard off-the-shelf technologies with their own patented inventions. They built complex software apps from scratch. They advised clients how to design and deploy new technologies. As a result, the project-specific contracts of the initial stages of information technology growth in India had been replaced by multi-year and multi-million dollar contracts to do work not only in India but in the client country as well; Tata Consulting Services is an example. A NASSCOM-McKinsey report (Kaka 2009) predicted that the value of Indian tech services was expected to exceed US$60–80 billion by 2010.

As the IT industry grew, it transformed from Body Shops, the two-third world without much creativity, to Brain Shops adding new technology and process excellence capabilities. They took advantage of the beachheads that had already been established by American companies, like IBM, EDS, HP, Accenture, and also organized around other vertical businesses in telecommunications, manufacturing, and retailing. As Hamm (2007) posited, the internet made the Indian mind and intellect available to western businesses. More than 700 Indian tech services companies, 'a new breed of tech companies' were providing vital, 'high-quality' brain work for large American, European, and Japanese companies. The inexhaustible supply of raw talent in 120,000 IT and other relevant undergraduate college graduates (according to NASSCOM), meant that there was a 'wealth in intellectual capital' (Hamm 2007: 3–4). Besides, the Indian companies had a cost advantage (pay was about 20 per cent of their comparable western counterparts) over western companies such as EDS, IBM, and Accenture.

On balance, advantages in cost and labour supply led to the Indian IT corporations being transformed from local outfits into global, virtual corporations and exponentially increased the cache of IT education and employment. It also created the ideal IT employee who could work transnationally, independently or in a team, and learn new technologies proactively to adjust to the changing business environments.

Wipro's management principles and their merit culture, as outlined by Hamm (2007), offer a good example of the IT merit culture making project. Guided by their business model of 'virtual and global collaboration', Wipro looks for a unique set of skills and even temperaments in their employees who can live up to their four pillars of strength: customer centricity, process excellence, people management, and career development. Their global foci required employees who had flexibility to cooperate with team members across different continents and time zones. Constant improvement and process excellence was emphasized at both the employee and company levels. Wipro aggressively adopted international quality standards by spotting and quickly adopting emerging standards in software programming and hardware R&D. And their employees were required to certify and recertify to keep up with the changing technologies. As a result, to any outside observer, the ambience in the company is one of perpetual transition, maintained through sheer will and determination. In the words of Wipro's chief operating officer, as quoted by Hamm, they 'will do whatever it takes to make things happen' (2007: 29). In this virtual, global set-up, IT Skills appear pre-eminent and out-shadow traditional Indian social vectors of caste/religion/communities. IT employees 'streamline' their multiple identities of class, caste, urbanism, religion, and gender to create a uniform set of norms and beliefs with which they can move quickly, easily, and pragmatically through geographic and virtual space. It is these streamlined merit norms, which have cache in the global IT sector, that privilege the *symbolic capital* of IT skills.

Yet, *streamlined merit* has also become a tool to manage the matrix of privileges associated with symbolic and material capital that intertwine and reinforce each other to create and sustain the merit IT culture. While honing their merit culture, IT professionals continue to be embedded in the 'gendered, religious, national, and class histories' of India (Radhakrishnan 2011: 5). It is in this complex socio-cultural context that questions about whether *pure IT skills* are the sole signal of 'Merit' or whether merit is also *holistic* and includes more subjective social markers take on significance.

Holistic Merit Criteria in the Indian IT Sector

Instructive in constructing the *multifaceted, holistic contours of IT merit* and the *potential caste loopholes* are the ground-level responses of IT professionals who spoke in the web survey about their work experiences. These professionals evaluated 14 different skills, *social and cultural capital* (Coleman 1988 and others), for their importance in the making of an ideal IT professional.[19] Their ratings fell into four unique sets:[20] Work Skills, Linguistic Cultural Capital, Social Comfort, and Social Background. These skills, which form the basis for judging and ultimately constructing

[19] To deconstruct the elements of 'merit' in Indian IT, a segment in the survey, which asked respondents about the characteristic of the ideal IT employee, were used. More specifically, the umbrella question in this survey segment read: 'Listed below are some characteristics of an excellent IT worker. Please check (X) how important each characteristic is on the scale provided'. The rating scale used: Not at all important, Not Important, Not Relevant, Important, and Very Important. A follow-up question gave the respondents an opportunity to add other relevant skills that make for an excellent IT worker. In addition to rating the 14 skill sets, the web survey also asked two open-ended questions to give respondents the opportunity to elaborate on the merit qualifications and also to probe more deeply into the question of work skills and education required. The specific questions read: 'What other skills do you think are important for an excellent IT professional? And why do you think so?' (Q15). And Q16, 'There are many who claim that the new information technology jobs are open ONLY to those who are qualified (they have the right education and skills) for the job. What do you think?'

[20] Results of the factor analyses conducted and statistical interpretations are presented in Table 2A.3.

'merit' in the IT sector, offered nuanced caste-embedded profiles of IT merit culture.

Besides, four major tropes that emerged in the narratives comments of rank-and-file IT professionals clarified the nature of merit in IT. It did not come as a surprise that the first trope to emerge was *pure merit* or the objective assessment of merit skills; it included technical skills and qualifications, as in job specific qualifications. However, the respondents extended the boundaries of merit by including more subjective merit measures that could be termed *Habits* of the Intellect (work habits), Mind (work ethics), and Spirit (Commitment). These 'habits' (to borrow from Bellah and Madsen [1996]) refer to a set of values, principles, and ways of being that shapes and reflects individuals' behaviour. Layered onto the merit criteria were *integration* (of degree, knowledge, and practice) and well-rounded with interest in *continuing/updating* their education/skills. The fourth major trope addressed *softer skills* such as English fluency, social skills, equality, and diversity. Taken together, it is these *subjective measures* of habits, integration, and soft skills, embedded in the matrix of *symbolic and material caste privileges*, that made for the porous contours of pure merit boundaries through which traditional caste and other considerations can enter into the IT sector.

Pure Merit as Human Capital; The Work Skills Factor

IT professionals, almost uniformly, deemed objective work skills, conceptualized as Human Capital resources, to be important, if not very important (Table 2.10). Shadowing the Wipro model, the ideal human capital skills included the following: Technical Skills; Ability to work well in a team; Willingness to put in extra effort; Shows individual initiative; and Being meticulous. For example, over 90 per cent rated these skills as either important or very important. However, there was some variability in the degree of importance the IT professionals assigned to the specific human capital skills. Not surprisingly, like with the Wipro labour model, two-thirds opined that technical skills (62 per cent) and ability to work in a team (65.8 per cent) were very important. A third rated these skills as important. Other human capital skills thought to be important (but not very important) were extra effort (54.7 per cent), individual initiative (58.6 per cent), and meticulousness (46.9 per cent); fewer (between 25–43 per cent) considered them to be very important.

Table 2.10 Merit: Human Capital Factor (Work Skills) (n = 488)

Human Capital Skills	Response	Percentage (n)
Technical skills	1 = Not at all important	0.2% (1)
	2 = Not important	1.2 (6)
	3 = Not relevant	1.8 (9)
	4 = Important	34.6 (169)
	5 = Very important	62.1 (303)
Ability to work well in a team	1 = Not at all important	0.0%
	2 = Not important	0.0
	3 = Not relevant	1.0 (5)
	4 = Important	33.2 (162)
	5 = Very important	65.8 (321)
Willing to put in extra effort	1 = Not at all important	0.2% (1)
	2 = Not important	3.7 (18)
	3 = Not relevant	5.9 (29)
	4 = Important	54.7 (267)
	5 = Very important	35.5 (173)
Shows individual initiat ive	1 = Not at all important	0.6% (3)
	2 = Not important	3.3 (16)
	3 = Not relevant	12.3 (60)
	4 = Important	58.6 (286)
	5 = Very important	25.2 (123)
Someone who is meticulous	1 = Not at all important	0.0%
	2 = Not important	1.0 (5)
	3 = Not relevant	4.3 (22)
	4 = Important	46.9 (241)
	5 = Very important	42.8 (220)

Source: Author.

Two other observations were note-worthy. One, technical skills, 'pure merit', appeared to stand apart in rendering who is meritorious. The technical skills ratings were the most weakly correlated with the other human capital skills like team work, extra effort, initiative and meticulousness.[21]

---

[21] Correlations of technical skills with the rest of the work skills were as follows: with ability to work well in a team = 0.16***; with extra effort = 0.14***; with meticulous = 0.18***; with individual initiative = 0.08 (*** denotes $p <= .001$. It applies to all similar occurrences in the text).

Second, there were shades of difference in the degree of importance attached to the remaining human capital skills. For example, positive ratings of one set, team work and extra effort ($r = 0.31^{***}$), or another set, team work and meticulousness ($r = 0.34^{***}$), were strongest and more consistent than with the other skills. If the professionals rated one as very important they were more likely to rate the other as very important also; this might say something about the dependence of a team's success on ability for team work, extra team efforts, and meticulous work.

The narrative comments offered by ground level IT professionals richly detailed what they meant by 'human capital skills'.[22] The meritorious professional was one who had the skills/qualifications (including job specific qualifications) that could be objectively measured. The ideal meritorious persona would also be someone who was an integrated (degree, knowledge, and practice) well-rounded person, interested in continuing and updating their education/skills. A more subjective set of criteria included 'habits,' work habits, work ethics, and commitment to work.

Objective Markers of Pure Merit. As they addressed objective markers, most IT professionals, in their own words, elaborated on the centrality of 'Technical Skills/Qualifications'. Some made general comments like, IT jobs 'need pure merit'. Another said, 'Right education and skills are basic requirements in information technology'. Other refrains included comments like: 'Education and skills are important to get jobs in IT'; one 'needs actual knowledge about his/her work' or 'I have experienced it while I was looking out for a job. Industries look for the right exact skills they need'. Commenting on what it takes to get an IT job are these professionals, 'qualification and skills are a must to work in IT', 'Employee should have right education and skills for the IT job', or 'the one who is well qualified should get a job' and 'the person should have at least the minimum qualification to do the job well'. To others, 'anyone with good education and technical skills can do information technology job' or 'I think it's open to all who have skills'; or 'only qualified persons will get good opportunities' or 'nowadays, for programming also, if he is well in a programming language, he will get a job', and that 'skilled persons are the need of the hour'.

---

[22] In the interest of authentic reporting, the written linguistic style of respondents has been largely left intact, except for minimal changes presented within '[ ]' to improve readability.

Offering reasons for their laser focus on IT skills were these comments: 'Skills are important to do the job. Education equips/enables one to develop the skill and qualification and hence it is important'. Emphasizing the globalized nature of IT work some said: 'Those who are not qualified, will get pushed out, even if they manage to get a job in an MNC' or 'Without knowledge it is difficult to survive in an organization specially during the time of such a recession'.

Still others emphasized 'degreed technical skills' with statements like: 'Academic competencies coupled with technical competencies will make the right mix and match to be the ideal candidate'. Or 'the ideal IT professionals should be Bachelor degree holders' or have 'technical and communication skills', or 'strong core technical skills' because to get hired into IT 'you must be technically strong' and that 'at least minimum degree is required to get job in a MNC'. Some IT professionals listed specific IT skills: 'Programming skill and logic thinking' or 'Business Analytical skills, and Testing'. In the words of an IT recruiter, 'In today's scenario as an IT Recruiter we should know all the skill sets to place different candidates at different places. All SAP working, Informatica, Coding (C++ UNIX ETC)'. In short, he said, 'ya definitely the right education is very important thing because they should know the basic things. After that once enter the IT industry they can become the professionals'.

There were those who advocated for pure merit 'in the interest of needs of the clients' when they said that IT professionals should 'try to understand the exact requirement of the customer to provide relevant solution for the problem'; or 'in IT, everything is based on the delivery performance in the project. If the job we are considering is related to customer project, qualification, and ability of the employee is vital. It can be relaxed for internal projects as internal trainings and upgrading the skill levels of employees will fill the gap'. Besides, technical skills are essential in IT to 'understand client requirement and finish things within time limit'. Others made reference to the work product. 'Technical know-how is important' because it 'reduces the learning time' and 'if we are qualified only then we can give best product'. Or that one needs the 'ability to listen and understand the exact requirement will help in reducing effort'. Also that there is the 'need to be able to communicate well and should think logically; an engineering degree provides you this' or that 'you need have the right basic skillset and then you can be expert/sharpen those skills on the job'.

Emphasizing the IT organization's needs for technically qualified workers were these IT rank-and-file professionals: 'Today's world is a competitive one, so no company would like to train and educate the unqualified and under qualified people and waste time on the same'; 'At this period of recession the company would like to cut the expenses on the training of employees'. Or that 'as most companies do not wish to spend on training and development, beyond their immediate project needs' and therefore 'many companies not willing to take freshers & groom them', because 'qualified people can grab things quickly and they are trained to do things in a better way. Yet all depends on how well the corporation shapes them up and polish them as a finished product as a fresher' or that skilled professionals' ... will help the company to move ahead quickly'. IT professionals also offered supply side arguments for why companies focus on technical skilled workers: 'With IT colleges mushrooming everywhere and Andhra Pradesh state alone churning out 1 lakh (100,000) engineers every year, added to several thousands of M.C.A.'s. Choosing quality resources from abundant quantity is a challenge, so qualifying parameters are a must'.

Many placed an added emphasis on continuing education to update their skills as yet another merit criterion. An IT professional should be 'technically updated to survive in the market and to develop their own skills' and that 'being willing/able to learn new skills is key: IT professionals must be able to learn new technologies, and they should be proactive in doing so'. As for the need for constant improvement, some noted that, 'It is important to update themselves with all the necessary skills, because everyday the skills keep changing and new things come up', and that an IT professional should have a 'desire to upgrade oneself to later and newer versions of a given technology' that is 'getting updated day by day', and therefore 'a person has to be current and up to date to find place in the new IT era' and 'never static'. In short, in a Wipro model, *IT* 'professionals should continuously update' their skill sets because: 'the technologies changes very fast and new technologies also will come very fast'. Therefore, 'Individual should have willingness and open to work on any technology or domain. This is required to survive in continuous changing market', and be 'competitive to survive with latest technology in his field'. As another noted, 'we have to agree with the fact that until and unless we are familiar with the updated technologies we cannot survive in this competitive world' and ergo the IT professional should have the 'ability to be an updated person in his field'.

How do IT companies manage their laser focus on degree credentials as indicators of 'merit'? Insights offered by survey respondents were noteworthy. For one, 'Recruitment is done only for the regular degree student'. And the emphasis on degree merit criteria is because 'Higher educational qualification will help the individuals to understand and complete the assigned task more effectively'. Also, 'In IT, interviewers look for the employees who can fulfill their posts'. Consequently, 'currently most jobs are given to engineering students only' or that 'nowadays jobs are given to students who have completed their engineering'.

Of course, there was nuanced dissent from the overwhelming support noted above for technical skills as a barometer of merit in IT. Many specified *boundary limits* (Powers 2010) to the role of technical skills in the IT merit metrics. Some boundaries were job specific or specific to the professional career histories of IT professionals. Other lines of dissent contrasted academic or degreed qualifications against skills, experience, training, effort, and interest/aptitude. As one said, almost tongue in cheek, 'Most of the right qualified peoples are unemployed'. On balance, the dissenters questioned, to varying degrees, the over-emphasis on degreed technical parameters for 'merit' in IT.

Drawing *job specific boundaries* between the core IT and non-tech sub-sectors, one stated, ' ... for software development job one needs to learn the technology or programming language though they come from different educational back grounds', because 'information technology jobs comprises all the jobs which is attached with the usage of computers; software programming is limited to those who are skilled in it. But other jobs like data entering etc. can be done with a person who has minimum educational qualification'. Other examples of job specific boundary limits on the relevance of education and skills in IT Merit were evident in these comments. 'No specific education and skill is required until and unless you are into core new developments project', or that 'Not all jobs require you to have technical background, there are still many jobs in marketing, finance, accounting sectors in these firms, however, the number of people who are willing to pursue career in these lines are less than those who are attracted towards the current high paying technical jobs'. Or 'like call centre jobs, they need only some computer knowledge and good communication skills in English'.

More examples of job-specific boundaries: specific skills are necessary, they said, 'for some specific jobs. If the project requires sound accounting

knowledge then the company may look for MBA or CA candidate who
has programming skill'. To others, 'It is depending upon the job nature'
as in 'If the job is for technical development role yes right education and
skills are important; but if the role is non-technical like operations, support, HR, IT Sales and then all it matters are general skills'. Summarizing
the general importance of skills in the IT merit construct was this respondent: 'Technical background appears to be most important in the career
of a professional; second, the educational qualification or the breadth of
knowledge'.

Some drew *boundary limits around the career histories* of IT professionals. Degrees are important, ' … especially if someone is looking for
his/her first job. But if he/she has working knowledge of the job, then I
believe it is not matter whether right education and skill is there or not'.
Other examples of career specific boundary limits were drawn around the
types of degree credentials required in IT merit: 'For freshers, nowadays
they started recruiting all graduates (BSC, BCA, BCOM). Before that
the preference was given only to BE, Btech, and MCA. But this is a good
move as talents are not only from the right education but from right way
of thinking and handling;' or ' … with proper training even regular graduates r getting the job now'.

There were also multiple lines of explicit dissent from the central role
of degreed technical skills in defining IT merit culture. One line of dissent
contrasted *skills versus academic or degreed qualifications*. As one noted,
'Anyone with any degree are getting such jobs. My degree is just waste
here', or 'He/she should be .com because they may be need to communicate with many people; according to me the companies they are looking
for the skills that person has rather than the qualification'. Or IT jobs 'can
be given to skilled people too. No need to have higher education'; or 'Even
though education matters, still skill/knowledge to put things into practice
are relevant'.

Preference for 'experience, over degreed credentials', in IT merit cal-
culations was another line of dissent. Some examples: 'Experience in the
IT field is enough, not more qualification'. Or 'if there is no qualification
also they can do it if they have experience'; or 'In every JOB requirement
qualification & experience is mentioned. But I believe experience matters a lot. We should consider the people more on experience & skills
they show in interview'. Or degreed education 'is important to a certain
extent, but there are opportunities for others too. With the right kind

of experience, qualifications may not be a relevant factor'. Or 'The degree and qualifications is not at all needed; only the potential experience, and knowing well behavior'.

Some even went to the extent of minimizing the role of degreed credentials in the Indian IT pure merit culture and drew other boundary metrics around 'interest/aptitude, effort, and training'. Some specific boundary examples that minimized degreed credentials: Interest/Aptitude: 'Anyone can do as long as interest is there'; or 'Anyone can do IT job who are interested in it', and 'I think this concept is wrong. Any person who is willing to learn new technology can be trained and suitable job can be assigned' or ' ... not all the companies demand [degrees] from an employee/candidate'. Other comments in a similar vein: 'The one who had good aptitude and attitude can excel in this field. Education and skill can play an important role but it is not correct that only those who are highly qualified will get a job'. Again, 'If they have the interest and talent, I do not think it requires only qualified People'. Emphasizing the importance of 'effort' and 'training': 'Anybody who can put in that extra effort is qualified'; or 'there is no limit to one's success if he/she is ready to put in 100% of their time and talents and are motivated and ambitious'.

Speaking explicitly about the limited relevance of degreed credentialed education in IT, were comments like these: 'I think skill set is more important than having right education. I mean even if person is having high school but he is good (had certifications and trainings) in certain technology in IT industry, it's enough for him to become IT professional. You don't need to have big engineering degrees of rocket scientist to succeed in IT'. Or 'Even though education matters, still skill/knowledge to put things into practice are relevant'. And 'we have people having diploma, and various people from irrelevant educational background. The point is if their logical and conceptual knowledge is good, he would fit any role'.

More generally, others who downplayed the importance of degreed education in the IT merit calculus, said, 'Education is optional, skill is mandatory', or 'Qualification is not important. Only the knowledge is important'. Or 'Today's IT jobs are open to anyone who can acquire the skills on job'. Or 'Your educated youth has less knowledge than the uneducated experienced worker', because 'If given proper training they will make it'. Others went on to say, 'uneducated can work if they are well known within that (like multimedia we should know how to work with that tools)' or 'people who have completed studies in open universities are not preferred in MNCs (multinational Corps) though they are capable'.

A few were more biting in their indictment of over-reliance on technical skills: 'Even a school completed candidate are working in S/W firms in India!!!' Or 'There is a possibility for a non-technical person to indulge in work and perform well'; or ' ... you learn on the job'. Indicting the Indian educational system as an explanation, one noted: 'The educational qualification is important. However, I am almost certain that today's education system in India does not develop with analytical skills'. Yet others, while agreeing that education and skills are required in IT, argued that other non-skill factors also come into play. Some nuanced their responses as: 'I think the right education and skills will be definitely needed for IT positions. But, the IT organizations will put effort on fake experience' and therefore, IT companies 'need to consider the ones who are not from very reputed educational institutes. It is the skills that matter'.

On balance, there was overwhelming consensus in the IT professional community about the objective markers of merit. In their words, 'Yes, they should have the right education and computer skills for the job' and these objective markers include technical skills and credentials and continually updating IT skills to keep up with the dynamic information technology environment. Even those who placed boundary limits on the relevance of objective merit markers were not negating the centrality of IT merit but were pointing to the complexity and breadth of the IT industry.

But, Merit Also Equals Habits of the Intellect, Work, and Spirit (Soft Merit Markers)

And herein lay the loopholes through which caste considerations can enter into merit construction. For, in addition to objective merit markers, many stressed 'soft' traits (soft because of their subjective nature) that are best described as 'habits' of the intellect or mind, work, and spirit. In the Bellah and Madsen tradition, habits comprised a set of values, principles, and ways of being that undergird and reflect lived experiences.

'Habits of the Intellect' were reflected in these comments: 'Having the right set of skills is definitely important, but that's not everything. Being in IT field we will come across many new technologies which we have not heard about, but we will start working on them and sooner we will have to be open to getting hold of it and master the art of implementing it for better use', or that IT professionals 'need to have basic logical skills but also an interest in "taking new challenges," and "an urge to learn new technologies that increase the productivity of the person and work done"'.

Others underscored additional markers of merit best characterized as *'ways of thinking'*. Some examples: 'The two most important skills I would look for is: 1. Ability to learn; 2. Ability to work in teams', and that a new hire 'Should be a quick learner and easily adopt to new environment or technology'. Also important are the 'ability to work with a team, ready to learn new things' because 'logical thinking, innovative ideas will bring quick and quality work'. Others noted, 'The person's knowledge is required, but above all his openness and interest, and determination in his career'; 'Commitment to the work', and 'ability to think different types of solutions for a single problem and also ability to choose the best among the options'. Such flexibility requires 'better grasping capacity', 'ability to understand & problem solving techniques', or 'Lateral thinking and urge to excel plus adaptive nature'. Analytical and logical skills are important said others, 'because that determines the complete output and IT related milestones' and is needed 'to guide the team appropriately' and for 'self-achievement'. Ranking these soft criteria one noted, 'Attitude. If you watch all successful people in IT they have great attitude towards the work what they are doing, that makes huge difference, then Problem Solving, Flexibility, self branding, etc.'

Work Habits

IT professionals also seem to imply work habits that are *results oriented* so that they can understand 'customer business requirements' and 'work toward customer satisfaction'. Some opined that the ideal professional should be able to 'Work under stress, Team work, helping others'; 'Managing and handling any type of situation is very important. It is good to be smart worker than a hard worker', be 'hardworking, keeping target etc.', or needs 'concentration, dedication and majorly responsibility.'

Some went further, when they listed 'Ability to learn new technologies, Ability for work life balance', 'Technical skill, team work, ability to communicate-I feel these skills are very important'; 'Managerial skill (needed for promotion), Team working, Domain knowledge'; 'He should understand the business process before developing any new requirement and should think out of the box to provide the solutions'.

Some emphasized multi-tasking skills as in the need to 'Stretch to finish tasks, be diplomatic and work well with teams' and 'flexibility is needed in IT'; 'I believe one has to take additional responsibilities and should ready to stretch few hours more'. Others noted, 'Need to have innovative skills to achieve the target'; 'Working smart with a difference'; or 'Deliver right the first time,' should be good learner, that helps to become an excellent IT professional today'. To yet others work habits meant, 'do the work in an effective manner without any distraction' or that 'systematic way of approaching the work is very important. Because, in IT field, everything can be done within time and with quality only if we are executing it in the systematic way'. To others, 'skills are important, but it matters how people implement their skills and knowledge' or 'armed up with up-to-date technologies … managing time at work is another important thing to have things completed efficiently; Innovative thinking which helps in doing things in a different way to save cost and time involved in it; and grasp them faster. It is not mandatory for a person to have all the skills before taking the job'.

A few delineated career position specific work habits: Speaking of managers, 'having charisma to lead IT teams on projects because most IT projects are team oriented in this age and are global'. 'Managements Skills are also important to lead his team', or 'Decision Making-inter personnel' relationships are markers of a leader; 'if we have no leadership quality, all our teams work will be topsy turvy'. In short, '"Leadership, Communication" go together', said another.

Habits of the Spirit

Some cited habits of the spirit that are 'needed to survive in the IT' industry: 'Need to have an Attitude to take things positively, he should be prepared for a change, should be a front seater whenever involved in meetings or sessions, should have an attitude to appreciate and share the knowledge with his peers, should get updated with latest technologies before your updated, should have Right Personality and should be organized; all these above characteristics will make him a complete IT Professional'. 'Ability to appreciate business/client requirements and willingness to meet them'; and 'interest to learn new things' is an added bonus. A few other traits listed were: 'Maturity', 'Always stay cool, keep cool head in work, ready to learn new things at any time', 'Patience is very important in the IT field; and he/she should be able to find the solution in many different situations for a single problem', "Trustfullness, Honesty to all, unselfishness, not forgetting our culture', 'Right Attitude and selfless service as this will be the main driving force to get any work done in a proper way', and 'sharing the work is very important, as such it will increase the Team spirit'. Others added: 'Must enjoy his/her work', 'Commitment', 'Self-motivation, ownership of task, think every problem has a solution', and even 'Humor' to succeed in IT. Also, 'listening skills are very much important. If the person cannot listen/understand actual requirement it would be the problem for him as well as team. Person should be proactive'. Others threw in, 'Patience ... Heroes are not born in day. Everyone needs time to come up in their life ... '; 'Should not boss around'; 'Good presentation skills, communication skills, highly adaptable'. And sounding a holistic note, one said, 'music for fun, sincerity shows how much you are lovable at work, Dedication shows how much you endure in work'. Another included, 'Need Exercise. It is important for the health of IT Professional because they are sitting in front of the computer without any body movement'.

Few examples of habits of the spirit related to client or customer needs: 'Adaptability, Domain/language/requirements of the client company keep changing faster in the IT field and you should be able to constantly learn and adapt to these changing needs'; 'Ability to understand customer needs and move/act accordingly'; and 'Attitude to adapt, aptitude to learn, willingness to share the knowledge ... needed in order to be an excellent IT professional as they help in demonstrating and delivering the required skills of an IT professional in a right way'.

To yet others, habits of the spirit meant balancing personal and professional life. In the words of one respondent, 'Not getting nervous if there is any critical issues comes up; instead person should have capability to make the stressful environment soothing. I think most IT Professionals in India are in mad rush and they are gradually losing their personal life ... there is no work life balance in India ... and tell you honestly there are two kind of professionals in IT industry in India ... group of people who are really very capable and work a lot and group of people who are simply baby sitter and work at very minimum level; no work life balance in India in more than 80% of IT companies'.

Another mentioned 'sincerity and straight forwardness. If you feel you cannot finish the work you need to admit. If you feel things are not going the way you expected you need to talk to your manager upfront instead of being in a shell'.

In conclusion, those who noted the importance of 'habits' did so not only for 'personal' reasons but also for a larger purpose, be it their 'team' or their 'company'. As one professional noted, even diploma holders (as opposed to the BTech degreed) with good technical and communication skill can survive if they have the 'moral flexibility to adjust, commitment, ownership, experience. All the above will help us to form a good team for smoother inception and closure'. Team spirit was a rallying cry, denoting the new work environments in the global, virtual IT world.

Integrated IT Professional, Another Soft Merit Marker

Another commonly noted 'soft' construct in the IT merit culture making project was the need to be '*integrated*'. An integrated IT professional was someone with the following attributes: 'willing to work, positive attitude, good team player, self-confidence, oral communication skills'. Others underscored the need for the strong IT professional to have not only technical skills but communication, team work, individual initiative, and dedication as well. The following comments also exemplified this integrated sentiment: 'Good technical skills, ability to work individually as well as with team, and good communication are the most important for IT professional'. Or 'Technical skill and dedicated to work ... because without skill and dedication, the work will go nowhere'. And 'to be in IT one needs to obviously have the right education and skills, but one also needs to tackle technical and managerial challenges every day', and 'good communication, leadership, flexibility to change according to need' are a must. And 'Dedication and Hard work. These two traits can overcome any practical shortcomings'.

Other details of the integrated IT professional included the following: One wrote, '5 Major Qualities are that covers all the aspects of Perfection. They are as follows ... Personality - Public Relations - Professional Ethics - Punctuality - Projection (Initiation & Innovation)'. Qualities needed to manage a team and a company were, 'Technical, Management, Marketing, Programming and Management Skills'. Or as one noted, ' ... technical skills are not sufficient. He or she should also learn how the business runs and for what they are working. He or she should have multiple skills in order to flourish in this competitive world'. And another added, '1. Initiative on working project. 2. Analyzing problems. 3. Must have ability of sharing knowledge on technology'.

In short, an integrated IT professional was someone who showed 'Initiative, willingness to work, ability to understand', had 'Logical Thinking, Ability to understand, Good Listener and Quick Learner'; or showed 'Professionalism at work, Team working, Focus more on Customer satisfaction' or a combination of 'Analytical/Research skills, Problem solving/Reasoning/Creativity, Teamwork, Reliability/Responsibility, Professionalism/Positive Attitude'.

Human Capital Merit: Linguistic Cultural Factor

The importance of English fluency that emerged as another criterion of holistic IT merit, was not surprising for a globalized, virtual industry. When respondents were asked to evaluate the importance of written and spoken English, an overwhelming (over 90 per cent) majority thought linguistic skills were important, if not very important (Table 2.11). The strong (r = 0.59) correlations between the two cultural skills indicated that to the Indian IT professional the ability to communicate in English, both written and verbal, were important indicators of 'merit'.

Narrative comments offered by IT professionals again illustrated the significance of cultural linguistic capital and the transnational communication skills that one accrues from English fluency. As for 'English Language fluency', one said, 'Good English with basic technical knowledge would do, team work, respect each and every one, speed, accuracy, experience will be added advantage'. Some offered a more contextual take on the importance of English fluency in IT: 'Like call centre jobs, they need only some computer knowledge and good communication skills in English'.

Table 2.11   Merit: Linguistic Cultural Capital Factor (n = 488)

Question	Response	Percentage (n)
Ability to communicate in English (written)	1 = Not at all important	0.0%
	2 = Not important	2.7 (13)
	3 = Not relevant	4.7 (23)
	4 = Important	46.1 (225)
	5 = Very important	46.5 (227)
Ability to communicate in English (verbal)	1 = Not at all important	0.2% (1)
	2 = Not important	2.9 (14)
	3 = Not relevant	5.5 (27)
	4 = Important	40.8 (199)
	5 = Very important	50.6 (247)

Source: Author.

The stress on English fluency was tied to the importance of communication in globalized business environments that require both on site and trans-anglo-continental team work. Some illustrative comments which underscored the importance of 'communication skills' in IT were: 'In most of the places communication skills play a major role'. Another said, 'without communication, it is difficult to service'; or 'Soft skills, personality development, and must be able to communicate fluently in English that is most required'. One even said, 'Communication, being sociable' is important; 'Communication, team work' were often repeated in narrative commentaries.

Others mentioned specific soft skills as in: 'Soft skills like communication skills, presentation skills, interpersonal skills and ability to work independently or in a team with very less supervision'. One elaborated on the importance of soft skills thusly: 'Eight Great Reasons to Develop Your Soft Skills 1. Certification is not an end in itself. Tech skills do matter. 2. Soft skills help advance your career. 3. Soft skills empower you and create opportunities. 4. Soft skills not only improve your career, they also offer personal growth. 5. Do you have more tech skills than sense? Work on communication and leadership. 6. Soft skills help you grow beyond money motivation. 7. Developing professional ethics is vital to your career. 8. Control co-workers' perception of you as a professional and an expert in your field'. And ultimately 'what matters more is your capability to showcase that you have the right education and skills'.

In addition to communication skills being important for team work and management, others cited monetary and social mobility benefits. Financial benefits that can accrue from being a good communicator are 'to show ability, to service and earn money'. And excellent communication and presentation skills will help one 'be a good team player and help for his career growth'. Others said, one 'must be able to gain their peers support and confidence through excellent communication' and 'gain their peers support and confidence', so that it will boost their promotion opportunities. Excellent presentation skills, 'because at the end of the day it is more of a show business ...'

One saw a delicate balance being drawn between technical skills and communication skills. For some, communication skills, while important, should not come 'at the expense of technical education and skill sets.' 'Yes it [communication] must be only if they have the right education and skills'; 'Communication Skills, Hardworking ability, but also Expert in technology'. On the other hand, there are those who felt that while 'good technical skills are needed, better communication skills, catching new ideas, ability to work as a team are more important than technical skills' because ' … good technical skill is of no use if he doesn't possess communication skills'. In the end, while 'willing to work, positive attitude, good team player, self-confidence, oral communication skills' are important, 'good communication skills and social skills are more important for clients'.

Merit Culture, Hard and Soft, by Industry sector and Education: Consonant with the boundary limits that IT professionals placed on work skills and English fluency, these merit criteria were not quite mono-lithically ascribed to across different sub-sectors in IT and educational backgrounds of respondents. Overall, on a scale of 1 (least important important) to 5 (very important), Merit/Skills (overall mean score of 4.37) and English language proficiency (overall mean score of 4.38) were ranked as important (Table 2.12). But, companies whose core compe-tency was solely BPO (mean score = 4.3) or solely ITES (mean score = 4.34) or solely IT (mean score = 4.34) placed slightly more emphasis on work skills than sectors that offered combination of services. It was not surprising that English proficiency was valued more in BPO sub-sectors

Table 2.12   Work Skills and English Proficiency Sets by IT Sector*: Mean Factor Score (Standard Deviation); Item Scale of 1 (least important) to 5 (very important)

	Factor 3: Work Skills	Factor 4: English Proficiency
All Sectors (n = 488):	4.37 (0.39)	4.38 (0.64)
1. Non-IT Other (n = 17):	4.60 (0.35)	4.38 (0.45)
2. Solely BPO (n = 24):	4.30 (0.46)	4.44 (0.73)
3. BPO with ITES (n = 49):	4.42 (0.42)	4.56 (0.59)
4. Solely ITES (n = 54):	4.34 (0.43)	4.28 (0.71)
5. IT with Other Services (n = 123):	4.40 (0.36)	4.32 (0.67)
6. Solely IT (n = 221):	4.34 (0.39)	4.38 (0.61)

Source: Author.

*Sector codes: 2 = Solely BPO (MNC Customer Service and MNC Financial/Back Office); 3 = BPO with ITES); 4 = Solely ITES (E-Commerce and Engineering Service); 5 = IT with other services; 6 = Solely IT (Programming, Infrastructure, and R&D); and 1 = Other non-IT.

(Sole BPO = 4.44 and BPO with ITES = 4.56) than in the hard-core sectors of the industry. BPO and ITES companies included call centre, data entry, and other services like medical transcriptions.

Furthermore, considering that the IT industry has a heavy engineering focus, be it hardware or software, the importance of work skills and English fluency in the IT merit culture were disaggregated by the engineering content of IT professionals' education. As might be expected, work skills and English Fluency were ranked somewhat higher by those with more engineering content in their educational background as well as by those who attended higher tier institutions of higher education (see Mean scores in Tables 2A.4 and 2A.5); the respective comparison groups were those who did not have engineering degrees or attended lower tier institutions. The emphasis on linguistic capital, English fluency, might reflect class and caste privileges, if not bias, in higher education.

Social Capital in Merit, Another 'Soft' Skills Marker

Since the 24/7 IT work often spills over from the office to social contexts, relevance of social criteria in the Merit metrics was important to evaluate. In addition to work skills and English fluency, respondents were asked to evaluate the importance of comfort in social environment and in social interactions as another IT merit criterion. The specific questions included comfort level in socializing with co-workers after work, in meeting respondent's family, and having a meal with his/her family. Unlike the first two merit skill sets (Work Skills and English Fluency), respondents were divided about the importance of social comfort as a criterion of merit (Table 2.13). A third to 40 per cent thought that their comfort level in socializing after work, and meeting or sharing a meal with their family were not relevant criteria. The rest were almost evenly divided between those who say it is important (20–39 per cent) or not important (28–38 per cent). The strong correlations among the three social comfort characteristics indicated the coherence in respondents' evaluations[23] of their relevance, or lack thereof, in IT. For some, all three social comfort

---

[23] The correlations: between socializing with respondent after work and meeting with respondent's family was 0.561[***]; between socializing with after work and family comfortable having a meal with was = 0.551[***]; and family comfortable meeting and Family comfortable having a meal with was r = 0.909[***].

Table 2.13   Merit: Social Comfort Factor (n = 488)

Question	Responses	Percent (n)
Comfortable socializing with after work?	1 = Not at all important	10.7% (52)
	2 = Not important	17.0 (83)
	3 = Not relevant	32.8 (160)
	4 = Important	32.4 (158)
	5 = Very important	7.2 (35)
Family comfortable meeting?	1 = Not at all important	17.4% (85)
	2 = Not important	18.0 (88)
	3 = Not relevant	39.3 (192)
	4 = Important	18.2 (89)
	5 = Very important	7.0 (34)
Family comfortable having a meal with?	1 = Not at all important	18.2 (89)
	2 = Not important	19.9 (97)
	3 = Not relevant	40.6 (198)
	4 = Important	13.7 (67)
	5 = Very important	7.6 (37)

Source: Author.

indicators as criteria for merit were irrelevant. For another third, social comfort was not (or not at all) important to judge merit. But, for the rest, social comfort with professional colleagues was important.

Social Background as 'Soft' Merit

As with the social comfort criterion for merit, the IT professionals were quite evenly divided in their assessment of the importance of social background in the IT merit culture construct (Table 2.14). A third to 40 per cent deemed these characteristics to be not relevant. As for the rest, they were almost evenly distributed among those who felt that these characteristics were not important (not or not at all) versus those who felt they were important (including very important). Correlations among these social background indicators (n = 488) were also quite strong indicating the coherence in the relevance or lack thereof, of social background in the IT merit culture.[24]

[24] Correlations of where the IT professional went to college with: which college they attended = 0.76[***], rural/urban location of upbringing = 0.497[***], and

Table 2.14   Merit: Social Background Factor (n = 488)

Question	Response	Percentage
Where went to college	1 = Not at all important	12.7% (62)
	2 = Not important	24.8 (121)
	3 = Not relevant	31.8 (155)
	4 = Important	25.2 (123)
	5 = Very important	5.5 (27)
Which college	1 = Not at all important	14.3% (70)
	2 = Not important	27.3 (134)
	3 = Not relevant	32.6 (159)
	4 = Important	22.3 (109)
	5 = Very important	3.3 (16)
Whether grew up in rural or urban area	1 = Not at all important	25.2% (123)
	2 = Not important	32.4 (158)
	3 = Not relevant	30.9 (151)
	4 = Important	8.0 (39)
	5 = Very important	3.5 (17)
Someone from SC background*	1 = Not at all important	44.2% (73)
	2 = Not important	15.2 (25)
	3 = Not relevant	29.1 (48)
	4 = Important	6.1 (10)
	5 = Very important	5.5 (9)

Source: Author.

* Reduced sample size (n) for item, 'Someone from SC background,' which was answered only by 165 respondents.

Social factors, namely social comfort, that is, importance of socializing with the co-workers after work and family's comfort in meeting and having a meal with said co-worker, were rated as less important (overall mean = 2.64 or between not important and not relevant) in the merit construct than human work capital and English fluency. Social background, as in location of schooling and SC background, was also rated as less important in the merit culture. However, it was noteworthy that social background

---

someone from SC background = 0.404[***]; Correlations of which college with rural/urban location = 0.583[***] and someone from SC background = 0.474[***]; Correlations of rural-urban location with SC background = 0.649***.

(mean = 3.15) and social comfort (mean = 3.54) were more likely to be deemed 'not relevant' by the BPO sector respondents than those in the IT and ITES sectors (Table 2.15). Perhaps, the *lack of cultural symbolic legitimacy* for those employed in non-traditional, call centre like, working conditions of BPO companies, might explain why the BPO workers think social comfort and social background were not as relevant in the IT merit culture matrix.

The social background and social comfort factors were also rated as less relevant (important) than human (work skills) and linguistic (English fluency) capital across all educational sectors (Table 2A.6). Yet, it was noteworthy that IT respondents whose educational background did not have an engineering focus, for example a non-engineering master's degree, rated social background (mean = 2.91) and social comfort (mean = 3.0) somewhat higher than the engineering graduates. And those who were educated in Tier 6 institutions, non-technical institutes, rated social background (mean = 3.00) and social comfort (mean = 3.01) as more important to consider in the merit culture than those from higher tiered educational institutions (Table 2A.7).

Table 2.15　Social Background and Social Comfort Sets by IT Sector: Mean Factor Score (Standard Deviation); Item Scale of 1 (least important) to 5 (very important)[*]

	Factor 2. Social Background	Factor 1. Social Comfort
All Sectors (n = 488)	2.64 (0.92)	2.87 (0.99)
a. Solely BPO (n = 24)	**3.15** (1.02)	**3.54** (0.79)
b. BPO with ITES (n = 49)	2.52 (1.01)	**2.95** (1.17)
c. Solely ITES (n = 54)	2.61 (0.89)	2.88 (1.08)
d. IT (n = 123)	2.59 (0.09)	2.83 (0.97)
e. Solely IT (n = 221)	2.60 (0.88)	**2.77** (0.97)
f. Non-IT Other (n =17)	3.00 (0.95)	**3.14** (0.62)

Source: Author.

[*]Sector codes: a = Solely BPO (MNC Customer Service and MNC Financial/ Back Office); b = BPO with ITES; c = Solely ITES (E-Commerce and Engineering Service); d = IT with other services; e = Solely IT (Programming, Infrastructure, and R&D); and f = Other, non-IT.

The narrative comments of survey respondents offered more elaborations on the social skills dimension of 'merit' in the IT professional culture. Some examples of specific 'Social Skills or Social Relationships' in IT merit thinking were: 'Good interpersonal skills'; or being 'Sociable, optimistic, balanced and well-mannered because such behavior is also equally important with skills'; or understanding 'the feeling of other, shouldn't be selfish'. Others expanded on the 'utilitarian benefits' of social skills as: 'Respect each other and ability to listen what others say' is critical in IT.

Porous IT Merit Boundaries: The Conduit for Caste Reproduction

As IT professionals engaged in the merit construction project, it became clear that merit, even when valorized, was more than *streamlined pure merit* or just technical work skills. They also listed a *holistic set of social and cultural capital skills* (Coleman 1988 and others) that included, among others, social skills, soft skills, team work, communication, leadership, and workplace social responsibility. They confirmed the importance of English fluency and soft skills, such as habits of the Intellect, Mind, and Spirit, which are subjective at best. More important was that such soft criteria open up opportunities for caste considerations, through *caste and class positionality, pattern recognition,* and *filtering,* to enter into the applications of merit criteria and represent a slippery slope towards accusations of discrimination and exclusion. For one, these subjective 'soft' traits are open to multiple, often conflicting, interpretations. Yet, soft skills were quite important to IT respondents; they spent a good amount of time opining about them.

Glimpses of conduits for caste introduction into Indian IT were found in the *philosophical* approach some adopted to their social skill reasoning. 'Studying well won't give a successful life; making money won't give a successful life', or 'working MNC company won't give a good or successful life'. What is needed is 'to share good and well known information to others; we have to share money to others; we have to make good relation with others without any expectation'. Other statements represented similar philosophical thinking. 'Work sincerely. To think emotionally, after all should be a good human being'.

It was also meaningful to ask more pointedly about whether caste and other traditional social vectors (class, gender, and urbanicity) dynamics have entered and found their place into the new arena of Indian IT. It is important to remember is that the responses detailed in this chapter were to questions that did not make explicit reference to caste or any other traditional social vectors.[25] Only a few (n = 20 of 514), when not prompted specifically about caste or gender, offered early glimpses into the caste, equality, and diversity dynamics at work in the IT world. That all, except two respondents, who commented on caste issues in IT listed their caste as SC is also relevant.

The few specific narrative examples of the caste entering the construction of the merit culture thesis were illustrative. Hinting at a differential application of 'pure merit and reservation merit', one professional noted, 'education and skills are additional to social stature and integrity. But, an upper caste Brahmin reported that he runs a company of IT, his qualification is BA (English); a scheduled caste has a BA (English) but forced to make a living as petty thief' (Dalit/SC respondent). Another SC IT professional added, 'an IT professional needs skill adjustment, yes, but a scheduled caste also has to be man of the boss, do more work and be a follower, not a leader'. According to another, 'one must belong to caste of your senior [*pattern recognition*], if possible and be very submissive and apt at flattery'. Yet another, downplaying the 'merit' persona in the IT culture retorted, 'This is just rubbish. You need only minimum knowledge. But most importantly you need to have strong reference [*networks, pattern recognition and homo-social reproduction*] from upper castes'. When it comes to list of qualifications, 'communication skills and Knowledge is last' lamented another SC professional.

Others elaborated on the *class-power-caste nexus* in Indian IT arena. As per a Dalit respondent, 'in socially divided society where concentration of power, income, wealth and education is aligned with certain upper caste, chasm is going deeper'. Speaking to the intersection between urban location and caste another reported, 'schools in cities where upper class people study are the best. Other schools and colleges are neglected. Hence by filtering talent, we are filtering actually caste of candidates'. Or 'White face,

---

[25] To reiterate, the specific narrative questions asked: 'What other skills do you think are important for an excellent IT professional? And why do you think so?' (Q15). And 'There are many who claim that the new information technology jobs are open "only" to those who are qualified (they have the right education and skills) for the job. What do you think?' (Q16).

Brahmin caste, or any other upper caste, black face, lack of confidence, will cause isolation for anybody'.

A few who did not list their caste status, noted other types of inequalities, mainly class and educational inequalities. More generally one stated 'But the right to education should be opened for all. IT is not only created for qualified people'. To another, 'To help the poor people, I spend 10% of my salary'. Or 'The new information technology should be made easier and simpler and available to the common man'.

Others specifically touched on *diversity* in the workplace as harbingers of porous boundaries and contested social relationships (be they caste, religion, region, or class based) in the Indian IT sector. Sample comments that reflected these sentiments: the meritorious (ideal) IT professional should have the 'Ability to work with diverse teams, tolerance for cultural diversity should be very, very high'. Another said, 'communication is well & good but we need to take care (of) poor background & talented in mind'. Also needed are 'Good mannerism, social activities, helping mentality, equality with all other people, spending time with family members, taking care of children, house maintenance etc.' and an excellent IT professional should be able to work in 'a diverse team - people from different cultural, ethnic and regions'.

Yet, as might be expected, there was pointed dissent about the relevance of caste in the IT merit rink. 'People should communicate with open mind, they should not have any gap on the basis of caste, region or any other. Performance review should be discussed under the presence of employees- immediate manager should not have all rights to review it & give the numbers. In that case employee will feel comfortable while working over there'. Or 'Make a portal to discuss the updates & issues. HR or management should take active actions in case if any personal issue is reported'.

Theoretical and Empirical Reflections on Caste Loopholes in IT Merit

In the lived work experiences of Indian IT professionals, 'IT Skills', at one level, appeared central to the *pure merit culture making project* and seemed to out-shadow traditional Indian social vectors of caste/religion/communities.[26] Valorization of 'Pure merit' confirmed observations offered by

---

[26] Traditional social vectors like caste were not explicitly mentioned in this set of survey questions.

Upadhya (2007a) and other scholars. *Streamlining* and creating *appropriate difference* between the IT and non-IT economic habitus, the respondents rationalized their laser focus on skills in the interests of efficiency and needs of western clients. That the IT professionals, who offered their observations about IT merit construction were quite representative of the Indian IT industry can be seen in the broad industry structure in which the respondents worked. Their IT companies were not monolithic in their core competencies; they ranged from companies that offered core IT functions (such as programming, Infrastructure, and R&D) to ITES and BPO companies (www.NASSCOM.org).

However, it is the *subjective markers of merit*, such as, English fluency, habits of the mind, intellect, and spirit, and other 'soft' skills of communication, that offer entry points through which traditional social vectors of caste, community, and religion can make their way into the IT occupational habitat. In fact, it is quite likely that 'caste' has entered into the IT Merit construction project. For one, the IT professional respondents spent a good amount of time opining about them. Also, as will be elaborated in the next two chapters, 'soft skills' are often the prerogative of members of the upper castes, classes, and urbanites. If the logic and tools of '*pattern recognition*' (Baron 2006) in hiring and promotion are used in the IT sector, it stands to reason that caste-class hierarchies are reproduced in the new occupational sector setting the stage for transference of caste inequalities and caste reproduction in the IT occupational structures.

To be clear, no one questioned the centrality of 'merit' and associated technical skill sets in the IT world. But, there was no agreement about what pure merit really means. Is merit pure only if it is earned outside of the public sector education system where quotas and earmarked reservations for SCs and other minorities are used? If so, is the IT sector's sole *raison d'etre* for its caste-neutral claim that they do not use reservations or earmarks for minorities? Seldom heard in the narratives were the hidden and almost naturalized caste and class privileges in which pure merit is deeply embedded. And when questions were raised about the embedded caste privileges the conversations became heated taking on the tone of a blood sport pitting caste versus merit. It is in the unpacking of the embedded sources of merit that the window opens wider into how caste hierarchies can be imported into the IT social habitus, creating a new vector of inequality. It is to these and related questions that we next turn.

Appendix: Table 2A.1 India Human Development Survey (IHDS) 2005, Government Resources by Caste Status and Northern vs. Southern States

	Southern States*			Northern States*		
	FC and Religious Minorities	OBC	SC/ST	FC and Religious Minorities	OBC	SC/ST
School type† (CS3‡):						
	(n = 4,986)	(n = 5,946)	(n = 3,499)	(n = 15,750)	(n = 11,478)	(n = 10,784)
Government school	**56.3%**	62.7%	74.7%***	50.3%	64.3%	**75.0%*****
Private school	32.9	26.8	16.5	39.0	29.3	19.9
Post-secondary/College	10.8	10.5	8.7	10.6	6.3	5.1
Job: In Government (WS12A)						
	(n = 4,676)	(n = 7,311)	(n = 5,741)	(n = 9,546)	(n = 8,714)	(n = 12,389)
0 = No	84.8%	90.2%	92.1%***	74.9%	87.7%	**88.5%*****
1 = Yes¥	**15.2**	9.8	7.9	25.1	12.3	**11.5**
Receive Government Benefits (INCGOVT)†‡	(n = 20,850)	(n = 24,936)	(n = 12,772)	(n = 60,096)	(n = 45,678)	(n = 45,076)
0 = No	94.4%	91.6%	81.9%***	89.8%	82.9%	**78.2%*****
1 = Yes	**5.6**	8.4	18.1	10.2	17.1	21.8
Number of Government Involved Services**	(n = 22,083)	(n = 27,222)	(n = 15,599)	(n = 60,096)	(n = 45,678)	(n = 45,076)
0	79.4%	76.7%	66.3%***	74.7%	68.5%	**62.7%*****
1	19.7	21.8	29.7	23.2	27.4	31.7

(Cont'd)

Appendix: Table 2A.1 (Cont'd)

	Southern States*			Northern States*		
	FC and Religious Minorities	OBC	SC/ST	FC and Religious Minorities	OBC	SC/ST
2	0.9	1.5	4.1	2.1	4.1	5.6
3	0.0	0.0	0.0	0.0	0.0	0.0
X̄/Mean (sd)	0.22 (.43)	0.25 (.46)	0.38 (.56)***	0.27 (.49)	0.37 (.56)	0.43 (.59)***

Source: Author.

* Southern States = Karnataka, Tamil Nadu, Andhra Pradesh, Kerala, Maharashtra, and Goa; Northern States = remaining states.

† Government School = Government and Government aided; Private school = Private, Convent, Madrassa; Post-Secondary = Open or Junior college, Post-graduate, Tech Vocational <1 year, or Tech Vocational >1 year.

± Names in Caps in parentheses are SPSS variable names.

¥ Yes = Regular government job or receiving government support such as food for work.

†† Government Benefits include: Old Age Pension, Widows Pension, Maternity Benefit, Disability Pension, Annapurna, Other government income, and NGO income.

** Composite of Yes (1) on Government School type (CS3), Job (WS12A), and Government Benefits (INCGOVT).

*** Differences among caste groups, within regions (Southern and Northern) statistically significant at the p <=.001.

Appendix: Table 2A.2 Demographic Characteristics of Survey Respondents

	Total Sample	(1) Other	(2) Only BPO	(3) BPO with ITES	(4) Only ITES	(5) IT Plus 1–3	(6) Only IT
Age of Respondents:							
x̄ (SD)*	27.7 (6.3)	36.9 (12.1)	27.6 (5.9)	26.7 (4.5)	26.8 (6.9)	28.1 (5.8)	27.2 (5.8)
(n)	(480)	(16)	(25)	(48)	(52)	(123)	(216)
Currently Married†	36.5%	68.4%	28.0%	44.0%	31.5%	42.9%	30.7%
(n)	(499)	(19)	(25)	(50)	(54)	(126)	(225)
Number of Children:							
0	39.3%	30.8%	42.9%	36.4%	52.9%	36.4%	40.6%
1	40.4	38.5	14.3	45.5	29.4	50.9	36.2
2	17.5	30.8	42.9	18.2	17.6	9.1	18.8
3	2.2	0.0	0.0	0.0	0.0	1.8	4.3
4	0.5	0.0	0.0	0.0	0.0	1.8	0.0
(n)	(183)	(13)	(7)	(22)	(17)	(55)	(69)
Male	63.5%	52.6%	68.0%	74.0%	64.8%	78.6%	60.9%
Female	36.5	47.4	32.0	26.0	35.2	21.4	39.1
(n)	(499)	(19)	(25)	(50)	(54)	(126)	(225)

Source: Author.

* x̄ (SD)*: Mean and standard deviation.

† Omitted category = not currently married.

Appendix: Explanation of Clusters in Factor Analyses

The first cluster: 'Social Comfort' (social capital) was the most consistent set of characteristics identified by the survey respondents. The second cluster, 'Social Background' (Social capital); was next. The third, 'Work Skills and Style' (Human Capital) cluster was less consistent; and the fourth cluster, 'English Fluency' (cultural capital), was least consistent.

The cluster ranking does not mean that social comfort is more important than human capital. But, there are subsets or clusters of survey respondents who think they are important or not. For example, the social factors, the 'social comfort' cluster, followed by 'social background' cluster were the first two factors to be extracted. 'Merit/Skills' and 'English language fluency' were factors 3 and 4 respectively. This ordering does not mean that social factors were the most important characteristic set. Both had lowest mean factor scores (Comfort Mean = 2.87/sd = 1.0); and Background = 2.64/sd = 0.92) in the ranking of how important they were to the respondents. The corresponding mean importance scores for the Work Skills/Style cluster were (Mean 4.37/sd = 0.39) and English Fluency (Mean 4.38/sd = 0.64). What the cluster ranking does mean is the following: respondents were more uniformly likely to rank social comfort (2.87) and social background (2.64), but thought these skills were only somewhat unimportant (2) or neutral (3). On the other hand, while the average respondent ranked merit/skills and English Fluency as important (4) or even very important (5), the sample was less uniform in their high assessment.

In other words, the prominence of clusters measured the tightness (correlations) of items in the clusters. The clusters indicate consistency of traits. That is, respondents were consistent in how important or not important they thought items in each cluster were. The cluster order does not mean that the first cluster is most important or that the last cluster was least important. Rather, the first cluster, social comfort cluster, was the one where there was more consistency in the low importance placed by respondents.

Appendix: Table 2A.3 Factor Analyses of Ideal Characteristics of IT Professionals

Factor Analyses: Q14.a-j and l-n (14.k excluded)

Rotated Component Matrix*

	Component			
	Factor 1. Social Comfort	Factor 2. Social Background	Factor 3. Merit/Skills	Factor 4. English Fluency
Q14.a. Technical skills	-.072	.072	**.511**	-.090
Q14.b. Ability to work well in a team	-.020	-.091	**.631**	.266
Q14.c. Willing to put in extra effort	.193	-.039	**.642**	.109
Q14.d. Shows individual initiative	.106	.219	**.575**	.022
Q14.e. Someone who is meticulous	-.080	.073	**.627**	.214
Q14.f. Ability to communicate in English Written	.041	.078	.142	**.863**
Q14.g. Ability to communicate in English Verbal	.125	.044	.160	**.845**
Q14.h. Where went to college	.081	**.876**	.100	.091
Q14.i. Which college	.144	**.887**	.140	.074
Q14.j. Whether grew up in rural or urban area	.292	**.737**	-.018	-.025
Q14.l. Comfortable socializing with after work	**.722**	.189	-.020	.241
Q14.m. Family comfortable meeting	**.927**	.160	.038	.020
Q14.n. Family comfortable having a meal with	**.924**	.158	.059	-.037
Q14.k. Someone from SC background	**.498**	**.578**	-.013	-.076

Source: Author.

* Extraction Method: Principal Component Analysis; Rotation Method: Varimax with Kaiser Normalization; Rotations converged in 7 iterations.

Appendix: Table 2A.4 Work Skills and English Proficiency Sets by Engineering Education: Mean Factor Score (Standard Deviation); Item Scale of 1 (least important) to 5 (very important)

	Factor 3: Work Skills	Factor 4: English Proficiency
All Degrees	4.38 (0.39)	4.38 (0.64)
Undergraduate degrees, NOT Engineering (n = 68)	4.29 (0.44)	4.29 (0.63)
Master's degrees, NOT engineering (n = 62)	**4.47 (0.34)**	**4.47 (0.58)**
Master's, bachelor's, diploma in computer applications (n = 188)	**4.40 (0.39)**	**4.41 (0.64)**
MS or BE in engineering (n = 166)	**4.35 (0.37)**	**4.34 (0.66)**

Source: Author.

Appendix: Table 2A.5 Work Skills and English Proficiency Sets by Institution of Highest Degree: Mean Factor Score (Standard Deviation); Item Scale of 1 (least important) to 5 (very important)[*]

Institution of Highest Degree	Factor 3: Work Skills	Factor 4: English Proficiency
Tier 1 (n = 9)	**4.42** (0.35)	4.28 (0.57)
Tier 2 (n = 14)	**4.44** (0.36)	4.25 (0.73)
Tier 3 (n = 156)	**4.37** (0.42)	**4.41** (0.64
Tier 4 (n = 158)	**4.41** (0.38)	**4.41** (0.64)
Tier 5 (n = 122)	4.32 (0.37)	4.29 (0.62)
Tier 6 (n = 25)	4.29 (0.47)	**4.36** (0.69)
Total (n = 484)	4.37 (0.39)	4.37 (0.64)

Source: Author.

[*] Tier 1 = Established Engineering & Technical Universities; Tier 2 = Less Prestigious but Established Engineering & Technical Universities; Tier 3 = Established but General Universities/Colleges, not only Technical; Tier 4 = Technical/Engineering Colleges & Institutes, Less Established open/correspondence); Tier 5 = Universities and Engineering Institutes (Newer, Private, Unclear Technical Focus); Tier 6 = Institutes, Not Technical.

Appendix: Table 2A.6 Social Background and Social Comfort Sets by Engineering Education: Mean Factor Score (Standard Deviation); Item Scale of 1 (least important) to 5 (very important)

	Factor 2. Social Background	Factor 1. Social Comfort
All Degrees	2.63 (0.92)	2.87 (0.99)
Undergraduate degrees, NOT engineering (n = 68)	**2.71** (0.99)	2.83 (.96)
Master's degrees, NOT engineering (n = 62)	**2.91** (0.89)	**3.00** (0.95)
Master's, bachelor's, diploma in computer apps (n = 188)	2.56 (0.89)	2.82 (1.05)
MS or BE in engineering (n = 166)	2.58 (0.92)	2.87 (0.98)

Source: Author.

Appendix: Table 2A.7 Social Background and Social Comfort Sets by Institution of Highest Degree: Mean Factor Score (Standard Deviation); Item Scale of 1 (least important) to 5 (very important)[*]

Institution of Highest Degree	Factor 2. Social Background	Factor 1. Social Comfort
Tier 1 (n = 9)	**3.11** (1.35)	2.78 1.43
Tier 2 (n = 14)	2.09 (0.65)	2.74 (0.92)
Tier 3 (n = 156)	2.65 (0.96)	2.90 (0.99)
Tier 4 (n = 158)	2.58 (0.87)	2.83 (1.05)
Tier 5 (n = 122)	2.63 (0.88)	2.80 (0.91)
Tier 6 (n = 25)	**3.00** (0.88)	**3.01** (0.87)
Total (n = 484)	2.62 (0.92)	2.86 (0.99)

Source: Author.

[*] Tier 1 = Established Engineering & Technical Universities; Tier 2 = Less Prestigious but Established Engineering & Technical Universities; Tier 3 = Established but General Universities/Colleges, not only Technical; Tier 4 = Technical/Engineering Colleges & Institutes, Less Established open/correspondence); Tier 5 = Universities and Engineering Institutes (Newer, Private, Unclear Technical Focus); Tier 6 = Institutes, Not Technical.

3 Merit vs. Caste 'Blood Sport' in the IT Work Arena

Implications for Caste Reproduction

Unlike the mostly reasoned IT skills discourse detailed in the previous chapter, when rank-and-file IT professionals and their knowledge leaders[1] were pointedly invited to reflect on their views and experiences with caste in the merit construction process, the conversations became passionately vocal and sometimes even strident and combative, taking on tones of a *metaphorical 'blood sport'*. Do, and if so, how do, IT professionals and their leaders view and talk about the caste-merit dynamics in their occupational habitus? What do the terms, 'Merit' and 'Caste', mean to them? The word in research and in social

---

[1] Terms like knowledge leaders and key industry informants, that will be used interchangeably, refer to those who have worked or are working in the IT industry. Other key informants included educators, social commentators, and activists.

activist communities[2] is, that Dalits and other disadvantaged minorities have been excluded from (or discriminated against) the IT market that has taken the nation by storm. How can this be, they ask, particularly since the IT occupation purportedly does not have the traditional caste associations? Have the caste hierarchies and inequalities found their way into the functional organization of the new occupational sector? To this, the critics counter that if there are not many Dalits in IT that is because of *Dalit Deficits* in merit skills. In the absence of direct evidence on discrimination, deconstructing the *hidden, symbolic caste-embedded sources of merit*[3] offers an important tool to disentangle the competing arguments and foregrounding the caste inequalities, to the extent present, at the employee and management levels in the IT sector.

A central point of contention in the scholarly and public opinion circles is around why members of the Dalit communities lag behind in IT or for that matter the rest of the society. The respective arguments fall into two camps depending on their *caste positionality*. One, the *Merit Camp*, typically in the FC communities, points to *Dalit deficits* in the required skill sets, and not their caste background, for their slow progress and small *Dalit footprint* in IT. To this camp, Dalits do not pass muster on the 'merit' yardstick because they lack the necessary IT and other social capital to work in IT. They are constrained by their limited human capital, namely the appropriate IT education and degree from the 'right' institutions. Deficits on the holistic criteria are also noted. Dalits, they contend, lack the necessary cultural and social capital; they are limited in English language fluency and often do not have the right connections (*networks*) either to the regional communities in which new IT companies are located and/or to relevant hiring personnel and educational institutions.[4]

These deficit arguments are vigorously countered by the opposing *Caste Camp*. To the Caste Camp, speaking from their *caste positionality*, systemic casteism, discrimination, and prejudice rampant in the broader society have been transferred into, and replicated, and reproduced in the working structures and practices. The implicit or explicit *caste filtering* that

---

[2] See Chapter 1 and Appendix 1A.1 for more details.

[3] Bourdieu (1977, 1990).

[4] Lin's (1999) resources in networks, strong/bonding, or weak/bridging ties (Fernandez and Nichols 2002; Granovetter 1973).

occurs in the application of the holistic merit criteria in the sector has transformed IT into the new caste inequality vector.

Given the lingering historical legacies of caste inequality, it is not surprising that even transnational IT professionals and key industry informants, who spoke from their experiences, could not agree on how free IT is of caste considerations. They were quite vocally combative in their comments about the presence or absence of caste in the Indian IT. Taking on the tonality of a *metaphoric blood sport* were the caste-neutral proponents who emphasized their laser focus on IT merit while vehemently rejecting the notions that caste considerations have entered their work habitus. But, squarely on the opposite side were the passionate defenders of the explicit and hidden caste reproduction in the Indian IT sector. The force with which the caste-neutral IT space was defended by the Merit Camp, they said, does raise questions about the continuing resonance of caste in the IT sector.

Disentangling these competing contentions requires closer attention to the arguments on both sides of the merit-caste debate. Issues around the caste-merit nexus in Indian IT, take on urgency in a national context where historical caste inequalities coexist with the new economic juggernaut, the Indian IT sector. Why has not the bourgeoning new IT occupational sector become the new equalizer? Have the historical legacies of caste/class inequalities been transferred into the new IT sector? Is the IT industry not capitalizing on the full range of talent available in the country?

An obvious first step in the search for caste considerations seeping into and affecting the ostensibly caste-independent IT sector would be a census of the state of diversity in IT, be it caste, religion, gender, linguistic regions, or other relevant social vectors. Ideally, comparative assessments of the impacts of diverse versus monolithic workforces on the productivity and company bottom line can answer the IT caste inequality questions. However, as has already been noted, even a census accounting of the state of caste diversity in the IT industry was difficult to obtain. For a variety of political (like potential back lash for not following government caste reservation or earmark policies) and principled EEO policy reasons, privately owned and operated Indian IT companies did not officially maintain data on caste or for that matter any other social demographic characteristics of their employees. In the absence of hard data on the caste composition in Indian IT companies, evaluating whether the seemingly caste-neutral merit culture in IT is, in fact, caste-neutral in outcomes could only be explored deductively. Such an indirect deductive approach to exploring the connections between caste and the IT merit culture was the only methodologically tenable path.

The following questions guided the explorations of the contours of caste privileges in the IT sector. As rank-and-file IT professionals, key informants, and knowledge leaders constructed the IT Merit culture, how did they speak, or not speak, about caste in the IT work environments? What did the term caste, vis-à-vis merit, mean in the IT work space? How were the benchmarks of 'merit valourization' and of casteism juxtaposed in the Merit vs. Caste contestations? How did the merit-caste contrasts differ by caste positionality of employees? How did IT professionals explain the small Dalit footprint in Indian IT, if they even confirm it? How and why has the debate taken on the makings of a fiery, combative 'blood sport'? Finally, what implications can be deduced from these varied experiences about the caste influences in the IT sector?

Caste Violence in the Indian Society

A brief review of the violent caste dynamics in the Indian social fabric offers an instructive prelude into the fiery Merit-Caste debates in IT. Frequent reports of caste-based discrimination and violence in universities and local communities can be found in a search of the internet for news about caste in India. Of particular relevance to Indian IT, were reports of *caste bias and discrimination* in premier educational institutions for Technology. Public records are available of harassment or unfavourable treatment of SC/ST students in Indian Institute of Technology (IIT)-Roorkee in Uttarakhand, All India Institute of Medical Sciences (AIIMS) in New Delhi, and Amity University in Uttar Pradesh. Some of the litigated accusations ranged from announcing the names of the SC students in derogatory manner and passing derogatory remarks to segregating students in common facilities like hostels (residence halls), targeting them through ragging (bullying) or financial extortion, and differential treatment in sports/academic infrastructure. In the wake of such discrimination across the country, the University Grants Commission (UGC)[5] in 2012 defined

[5] The University Grants Commission of India is a statutory organization set-up by the Union Government in 1956 and is charged with the coordination, determination, and maintenance of standards of university education in India.

caste bias as an education malpractice and put in place a set of progressive measures to reduce caste bias in colleges and universities; the progressive measures included stopping grants or cancelling recognition of higher educational institutes engaging in such discrimination.[6]

On a systemic level, disastrous negative outcomes for SCs are found in the *disparate impact* of natural disasters on SC communities. During the heavy monsoon seasons, newspapers are replete with reports of floods destroying homes of SC families and their communities. Low-level (and less desirable) geographical locations of SC homes (compared to FC homes at higher elevations) rendered them more susceptible to flood impacted destructions.

That caste segregation operates in the daily lived experience of SCs was also evident in the stories the researcher heard in the field in southern India. A young SC female caregiver for elderly patients recounted her seg-regating interactional experiences while working in the home of a Brahmin female patient. Despite being the hired caregiver, she was not allowed to 'bathe her, feed her, or touch her'. Another SC male day labourer remem-bered not being allowed into the home of a Brahmin IT professional in his native village. Other domestic help, told stories, of being forbidden from entering Brahmin kitchens for fear (often unspoken) that the SC household help would pollute the food.

This segregated social interactional context is not limited to Southern India. A recent (11 May 2015) story in *The Indian Express* is illuminating. The report was about a Dalit groom in a village near Bhopal, Madhya Pradesh (northern India), who was forced to wear a helmet to his marriage ceremony because upper caste villagers stoned his marriage procession (baraat). The upper caste villagers had 'duly' informed the groom and his family that lower-caste grooms were forbidden to practice the traditional marriage ritual of riding a horse and take out a procession in the village. In response to the groom's father's request for police protection, the local administration had called the two sides for a meeting in which the upper caste villagers agreed to keep their doors closed so that they would be

---

It provides recognition to universities in India, and disburses funds to such recognized universities and colleges (Retrieved from http://mhrd.gov.in/univer-sity-grants-commission, 22 May 2015).

[6] http://www.jamshedsiddiqui.com/2012/06/ugc-plans-anti-caste-bias-regulations.html, retrieved on 21 May 2015.

spared the sight of a Dalit groom atop a horse. The upper-caste villagers kept their doors closed but when the procession reached the marriage site, the procession was heavily stoned, with more than half a dozen people sustaining injuries.[7]

These endemic caste inequalities in contemporary India come as no surprise to students of Indian society. The economic, social, and cultural capital deficits experienced by SCs and STs, despite more than half a century long government affirmative programs or quotas, speak volumes about the systemic nature of the caste problem. But, more to the point of this research monograph, are (and how) these inequalities reflected in the discourse of Indian IT professionals and knowledge leaders? What are the contours of the merit vs. caste debates and their caste implications for the Indian IT sector?

Given the purportedly caste-less background of IT, it is to be expected that the Merit Camp passionately, combatively, even 'bloody in rhetoric', portrayed the IT sector as caste neutral. And if there is a Dalit deficit in the IT ranks (as in, few SCs in IT organizations), the Merit Camp would attribute the small Dalit footprint to their merit deficits (following the 'merit' or *human capital* argument). On the other hand, the Caste Camp's equally passionate counter take ran as follows. The Indian IT industry, by virtue of its location in the private sector, is fertile ground for continuing the age old casteism and caste dynamics. The non-governmental or private sector nature of Indian IT excludes it from the constitutionally mandated hiring caste quotas for SCs, STs, and OBCs. Without active government interventions, the Caste Camp posited, there is no reason to expect that the lived segregation of SCs will not be transferred to the coveted IT job market.

Industry Perspectives on the Merit-Caste 'Blood' Sport

What do IT industry leaders (key industry informants and knowledge leaders) say about the caste-merit dynamics? Conversations with key industry informants about the merit-caste contest digressed, sometimes antagonistically, along multiple paths. The *overwhelming consensus* in these

---

[7] http://indianexpress.com/article/india/india-others/dalit-groom-forced-to-wear-helmet-as-upper-caste-villagers-stone-baraat/, accessed on 21 May 2015.

conversations[8] about 'caste in Indian IT' was that the term 'caste' meant 'SC/ST reservations' or earmarks. Their responses to the caste questions represented a mix of ambivalence, avoidance, palpable concern, anger, and sometimes hope. Ambivalence was reflected in the voice of one knowledge leader who sceptically asked: 'why do you want to study caste? It [caste] is not there, but is there'. Then there were CEOs and managers who talked around the issue, or would not mention the word caste; instead they focused on business imperatives (read Pure Merit pattern recognition) rather than caste. A few owners of small IT staffing companies worried about law suits and the 'media running with it'. There was 'palpable concern' that if the caste composition of their companies became publicly known, they will be accused of not hiring SCs and OBCs, even though as a private owned company they are not required to follow the government's reservation policies. Another group, albeit smaller than the caste deniers, were those who acknowledged that social vectors of community and religion[9] have indeed replaced caste in the hiring and promotion models.

Offering a diametrically contrasting, equally combative, viewpoint were the social activist key informants. To them, IT was clearly a barrier for SC/STs. They then immediately jumped to outline the multiple ways in which upper castes prevent the SC/ST from joining the new IT sector.

[8] To get an industry perspective on merit-caste debates in Indian IT, interviews with the 30 key informants typically started with the following set of open ended questions: 'Does caste play a role in Indian IT? If, Yes, how? If not, why do you think so?' The key informants (CEOs, HR managers, senior staff, consultants, and educators) were located in the metropolitan areas of Bangalore, Hyderabad, Chennai, and Trivandrum. These are Tier I IT cities in the four southern Indian states that either have IT hubs or emerging IT hubs. As promised at the start of interviews, the interviewees who were identified through snowball sampling were identified only by their position and sector names (like Director of an IT Staffing firm or IT Consulting firm). In the interest of authentic reporting, the written linguistic style of respondents has been largely left intact, except for minimal minor changes presented in '[ ]' to improve readability. Capitalization within quotes is present in the original written comments and has been retained.

[9] The pervasive role of religious traditions in non-religious environments was evident in the time spent in the field. Two examples: The politicians doing 'pooja' (prayers) in order to address political/community problems or a well-educated (had spent time outside India) businessman, organizing pooja to rectify a technical problem at a manufacturing plant.

In between the opposing camps was a small group that presented more nuanced understandings of the changing face of caste-merit dynamics in Indian IT. Their *contingent appreciation of caste-based affirmative programs* in IT required the candidate to have necessary IT entrance skills. Also *in the middle* was the informant-on-the-street who started the conversation talking about the quotas for SC/ST as: 'SC/ST given a lot of importance. We have kept them very high'. They then hastened to add that caste seems less important for the younger generation, Christians, and the educated Indian. In the final analyses, the phrase 'caste in Indian IT' meant different things depending on the *organizational* or *caste positionality* or 'standpoints' of key informants.

The Merit Camp: IT is Caste and Caste Reservation Neutral

Speaking from an organizational standpoint were the owners of, or managers in, the India IT sector who equated 'caste neutrality' with formal 'caste blindness' in their business policies and practices. Caste was not relevant (neutral) in their business operations because their EEO policies explicitly prohibit them (read did not formally ask) from knowing their employees' caste identity. At no time in the employees' associations with the organization, in their job applications, in the interview process, or in performance/promotion evaluations, are they asked to identify whether they belong to the dominant or scheduled castes. Besides, the largely privately owned Indian IT sector is not bound by or not accountable for the constitutionally mandated SC/ST reservations or earmarks in hiring and/or promotions. Even when community, religious, and regional backgrounds have replaced traditional caste hierarchies (as in Brahmin to SC status) business imperatives were cited for company 'caste neutral' (any caste is welcome) stances and 'caste avoidance' practices.

Skills, a Business Imperative

The *caste-neutral* (that they are not partial to any caste communities) key industry informants relied on global business practices to legitimize their stance. It is a functional IT business imperative, they said, to be caste neutral in the new globalizing world. It was not the traditional caste background (whether you were Brahmin, Shudra, or SC) that mattered in Indian IT. Rather it is the appropriate skill set that separated those who were hired, retained, and promoted from those who were not. In the words of a CEO of a specialty organization with deep ties to a local IT sector, 'competence has taken over from caste'. This key informant listed the core IT employee competencies required by the global nature of Indian IT businesses as: 'competency, skill set (content and tech writing writing) match; literate, hand-on experience in the field; science and computer science background; and motivation are the critical skill sets needed to succeed'.

Small and larger companies alike used the 'skill or merit capital' argument to justify their SC caste-avoidance in the work environment. Here is a CEO of a small staffing business (about 230 employees) in a southern Indian state who emphatically posited that, 'In IT, caste is no bar. No caste, no religion. Skills, what you can do is what is important'. Consequently, the company does not 'ask about caste. If we open up the issue, it will become an issue in the corporate sector'. This project-based staffing company recruited candidates, prepared them for interviews, and worked with US based or associated companies.

Similar 'human capital skill' based refrains were heard in mid-size IT companies. In a group interview with the CEO and other senior staff of one such IT staffing company located in a southern High Tech City, the skill or merit arguments were underscored around the conference table. They continued on, 'We don't know employees' caste. It is not legal to do so. If they put down "Reddy" or "Gowda" or "Kamma" [non-Brahmin forward castes][10] as their last name, one can figure out caste. But, the company will not ask caste status'. When asked to clarify the 'not legal' statement, the CEO noted: it is 'caste based discrimination [that is] is illegal in India and not whether employees are asked to identify their caste'. But, to avoid any semblance of caste discrimination, we choose to formally avoid [as in not asking] the question altogether. In fact, 'if someone complains [that we talked about caste in the company], we could be in jail'. They, however, did concede that caste considerations might apply at the individual and social levels (in marriage and social relations) but not at the corporate IT level. But, they also were quick to add: 'There are no questions about caste in the job application forms'.

One tool used by IT companies to pre-empt caste isomorphic considerations in hiring and promotions is EEO policies. They emphatically

---

[10] [ ] brackets are added within quotes to improve readability.

dismissed the relevance of caste in Indian IT because of EEO guidelines. In the words of an HR manager, who considered HR to be the upholder of company policies and image, 'caste is not at all relevant because we follow EEO policies'. Another, a high level administrator in a private professionally managed organization, said 'No place for caste/community. Companies do not ask personal information [like Caste]'. He too was quick to add that 'asking about caste is NOT ILLEGAL[11] in India. But, companies avoid the question because it goes against EEO policies'.

Transition from 'Caste' to 'Community' in Indian IT

An interesting caste-laden layer to the caste (SC) neutral stance presented above, were the key industry leaders who spoke on how caste in Indian IT operates through *community and linguistic social vectors* that are strongly tinged with dominant caste perspectives. The new dominant castes are not exclusively Brahmins but include other economically prominent non-Brahmin upper caste groups. While the language of caste may have been replaced by 'community' in the discourse of Indian corporations, the close connections between 'community and forward or dominant caste status' have continued to render caste relevant in Indian IT. As the female CEO of a specialty organization commented, 'They say caste is not important, but community, regional backgrounds have become more significant' particularly at the higher rungs of management.

The female CEO pointed to the 'Founder Effect' in operation in Indian IT, to demonstrate how 'caste' has been replaced by 'community' in Indian IT. Access to resources and networks in the founder's community have become the new social and cultural capital with cache for entrance into and promotion within Indian IT. In her words, 'top management is from the same community as the founder. If the founder is Reddy or Brahmin, senior management is Reddy or Brahmin, respectively'. In her experience the new preferred hiring rankings in Indian IT management looked like this: 'if the founder is from Hyderabad, Andhra Pradesh or Chennai in Tamil Nadu, the top management ranks are drawn from Telugu [language of AP] locals or Tamil locals [respectively], particularly those who have worked in USA and have global experience. Locals are given first priority in hiring; India expatriates second'. A senior manager of a BPO

[11] Caps were in the original written communication.

company confirmed the founder effect. To him, 'the founder's community background and linguistic origin, whether Gowda [a forward caste] or Brahmins [caste] or Telugu [language] has replaced caste and impact who is given preference at the senior levels of the company'.

Another key informant, with experience in both Indian and international businesses, spoke about the close connection between community and forward/dominant caste in Indian IT as: 'TCS management is dominated by Chennai Iyers [Brahmins]; in AP, it is the Reddys and Kammas [dominant non-Brahmin castes]'. He offered additional examples to illustrate the connections between caste, region, and community using the southern Indian banking institutions as examples.[12] 'Caste is closely linked with community. Canara Bank – very Konkan, Brahmin in top management; Mangalore Catholic Bank – Very Catholic; Syndicate Bank – mix of Konkan Brahmin and Catholic Brahmin; Corporation Bank [government owned] – mix of castes; South Indian bank-mainly Kerala upper caste'.

In other words, even though community and regional backgrounds have replaced caste hierarchies, *caste considerations have not disappeared* from the social and business organizing frameworks of Indian IT companies. When the key informants talk about 'community' they did not mean the age-old caste system, with Brahmins at the top, SC/ST at the bottom, and others in between. Rather, they were referring to a broadening of the top tier in the caste system by adding local wealth and landowning caste communities. The new dominant caste is not limited to Brahmins; it also includes the middle caste stratum around which local communities are organized. As one key informant noted, business owners of certain dominant castes (typically upper castes and non-SCs) and regions tend to hire from their own communities. The 'assistant' to one key informant had previously worked for her family-owned company and hailed from the same community (aka dominant caste background) as she does. Another senior HR executive for customer relations, while extolling the seminal role of appropriate skill sets, added parenthetically, 'Internally, natural bias is to own community'. His company, with a growth rate of 60–75 per cent, had clientele in USA and Japan.

---

[12] There is no reason not to believe that similar dominant/forward caste connections are also prevalent in northern India.

In short, these key industry informants confirmed the operation of caste or community resources in the hiring and promotion practices in Indian IT. Whether it is access to resources within one's *caste/community networks'* (Lin 1999), be they the '*strong, bonding personal/familial ties*' (Fernandez and Nichols 2002; Granovetter 1973) *or through community ties (weak, bridging ties), caste/community connections* are important to secure jobs in Indian IT. And when managers were promoted or hired, IT professionals operated from their caste/community positionality when they used caste/class tinged *pattern recognition* (Baron 2006) to evaluate the merit of IT professionals. In the final analyses, through a *caste/community homosocial reproduction* (adapted from Kanter 1977a) of employees and managers, existing caste/class hierarchies are transferred into the IT sector.

Community/Regional Isomorphic Foci Also Deemed Functional for Businesses

Even those key industry informants who acknowledged the shift from caste to communal/regional foci in the IT labour pool were quick to point out, 'but it is functional to limit to local areas; if local talent is available, why not hire them; can groom them, will be stable'. They deemed it *imperative* for Indian IT companies to have more control over their labour force, particularly when their clientele was external to India; these companies offered software solutions, development, support and consulting services to external (American companies) and internal markets. Besides, it is easier, they said, to recognize success patterns (read *pattern recognition*) in local employees with similar linguistic and community backgrounds.[13]

---

[13] During my field trips, it was interesting to observe and hear about other industries in India, like the hospitality industries, and their practices of hiring staff from other states in the country. In the guest houses where I stayed, the guests were typically hi-tech employees who were relocating with or without families. Because they liked the home like atmosphere of guest houses, many corporations (software, hardware, BPO, Call Centres, international—Oracle, Deloitte) used their services. The male kitchen staff of one guest house were primarily from Odisha (a northern state) and the supervisor was Muslim (Mohamedan, he says). When I asked, 'Why not hire locals', the supervisor responded, 'The guest house (there were five in the high-tech city) requires 24/7 service. Locals do not live at the guest house and they want leave every 15 days'. Besides, non-locals 'bring their own crews from their home state'.

It is worth noting that no matter their standpoints, these key informants, whether caste neutral or community focused, overwhelmingly heard caste as SC 'caste reservations'; they questioned the quality of merit gained in caste-based earmark programs.

Caste Camp: IT Embedded in the Caste System

At the opposite end of the spectrum were the activists, educators, and social commentators who lamented that 'business imperatives have turned discriminatory and reinforced casteism' against SCs even in the putative caste blind/avoidance IT environments. In their experiences, caste hierarchies have been transferred into the new occupational sector. Their 'caste is relevant' assessments in Indian IT ranged from intentional to unintended casteism. At the intentional end were those who accused Indian IT of blatant casteism for their small Dalit footprint. Others referred to Dalits lacking the *hidden symbolic qualifications*. In between were those who talked about the functional merit imperatives in Indian IT that have turned discriminatory. They acknowledged the traditional Dalit deficits in *pure merit* to be outcomes of casteism. But, they also saw indications that the dysfunctional, even when unintended, consequences of caste neutral business imperatives contributed to the reproduction of the broader caste/communal hierarchies in Indian IT. On balance, the recurrent endpoint in the casteism narrative was one of caste reproduction in Indian IT. Caste hierarchies in the larger society, with its unequal competitive edge for the dominant castes, have been constructed and reproduced in the much coveted Indian IT sector.

Functional Business Imperatives Turned Discriminatory

Even if dependence on the local or community labour force was necessary for Indian IT companies, the local 'qualified' labour force, interestingly, was often from the local dominant community, said two key informants who worked in Indian IT. At the time of the interview, these interviewees were senior system analysts with an offshore arm of a multinational electronic production corporation. While the electronic production company is very strict, they said, about not having workplace discussions about caste and background, in their estimation about 70–80 per cent of the company's Indian employees were Brahmin. If not caste, it was the *dominant communal or regional vectors*, one stated. Alluding to the *caste-homosocial reproduction* of the staff and managers, 'Birla/Tata companies hire primarily Birla/Tata community members'.[14] In his first job in an Indian IT company, he (from the southern state of Tamil Nadu) recalled, being sent to Hyderabad (in Andhra Pradesh). Although he was promised staff, he ended up doing everything by himself. When he inquired about the staff, he was told 'no, you have to go solo'. His interpretation: 'they did not want to assign Hyderabadis to be [work] under him, a Tamilian. So, I left that company'.

But for the Dalit Merit Deficit

Others, even while conceding the relevance of caste hierarchies in Indian IT, put the onus on Dalits for falling short on the mandatory pure merit-skills criteria and the consequent small Dalit footprint in Indian IT. An example was an administrator in a private professionally managed organization who did not categorically affirm a caste-neutral stance, but made the Dalit skill deficit argument for the absence of SCs in Indian IT. He wrote, 'skill based, scale of global operations limit anything but quality and skills ... English is lingua franca in corporations; will be difficult for SC/ST'. Associating *reservation-merit* with the limited presence of SC/ST in the IT labour force, the administrator went on to add, 'They do not have qualifications. They go to government schools which have poor quality education'. He continued to lament, 'Most SC/STs do not qualify in the company interviews'. But suggested that, 'Organizations should be proactive about affirmative action. Not gone far enough because of political issues; buying SC status. Root causes need to be addressed. Why don't Dalits have social and cultural capital?' he asked rhetorically.

Indian IT Embedded in Casteism: A Blunt Assessment

Most key informants in the Caste Camp were even blunter about the *explicit casteism* in Indian IT. Just as some categorically affirmed the caste

---

[14] The Tata family belongs to the well-defined Parsi community legendary for its economic wealth. They are not a 'caste' group per se because they are not Hindus. The Parsis are an immigrant community, who practice the Zoroastrian faith, possibly from Persia, and are now located in Mumbai, Maharashtra.

neutrality of their companies, others, particularly those from SC or minor-ity religious communities, were equally adamant that caste discrimination in Indian IT was not just implicit, rather it was quite blatant.

Poignant examples offered by key informants in this camp lucidly illustrated the *explicit casteism* arguments. An IT engineer, a Dalit (who has an MS from the prestigious IIT) wrote that the 'Indian community here will deny any "caste" bias as usual; the cream of the society in India always denies there is caste. However, it is the cream that helps maintain the caste, funding caste-based organizations with their economic power. The cream does not know what they are doing - as their caste status gives them so much "cultural capital" that they enjoy without knowing it'. Speaking more pointedly to his experience with how casteism operates in Indian IT was this manager (from a southern backward caste community) at an off-shored American ERP systems corporation. He recounted the following scenario. During a job interview in India, the interviewer got a call from a member of his dominant community. When the conversa-tion was over, this interviewee was plainly told that the position was closed. Another high level administrator (a Catholic) in an India-based international IT company ironically observed, 'Brahmins will be the ones to complain about questions about caste; Most managers are Brahmins'. Yet another SC key informant, albeit based on the experience of his IT friends, affirmed that 'there is a Brahmin domination in IT industry'.

'Unsolicited comments' from a non-Indian IT professional about how caste relations might play out in the social dynamics in the IT workplace were also informative. During his long years in IT in the USA, as a techni-cal team lead, project manager, and system administrator, he said he had hired many Indian IT professionals in the USA and had also worked with (and sometimes for) Indian IT companies. He wrote, 'I was always fas-cinated by the cliques and communication patterns I observed in groups of Indian professionals. Along with the language and regional differences, issues of caste always seemed to be a specter that loomed over interper-sonal and professional relationships'. Although he did not explicitly inquire into the caste status of his co-workers, he was always amazed, he wrote, 'at the variety and complexity of interaction between my Indian coworkers. There were those who always seemed to be in control (of themselves and all around them) and they were generally deferred to by others. Some, few, at the other extreme always seemed in need of bowing and humbling themselves before everyone else. These behaviours were so strong and automatic that I always felt they had to be the result of lifelong training and expectation.'

'The Dalit activists and social commentators' were also explicit in their observations about centuries-long caste inequalities and tensions being transferred into the new IT sector. The Editor of *Dalit News*, an Indian magazine, started by categorically negating the claim that caste is not relevant in Indian IT. It is all 'bogus', he cynically noted. 'Caste is still very important', and he went on to detail, 'in Indian IT 50-60% is Brahmin. Many claim that SC/STs are not qualified. Yes, but how will they be, if the schools in rural areas do not teach and most SC/ST live in rural areas which have poor quality schools'. And, 'Even if SC is hired, life will be difficult and they most likely will leave the job'. When asked how Indians know someone's caste/community, he responded, 'In the north, by family name. In the south (of India) by community name: Andhra Pradesh (Reddy), Kerala (Nair). SCs often used initials of their family names as in P. Raja. Skin color is sometimes another giveaway; SC/STs are often darker'.

As the key informants reflected on the relevance of caste in India, the importance of *caste/community positionality* and the cache that *embedded hidden symbolic capital* had in IT became clear. And, irrespective of whether caste has been reproduced or not, the intense, metaphorically bloody, nature of the caste vs. merit debate was not lost on these key informants in the Caste Camp.

Industry Perspectives on the Merit-Caste Debate: Concluding Reflections

Several theoretical insights were gleaned from the Merit-Caste commentaries offered by key industry informants. One, their interpretation of the 'caste in IT' question varied depending on their organizational and/or caste vantage points (*positionality*). Those in management positions categorically posited that Indian IT was caste-neutral either because of their EEO policies or because caste (read SC/ST status) was not a relevant hiring criteria. Their caste neutrality argument hinged solely on the fact that, unlike the government sector, they did not hire or keep records of employee's caste status, be they from SC or any other higher or middle caste backgrounds. Besides, they emphasized the importance of the *pure merit metric* in their operations.

But, to the Caste Camp, these stated reasons for caste-neutrality or caste identity avoidance practices begged the question about the connections between *caste neutral policies* and *caste neutral outcomes*. Even if caste (whether SC or other castes) was not an official hiring criteria in IT companies, how can one be definitive, they asked, that the outcomes are caste neutral? If there are no records maintained of employee caste background, not only of SCs but also of upper castes or founder's caste as the case may be, how does one prove or disprove claims of caste neutrality in hiring and in the workplace caste composition? How do neutrality claims operate in compensations and promotions in the company? To the key informants in the Caste Camp these questions became more urgent because of the overlapping and interlocking connections between dominant caste status of IT company founders, their management, and other 'local' employees. *In other words, as long as IT merit is embedded and hidden in the unequal social and economic structures in India, merit cannot be caste neutral.*

But, why 'should IT companies be concerned about engaging, and resolving, the merit-caste debate?' At the very least, questions about caste neutrality in the activist and scholarly communities might be effectively countered only when companies figure out ways to systematically account for both merit-skills and personal backgrounds (including caste and community) of their employees. At best, such information will provide evidentiary proof for the successful outcomes of their caste-neutral EEO policies that theoretically open up the talent pool, irrespective of caste, community, religion, or region.

What does 'the future hold for the Merit vs. Caste debate' in Indian IT? Here, too, the intensity of the debate was evident in the remarks of key informants who returned to the problematic nature of SC reservation or earmarks in the private sector. For example, the administrator in a private professionally managed organization, reflecting on the future of caste in the private sector, offered some dire predictions: 'Of late, there is discussion of employment and education quotas for SCs in the private sector. There is backlash against it ... it is a non-starter; reason why the private sector is resistant because it will open a Pandora's box. Once quotas for SC/ST are instituted in the private sector, there will be a quick downgrade, slippery slide into religion, language. If government mandates SC quotas, Indian IT companies will relocate', he warned.

Other commentators, two entrepreneurs in particular, outlined 'boundary limits' (Powers 2010) in their predictions. They saw the combative

Merit-Caste blood sport being limited to the engineering sectors (or KPO) in Indian IT. While confirming the subordination of SCs by the dominant castes in the IT sector, they suggested that the BPO sector currently is, and might be, more open to SC/ST than the KPO companies. In their experience, BPO employees often do not require engineering degrees. Instead some college education and short training in accent modification were sufficient in the BPO sector. Consequently, SC/STs might do reasonably well in those working environments, they opined. But, that is not the case in KPO, they added. In the KPO sector that requires a bachelor's degree in Technology (BTech) or higher engineering degrees, only 1 per cent of their employees might be SC/ST.

Another future track in the Merit-Caste debate was affirmed by social commentators who were sympathetic to the SC cause, while simultaneously recognizing the merit imperative, albeit of the *holistic* kind, in the IT sector. A high level administrator of secondary high schools in South India spoke from her professional experience, 'in the private IT sector, more significant than caste is knowledge, ability to "*communicate*", deal with people. If SC/ST have those "soft skills", it will give them an advantage'. An engineer in an international manufacturing company concurred, 'If 2 candidates with similar qualifications, SC/ST should be given preference because they have suffered much'. Both also saw glimmers of hope in the youth and urban educated segments of India to whom caste, they noted, was not as significant as it was in the previous generations.

Is Indian IT a Neutral or Contested Space for Caste? Ground level Perspectives

The arguments in the lived experiences of rank-and-file IT employees, about whether IT was caste neutral or a new caste vector, were more contentious and visceral than in the key informant community.[15] On the

---

[15] To understand the lived employee experiences on the caste vs. merit debate in Indian IT, the original web survey (Appendix 1A.2) was designed to probe responses to a set of seven open ended questions about caste. The specific questions were: 'What are your thoughts on the statement that caste/community is no longer a barrier to work in the information technology sector in India' (Q21)? 'In contrast, what and why do you think about those who posit that too many, or too few, jobs in high-tech companies are offered to members of the scheduled caste

one hand, the-rank-and file IT professionals, like the industry informants, aligned themselves into the Merit versus Caste camps. IT professionals in the Merit Camp *valorized merit* and clearly distinguished it from *reservation-merit*, all in the name of a globalized work environment where caste is irrelevant and even inefficient, they said. Vociferously countering the caste-free narrative, the Caste Camp proclaimed that caste was alive and well in Indian IT backing up their claims with the *symbolic, hidden nature of merit,* and *caste filtering* in hiring and promotions at different levels in Indian IT.

Caste, a Third Rail: Methodological Lesson

The highly contentious nature of ground level discussions about caste in India or in the IT sector became evident early in the web survey data collection process. Initially, potential web survey respondents were identified through snowball sampling methods. Many of these IT professionals (out of the 149) who completed the original long form (Appendix 1A.2) expressed serious reservations about the caste and even the specific SC questions. They either left the questions blank or expressed their anger and displeasure at having to respond to questions about caste. A common refrain read like this: caste discrimination is illegal in India; moreover, SCs/STs have been given preferences in education and jobs since India became independent in 1947, at the expense of middle and upper castes. So, why are we being asked to talk about caste and caste discrimination in Indian IT?

Similar reservations were heard when arrangements were being made for fielding the survey, either through HR offices of Indian IT companies or through snowball sampling methods. Caste, an educator said 'has become a lightning rod. Just mentioning caste has become a "show stopper,"

---

groups' (Q22–24)? 'There are many who think that hiring managers will hire mainly people from their own caste/community; what do you think' (Q25)? 'And finally, based on your experience, to which caste/community do hiring managers belong' (Q26)? 'At the end of the survey, the respondents were invited, if they chose to do so, 'to identify their caste status' (Q27). An overwhelming majority (86 per cent or 128) of the 149 respondents who completed the long version of the survey responded to Q27, what is your caste, if you don't mind ...).

a "No Go" word; you say caste and they hear SC/ST. People get worried about why one is doing a study of caste'. In fact, the initial set of HR managers who reviewed the survey politely refused to distribute a survey that included questions about caste to their employees. An HR manager of an IT staffing company explained his reluctance in sending out the long (original) form to employees as: 'as a manager, if I send this survey out, employees will wonder and also talk amongst themselves about why caste questions are being asked when caste is not part of the hiring criterion in private companies. Employees will not distinguish a third party researcher from the manager who will distribute the survey. They will think that the manager wants to know their caste, caste of managers, etc. and that could be an issue that unnecessarily raises tensions'. Another manager responded, 'Out of curiosity I looked at the survey, we may find some of the questions not acceptable'. Another had to be reassured a few times that caste specific questions will be deleted before agreeing to distribute the survey to potential respondents. In their judgement, the term 'caste' was to be avoided because it (the term caste) is frequently equated with SC/ST reservations.

In response to these concerns, the original survey was stripped off of all, except one (out of 7), of the caste questions. The question (Q21) that remained was: 'There are many who claim that caste/community is no longer a barrier to work in the information technology sector in India. What do you think?' This abbreviated survey (see Appendix 1A.3) was completed by 365 (71 per cent) out of 514 IT professionals. In both versions of the web survey, no identifying information about the respondent (their name and the company they worked for) was collected to enhance and honour the confidentiality/anonymity rule in data collection.

However, one would be remiss if mention was not made of the positive comments (about the original long-form survey) that were offered by some in the SC community. Two examples: An IT engineer in the USA (a Dalit who has an MS degree) who responded to the web survey thought the survey was light or generic about caste. He emailed, 'Your survey is generic. It has common questions. I went through 3 pages and could not go on as it does not address the main issues titled as "caste in IT". Perhaps the 4th page may have some questions. I am confused. Are u looking for "caste" in IT or in general?' Another, a Dalit lawyer, wrote, 'I was very happy to see the link on the on Dalit Voice website for your survey on

Caste in Indian IT. This was a survey or a study supposed to happen long time back.'

The Caste versus Merit Blood Sport Tropes

As in the key industry community, two major conflicting tropes emerged in the reflections on ground level experiences with the place of caste in the IT social space.[16] There were those who squarely positioned themselves in the Merit Camp while the others were in the Caste Camp; the Merit Camp made arguments for a caste free IT social space while the Caste Camp countered with 'caste filtering' based on 'caste positionality', and embedded symbolic content of IT merit.

Among the 404 who commented on the relevance of caste in IT, 63.9 per cent (258/404) either declared that 'Caste was not a barrier (period)' or went on to 'Valorize Merit, IT skills, and knowledge'. Many in this camp extolled that 'IT has no religion, caste or creed; it is education, knowledge, skills, merit, ability that matters'. Such valorization of the IT meritocracy coupled with declarative, vehement portrayals of a caste-no-bar IT, comports with the national rhetoric that has equated caste reservations/quotas for SC/STs with weakening of merit standards. Stated differently, the vocal disassociation between IT and caste considerations meant that the private IT sector, unlike the government, did not give preference to SCs or Dalits for fear that IT's 'Pure Merit' standards will be diluted. And if there is a small Dalit footprint in IT, it has to do with a 'Dalit Merit Deficit' than because of the traditional caste discrimination. One IT professional summarized the Merit Camp argument as: 'I think there's no discrimination against lower castes inside an organization. Caste is a non-issue when it comes to getting a job done. However, you may see fewer lower castes in these jobs because they have some criteria like having an ability to speak English, being urbanized—lower castes may be out of touch with these things so they probably have less chance making it through the interview process. However, there are no binding rules or strict trends. Any lower caste who is educated enough and can speak English well, will not be discriminated against anyway (a self-identified Brahmin-upper caste)'. Irrespective of the Merit Camp's caste-neutrality portrayal of Indian IT,

---

[16] These are compiled responses to survey statement about caste not being a barrier in IT (Q21).

they seemed *'unaware of or "misguided"'* (per Bourdieu 1990) about of the *'embedded nature of their privileged pure merit'.*

On the other hand, there were a sizeable number of voices, some equally forceful, others more nuanced, positing that *casteism was alive and well* in the IT sector (36.1 per cent of 404).[17] 'Caste matters in IT' these respondents cried, whether it was with a simple, declarative 'Yes' or more detailed exposition of how caste discrimination and casteism has come to operate in Indian IT. To them, when no special allowances (like no SC reservations in the IT sector) are made for the marginalized castes, who continue to endure inequalities in ownership of merit related wealth, societal prejudices and resulting discriminatory practices are bound to reproduce casteism in the IT sector.

To the Merit Camp: It is Merit, Not Caste

Despite the initial reluctance to answering questions about caste, a majority (79.6 per cent of 514) offered some response, even if brief, to the one remaining statement 'There are many who claim that caste/community is no longer a barrier to work in the information technology sector in India. What do you think?' (Q21).[18] Only a fifth (21.4 per cent) left the question blank.

Preliminary Comments: Merit and Not SC/ST Reservations.

Like many of the key informants, about two-thirds of the IT professionals who responded to the survey posited that caste was not a barrier in Indian IT. They characterized the *IT work space as one organized around 'Skill based Merit' and not 'Caste'*. However, it became clear that when respondents delinked merit from caste, they meant that Indian IT did not follow the constitutionally mandated reservation policies for 'SC/ST' (quotas for SC or ST) and not that caste considerations operate

---

[17] Percentages throughout the rest of the chapter sometimes add up to more than 100 per cent because of multiple responses.

[18] To recap, 365 respondents (71 per cent out of 514) completed the short form with only 1 explicit caste related question, Q21. The rest, 149 or 29 per cent, who completed the long form, had the opportunity to respond to 6 more questions, in addition to Q21.

in Indian IT. Since quotas and reservations typically involved lower/ reduced merit standards for the SC/ST applicants, it was understandable (even if not historically justifiable) that, in an environment that valorizes skill based merit (see Chapter 2), disconnecting merit from caste was equated with caste neutrality. Their argument went like this: IT's 'merit' reputation is not sullied because they do not (are not required to) follow the constitutionally mandated reservations/quotas for SCs as is the case in the public sector. In other words, when IT professionals, like the key informants, say 'caste is no barrier' in Indian IT, they meant that no special allowances (no reservations) are made for the SC/STs, unlike in the government sector where merit requirements are relaxed for SC/STs.

In fact, some respondents complained that asking caste related questions just reinforced an outdated, bad, practice. Some (even in the short form pools) seemed angry that even one question (Q21) about caste was asked. There seemed to be an unwritten assumption that not talking about caste would make caste tensions disappears. Interestingly, they were more comfortable talking about gender issues in Indian IT than caste (see Chapter 5 for more details).

Unpacking the 'Caste Not Relevant' Discourse in Indian IT: Declarations.

A plurality (39.5 per cent of 258), of those who made the declaration or affirmed the statement that caste is not a barrier in Indian IT, did so without much explanation. The monosyllabic responses included words like, 'True', 'Correct', 'Yes' or 'Right' or 'agree'. Others qualified their monosyllabic assent to the caste-no-barrier in IT statement with phrases like the following: 'yes very much true', or 'of course yes'; or 'True absolutely'. Others said, caste 'is not important' or 'it is not all important' or 'The statement is right!' Other sample responses in a similar vein: 'yes, it's not needed' or 'yes, caste/religion/state doesn't matter'. Adding a few emphatic qualifiers to their declarations of a 'caste-not-a-barrier' IT, were those, who responded with comments like, 'Obviously there is no such discrimination'; or 'I don't think caste/community is a barrier to work in the IT field'; or that the caste-no-bar statement 'Makes a lot of sense'. Sarcastically, one asked 'It's not a barrier, who don't know that?'

Of those who self-identified their caste status,[19] there were four Brahmins who gave monosyllabic certification of the veracity of the caste-is-not-a-barrier statement (Q21). A Christian Vanniyars[20] also confirmed, 'Yes, caste/ community is not a barrier'. Interestingly, among those who affirmed, 'Yes, We need not to worry about this', was one who claimed 'I am first a man' as his caste. Another who said 'I am a human of masculine gender' was vehement in his comment that caste is 'Definitely not' relevant in IT.

Some caste-no-bar respondents hastened to note that they were talking about Indian IT when they referred to the apparent incongruities between merit culture and caste reservations. 'That is true. No one asks about caste nowadays and there is no caste reservation for IT jobs', said one respondent. Other comments in a similar vein: 'ya, ... caste and community is not a barior for skilled people' or that 'Definitely caste and community is not a barrier to work in IT sector'. Or 'They are right ... Caste has nothing to do with any job, so as with IT'. One IT professional [who maintained that 'I am from the Catholic community, if that can be called community, and I don't know my caste'] added: 'In my view, caste or community is not a barrier to work in the IT sector in India'. Yet another asserted, 'Not at all. Caste, religion and regionalism is not at all a barrier. There might be some personal favouritism which cannot be neglected' said one who viewed self as 'I am an Indian and Software Engineer is my caste'. Taking a societal perspective, were those who wrote: 'Yes it [caste] is not. I don't think it was ever a problem' or 'Yes. People don't look into Caste/Community ... ' Few were grateful in their responses as in, 'Yes, No more community' or 'Yes, caste/community is not needed anymore [self-identified BC, backward caste, Christian]'.

---

[19] Self-identified caste background of IT professional respondents is noted when available. As was mentioned earlier in this chapter, the caste identity question (Q27) was asked only of the 149 respondents who completed the original long version of the survey. Close to 40 per cent (n = 56 or 38 per cent out of 146 with valid responses) identified their caste.

[20] Traditionally most Vanniyars (the largest single community in Tamil Nadu) are agricultural labourers; the community now owns 50 per cent of the lands of the traditional landowners. In the 1980s, they had their caste classification changed to Most Backward Caste to avail of government benefits (https:// en.wikipedia.org/wiki/Vanniyar).

Pure Merit Valorization

As with the key industry informants, IT professionals' explanations for their 'caste was not a barrier in Indian IT' stance revolved around 'Pure Merit'. Some explicitly 'streamlined' pure merit when they juxtaposed valorized merit (education, knowledge, and talent) against caste or community while simultaneously linking merit to the needs of a globalized IT work environment and delinking IT from the government social vector where SC reservations matter.

They typically *equated merit with technical and analytical skills, knowledge, and higher education*. In their affirmation and confirmation of the statement that caste is not a barrier in Indian IT, they specifically noted: '"Because for working, talent is enough" [respondent self-identified as "all are human beings"]' or 'Yes, IT is concerned only with technical and analytical skill' or 'only technical skills matter', or 'individual ability' or only 'talent' matters, because 'nothing else is countable'. And, 'only skills matters, any one with qualification & work experience can fit in IT jobs'. On balance, these respondents, who valorized merit and knowledge as the only things that matter in the Indian IT work environment, were loud and clear about the irrelevance of caste even when they did not explicitly mention the word 'caste'. Taking a universal tone were those who wrote: 'True. Mind and willingness has no barriers'; or 'Any job requires brains to work, as long as they got brains, they are fit'.

Those who *explicitly streamlined and juxtaposed* valorized merit (education, knowledge, and talent) against caste or community has this to say: 'I think IT jobs are skill based and cast/community is never considered'; 'There is no difference for the caste in IT jobs'; 'caste is not a matter; communication and Knowledge is primary'; 'Only knowledge matters not caste' or 'Caste/community does not matter, it matters how eligible you are for that job'. Some sounded indignant when they responded: 'No community in work place'; 'Yes, the term CASTE is never used in IT sector of India'; 'Quite right. There is no caste and community comes to picture when performance is concerned' ['I am an Indian' in response to the caste identity question]. Others noted that there is 'no need to look for caste/community. Only quality is needed', or 'only the skill is needed', or 'caste/community does not come into picture in the current working environment'. In short, to quote two more, 'No IT don't think about caste/community' and 'there is nothing like caste, community to work in IT

Industry. There is only one thing is important that is the person should be well qualified with good Skill'.

Such confirmation that caste was not a barrier (or that there was no caste-based reservation) in Indian IT was heard *irrespective of self-identified caste background* of respondents. One IT professional who claimed, 'I belong to Jainism and i am proud to be Jain' [a religious minority], also added:'If you are well qualified and technically sound person then it hardly matters to which caste you belongs to'. A Hindu Tamil-speaking-Brahmin concurred,'As long as requisite skills are present anyone can do the work. Nobody considers caste to recruit in IT'. Other respondents, who claimed backward caste (BC) as their background, affirmed that caste is not a barrier in Indian IT. One noted, 'IT sector skills are important and not the caste'. To another who was from the OBC community, 'They [caste] are not needed for IT'. Yet others who chose non-caste vectors to describe their social status also agreed, 'Yes. Caste/community is not a matter to work in IT field', and 'I am happy with my family life' was the response to caste identity.

Intimating fears that 'caste reservations will be seen as equaling weak merit' were sample comments by those who wished to distance their success in IT from their caste identity. 'No caste or community, only skills' said one who noted 'I belong to BC, good enough with my qualification and experience'. 'People are placed based on qualification and skills that they have. I was not placed based on caste/community background. So nothing to say about it', said another. One professional, ['I have been categorized as belonging to Forward caste/Brahmin community'] who was surprised the caste question had come up in this survey, noted 'Caste/Community is not important in the IT field, the knowledge/skill/qualification is what matters'. Or 'Caste/community is not needed … only the output is needed. I don't want to say anything about caste and community. It is not needed and must not be about the caste/community background' and that 'Only performance and capability speaks rather than all these useless stuff'.

In fact, a few went a step further opining that 'caste identities are detrimental to productivity' in Indian IT. In their words, 'Yes of course, caste/community is not a barrier, because in IT we need technology, experience to give productivity, caste/community will not give any productivity'. Or another, 'we are here to work, not to form or run any social community or organization'. Or 'Because caste/community will not help an employee to complete the job; only the experience', or that 'it is outdated and not required at all in order to achieve'. Another respondent who claimed to be 'Multicaste - Hindu by birth, Christian follower' lamented, 'If caste is considered as one of the criteria, product qualities would deteriorate and would impact business which none of the companies would be ready to take this hit'; another asked, 'How long you will be able to remain in IT sector if you are hired because of your caste and not merit?'

Globalized IT Work Environment

Another sub-trope in the Merit Camp in Indian IT was the indispensable link posited between 'pure merit' and the demands of the globalized nature of IT work. In addition to the requisite educational credentials, they added good team work, deliverables, and communication to the merit criteria if one is to succeed in Indian IT: 'I never feel caste will be the problem in IT industry. I think most of the people will come into this field with high qualification. So obviously they know how to corroborate [collaborate] with each other'. Said another, 'Irrespective of caste, we work on a common platform. We do not care it at our workplace'. Along the same lines another added, 'caste is no need in Workstation ... ' To others, 'Yes, IT company need only the people with good communication and having good technical skills'; 'Yes, only the technical knowledge is required for giving delivery' [one who listed caste as Hindu]; 'IT means Team work'; 'Here only attitude, technical skills, communication skills and ability to work in a team matters'; 'Which [caste] is not barrier, they need Dedication, Good Team Player, Commitment, Ability Understand New Things Easily, Patience'; or that 'Qualification, experience and ability are the important factor in IT field. So caste/community doesn't have any role in this field'. In short, the IT environment claimed one IT professional, 'is fairly cosmopolitan so even hiring managers are from different social backgrounds'.

Yet others reflected on the 'creative, dynamic, competitive nature of work' in the new IT occupational structure as limiting caste considerations with comments like: 'IT is an area where the talent is really encouraged and create opportunities'; or 'sure because if you do not have talent you will come and go, that's all, [not caste] is needed'. Others said, 'Absolutely. Your ability is the only criteria in this competitive world'; or 'IT's based purely on merit/skills/ability to perform under stress and constrained

environment, etc. that matter the most and not caste etc'. In this competitive work habitus 'community is not at all concern in IT sector where we
only concern about talent and dedication'. A bit more realistic was one
who claimed 'Muslim' as his caste: 'Of course there can be a case here and
there, where people feel discriminated, but that's in all the fields and in all
the countries'.

Emphasizing *caste neutral hiring practices* in globalized Indian IT were
these sample comments. 'In IT Tech, hiring people is not based on caste
or community. Caste or community is not a matter in IT. The person
must have ability to work and qualified'. Another seemed surprised, 'Why
would caste/community play a role in the selection? It is a global platform and people should have equal opportunities'. To a Telugu-speaking
Hindu respondent, 'in global IT there is no discrimination in hiring with
respect to caste/community'. Or simply put, 'It is of course not a barrier as
there is no discrimination in hiring in information technology' or because
'Nobody even care to know all those information' [a self-identified member of a lower caste].

Some utilized 'experiential evidence' for their caste-is-not-relevant case
in Indian IT. 'I have not come across any instances' one said. Or to another
'I have never heard of such an instance when caste/community are given
preference when considering for IT job'; or that ' ... no one has asked me
my caste and none of them is interested even when I have said what my
community is'. Another piece of supporting evidence in the caste-no-bar
argument was that 'almost all types of society people are working in this
sector' or that the respondent has not seen 'caste / community, etc. play
a part in any developed company' because to another 'as true as sun rises
in east. No employee form has details about caste'. A Hindu Brahmin
agreed, 'Individual calibre matters more. Don't know of any companies
that ask for that [caste] data when they review applications'. To another,
'after working in this field of IT industry, I haven't come across a situation
where-in I had to disclose my community or cast officially for any reason'.
An IT professional from a backward community confirmed, 'Great. I
adhere to the no-caste in IT' argument.

Profit and Practicality

These were two additional incentives offered by the caste-no-bar proponents. One IT professional was direct, 'Information Technology

companies are mainly targeting only those with talent, performance, and the stuff what a person have ... They are not considering about caste/community. It's a practical question'. And, 'In an IT organization Caste/Community is no longer a barrier to work in India. Because management is only hiring talented and skill matching people. That leads organization in good and profitable way'. Consequently, 'there is no discrimination in caste in private sector'.

Taking a philosophical tone were these responses: 'there are no caste or community in IT. Technology is the same for everyone' because 'all are the same', and therefore 'this question is irrelevant. All are equal and no barrier, we are all one'. Another IT professional who claimed 'I don't have any caste, I am an Indian' stated, 'Yes, all people are common'. Another who thought caste questions 'should be removed from the survey', said 'Caste/community is not required. All are human being'. With sardonic humour another added, 'I think it's not a barrier in any sector in India. All have 2 hands, 2 legs, 2 eyes etc ... It's the brain and how well it's used that makes a good programmer'; this respondent also felt the caste 'Question is irrelevant' because to another 'Secularism is in India'.

There was also an *ethical or even moral undertone* in some survey respondents' assessment of no-caste considerations in IT. Some sample comments: 'This is the right way' and that 'We need to stop thinking about caste and community. Need to grow up'. Another, 'one should not discriminate using the term caste. It's a biggest sin'. Or that 'Caste is waste, Community is Immunity' or 'Caste/community are never a barrier and should not be', and 'Not a relevant question. I don't believe in caste'. Indicating that caste is 'highly un-ethical in the IT sector and should not be encouraged in any way', another confirmed that 'Certainly, there is no barrier in the IT sector, only qualified and hard working professionals reach the top'.

Offering yet another take on the no-SC-caste-bar IT argument were those who accused the IT world of *reverse casteism*, 'Yes, now a days the people from low caste gets more opportunities than other caste people'. Or 'the lower castes and backward communities get opportunities to study in the best institutions, often at the cost of the more deserving general category students' [self-described Upper class member].

Another interesting juxtaposition between pure merit and caste was found in comments that offered a *cost-benefit analyses* of a multi-caste IT social space for the company vis-à-vis the individual employee. Extolling benefits to a company, one noted, caste 'is not a barrier. When we work on a team there are many other having different caste and community. But while we are doing work everyone wish to complete their work as a team player'. In fact, another claimed, 'caste is not at all a barrier to work in IT, as Work place should be flexible to be associated with multi-cultural people and people should feel good to be associated with such environment and it also makes employees to respect different cultures across the globe which ends in unity'. In contrast, to a self-identified SC respondent, affirming an open multi-caste environment might be positive only in the ideal. As this respondent went on to write, 'Caste and sub-caste if known in the private company will become a barrier to work place advancement and career prospects in the company'.

Caste (SC Reservations) Stops at the IT Merit Gate

In their attempts to clarify merit valorization in Indian IT, some,[21] similar to the key informants, explicitly drew *boundaries* around the IT sector to *streamline* and distinguish it from non-IT workplaces. Even as they drew these boundaries, it became clear that to them the term caste meant government SC/ST reservations and associated questionable merit. Some differentiated the IT sector from the government sector in Indian society where caste reservations are in effect. Others separated the IT sector from rural, less cosmopolitan, segments in India.

Depending on the contrast reference points, IT professionals used different, even if related caste metrics. When contrasts were drawn between the IT sector and the government sector and political institutions (n = 25), they used caste reservations as the distinguishing metric. But, when the comparison points were with rural or educated segments, or even their personal life (n = 26), general casteism seemed to be the guiding principle.

The Government Sector vs. IT

Responding to the caste relevance in IT statement were these sample comments that separated the 'caste-no-barrier IT from the government

---

[21] This group included 51 of the 258 respondents who held that caste was not a relevant factor in Indian IT.

sector'. 'These are not government jobs where such barriers to growth and recruitment could be having a good playground. IT is the reflection of the modern world in Indian society'. To another, 'Anyone who is educated and qualified can get into and start working in the area of his/her choice. India, like many other great countries, is coming out of this social divide. Only when it comes to Government jobs, it prefers few caste and tribes. However, this doesn't apply to other places as qualification is the only criteria here. Presently, there is a lot of debate going on to consider economy status of people instead of caste or community for such preferences'.

Others spoke to the 'private nature of the IT industry' (vis-à-vis the public government sector) as a reason for IT not being under the purview of the constitutionally mandated SC reservation policies: IT companies are 'fully owned by private ltd, Pvt (private) company need only skilled person to help company'. 'In non-IT field, reservation helps lower caste to get a preference. In IT, it is not so. All are equal' and that 'for any non-government Organization, irrespective of IT or Non-IT, caste & community is no longer a barrier'. In short, 'In private organizations there is no caste barrier … those who have skills … he/she will succeed'.

Speaking directly to the 'caste-based quotas' in the government sector were some IT professionals who commented: 'Only in govt jobs we have that nasty history of taking people based on caste which I completely oppose. In IT no one would be appointed based on caste. Resume of an IT professional never speaks about his caste'. Another elaborated, 'In Govt sector, caste or community counts since there is reservation etc. But for IT profession only the technical capability matters'. One IT professional used the example of Infosys (a global IT services company) to make the caste-no-bar in IT case: 'Unlike Government sectors caste doesn't matter in IT, and no reservations as well. Infosys CEO [former] Narayanamurthy refused to reserve jobs for Karnataka natives. This proves that IT have no Communities, No Caste, No religion'.

Explaining why caste should not matter in privately owned IT sector, was another IT professional who wrote, 'SC/ST students get first preference in all sectors. And so it is right' that IT does not consider caste.

In summary, to respondents who contrasted the IT sector with the government sectors, caste explicitly meant *SC reservations-earmarked merit*. The constitutionally mandated reservation quotas for SCs are mandatory in government jobs but not in non-government or the private sector where Indian IT is situated. In contrasting government jobs with the privately owned IT sector, they placed IT squarely outside the occupational boundaries of constitutionally mandated SC reservation quotas. In their thinking, caste reservations diluted merit standards; hence, the merit standards and culture in IT precluded SC caste-based reservations. In fact, 'everything is open to everyone in IT but not elsewhere; Conducting such survey is waste of time and makes no sense', or 'Yes, caste or community is no longer a barrier to work in the IT field. There are some fields where people really consider caste or community for working but not in IT field'.

Other Social Vectors vs. Indian IT

Some survey respondents, like the key informants, differentiated the caste-no-barrier Indian IT sector from other vectors in the Indian social hierarchy. Separating the IT sector from political institutions, less educated segments, and rural communities they, once again, underscored the absence of SC reservation theme in their IT caste-no-bar discourse. 'Caste/community is never a barrier in IT sector. It might be a barrier in politics[22] :-)' and that 'It is not known in large companies'. While conceding that 'Caste/community divisions can be there in the rural areas, but not in the technology/company levels'. Explaining a caste neutral IT stance was another IT professional who spoke to broader regional differences. 'In fact people like me who are brought up in big city, don't even understand them. Also North India person has no idea and is least bothered about a caste system in south and vice-a-versa. I don't think it's a barrier'.

Multiple interlocking boundaries were drawn by some respondents to separate Indian IT from non-IT sectors: 'At least in the IT sector, it's just your work that speaks. Get promoted on performance not caste. I am Kayastha.[23] BTW, I agree that caste still needs to be eliminated from rural and uneducated areas, but doesn't exist in IT sector'. Or 'I do not think caste has any influence on this. May be this factor has

[22] Underlines added to denote examples.

[23] Kayasthas are considered to be members of the literate scribe caste and have traditionally acted as keepers of records and public accounts, writers, and administrators of the state. They are considered a 'mixed' caste, having been recruited from Brahman-Sudra (lower caste) and sometimes Kshatriya as well (Kaminsky and Long 2011: 403–4).

some influence in India but not anywhere else, as in IT'. This respondent added, 'Even though my community doesn't recognize caste, we claim were from upper caste'. Combining the boundary caste limits with a cultural deficit argument was another who wrote: 'I feel that caste/community may not be a barrier in the long run if the person is trustworthy and satisfies other requirements. But, caste and community is still a barrier in many sections of society in India but not so in the reputed and professional companies' [a self-identified 'zoroastrain [Parsi] married to a gujarati hindu'].

Summary Reflections from the 'It is Merit, Not Caste' Camp

For one, it was when the IT professionals explained their 'caste was not a barrier in Indian IT' stance that it became clear that they *equated 'caste' with 'earmarked reservations'* for SC groups. That is, when these professionals said that caste was not a barrier in Indian IT, they meant that there were no job reservations or quotas for SCs in IT. To them the government sector, be it in education or employment, diluted merit when they used reservation policies. Consequently, reservations were antithetical to the IT merit culture. It is this ostensible contradiction between a merit ideology and caste-based reservations, which renders caste (read SC status) to be unacceptable in IT. In fact, caste reservation, they held, was more a liability than an asset in the globalized and dynamic nature of work in Indian IT. And because the Indian IT sector does not have to, in principle and in practice, follow the government's reservation laws (that is, hire and promote people based on reservation quotas), IT was deemed to be a caste neutral environment. It was interesting that *hidden symbolic caste privileges* of dominant communities were seldom heard in this caste-no-bar discourse. Furthermore, if there was a *small Dalit (SC) footprint* in Indian IT, they said, it was the result of their IT merit deficits and not caste discrimination.

In short, those from the 'upper or forward caste' backgrounds were typically the ones to 'vociferously claim that caste did not matter' anymore in IT. On the other hand, 'many SCs or Dalits seemed more aware' of their caste status and were willing to name their caste. Another boundary lay in the 'respondents' tenure in IT companies': those who were fairly new or young in the workplace proclaimed that they got the job because of their pure merit and were not aware of caste dynamics at work. It was the more senior employees who had more realistic insights into the workings of caste dynamics even when the company claimed it was caste neutral.

The Caste Camp Counter: Caste Reproduction in IT

Unlike the Merit Camp that valorized merit in Indian IT, were those (36 per cent or 146/404) who denied the veracity of the caste-is-not a barrier statement in Q21. This group equated the term 'caste' to the *broader casteism*, and *not to caste reservations*. They countered the caste neutral merit culture by either categorically affirming the presence of caste hierarchies in Indian IT (62 per cent out of 146) or pointing out cracks in the IT no-caste firewall (25 per cent out of 146), or acknowledging the history of caste (13 per cent out of 146). Caste inequalities that are reproduced in Indian IT through *caste filtering* and *discrimination* were the most common reasons offered in support of their caste tinged opinions about Indian IT. Those who provided detailed explanations for *Caste Inequality* touched on *embedded cultural and social capital deficits* for SCs lagging behind in education based merit.

Cracks in the Indian IT Merit Firewall

That the merit-culture firewall against caste in Indian IT is not as solid or stable were reflected in phrases that denied the overwhelming negations of caste in the Merit Camp. Sample responses against the caste-not-a-barrier-in-IT statement were typical of respondents who did not fully endorse the 'caste-no-bar' portrayal of Indian IT. They said, 'To some extent yes' [Hindu from south India]; or 'May be', or 'To some extent yes, but now a days people don't consider caste as prime important thing to get a job', or 'I agree most of the time' [self-identified upper class].

'But, Caste is Alive in Indian IT', said most rank-and-file IT professionals in the Caste Camp. They said so in simple, declarative statements while others provided more detailed, nuanced responses. Some made their declarative negations without any further elaborations. 'No', or 'I don't think so', or 'Sorry, it is not so' were typical. Others said: 'Caste/community, linguistic backgrounds still play an important role in IT sector in India' or 'Caste is still a barrier in the IT industry'.

Those who offered details about their case that caste is relevant in Indian IT (to Q21), cited *caste isomorphic practices* (61 per cent of 56) in hiring, if not in promotion, opportunities in Indian IT. The statement about caste not being a barrier cannot be true, they professed, because casteism, deeply rooted in Indian social fabric, has seeped into Indian IT.

A few sample narratives: 'Caste is everywhere and in every sector in India', proclaimed a Dalit Christian. 'In India caste factors are deeply rooted in humans' noted a scheduled caste, 'Mahar' community member. 'In India caste factors are deeply rooted in humans, some exceptional are always everywhere' [SC]. A few others denounced the permanence of casteism and noted, 'That's INDIA- Cannot eliminate caste/community factor' [a Roman Catholic IT professional]. Another alleged, 'people from high caste are more employed'.

With 'moral outrage' others noted: 'There is caste in the IT sector in India coz the caste system is backbone, it shows the more evil face of real India and its dirty culture which some Indians carry wherever they go. Cry foul about Racism in the world and keep silent about the existence of caste system which is bigger devil here than Racism. I proudly say that I hail from India and true Indian of this soil belonging to Minority Community of Buddhist the path of enlightenment which has given India its international name and fame'. Another noted, 'still there are Brahmin ... who believe in the caste system. We are not lower in the society. We also have the same rights and beliefs as higher caste ... have'. Another wrote, 'India has been providing reservations to social/economical backward classes since the last 60 years and so is USA where they have reservations/quotas for Minority owned business/Woman owned/Veteran owned/Asian American owned/Hispanic owned and a bunch of other categories which is a living testimony that discrimination exists; the state has to impose certain laws to provide justice. So the fact is the barrier exists', and ' ... even the so called "*very educated*" and matured people still believes in casteism'.

Caste Filtering and Pattern Recognitions in Indian IT

The Caste Camp saw 'caste filtering' to be one prime mechanism through which societal caste hierarchies are reproduced in the IT work sector. Hiring and promotion tools like '*pattern recognition*' (Baron 2006), while seemingly caste-neutral, reproduce casteism in Indian IT, in much the same way that that Kanter (1977a) spoke about the '*homosocial male reproduction of management*'. The workings of caste filtering were illustrated in the sampling of answers presented below.

At the initial hiring stages in Indian IT, 'Most of the time it's not. But you know, the roots can never be uprooted that easily. There will definitely be some effect, or I should say a small "inclination towards the same caste/clan" will be always present and that will never disappear from India'. Another concurred that while caste discrimination is not prominent, 'preferences r shown depending on the manager or head" and "Caste plays an important role in getting jobs' [OBC].

Speaking to the *hidden, symbolic* nature of caste filtering in hiring into Indian IT were these respondents. Even at the initial interview stages, said one, 'there are some people who look and have soft corner into caste/community while at the part of Interview'. And once inside the company, experience taught them that caste preferences and discrimination 'still exists in India. As it is a private sector ... This won't come out'. A variation on this theme was 'Plainly you can say yes but when you actually start working you will feel that you are getting low treatment than others' [self-identified Buddhist].

Lack of *appropriate employment references*[24] was a concrete example of caste tinged pattern recognition dynamics that excluded SCs from being hired. Hiring is 'based on reference. The caste Brahmins refer their relatives and friends, while the low caste have no reference in the IT sector. So IT companies are full of high caste brahmins'. And that 'not even 1% of IT companies has low caste SC/ST though they have passed Engineering and have qualifying marks ... Reason is lack of reference in the org which other caste have who pull them in to org. I am from low caste and have experienced the same. Low caste no matter if passed with distinction, is incompetent whereas an upper caste is born intelligent'.

Another organizational layer where caste filtering operates is in promotions to the management ranks. *Caste-based preferences in promotions* have become a glass ceiling hurdle for SCs and OBCs in Indian IT. A few sample comments about the management ceiling encountered by SCs and OBCs: 'Caste/community is an important unofficial factor in almost every employment sector. Your promotions, increments, etc strongly depend on your "caste as top post holders" are mostly from higher castes' [an OBC

[24] References are resources available within one's networks (Lin 1999), be they through personal/familial (Granovetter's 1973 strong, bonding ties) or through community ties (weak, bridging ties) are critical for success in the educational and labour market.

member]. Another wrote, 'Unlike other industries, caste/community barrier is less in IT since it is knowledge based. But I still feel there is discrimination towards oppressed castes on promotions and incentives' [said a member of a backward class called Dekhani Muslim, South Indian Urdu Speaking Muslim]. Or 'Yes, till you reach Management level there is no caste or community. But for higher posts like AVP, VP, COO, CEO; the caste factor still plays the significant role. But IT's based on who owns the company'; or ' ... these things come into picture with vengeance for higher level in management. Max till Tech lead it will not be a problem :) ...'

Others offered *caste pattern recognition* for possible caste reproduction in Indian IT. Alluding to the founder effect in caste transference into Indian IT management, was one respondent who said, '100% of IT companies are owned by upper caste, so working under them has no barriers. Until we ask for promotions and protest against underpay, then we are stopped. Even in multinational companies, all higher positions will be to upper caste, mostly Brahmins, then Marvadis, and then Kshatriyas; watchman and cleaning posts go to shudras'. Even in MNCs, with offshoring presence in India, 'many MNCs recruitment is based on caste. Many MNCs takes upper caste people since the top management is upper class' [said a BC member]. Speaking to *hidden social and cultural privilege* of the FCs in the IT workplace was the respondent who wrote, ' ... most of entrants are from given upper castes and show sort of uniformity among them. But odd caste groups attract derision and unwillingness and sometimes social discrimination' said a respondent who identified self as a 'so-called scheduled caste'.

Caste by another Name in Indian IT was another narrative that alluded to the new ways dominant caste preferences infiltrate into and perpetuate caste/class inequalities in Indian IT. These professionals, like their key industry informant counterparts, held that caste hierarchies and associated discrimination are alive and well in Indian IT. Some sub-tropes with examples of *caste being replaced by Other Social Vectors* were comments like: 'I haven't come across any caste issues. But have seen regional barriers cropping up' [wrote a Catholic Anglo Indian OBC]. Caste 'is no longer a barrier, but there is a tendency to select people who are from the same region / speak same language though; Yes, it is no longer a barrier, but I feel still linguistic bias is there'. Expanding on this theme was this respondent: 'That's true it is not the barrier now. But I feel odd when I am not able to discuss the issue properly because people around me are speaking

Telugu which I do not know. Many times other person is not able to explain the issue, reason & solution because they cannot communicate properly in my language Hindi or English. Some people who are not open minded they pass the comments in their mother tongue- Telugu as they know she cannot understand this & make the fun of this. But all are not same—its totally depend in which environment you are working. People should become open minded & management should make the rules so every person will feel comfortable while working over there'.

A few other variations in the Caste-Is-a Barrier narrative went as follows: A tenth of IT professionals who disagreed with the caste-not-a barrier statement acknowledged that *casteism is historical fact*, even if might no longer pose a barrier in IT (34 per cent of 56). A small group, while recognizing the extant caste barrier in Indian IT, expressed moral dissonance with the prevailing caste dynamics. 'Yes, there should not be a barrier of cast/community to person who would like to work in IT' because 'India is a country free from any type of discrimination against humans' and therefore 'there should not be any difference in caste/community. Everyone should be treated equally'. And 'It is still visible in some areas but that cannot be considered as a wholesome view' and hoped that casteism' ... it SHOULD NOT and it WILL not ...'

Small SC Footprint in Indian IT[25]

Irrespective of whether they thought that the IT environment was caste neutral in policy or caste imbued in reality, there was consensus on the IT ground that the *Dalit footprint in Indian IT was small*. However, they 'disagreed in their reasoning for the small Dalit presence' and disagreements aligned on either side of the Merit-Caste debate. Distinctions between caste-neutral policies and caste-neutral outcomes emerged in comments that acknowledged a small Dalit footprint in Indian IT. In the Merit Camp, it was the *merit deficit* that was responsible for the small SC footprint in Indian IT. Their argument went as follows: Caste is not a barrier in Indian IT and if there are not too many Dalits in IT jobs it is because they do not meet the IT merit criteria. On the other hand,

---

[25] This and later sections drew on national data and on responses to questions Q22–Q24 that asked about the reasons for the small or large SC footprint in Indian IT.

the Caste Camp attributed the limited presence of Dalits in Indian IT to *casteism, caste-based discrimination*, and *communal pattern recognition* bias in IT hiring, promotions, and in access to quality educational opportunities. In other words, the small Dalit IT footprint in Indian IT and even the alleged SC merit deficit was attributed to their limited caste privileges.

National Evidence on *Dalit Deficit*

What clues do the available national data offer about the potential for Dalit deficit? As seen in the evidence presented below, Dalits and OBCs are relatively disadvantaged compared to the forward castes or FCs, despite over a half century of government-sponsored programs for SC and OBC communities.

Caste Disparities in Individual Educational Capital

The educational disparities presented in Table 3.1 by caste background (FC, OBC, or SC communities) are both the products and reasons for the inequalities in family wealth and standards of living. No doubt, irrespective of caste background, the average Indian in all caste groups, had barely matriculated. However, irrespective of the family member whose education (highest educational level completed) was used as a marker, caste rankings followed the expected caste hierarchy: FCs were the most educated, the SCs the least, with the OBCs falling in between.

Two examples from the Southern States[26] (Table 3.1): the highest educated adult in a FC household had finished 9.6 years of schooling. In contrast, the comparable level in SC households was only 6.3 years; OBC levels were 8.4 years. Women were less educated than men, but were much less so if they were SCs; FC women had finished 7 years of schooling, OBC women 5.7, and SC women only 3.5 years. And the household

---

[26] In keeping with the Southern Indian Information Technology focus of this research, data for the four southern states of Kerala, Tamil Nadu, Karnataka, and Andhra Pradesh were examined separately from the northern states. When relevant, comparisons with the northern Indian states were also assessed. In the four Southern States of Kerala, Tamil Nadu, Karnataka, and Andhra Pradesh a sizeable plurality (42 per cent) were OBCs. A third (34 per cent) belonged to forward castes or dominant religious groups. Only a quarter (24 per cent) were SCs and STs; they were also more likely to be rural. See more details in Table 3A.1.

Table 3.1 Socio-Economic Characteristics by Caste Status and Northern vs. Southern States, India Human Development Survey (IHDS) 2005

$\bar{X}$ (sd)[†]		Southern States*			Northern States*		
		FC and Religious Minorities (n = 22,083–21,349)	OBC (n = 27,202–26308)	SC/ST (n = 15,593–14,988)	FC and Religious Minorities (n = 60,096–58,169)	OBC (n = 45,625–44,353)	SC/ST (n = 44,994–43,647)
Individual Members	Highest educated adult Range 0–15± (HHED5ADULT¥)	9.6 (4.2)	8.4 (4.7)	6.3*** (4.9)	8.9 (5.1)	7.5 (4.8)	6.0*** (4.9)
	Highest educated Male (HHED5M) Range 0–15	8.9 (4.5)	7.7 (4.8)	5.8*** (4.9)	8.5 (5.1)	7.3 (4.8)	5.8*** (4.9)
	Highest educated Female HHED5F) Range 0–15	7.2 (4.8)	5.7 (4.9)	3.5*** (4.5)	5.9 (5.4)	3.9 (4.7)	2.9*** (4.3)

(Cont'd)

Table 3.1 (Cont'd)

$\bar{X}$ (sd)[†]	Southern States*			Northern States*		
	FC and Religious Minorities	OBC	SC/ST	FC and Religious Minorities	OBC	SC/ST
	(n = 22,083–21,349)	(n = 27,202–26308)	(n = 15,593–14,988)	(n = 60,096–58,169)	(n = 45,625–44,353)	(n = 44,994–43,647)
Education of Survey Respondent (ED5) Completed Years Range 0–15	6.1 (4.8)	5.3 (4.7)	4.0 (4.3)	5.4 (5.0)	4.2 (4.4)	3.4 (4.1)
Age of survey respondent (RO5)	29.9 (20.1)	29.9 (19.6)	27.8*** (18.9)	27.4 (19.4)	26.3 (19.3)	25.4*** (18.7)

Source: Author.

* Southern States = Karnataka, Tamil Nadu, Andhra Pradesh, Kerala, Maharashtra, and Goa; Northern States = remaining states.

† $\bar{X}$(SD): Mean and (standard deviation).

‡ Education values: 0 = none, 10 = Matriculation; 12 Higher secondary, 15 = college graduate.

¥ Names in Caps in parentheses are SPSS variable names.

*** Differences among groups, within regions (Southern and Northern) statistically significant at the *** p <= .001.

member who responded to the survey was older and more educated if they were from FC households than from OBC and SC families. Similar educational disparities along caste status lines were seen in the Northern States.

Wealth Inequalities

That the educational Dalit deficits have been endemic in Indian society are seen in the *distressed wealth and socio-cultural capital of SCs*. Whether measured by income, wealth, access to non-economic capital, or health care, SCs/STs, as recently as 2005–6, fared worse than the forward castes and OBCs. Wealth disparities also exit at the family and individual levels (see Table 3A.2). *SCs were also the least wealthy*, per both, the IHDS and NFHS surveys. Total household income in rupees (INR) of southern SC/ST households (Rs 40,800) were, on average, Rs 37,000 less than the Rs 77,435 reported by FC households; the income of OBCs fell in the middle (Rs 52,249). Lower asset levels of SC/ST households corresponded with their income levels. For example, SC/ST households in the southern Indian states had only 9.8 (out of 30) assets; the comparable asset rates of FCs were 15 (out of 30 assets) and 12.8 for OBC households. Of the three caste groups, SC/ST homes in the north were also the least wealthy.

A similar profile of caste-based wealth stratification emerged when the NFHS wealth index was used. While three quarters (74.5 per cent) of FC households in southern India were classified as rich or richer, only a little over a third (38.2 per cent) of the SC/ST households were in the upper ranges of the wealth distribution. The OBCs were middle class or higher. And while the overall caste-wealth distribution in the northern states was similar to the south, the northern OBCs and SC/STs were in the middle or lower rungs of the wealth ladder. When looking at the bottom wealth rungs, it is not surprising that the SC/ST communities, in both regions, had more households in poverty than the other two caste groups. In fact, the SC/ST poverty rates in the south were double (29 per cent) that of the FCs (17 per cent) or OBCs (15 per cent).

Caste Stratified Cultural Capital Resources

Caste-based stratification, with SC/STs at the bottom of the ladder, had the expected ramifications for lifestyles and access to cultural capital

(Table 3A.3). Two thirds (63.9 per cent) of the southern FCs had highest standards of living. In contrast, two thirds of the SCs/STs had low (31.5 per cent) or medium (34.9 per cent) living standards.

Corresponding inequalities in access to newspapers (cultural and social capital) and health care access were also evident. For example, FC respondents accessed news outlets (reading newspapers, or listened to the radio, or watched television) more frequently than SC respondents. FC Mean ($\bar{X}$) of 1.44 represented news access between less than or at least once a week; the comparable average of 1.1 for SC respondents meant they accessed news less than once a week.

The health care barriers identified ranged from getting permission to seek treatment or securing the money needed, distance to health facility, concerns that there was no female health provider, or that there was no provider, and that no drugs were available (see footnote 4 to Table 3A.3 for full list of barriers). Among the different health care barriers about which the NFHS inquired, FC respondents were more likely to report 'no' barriers to six of the eight barriers ($\bar{X} = 6.1$) than SCs ($\bar{X} = 5.1$). And when asked to rate the number of big healthcare barriers, SC respondents were twice more likely to list at least two as big barriers (FC $\bar{X} = 0.7$ versus SC $\bar{X} = 1.6$). In short, barriers to health care followed unequal caste patterns in economic and cultural resources.

The Merit Camp Take on Dalit Pure Merit Deficit

How did IT rank-and-file professionals see these *limited social capital resources translate into the Dalit Deficit?* Those in the *Merit Camp* explicitly used the Dalit Pure Merit Deficit argument to explain why they were not many Dalits in Indian IT and why caste is not a barrier in Indian IT. Starting with 'No, there are not many SCs in Indian IT' they explained their observations as: 'They do not have right opportunities and skills to enter into IT. This is very true in every profession. Caste is the bed rock for anything in India' and because 'Private sectors work on performance only' [a Roman Catholic] or 'High-tech companies mainly concerned with the skilled employees' [a 'proud' Jain], therefore the Dalits are disadvantaged in Indian IT. To others, deficits in cultural merit deficits were manifested as the Dalit Deficit in IT: 'It's just that these people are from backward communities and have little incentive to move ahead in life' [a self-identified Brahmin-upper caste]. Another used *lack of bridging network resources:*

'They do not have good references. The SC and ST members long for the government jobs and also their parents and relatives are not there in the IT jobs ... where the right skill and education and experience play the major role'.

That the 'Dalit merit deficit starts early' was acknowledged by two IT professionals. 'Dalits due to their economic condition do not have the opportunity to go to right education. This is a major factor not only in IT but in all domains. But fortunately the situation is changing'. In a similar vein, one said, 'percentage of the so called lower cast students studying IT almost negligible. In my college which is one of most reputed private college in India, I was the only student belong to SC community out of 60 students'. In short, whether explicit or implicit, these respondents did not expect to see too many Dalits in Indian IT because Dalits fall short in a market where only the qualified by the *pure merit metrics* are selected.

Others clearly pushed back on caste reproduction thesis in Indian IT; they cited 'checks and balances against caste isomorphic pressures in the hiring process'. They wrote: 'My point of view there is not such a partiality and all. High-tech companies no chance, because of campus interviews'. In a similar vein, were these two comments: 'One good thing in IT is the application does not contain any question on the caste wherein most of the other profession there would be a mandatory question on caste ... considering the formal interview panel wherein individual influences does not work' [a Multi-caste: Hindu by birth, Christian follower]. A second expounded further, 'At least in the IT sector, it's just your work that speaks ... [27] This doesn't happen anywhere, tho sometimes they may choose to go out of way to hire somebody related to them and hence belong to same caste. But this then is a connection issue not a caste issue. Also, even this happens very rarely, as a candidate has to clear multiple interviews. I know specific case in which my manager had to decline our group director's nephew as he was not qualified enough. No specific caste; get promoted on performance not caste. I am Kayastha. BTW, I agree that caste still needs to be eliminated from rural and uneducated areas, but doesn't exist in IT sector'. In short, they argued, 'caste is not a barrier

[27] This respondent complained that 'No there are not many; Again, a weird question! I didn't keep a statistical table of my colleagues' castes. Surveys like this do a disservice to the sense of community, as they force you to think on caste lines'.

in Indian IT because companies see qualified people not the caste' and 'as long as requisite skills are present anyone can do the work. Nobody considers caste to recruit in IT. I am not aware of who was a scheduled caste in my peer group through out my work. So I cannot comment on this'.

But, in the context of empirical evidence for the continued prevalence of caste inequalities in contemporary India, the debates about caste neutrality in Indian IT are far from settled. Nationally, Forward Communities continue to be privileged in education and in wealth; some would say that they have earned these privileges. In this stratified social context, the absence of caste-neutral outcome evidences from the IT sector, render questionable the merit deficits explanation for the small Dalit footprint in Indian IT. Besides, caste continues to be relevant even in the modified social hierarchy in Indian IT; the upper caste stratum, that historically was limited to Brahmins, has been broadened to incorporate the dominant regional community (say the company founder's community). But even in this revised caste system, the lowest stratum remains intact; SCs are marginalized because of their limited, whether real, and/or perceived skill levels. It is in this evidentiary context that the Caste Camp's counter arguments take on added weight.

The Caste Camp: Caste Filtered Bias and Caste Reproduction

While both the *Merit and Caste Camps* agreed that there was a Dalit Deficit in Indian IT, the Caste Camp, unlike their merit counterparts, used *discrimination, communal bias,* and *ultimately caste positionality and filtering* to illustrate *caste inequality diffusion and reproduction in Indian IT.*

Some examples of explicit *caste filtered discrimination in Indian IT*: An OBC IT professional explained the small Dalit footprint in Indian IT as, 'discrimination usually'. As to how caste filtering operates in hiring, one SC IT professional reflected: 'despite their merit and qualification, they are recognized by surnames and if openly known not given opportunity. This is a fact'. Consequently, a self-identified upper class respondent surmised, 'I still think Dalits are held back'. And even if 'Unlike other industries, caste/community barrier is less in IT since it is knowledge based, there is discrimination towards oppressed castes on promotions and incentives' said another. *Caste or communal filtering, pattern recognition, and associated bias* in hiring was clear in these comments: 'few of them choose their own caste/community people'. 'Partial world' said another. One more, 'Your promotions, increments, etc. strongly depend on your caste as top post holders are mostly from higher castes. Caste plays an important role in getting jobs too. Yes upper caste people do that'.

Explicitly attributing IT *Dalit Deficit to caste filtering in the referral/ recruitment* processes was this IT professional who attributed the low proportion of qualified SCs in Indian IT to lack of *references or networks:* ' ... Jobs are open but mainly filled by reference and guidance. Low caste don't have any reference in the org and guides to the org though they are equally qualified ... low caste suffer from stereotype that they are incompetent and Brahmins are more [competent]; non-Brahmins also influenced by brahminical ideology which does not accept low caste in main stream'. Another said, 'caste discrimination seldom happens very overtly'.

Others offered examples of *caste, communal, or regional pattern recognition and filtering in the referral and recommendation process* commonly used in IT. Speaking to *caste bias* were these respondents: 'In current recruitment, many interviews are telephonic and there is no opportunity to identify based on caste unless it is by referral. Referral recruitment is always based on biases'. Confirming the caste bias in IT hiring was this respondent: 'On recommendation basis. High Caste with recommendation; others not needed and not welcomed'.

Accusations of *communal bias* were clear in these comments: 'based on the recommendation they select people. It is a Christian Institute, so many are Christians'. Regional bias was another reason, said another; 'Partiality yes, usually people get attracted to people belong to their caste or home town'. And 'there may be a certain bias towards this in any sector, but the IT industry as a whole has more people from south India - a sector of people who have the highest literacy rate in the country and are also extremely hard working and honest' [a Zoroastrian Parsi]. Other comments, 'Yes, only their relatives and neighbours are being taken for the company'; or 'I have heard of people being hired because they speak the same language. In my case, they are from a different community' [a Catholic Anglo Indian]. And 'There are few cases like, a Tamil manager will hire only tamil IT people, but not in all the case'.

In the Caste Camp's final analyses, no matter whether the *source of the small Dalit footprint* was *caste tinged pattern recognition, caste filtering, and discrimination,* the end result was systemic casteism or communalism being reproduced in Indian IT. Alluding to the *systemic casteism* or *caste reproduction* in Indian IT were the following respondents who commented:

'Right from its inception till date this sector has been exploited by upper caste communities, and only a handful of SC professionals have been able to meager survive and I say meager survive coz all the future doors are systematically closed for scheduled caste professionals. So in no case there are many jobs offered in high-tech companies to scheduled caste, I would say it is just fooling the masses by showing handful of examples'. To another IT professional, 'There are no proper representation to these people. It is obvious as I know Indian minds are polluted with caste cultures. Why owners will offer the high post to these people Brahmins, Kshatriya, and Vaisya. I belong to Scheduled caste, community "Mahar"'. Or 'around 30-60% of the people in IT belong to Brahmin community only. But their total population is small. If people are available from their community, definitely they will go for their own caste/community. This is especially 100 % true for promotions opportunities'. And 'the management is occupied by the high caste who gives opportunity only to the high caste'. Sarcastically another wrote, 'please ask these questions to the Brahmins who have occupied the jobs in private company'.

To summarize the Caste Camp argument using a point-by-point elaboration of the workings of casteism in the IT organizations offered by one professional: '1) Omnipresent: Interview panels and HR are dominated by Upper Castes; 2) Upper Caste's superiority complex: Many Upper Castes still believe that they are a superior race and Scheduled Caste candidates cannot perform well in IT; 3) Selective discrimination: Upper Caste want Schedule Caste people to remain their slaves (3000 years of slavery and Masters cannot afford to see their slaves shining in their lives and careers). While absolutely wrong, a hiring manager will select a candidate from his own community if he has to select one from two probable candidates. That is one of the reason why Indian IT companies are dominated by micro-minority Upper Castes (around 75%). Most of the HR professionals, especially Managers belong to the Upper Castes Hindu-Brahmins. Approximately around 75% of the hiring managers belong to Upper Castes. I belong to a backward caste called Dekhani Muslim' [South Indian Urdu-Speaking-Muslim].

Does Caste Reproduction in IT Start at the Top?

While the IT professionals profiled above focused primarily on the caste background of the rank and file in Indian IT, answers to a question specifically about the caste of an IT hiring manager (Q26 only in the long form survey) offered another look at caste reproduction and casteism in the management ranks. The analyses presented below are based on the responses of IT professionals who responded to the manager's caste question (Q26) in the long form survey; nearly all 144 out of the 149 offered a response.

Like the comments about the caste identities of rank-and-file IT employees, the responses to the managers' caste question also fell on opposite sides of the *merit-caste debate*. Here too, on one side were those who *valorized merit* and spoke in 'caste neutral' terms. On the opposing side were those who identified the hiring managers' forward caste status and spoke to its implications for *reproducing casteism* in Indian IT. There was also a plurality of respondents (41 per cent of 144) among those who completed the long form survey, who wrote that they did not know the caste of hiring managers. They either did not ask or were not interested in the manager's caste. But, the rest who did comment were evenly divided between the two camps in the Merit (26 per cent of 144) vs. Caste (24 per cent) debate. The remaining few pointed to regional or religious bias in the management hierarchy.

It is Merit and Not Caste in the Management Ranks

For the most part, those on the Merit side of the divide declared that they did not care about caste, or did not believe in caste, or were unaware of the caste in the hierarchy (32 out of 38). The rest explicitly identified 'pure merit' as the foundational principle not only in the rank and file but also in the higher levels of the IT hierarchy.

Suggesting that caste was no barrier at management levels of the Indian IT organizations were these professionals who said: 'I don't think there was a dominant caste' [by a Hindu Tamil Speaking Brahmin], or 'There's no way to tell Brahmin-upper caste manager from another' [a Jain], or a Muslim who wrote, 'I have seen managers from all the castes', or that the position of 'managers are open to all castes' [Catholic respondent]; sarcastically asked an OBC professional, 'A very stupid question. You don't ask these things to the hiring manager, do you?'

Some specifically identified *merit as the qualifier for a manager's* background: 'Knowledge and experience makes a manager'; or managers are 'Those who have the knowledge and experience' [Brahmin]. Another said, 'managers are hired based upon their qualifications' [Roman Catholic] or that 'It's all about how you perform. I don't believe at all on cast for IT positions' ['I am an Indian').

But, Hiring Managers are Brahmins or Upper Caste, say the Caste Camp

In contrast to this caste neutral merit-based management portrayal were the IT professionals (n = 35) who had a clearer sense of the caste, if not community, background of hiring managers in the IT sector. Firmly pointing out to Brahmin, if not upper caste, domination of those in the hiring position in Indian IT, they strongly hinted at *diffusion of caste inequalities* in the top rungs of the hierarchies in Indian IT sector.

One upper caste IT professional, speaking about the caste of hiring managers, said, 'normally they are from the upper castes. Caste plays a major role when it comes to selecting from First among Equals'. Others (n = 13) were more exact in naming Brahmins as the dominant caste in the managerial circles. Another 22 survey respondents mentioned forward castes of managers; a few included Brahmins in the forward caste category.

In their own words: 'Hi caste people hiring managers' [no caste mentioned]; 'Managers are the people who are in high caste' or 'we have The Brahmin, Upper caste Manager'. Two combined caste and class hierarchies in management thusly: 'Managers: Mostly the upper castes and classes'; or that 'the top management is upper caste and class'; and 'based on my experience most they belong to Upper caste, elite community'. Another wrote, 'Managers vary B/W Ksahtriya and Brahmin'; both are dominant castes. Most of these IT professionals were from self-reported Dalit or OBC communities or Buddhism. However, even those who did not specifically disclose their caste identity ['Human Kind' or Indian] also noted that hiring managers were typically 'Hindu Upper caste managers'.

Speaking to the new regional and other community anchors in Indian IT (heard earlier in narratives of both the key informants and IT survey respondents), were those who identified hiring managers either by their regional (n = 7) or religious (n = 5) background. When respondents identified managers by their regional identity, they combined it with upper caste status. Two examples: A Telugu-speaking (from Andhra

Pradesh) Hindu said, the managers in his company were 'Iyer' [Brahmin from Tamil Nadu] 'or Malayali Brahmin' [from Kerala]. According to another, 'Hiring managers in Christian founded IT organization were Christians'.

Reviewing Scores on the Merit vs. Caste Blood Sport in Indian IT: And the Winner Is ...

Despite more than half century long government affirmative programs or quotas, caste inequalities continue to prevail in contemporary India. Whether measured by education, economic, or other social indicators, SCs/STs (or Dalits) are less privileged than the forward castes. To the point of this monograph, to what extent are these inequalities diffused and reproduced in the Indian IT sector? And if so, what do caste reproductions look like from the point of view of those who are involved in the IT sector? A play by play of the arguments in the 'blood sport' like Merit and Caste debates offered a window into how Indian IT has become the new caste frontier.

The Caste Neutral Merit Camp

According to the 'Merit' camp, Indian IT is unconditionally caste neutral on many fronts. As a matter of principle, the only valued currency in IT sector is *Skill based Pure Merit*, and definitely *not Caste*. Operationally, merit is caste neutral because private IT companies, unlike the government sector, are not bound by, and do not practice SCs and ST *reservations* because such practices lower IT merit standards. Rather private IT companies are guided by EEO principles, which stand in stark contrast to the government sector's caste reservation metrics in hiring and promotion.

Indian IT's caste neutral operations are justified on 'ideological' and 'functional' grounds. With ideological fervour, they vehemently paint caste reservations as antithetical to the merit principle because group benefits weaken the stringent merit standards that the IT sector applies to individuals. Besides, the 'merit' standard, delinked from caste and stripped off caste and other restricting social vectors, is a functional pre-requisite for the successful operations of IT corporations in a globalized economy. Caste neutral merit, has the added advantage of opening up the job market to all, irrespective of their particular (aka caste or communal) identities. Consequently, there is an urgency to valorize merit and to delink IT and its 'pure merit' standards from caste metrics. In the 'merit camp', if there are few Dalits (SCs) in IT that is because they do not meet the stringent individual merit criteria.

Theoretically speaking, the *valorization of merit* in the Merit Camp can be explained as follows: In a growing technological world, the *symbolic and associated material privileges* associated with the competitive IT sector have been authorized as valuable by the global IT society in which the Indian IT companies operate (Reich 1991).

Consequently, IT engineers, analysts, or knowledge professionals are highly regarded globally and in India. But, merit valorization, with its dominant-forward caste undertones, has echoes of Bourdieu's (1977, 1990) rendering of the *symbolic and hidden nature of capital resources* (be it education, income, urban location, language, culture): ownership of resources is symbolically 'natural and permanent' (even though Bourdieu would say it is misguided). In this scenario, it is but natural that those who have the resources (as in the case of forward castes) are also dominant in the IT industry. Those who do not have the 'natural' talent and skills, either do not have them (as with lower entrance scores of SCs that bar their access into higher educational institutions) or do not want it even though they are available to all who desire them (as in the case of lower castes who have become dependent on government assistance) or are not qualified enough (due to weak English fluency and other needed social skills).

The Caste Camp Says It Is Casteism

But, the Caste Camp rejected outright the caste neutral merit argument. To them, *societal casteism has been reproduced* in the IT sector *through caste filtering and pattern recognition processes in hiring and promotion*. In the original and modified representation of caste in Indian IT, SCs are at the bottom of the hierarchy. In the modified form, the top caste tier in Indian IT has been expanded to make room for other dominant castes, 'communities', into the top tier of a resource intensive IT sector. Caste communities (like Kammas or Reddys) that traditionally ranked below the Brahmins in the ritual caste hierarchy have been able to use their landed wealth to start IT companies in India and rise to the top of the caste hierarchy in Indian IT.

Even in this slightly restructured caste context in Indian IT, the Caste Camp continued to point to the *misguided roots of quality and power* (per Bourdieu, particularly 1990 and other publications) that dominant castes exert in the IT sector. They remind us that *dominant caste privileges are misguided, hidden, and obscure* (as per Bourdieu, particularly 1990 and other publications). Merit was not solely the product of individual talent but was mostly enabled by family wealth and privilege. To the Caste Camp, merit, symbolically and socially constructed, is largely a byproduct of inherited resources. Therefore, the *small Dalit footprint at all levels* of Indian IT is squarely the result of the *enduring caste inequalities.* Disparities in ownership of merit related wealth, societal prejudices result in discriminatory practices in educational preparations for and hiring into the IT sector. When merit is valorized, the Caste Camp argued, it is as if 'earned' merit is compartmentalized and separated from the very socially rooted privileges that have largely enabled the dominant caste members to study at the best schools, be hired into high paying jobs and move up the occupational ladder in a company.

On the operational level of caste reproduction, *the Caste Camp did not see Dalit deficits in Indian IT as shortfalls in merit.* Rather merit practices become discriminatory when Dalits are not hired or promoted because they lack the needed *social network connections* and *referrals* in the IT industry to gain entrance into, and to move up the career ladder, in the coveted IT sector. And when managers hail from the forward, and even if not always Brahmin, castes, *implicit caste filtering* in recognition of appropriate qualifications (Baron's *pattern recognition,* 2006) made it highly unlikely that SC merit will be judged to be equal to others, leave alone first among equals.

Under these unequal circumstances, *if no special allowances (like SC reservations in the IT sector) are made for the marginalized castes, casteism is bound to be reproduced* (in a similar vein to Kanter's homosocial reproduction of management, 1977a) in the ostensibly caste neutral Indian IT sector. Even if caste has been replaced by wealthy dominant communities, it is noteworthy that it is not the SCs who have founded IT companies. Rather the founders belong to land and wealth owning caste communities (Reddys or Kammas), who, along with Brahmins, have been elevated to forward, dominant caste status.

In short, *caste dynamics,* the Caste Camp asserted, has not disappeared. *Societal casteism has been introduced and reproduced in the IT sector* either in its *original or modified forms*. In the original representation of caste in Indian IT the Brahmins are at the top of the IT organizational hierarchy while in the modified form, the top caste tier has been expanded to make room for other dominant castes, 'communities', into the top tier of a resource intensive IT sector. In either case, SCs are at the bottom of the hierarchy.

Stalemate in the Merit vs. Caste blood sport in Indian IT

The marker used to referee the coveted Merit-Caste contest was the IT 'merit culture making project'. In what ways did the laser focus (real or putative) on 'Pure Merit', the currency of the IT workplace, make the Indian IT social space caste free or caste neutral? *If the socially constructed IT 'merit' culture, by virtue of how merit is defined and acquired, favours the FCs and other privileged segments, IT cannot be truly caste neutral.* But to many, caste neutrality simply meant that the private sector Indian IT did not reserve jobs for SC/STs as the government sectors are mandated to do. The extent to which the merit deficit explanation for the limited SC footprint in the Indian IT sector has become a rationale for keeping the IT social space free of SCs and of the contentious caste-related social dynamics in the larger society remains an open question. Comments shared by rank-and-file IT professionals and industry informants, as they reflected on caste and related issues in the new occupational sector, offered a test of whether the IT social space is *caste-neutral* or is *embedded within the existing caste hierarchies* were *contingent on the caste and organizational positionalities* of the respective camps.

At first glance, the Merit vs. Caste discourse in the Indian IT world seems to be at *a stalemate*. The Merit Camp passionately claimed to be guided by the 'ideals of meritocracy and equality'. The associations they critically drew between caste reservations and diluted, even lack of, merit rendered caste discussions to be a 'non-negotiable topic' to the Merit Camp. With equal fervour, the opposing camp rejected outright the merit views of the other. To the Caste Camp, the point of truth is that the *merit culture and norms* constructed by the privileged 'have never been equal'. Rather, the practice of merit culture is just another conduit through which caste has been diffused into Indian IT leading to 'casteism' in the sector.

As the debate in the merit-caste discourse combatively rages past each other, both camps claim victory. *The Merit Camp is a winner*, if only because there is no hard evidence to assess the outcomes of their caste-no-bar policies. But, *the exclusionary construction of the 'merit' terms in India IT (that favours the dominant castes and excludes the disadvantaged castes) all but ensures that casteism has been isomorphed and reproduced* in the self-professed caste neutral Indian IT sector. The Caste Camp wins their argument, even if indirectly, that the IT sector has become the new caste frontier.

However, the empirical quality of the 'win' on either side will remain questionable until evidentiary ways to directly test the competing con-clusions are developed and implemented. There certainly will be 'bloody' resistance from the Merit Camp to any talk of collecting and scrutinizing the empirical outcomes of their caste-neutral policies. And it is highly likely that the Caste Camp will walk away from the ring because they per-ceive the status quo to be beneficial to them. But, as an activist informant asked, will it take their global multinational parent or partner corpora-tions, or even the government, to pressure the Merit Camp back to the IT mat?

From a business perspective, a continued stalemate will be less than productive, to say the least. There is growing recognition in the global business sector that diverse workforces are not merely strategic business imperatives but also their civic and social responsibilities. A diverse and inclusive workforce offers companies access to a wider talent pool and associated innovative ideas that can sharpen a company's competitive advantage and sustain excellence (Cox 1993; Ely and Thomas 2001). Positive diversity climate in an organization is also linked to greater employee satisfaction, intent to stay at the company, and limiting employee turnover in a rapidly changing IT employment environment (Goyal and Shrivastava 2012–13). Besides, irrespective of the functional or principled reasons that Indian IT companies have for not considering employee caste background, if the primary evidence for caste neutrality is not available (because companies do not ascertain caste identity), claims of caste irrelevance or caste neutrality will remain only assertions that cannot be empirically evaluated, settled, or become the basis for produc-tive transformations within businesses.

The contours of some proactive policy solutions will be further explored in Chapter 6. For a sector that prides itself on being at the forefront of the technological revolution, being proactive about evidence-based initiatives that strategically leverage the business values of caste diversity and inclusiveness should be appealing. A good first start will be shining sunlight on the caste, and other diversity and compositions of IT companies. But, if IT companies are to be coaxed into reviewing their personnel files, there will have to be a government endorsed moratorium on legal challenges to companies that show good faith attempts to engage in evaluating and revamping their exclusionary practices, if that is deemed to be the case. Having evidence on the socio-demographic (caste, religion, and gender) composition of their IT workforce, could become an asset in burnishing their claims to be an EEO and caste neutral work environment. Companies that fall short of their EEO ideals can use the extant evidence for an honest assessment, and re-crafting, of their hiring policies. Some unintended positive benefits might be that, in the long run, evidence of such transformations might even reduce legal allegations of caste discrimination and become an integral component in business productivity improvement strategies.

Appendix 3A.1: Demographic Profiles: FCs, OBCs, and SC/STs

In the four southern states[28] surveyed in the 2005 IHDS (Table 3A.1), the caste distributions were as follows: Of the 64,904 respondents from the southern states, a sizeable plurality (42 per cent) were OBCs. A third (34 per cent) belonged to the forward castes or dominant religious minority groups not classified as OBCs. Scheduled Castes and Scheduled Tribes represented a quarter (24 per cent). In the FC/religious groups, high-caste non-Brahmins (49 per cent) predominated, followed by non-OBC Muslims. Three quarters (76.6 per cent) of the SC/ST grouping was SCs. In contrast, there were more FC respondents (39.8 per cent) in the northern Indian states than OBCs (30.3 per cent) or SC/STs (29.9 per cent). And the forward caste grouping in northern India had more Brahmins (17.9 per cent) than in the southern states (6 per cent). Also, there were more SCs than STs in both regions; counts of southern SCs were 76.6 per cent and northern SCs 69.5 per cent.

[28] In keeping with the southern Indian Information Technology focus of this research, data for the four southern states of Kerala, Tamil Nadu, Karnataka, and Andhra Pradesh were disaggregated by caste status. When relevant, comparisons with the northern Indian states were also assessed.

Appendix: Table 3A.1 Demographic Characteristics (Northern vs. Southern) by Caste Status, India Human Development Survey (IHDS) 2005*

	Southern States† (n = 64,904)			Northern States† (n = 150,850)		
	FC and Religious Minorities	OBC	SC/ST	FC and Religious Minorities	OBC	SC/ST
Caste (GROUPS 8)	34.0%	41.9	24.0	39.8%	30.3	29.9
	(n = 22,083)	(n = 27,222)	(n = 15,599)	(n = 60,096)	(n = 45,676)	(n = 45,076)
1 = Brahmin	6.0%	—	—	17.9%	—	—
2 = High caste	49.3	—	—	41.0	—	—
3 = OBC	—	100.0%	—	—	100.0%	—
4 = Dalit	—	—	76.6%	—	—	69.5%
5 = Adivasi	—	—	23.4	34.5	—	30.5
6 = Muslim	31.3	—	—	5.7	—	—
7 = Sikh, Jain	1.1	—	—	12.2	—	—
8 = Christian	12.2	—	—	—	—	—
2001 Census Village/town (URBAN)±						
0 = Rural	54.9%	65.1%	71.9%	56.0%	73.7%	77.7%
1 = Urban	45.1	34.9	28.1	44.0	26.3	22.3
Number of persons in household (NPERSONS) (n range)	(59283–)(59117)	(26410–(26347)	(14512–(14504)	(57909–(57822)	(59608–(59552)	(69181–(69181)
Mean ($\bar{X}$)	5.9	5.6	5.8***	6.6	6.9	6.4***
(SD)¥	(2.8)	(2.9)	(2.9)	(3.2)	(3.5)	(2.8)

(Contd)

Appendix: Table 3A.1 (*Cont'd*)

		Southern States† (n = 64,904)			Northern States† (n = 150,850)		
		FC and Religious Minorities	OBC	SC/ST	FC and Religious Minorities	OBC	SC/ST
Number of adults 22+ (NADULTS)	Mean ($\bar{X}$)	3.3	3.3	3.0 ***	3.4	3.4	3.0 ***
	(SD)	(1.6)	(1.8)	(1.5)	(1.8)	(1.8)	(1.5)
Number of children (0–14) (NCHILDREN	Mean ($\bar{X}$)	1.8	1.6	1.9 ***	2.3	2.6	2.4 ***
	(SD)	(1.6)	(1.5)	(1.7)	(1.9)	(2.1)	(1.8)
Adult–Child Ratio††	Mean ($\bar{X}$)	1.8	1.9	1.6 ***	1.6	1.5	1.4 ***
	(SD)	(1.2)	(1.2)	(1.0)	(1.2)	(1.1)	(1.0)

Source: Author.

* Except when otherwise noted, data are from 2005 IHDS.

† Southern States = Karnataka, Tamil Nadu, Andhra Pradesh, Kerala, Maharashtra, and Goa; Northern States = remaining states.

± Names in Caps in parentheses are variable names.

¥ sd = standard deviation.

†† Adult to Child Ratio = NADULTS 22+/NCHILDREN 0–14.

*** Differences among groups, within the two regions (Southern and Northern) statistically significant at the *** p <= .001.

Appendix: Table 3A.2 Household Wealth by Caste Status and Northern vs. Southern States, India Human Development Survey (IHDS) 2005 and National Family Health Survey (NFHS–3) 2005–06*

	Southern States†			Northern States†		
	FC and Religious Minorities	OBC	SC/ST	FC and Religious Minorities	OBC	SC/ST
	(n = 22,083–21,349)	(n = 27,202–26,308)	(n = 15,593–14,988)	(n = 60,096–58,169)	(n = 45,625–44,353)	(n = 44,994–43,647)
Mean $\bar{X}$ (SD)‡: Total household income in INR (Rs): (INCOME)¥	77,435 (115,439)	53,249 (73,363)	40,800*** (45,448)	78,503 (127,048)	52,009 (65,936)	43,978*** (73,134)
Mean $\bar{X}$ (SD): Assets on a range 0–30 (HHASSETS)††	15.2*** (5.4)	12.8 (5.4)	9.8*** (5.2)	14.6 (6.3)	11.3 (5.8)	9.8*** (5.7)
Wealth Index** (V190–NFHS-3):	(n = 18,361)	(n = 26,410)	(n = 14,512)	(n = 57,909–56,812)	(n = 59,608–58,599)	(n = 69,181–67,410)
1 = Poorest	3.2%	6.7%	15.8%***	8.4%	20.2%	26.4%***
2 = Poorer	7.4	14.2	20.3	12.5	22.2	22.0
3 = Middle	15.0	23.8	25.7	18.0	21.4	20.7
4 = Richer	30.4	28.9	23.0	23.2	20.8	18.4
5 = Richest	44.1	26.5	15.2	37.9	15.3	12.5

(Cont'd)

Appendix: Table 3A.2 (*Cont'd*)

	Southern States[†]			Northern States[†]		
	FC and Religious Minorities	OBC	SC/ST	FC and Religious Minorities	OBC	SC/ST
Percent Below poverty line (POOR):	0.17	0.15	**0.29**[***]	0.16	0.26	**0.36**[***]
	(0.37)	(0.36)	(0.46)	(0.37)	(0.44)	(0.48)

Source: Author.

* When not specifically noted, data are from IHDS.

[†] Southern States = Karnataka, Tamil Nadu, Andhra Pradesh, Kerala, Maharashtra, and Goa; Northern States = remaining states.

± $\bar{X}$(SD): Mean and standard deviation.

¥ Names in Caps in parentheses are SPSS variable names.

[††] HHASSETS: Number of household goods & housing owned with a minimum and maximum range was 0–30; some examples were: Cycle/bicycle, Sewing machine, Generator set, Mixer/grinder, Motor cycle, B/W TV, Colour TV, Air cooler, Clock/watch, Electric fan, Chair/table, Cot, Telephone, Cell phone, Refrigerator, Pressure cooker, Car, Air Conditioner, Washing machine, Computer, Credit card, 2 sets of clothes, Footwear.

** Wealth Index (Range 0–33) constructed by NFHS-3 combining information on 33 household assets and housing characteristics such as ownership of consumer items, type of dwelling, source of water, and availability of electricity into a single wealth index. The household population is divided into 5 quintiles (equal groups of 20 per cent each) on the wealth index at the national level from 1 (lowest, poorest) to 5 (highest, wealthiest).

*** Differences among groups, within regions (Southern and Northern) statistically significant at the *** $p <= .001$.

Appendix: Table 3A.3 Economic and Cultural Capital by Caste Status and Northern vs. Southern States, National Family Health Survey (2005–06, NFHS–3)

% and X̄ (SD)[†]	Southern States[*]			Northern States[*]		
	FC and Religious Minorities	OBC	SC/ST	FC and Religious Minorities	OBC	SC/ST
	(n = 17,918)	(n = 26,006)	(n = 14,250)	(n = 56,812)	(n = 58,599)	(n = 67,410)
Standard of Living Index (SSLI)[±]:						
1 = Low	7.9%	15.3%	31.5%[***]	13.6%	24.0%	33.7%[***]
2 = Medium	25.2	33.3	34.9	25.9	37.4	37.1
3 = High	63.9	48.7	30.8	57.6	35.2	26.8
7 = Not dejure resident	3.0	2.8	2.8	3.0	3.5	2.4
Average frequency of access to Media Outlets[¥]	**1.44**	1.32	**1.1**[***]	**1.2**	0.69	**0.77**[***]
	(.84)	(.82)	(.83)	(0.86)	(0.74)	(.75)
# of no barriers to health care (Range 0–8)[††]	**6.1**	5.5	**5.1**[***]	**5.3**	4.3	**4.0**[***]
	(2.4)	(2.6)	(2.7)	(2.6)	(2.7)	(2.6)
# of big or small barriers to health care (Range 0–8)[**]	**1.8**	2.5	**2.9**[***]	**2.7**	3.7	**4.0**[***]
	(2.3)	(2.6)	(2.7)	(2.6)	(2.7)	(2.6)
# of big barriers to health care (Range 0–8)[±±]	**0.7**	1.2	**1.6**[***]	**1.1**	1.6	**1.9**[***]
	(1.6)	(2.0)	(2.3)	(1.8)	(2.1)	(2.2)

(*Cont'd*)

Appendix: Table 3A.3   (Cont'd)

Source: Author.

* Southern states = Karnataka, Tamil Nadu, Andhra Pradesh, Kerala, Maharashtra, and Goa; Northern states = remaining states.

† $\bar{X}$ (SD): Mean and standard deviation.

‡ SSLI: constructed by NFHS-3.

¥ Average Frequency of access to Media Outlets: Reading newspaper or magazine (V157) + listening to radio (V158) + watching television (V159)/3; Frequency: 0 = Not at all, 1 = LT once a week, 2 = At least once a week, and 3 = Almost every day.

†† Count of number of no (0) barriers to health care access for respondent, such as getting permission to go (V467B), getting money needed for treatment (V467C), distance to health facility (V467D), having to take transport (V467E), not wanting to go alone (V467F), concern no female health provider (V467G), concern no provider (V467H), and concern no drugs available (V467I).

** Count of number of big (1) or small (2) barriers to health care access.

‡‡ Count of big (1) barriers to health care access.

*** Differences among groups, within regions (Southern and Northern) statistically significant at the *** $p <= .001$.

The IHDS surveyed households, were overall from rural areas (64 per cent). But, the likelihood of rural living was highest for the SCs/STs (71.9 per cent in the South and 77.7 per cent in the North). FCs, on the other hand, were more likely to live in urban locations (Southern 45 per cent and Northern 44 per cent) than in rural areas.

As for household composition, SC/ST households in the South were slightly smaller, both in terms number of persons in the household and adults over 22 years old. But, SC/ST households had more children aged 0–14 (1.9) than FC (1.8) and OBC (1.6) homes. While there were approximately two adults to a child (aged 0–14) across all three caste groups, the ratios were slightly smaller for the SC/STs (1.6) than in the FC (1.8) or OBC (1.9) households. Similar patterns applied to the northern states.

4   Information Technology Education

Prelude to the Caste-Merit 'Blood Sport' and Caste Reproduction

The seeds of the Merit-Caste debate in the merit IT culture making project, the conduit for caste diffusion into IT (detailed in Chapters 2 and 3), are sown in the rink of the technical education system. This is where IT professionals start crafting their 'pure merit' skills in preparation for lucrative careers in IT. As the CEO of a specialty organization with ties in the local IT sector, noted, 'All want to be in IT, pays better; they seek technical education.'

Three key industry informants who are CEOs of their respective companies outlined the different combinations of must-have credentials, both of the pure and soft kind, to be hired in IT companies.[1] In their 'pure' merit

---

[1] The typical education system is referred to as 'the ten + two + three' system. The first ten years of education are theoretically obligatory, followed by two years of secondary schooling and three years of bachelor's degree.

construction, the basic hiring filter for R&D positions in Information Technology is a BTech or BE[2] degree. More important are additional skills sets in particular software (ERP systems like Oracle, SAP, BaaN) or hardware. Employees acquire these skills through their formal BTech, other formal training, or in training institutes. A diploma in engineering or a polytechnic certificate or infrastructure certificate (10+2 or 10+3) is also typical for entry-level positions. A BTech or BE with MCA (masters in computer applications) or programming languages (like C++, Java, Java Script, PHP, SQL) is better for moving up the management ladder. After this credential starting point, the job interview process becomes the next filter through which companies further differentiate using 'soft skills' like communication style, English fluency, and grooming potential. Ironically, as noted in Chapter 3, the soft skills requirement in hiring and promotion open up loopholes in the streamlined merit construction through which caste/class considerations are filtered into the workings of the IT work habitat.

But, competence and right skill sets, the mantra in the Information Technology social habitus, are initially learnt in institutions of technical higher education. *Streamlined*[3] educational credentials, be they in the form of degrees, diplomas, or certificates, are a simple but favoured administratively robust tool used by IT companies to appropriately differentiate competence, eligibility, merit worthiness, and qualification to enter the coveted IT work arena. However, the *symbolic nature of merit education*, be it the pure or holistic kind, and the social-cultural structures in which merit is embedded, are 'hidden' and 'seldom acknowledged'. It is this hidden caste/class nature of pure merit education that becomes an 'early conduit for caste norms and practices' to enter into Indian IT. In addition to ratifying 'pure merit' credentials, technical educational institutions open up job *networks* that are critical for success in the IT labour market. These credentials and networks, by creating a framework for successful *pattern recognition* by alum in the IT labour market, make further room for *caste-class social reproduction in Indian IT*.

[2] BE = bachelor's degree in engineering.
[3] Theoretical concepts drawn from Radhakrishnan's cultural streamlining (2011); Lin's (1999) network resources and building weak (Granovetter's 1973) and bridging ties (Fernandez and Nichols 2006); Baron (2006); Bourdieu (1990); and Kanter (1977a, 1977b).

In an IT credential frenzied environment, it is not surprising that the number of institutions in the higher education rink, particularly those that offer technical degrees, has soared.[4] During the first decade of the twenty-first century, India's higher education system was one of the largest in the world; there were 378 universities, more than 18, 000 colleges, 14 million students, and about half a million educators. The 11th Five-Year Plan of India, 2007–2012, dubbed the 'education plan' had the goal of turning India into a knowledge society. Not surprisingly, the growth has been concentrated in the technical and professional fields with potentially lucrative credentials. For example, the number of degree level technical engineering institutions in India rose from a mere 50 in 1950 to 337 in 1990 and then grew dramatically to 3,384 in 2013–14. And this growth has been primarily in southern (AP, TN, Pondicherry) and South-West states (Karnataka and Kerala); in 2007, of the 1,668 institutions, 593 were in the southern and 234 in SW states.[5] In addition to the traditional university campuses, a popular new institutional option has been that of distance education, offered through the state-run Open University system; Indira Gandhi National Open University or IGNOU is the lead university in this sector. The insatiable hunger for credentialing education is reflected in enrolment growth trends. Enrollment in Engineering Programs grew 54 per cent between 2001 and 2007, even though India's GRE (gross enrollment ratio) of 11 per cent is one of the lowest in the world[6] and undergraduate enrollment in general degrees like BA, BSc, or BCom has stayed flat. By the middle of the 2001–10 decade, a third of total enrollment was in government sponsored open universities.

Aside from the government sector educational options, there has been unprecedented growth in the *for-profit private* sector which offers technical degrees, diplomas, and certificates. The share of private engineering

---

[4] Education trends in this section were drawn from Deshpande (2012) and UGC reports (http://www.ugc.ac.in/pdfnews/6805988_HEglance2013.pd and http://www.ugc.ac.in/oldpdf/pub/he/HEIstategies.pdf). For purely practical reasons, June 2015 was the cut-off date used for the secondary education data presented and analyzed in this research. While acknowledging changes since the cut-off date, they do not seriously alter the patterns noted in the analyses.

[5] http://www.aicte-india.org/downloads/Growth_Technical_Institutions_310514.pdf

[6] Enrollment in BE or BTech degrees rose from 418.2 to 1,777.7 in '000s.

institutions has grown from 76 per cent (out of 669) in the 1999–2000 period to 85 per cent of 1,265 institutions in 2007; during the same time period the share of student enrollment has kept pace; 77 per cent out of 17,418 enrollees to 85 per cent of 380,803 enrollees. There is general agreement in academic and policy circles that the paucity of government funding for higher education, combined with the government's liberalization policies in 1991, were the prime reasons for the growing privatization, be they for-profit and non-profit, of educational institutions.

Even with this expansion of educational options in technical higher education, the demand for seats far outstrips availability. No doubt, the popularity of 'lucrative' information technology jobs in India has made technology education the degree of choice. Sheer population growth is another factor fueling demand. The population in the age-group 15–34 years was expected to increase from 353 million in 2001 to 430 million in 2011 and then continue to increase to 464 million in 2021, before declining to 458 million only in 2026; this young population comprises 35 per cent of the urban population and 32 per cent of the rural population[7] (Jayaraman 2013). And, the more prestigious the institution, as in the state sponsored (autonomous) IITs, the greater the demand for admission.

It is the growing unmet demand for technical education coupled with the intense competition for the limited 'open seats' in coveted technical institutions that has transformed education in India into the competitive 'blood sport' it has become. To recap,[8] 'Open Seats', in government-sponsored, government-run, or government-aided educational institutions are those that are not assigned to or reserved (up to 49.5 per cent) for the historically marginalized students from the SC, ST, and OBC communities provided they secure at least the cut-off in the aggregated marks in the Class XII secondary school board examination and JEE (Joint Entrance Examination) or other exams.[9] In order to preserve the original intent of

[7] Jayaraman in the *State of the Urban Youth, India 2012*; retrieved on 29 May 2015.

[8] See Chapter 1 and Appendix 1A.1 for more details. The three reserved groups comprise more than half the country's population; SCs 16 per cent, STs 8 per cent, and OBCs about 36 per cent. The reservation quotas for SCs and STs are approximately proportional to their share of the population, but not for OBCs (27 per cent).

[9] For example there is a two-tier entrance system for admission into the IITs. In 2015, only the top 150,000 candidates (out of 14 lakhs) in the JEE Main exam

these redress policies, these seats are expected to be left vacant even when they are not filled by those for whom they are set aside. Despite being in existence for more than half a century, the constitutionally enshrined reservation system has survived multiple legal challenges.[10]

These reservation or earmark policies leave only half of the seats available to open competition in public institutions of learning. That the non-reservation castes have access to only half the pie of the coveted technical education opportunities is only part of the intense grievances of dominant caste communities. Bitter allegations (at least in a narrow test score sense) also abound that open or general seat candidates are rejected for admission only because they are displaced by 'less qualified' reserved candidates who are admitted with lower scores on entrance examinations. Begrudging awareness that the reservation social redress policies have no shelf life has further deepened the resentment. Intensifying these caste tensions in higher education are the growing costs of private sector education, which to many IT bound hopefuls is the only alternative to public sector institutions.

It is in this contentious background that the 'blood sport' of access to technical education and caste diffusion potential are located. A historical review of the Indian technical education system shed light on the deep roots of meritorious technical credentials construction. But, the more recent trends in expansion of for-profit, expensive, private technical education options have raised concerns about delinking of credentials from quality, re-crafting of the merit culture making project, and opening loopholes for caste inequalities to be transferred into the preparation for employment

---

and those who receive more than 75 per cent (70 per cent in case of ST/ST) in their class 12 exam (common merit score with a maximum 360 points) can do the second stage of the IIT JEE advanced exam. About 75,750 (50 per cent) who topped the common merit list. Corresponding top percentages for SCs is 22,500 (15 per cent), for 11,250 (7.5 per cent for STs, and 40,500 (27 per cent from OBCs. Considering that there are only less than 10,000 seats at all IITs combined, the competition is quite stiff; 140 competing for 1 seat (admission. aglasern.com). Other public colleges and universities have a similar process, even if they use a different entrance exam system. So do private institutions, except that they are not required and do not reserve seats for SCs, STs, and OBCs (IIT websites).

[10] See Appendix 1A.1 for details.

in Indian IT. Assessments provided by rank-and-file IT professionals and key industry informants were used to illustrate the credentials–quality rifts. The chapter ended with a discussion deconstructing and revealing the caste dimensions in the competitive 'Blood Sport' around 'pure merit' waged in the rink of technical education.

History of Public and Private Indian Technical Education and Construction of IT Merit

Technical and engineering education in India is nothing new. It certainly did not start with the Information Technology invasion into India in this century. Professional engineering education institutions in India were started by the British in the nineteenth century to groom civil and mechanical engineers to work on their infrastructure (dams and railroads) projects. After the country became independent in 1947, the Indian government was a pioneer, among developing countries, to take deliberate policy and institutional measures, as early as the mid-1960s, to develop an electronic production base. The government heavily invested in education and technical education to meet the need for technically qualified individuals (Joseph 2009).

Overview of Technical Institutions in India[11]

A historical review of government sponsored higher education and technical institutions in India are essential to understand the foundation on which the 'private' IT sector is built and the ensuing merit-caste blood sport is waged. The list of the who's who in the long-standing engineering institutions in India was all associated with *the central or state governments*. Under British rule, universities provided engineering degrees, most often in civil engineering. Post-independence, these institutions were transformed into prestigious engineering and technology institutions. It is the public nature of elite technical institutions that made them one primary site where the Merit-Caste blood sport is waged. The competition for education in these elite public institutions, which is relatively

[11] Information extracted from respective university websites and http://www.mhrd.gov.in/higher_education; http://www.ugc.ac.in/; http://www.aicte-india.org/.

cost-effective, is intense because of the limited availability of seats; 50 per cent are 'open seats' while the rest are 'reserved' for SC/ST and other marginalized communities.

The very first government engineering college in India, Thomason College, was established in 1847 at Roorkee, Uttar Pradesh, (predecessor of the current IIT Roorkee), to train civil engineers for the Upper Ganges Canal. The British rulers opened three additional engineering colleges by 1858 in the then three Presidencies. The Calcutta College of Civil Engineering in the Bengal Presidency, established in 1856, later became the Indian Institute of Engineering Science and Technology (IIEST, Shibpur in West Bengal). The Overseers' School at Pune in the Bombay Presidency, around 1858, became the College of Engineering, Pune (affiliated with Bombay University, Maharashtra). In the Madras Presidency, was the industrial school serving the Gun Carriage Factory (around 1858–61) which became the College of Engineering, Guindy, affiliated to Madras University. In addition, a fifth pioneering engineering college established in 1917 was the Visvesvaraya College of Engineering (VCE) under the University of Mysore, Karnataka; VCE was set up by Sir Mokshagundam Visvesvaraya, a notable Indian engineer and first Minister (Diwan) of Mysore with generous support from the Maharaja of Mysore, Krishna Wodeyar IV.

More colleges of engineering and technology in southern India followed with funding from visionary maharajas of local kingdoms. The College of Engineering, Trivandrum, Kerala, was established around 1939, under the rule of the Travancore Maharaja, Sree Chitra Balarama Varma. In Tamil Nadu the Alagappa College of Technology, funded by the philanthropist Alagappa Chettiar in 1944, was formerly affiliated with Madras University and now with Anna University. By 1956, the state of Karnataka had two Government and three private engineering colleges.

While initially set up to provide civil, mechanical engineering, and architectural degrees (BE, ME, BArch, MSc Engineering, and PhD), with the revolutions in computer technologies, these institutions have added degree programs in computer science and related fields; available degrees are BTech; MTech degrees in computer science engineering, electrical and electronics, electronics and telecomm, and information technology; and bachelor's and master's degrees in computer applications; among others. More recently, these colleges have gained 'autonomous status' with affiliation to their respective local universities. As 'autonomous organizations' or 'autonomous institutes', they are publicly funded by either the central or state governments but have freedom to set their own curriculum, evaluate student learning, and manage its own finances.[12] For example, the College of Engineering, Pune, is an autonomous engineering college (autonomy from the state government) but with permanent affiliation to the University of Pune, in Maharashtra, India.

The relative newcomers, even if only in their structural investitures, were the IITs and Indian Institutes of Management (IIMs).[13] IITs are 'autonomous organizations' or 'autonomous institutes'; they have the freedom to set their own curriculum and manage its own finances. But, they are funded by the central government and fall under the administrative control of the Central Department of Higher Education.

The IT boom has also brought with it a *proliferation of private technical institutions*, either as add-ons to existing engineering institutions or as standalones. An evaluation of excellence in the 'pure merit' quality of the credentials (be they degrees, diplomas or certificates, and comparative standings of the myriads of technical schools) requires a brief review of the history of the system of education and the accreditation bodies that are charged with coordinating and maintaining educational standards in post-independence India. Except for institutions created through Acts of Parliament (central government), accreditation through the National Assessment and Accreditation Council (NAAC established in 1994) has now become mandatory for all higher education institutions in India. Without accreditation, these institutions have no legal right to call themselves a University or award 'Degrees' (per UGC[14] rules); unauthorized credentials are not valid for academic and/or employment purposes.

---

[12] In the traditional model, learning and teaching happens in the colleges affiliated with universities with syllabi and tests/evaluations done by university. Guidelines for qualifying for autonomous status include qualified teachers, consistently good academic record, and necessary physical and teaching infrastructure.

[13] http://www.mhrd.gov.in/higher_education and http://www.ugc.ac.in/.

[14] To reiterate, the University Grants Commission (UGC) of India is a statutory organization set up by the Union government in 1956 and is charged with the coordination, determination, and maintenance of standards of university education in India. It provides recognition to universities in India, and disburses funds to recognized universities and colleges. Available at: http://mhrd.gov.in/university-grants-commission. Retrieved on 22 May 2015.

Higher Education System in India[15]

Higher education in modern India is provided in a variety of institutional settings. There are four types of universities: central, state, deemed, and private universities. While the Central and State Universities can be unitary, most also have affiliated colleges. Of particular significance to the information technology sector are Institutes of National Importance. Open Universities are a recent addition to the education offerings; they offer a distance education model based instruction. The Indira Gandhi National Open University (IGNOU), started in 1985, is the best-known Open University with national jurisdiction; there are 13 state open universities. On balance, the higher education system in India has grown rapidly; the number of universities in India has increased from 20 in 1950 to 677 in 2014, while the number of affiliated colleges has risen from 500 in 1950 to 37,204 in 2013.[16]

Central and State universities, in their unitary or affiliated forms, are those that have been established through and are supported by State Legislative Acts. The Central government, through the UGC, financially supports Central and Deemed Universities recognized for their high performances as well as Institutions of National Importance. Private universities/Institutes, while founded by private sponsoring bodies, like a Trust or Religious Organization, are also established through state or central legislation. An important player in the private technical university sector is the Birla Institute of Technology and Science (BITS); the institute's transformation from a regional engineering college to a national university in 1964 was financially backed by industrialist G.D. Birla. BITS currently has centres at Pilani, Goa, Hyderabad, and Dubai.

Within each state and central affiliated university are the *affiliated colleges* that also provide instruction. The vast majority of colleges in India are affiliated colleges which follow their affiliated university's curriculum, examination structure, and grading protocol; but transcripts and degrees are awarded by the university. Colleges that have been granted *autonomous status,* are overseen by universities, but can set their own curriculum, admission requirements, and award provisional certificates with the name of the college printed on the transcripts.

---

[15] Sources: University Grants Commission (http://www.ugc.ac.in) Annual Reports; The Department of Higher Education in the Union Human Resources Development Ministry (http://mhrd.gov.in/), and Mishra (2003).

[16] Available at: http://www.mhrd.gov.in/higher_education. Retrieved on 3 June 2015.

The educational quality of institutions of higher education in India is coordinated and monitored by the national UGC, the statutory regulatory body of the Ministry of Human Resource Development (MHRD). The UGC, established by an Act of Parliament, the University Grants Commission Act of 1956, is the apex body that determines, coordinates, and maintains standards of teaching, examinations, and research in university education in India. Serving as an important link between the central and state governments and other institutions of higher education, the UGC assesses the financial needs of universities and allocates/disburses grants to universities and colleges. The UGC, in the mode of self-study and external quality assessment to promote continuous improvement, recognizes and provides grants to existing universities and their affiliated colleges to update their educational quality, be it the curriculum, teaching and student assessment, research capacity, infrastructure and resources, student support and progress, and institutional management, among others.

The UGC, through its many cells, also monitors compliance with quality and social justice issues. For example, the SC/ST/OBC Cell of UGC monitors the effective implementation of the reservation policies in admissions and appointments in the university system. The Cell against Malpractices deals with the existence and mushrooming of Fake Universities and degrees; in its 2011–12 annual report, this cell identified 21 institutions and initiated action against them. The Vigilance Cell of UGC fielded and dealt with 108 complaints from the MHRD, Universities and Colleges and other agencies during the reporting period. The Cell against Sexual Harassment of Women at Workplace received one complaint from a woman officer of UGC during 2011–12. On balance, the ultimate education mandate of the UGC is to transform existing institutions and developing new institutes with world-class standards in their domains that meet the needs of the relevant stakeholders—the government, students, and employers.

As of 31 May 2015, the MHRD and UGC websites[17] listed 719 universities, 36,671 colleges affiliated with universities, and 11,445 standalone (diploma granting) institutes of higher education. Over a quarter of

---

[17] Available at: http://mhrd.gov.in/sites/upload_files/mhrd/files/statistics/ EAG2014.pdf; http://www.ugc.ac.in/alluniversity.pdf; http://www.ugc.ac.in/ oldpdf/colleges/list_of_colleges_as_on_31.05.2015.pdf; http://mhrd.gov.in/ sites/upload_files/mhrd/files/statistics/EAG2014.pdf; and http://mhrd.gov. in/sites/upload_files/mhrd/files/statistics/AISHE201011_0.pdf.

the 719 universities were located in the southern states: Tamil Nadu = 48; Karnataka = 45; Maharashtra = 42; Andhra Pradesh/Telengana = 44 (AP = 25 + Telengana = 19); and Kerala = 14. The 719 universities operated under four institutional structures: central (46), state public (330), deemed-to-be universities (128), and private universities (215). Central Universities (46 CUs) are established by Acts of Parliament in the central government) and receive funding from the central government for their maintenance and development. The University of Delhi, Jawaharlal Nehru University (JNU), and Aligarh Muslim University (AMU) are examples of Central Universities. The State Public Universities (n = 330)[18] are set up and funded by state legislative acts. The oldest state universities were the University of Mumbai, University of Madras, University of Calcutta (all circa 1857), and the University of Kerala (1937); they were originally set up to provide a liberal arts education and other specialization such as engineering and/or medicine.

'Deemed Universities', about 128 as of 2015, are institutions of higher education which have been granted autonomous status by the UGC in recognition of their long tradition of teaching or specialization and excellence in a particular area of knowledge. Such institutions, in recognition of the high caliber of their educational standards, enjoy autonomy in developing and implementing academic programs and have the power to grant their own degrees, just like the central/state Indian universities. These 'deemed' universities are not established as Universities through legislations. Rather they are declared as deemed to be universities as per Section 3 of the UGC Act. On the other hand, the central/state universities are legislatively acted upon by the government. The autonomy granted, by the Department of Higher Education under the advice of UGC, to Deemed Universities allows them full autonomy in developing courses, curriculum, syllabi, pedagogies, admissions, setting up fee structures, and awarding degrees; examples of deemed universities that provide technology related education are the National Institutes of Technology (formerly known as Regional Engineering Colleges), the Indian Institute of Information Technology and Management and the Indian Institute of Science (both in Bangalore), and Christ University in Bangalore (2008).

Private Universities are also established through state or central government legislation on behalf of an established sponsoring public trust,

---

[18] Available at: www.ugc.ac.in/print_stateuniversity.aspx.

society/association such as a literary, scientific, or charitable purposes (registered under the Societies Registration Act, 1860). They are approved by the UGC which lists 215 private universities as of 2015. Private universities, once approved by the UGC, can grant degrees but they are not allowed to have off-campus affiliated colleges. For example, BITS at Pilani in Rajasthan, funded and run by the Birla Group Trust, became an officially recognized university in 1964. Many private universities offer multidisciplinary professional courses similar to state funded universities. Some offer single stream specialization programs, like Mumbai Film Academy, known as one of the best institutes in India offering film study courses.

In addition to the UGC approved universities, of particular relevance to technology education in India are the Institutes of National Importance (INIs) that were set up by an act of central parliament to receive special recognition and funding. These INIs (n = 68), while not called 'university' by name, are granted permission to autonomously award university level degrees. They usually fall under the administrative control of the central government's Department of Higher Education. In official documents they are called 'autonomous bodies' or 'university-level institutions', or even simply 'other central institutions'. They are established by the central government, are centrally funded, and managed by the Indian Ministry of Human Resource Development.

The history of technology-focused INIs, like the IITs considered to be the premier Indian institutions for technical education, illustrates the Indian government's investment in technology related education. The Indian Institutes of Technology are governed by the 1961 Institutes of Technology Act which declared them as 'Institutions of National Importance', and lays down their powers, duties, framework for governance and so on. Recognition that technical education is fundamental to meet the atomic, technological, and economic development needs of the country is evident in technical education goals and funding being integral parts of the nation's Five-Year Plans since Independence. Major categories of the technology institutes, among others, are the following:

1. *Indian Institutes of Technology* (IITs), a group of elite autonomous engineering and technology-oriented institutes with special funding and administration (set up under The *Institutes of Technology Act, 1961*), are perhaps the best known of the existing technology

and engineering institutions in India, for the elite quality of their credentials. The IITs, deemed 'Institutes of National Importance', were approved by the Indian Parliament between 1951 and 1961 (http://mhrd.gov.in/technical-education-2); initially five IITs were set up and 11 more were added since 1994 (Parthasarathy 2012; UGC website). Even though liberal resources are provided by the central government, each IIT has autonomous curricular and governance structure, apolitical leadership, elite faculty, and world class education, at least in the original IITs.

The original five IITs were in: Kharagpur, West Bengal, in 1951; Bombay, Maharashtra, in 1958; Kanpur, Uttar Pradesh, in 1959; Madras, Tamil Nadu, in 1959; and Delhi in 1961. These are the elite, Ivy-league institutions in technical education, with high entrance qualification standards, rigorous curriculum, and high standards. Three more IITs were added during the late 1990s and early 2000s: IIT Guwahati, Assam, the sixth member of the IIT fraternity, was established in 1994; IIT Roorkee, Uttar Pradesh, formerly The Thomason College of Civil Engineering in 1854, and in 2001 elevated to Institute of National Importance; and IIT Varanasi, Uttar Pradesh, former Benares Hindu University, designated IIT in 2012. Remaining eight include IITs in: Bhubaneshwar, Orissa; Gandhinagar, Gujarat; Hyderabad, Andhra Pradesh; Indore, Madhya Pradesh; Mandi, Himachal Pradesh; Patna, Bihar; Jodhpur, Rajasthan; and Ropar, Punjab.

2. *Indian Institutes of Information Technology* (IIITs) are a group of autonomous information technology oriented institutes with special funding through The Indian Institutes of Information Technology Act. Currently there are four central (at Gwalior, Allahabad, Kancheepuram, and Jabalpur) and 16 Public Private Partnerships (PPP) IIITs.

3. *National Institutes of Technology* (NITs),[19] a group of engineering, science, technology, and management schools which were

---

[19] The other INIs are: the Schools of Planning and Architecture (SPAs); All India Institute of Medical Sciences (AIIMS), a group of autonomous public medical colleges of higher education; and National Law Universities (NLU) for the promotion of legal research and legal profession in India. Like the technology INIs, these premier centrally funded institutions were established by the

originally established as state-funded 'Regional Engineering Colleges', were upgraded during 2003–07 to national status and received funding from the central government; NITs (20 NITs with plans for ten more) were established through parliamentary acts at the central government level.

4. *Indian Institutes of Management* (IIMs) are a group of business schools created by the Government of India. IIMs are registered Societies governed by their respective Board of Governors. The Department of Higher Education lists 13 IIMs.

5. *Indian Institutes of Science Education and Research* (IISERs) are a group of five institutes established by the MHRD, on the model of Indian Institute of Science, devoted to science education and research in basic sciences.

Credential Quality Assurance and Sustained Excellence[20]

Accreditation, used to regulate, monitor, and safeguard the *pure merit culture making project*, has become the buzz word in the technology education and occupational sectors. As per Sinha and Subramanian (2013), the preferred applicants for hiring and promotions in Indian IT companies are those who gained their credentials from a university, institute, or college that has the proper accreditation (read quality of 'pure merit') status.

An important measure of a public or private institution's educational quality is whether they have been recognized in an initial one-time review by the UGC and accredited, through periodic evaluation, by the relevant accrediting professional agencies. Sixteen autonomous statutory professional councils, under the aegis of the UGC, are tasked with accreditation of higher education institutions, except those established by acts of the central Parliament like the Central Universities and IITs. For example, the All India Council for Technical Education (AICTE) and the Department of Electronics Accreditation of Computer Courses (DOEACC), through the National Board of Accreditation (NBA), are

---

Ministry of Human Resource Development of the Government of India. All the SPAs are premier centrally funded institution.

[20] See http://www.mhrd.gov.in/higher_education; http://www.ugc.ac.in; and Sinha and K. S. Subramanian (2013).

two of the bodies responsible for ensuring quality in technology focused institutions of higher education by recognizing, or de-recognizing, when needed.

In addition to the accreditation process, the UGC uses several tools to ensure educational quality of the credentials institutions offer their students. For one, as per the UGC, no institution other than a university established by or incorporated under a Central Act or a State Act is entitled to use the word 'University' associated with its name. The UGC also periodically, usually on 5-year cycles, assesses institutions as fit to receive (or not as the case might be) funding assistance, UGC grants, from the central government.[21] As an example, individual colleges affiliated with universities are given 5-year grants under the scheme 'Colleges with Potential for Excellence'. As of January 2015, 172 affiliated colleges were selected for the potential for excellence program. After the initial grant, colleges can be upgraded to 'College of Excellence' status; there were 14 affiliated colleges listed in the upgraded list on 1 January 2015.

Furthermore, because of the proliferation of unrecognized institutions that claim to offer post-secondary education in India, the UGC periodically publishes on its website, an updated list of 'fake' universities that do not meet the originally approved standards. The AICTE maintains a similar e-list of institutions that offer technical education, both of council approved and unapproved programs. Penalties for unapproved programs diluting quality include financial and jail sentences.

Technical Institutions: Home to the Education 'Blood Sport'

In the final analysis, despite the exponential growth in institutions that offer technical education, the demand far outstrips availability of seats. A combustible mix of factors, like popularity of lucrative IT jobs, limited 'open seats' in prestigious educational institutions, prohibitive costs of for-profit private technical education, and population growth, have transformed the search for higher education into a metaphorical 'blood sport.'

---

[21] Exceptions are the 37 institutions established under State Legislature Act and are being funded by the concerned Central/State Ministry or Central/State Statutory Bodies.

Lost in this mix is the contrast in the quality education offered by public or publicly funded institutions versus the questionable quality associated with for-profit institutions and the resultant delinking of quality from credentials.

'Market Value' of Credentials as Experienced on the IT Ground

One marker of the market quality of IT education is the types of IT jobs into which students can parlay their education. What is the market potential of these credentials? The rank-and-file IT professionals who responded to the web provided clues into the credentials needed for different types of IT work. The workplace marketability of education credentials was evident in the educational backgrounds of these IT professionals. Their experiences also indicated that the *merit-caste dynamics in technical education* is not just in rhetoric, but have consequences in the lived experiences of IT professionals.

Educational Capital of Rank-and-File IT Professionals

Of the 495 IT professionals who responded to the web survey and for whom education data were available, 62 per cent had completed their high school in a city or urban area (38 per cent in a village), primarily in South India. About 37 per cent went to a high school in Tamil Nadu, and 23 per cent in Kerala. Andhra Pradesh, with 15 per cent and Karnataka, with 13 per cent, followed.

Highest Degree Completed

Confirming the observations of key industry informants, the most common technical degree (Table 4.1) that IT professionals had was either a bachelor's degree in engineering, computer science, information systems or data base management (29.6 per cent), or an MCA, master's degree in computer applications (28.2 per cent). Another third (27.0 per cent) had a variety of non-engineering degrees; the most common degree in this group was the 14 per cent who had a bachelor's degree in a non-engineering field and another 7.5 per cent had an MBA.

Table 4.1. Type of Degree Completed (n = 495)

Type of Degree	Per cent
1 MS engineering, IT, CS, IS, DBA	4.8%
2 BE (engineering, IT, CS, IS, DBA)	29.6
3 MCA	28.2
4 BCA	7.3
5 Diploma (DIT, DCT)	2.8
6 Other advanced degrees—CA, FCA, MPhil, MAEd, LLB	2.8
7 MBA	7.5
8 MA, MSc Not in engineering or technology (Comm, Arts, PubAdmin, Commerce)	2.8
9 BA/BSc/PUC/BCom NOT engineering or technology (Comm, PubAdmin)	13.9
10 HSC	0.3
Total (495)	100.0

Source: Author.

Higher Education Institution Attended

Quality of technical education institutions, from where IT professionals got their technical credentials, was evaluated using the Career360.com[22] ranking of higher education institutions. This ranking covers the quality of admitted students and a combination of factors including faculty research output, industry interface, refereed publications, and academic productivity. At the top of the hierarchy was the *AAAAA* group, '*the Leaders*', which included only five institutions—the established IITs—Bombay, Delhi, Kanpur, Kharagpur, and Madras. The second tier was labelled '*AAAA+*' or '*the Challengers*' and included only 28 engineering colleges (0.81 per cent) in the country; there was an even mix of public and private challenger

---

[22] Available at: http://www.engineering.careers360.com/articles/top-engineering-colleges-in-india-2015 is used by aspiring engineering students and their families. While Career360 grouped institutions into nine ranked categories, only four of their groupings were used in this analysis. The fifth group, even though it was not ranked, was the national and state Open University attended by 72 respondents. And the sixth group was management institutes that 16 respondents had attended.

colleges in Tamil Nadu, Andhra Pradesh, and Karnataka and was dominated by the newer IITs, Tier-1 NITs, a few IIITs, Manipal Institute of Technology (MIT) and Vellore Institute of Technology (VIT). The third tier 'AAAA', '*the Strivers*' (n = 372), admit students in the 99th percentile but their research productivity is nascent. The 'AAA+', '*the Soldier Ants*', had over 100 high-quality affiliated colleges that are fine teaching institutions and are making successful forays into research activities as well. This cluster also included a number of young deemed universities, which were good teaching institutions in their previous form.

From which of these institutions did rank-file-IT professionals get their educational credentials? Given the ubiquity of private, university affiliated colleges (AAA+), it was not surprising that a plurality (43.5 per cent) of survey respondents had received their highest degree from these colleges (Table 4.2). The second most common type of higher education institution was the AAAA or the Strivers (34.3 per cent). About 15 per cent had attended IGNOU. The rest, albeit in small percentages, had graduated from either AAAA+ Challenger institutions (2.4 per cent), AAAAA leader institutions (1.8 per cent), or management (3.3 per cent) institutions.

Table 4.2. Institution Type* Attended for Highest Degree (n = 492)

Type of Institution	Per cent
AAAAA (Leaders)	1.8%
AAAA+ (Challengers)	2.4
AAAA (Strivers)	34.3
AAA+ (Private Affiliated Colleges)	43.5
IGNOU	14.6
Management Institutes	3.3
Total (492)	100.0

Source: Author.
* Refer to text above for descriptions of Institution Type.

IT Education and their IT Job Market Potential

Connecting the educational background of survey respondents with specific IT Sub-Sectors[23] in which they worked offered further insights

---

[23] As was noted in Chapter 2, survey respondents worked in a variety of sub-sectors in the Indian IT occupation: 44.9 per cent in companies whose core

into the *job pay-offs of credentials* from different tiers of educational institutions. Several revealing patterns were evident in the data presented in Table 4.3. *First*, irrespective of their alma mater's ranking, those who had a degree in engineering or technology, whether a ME or BE, or degree in computer applications were more likely than not to find employment in IT companies whose core competencies were solely hardware, software, or solely IT R&D. For example, 56 per cent of the 72 respondents with a MS/BE from the AAAA-Striver institutions were working in IT companies whose core competencies were hardware, R&D, or software development. The corresponding percentage for the private colleges (AAA+) was 47.6 per cent. Three of the seven (42.9 per cent) from the AAAAA-Leader institutions graduates and two of the four (50.0 per cent) from the Challenger-AAAA+ institution graduates were also employed in core-IT companies.

Second, similar patterns were true of those with degrees or diplomas in computer applications. About half of the 91 survey respondents who obtained degrees from private colleges (AAA+ = 51.6 per cent) or the 40 striver graduates (45.0 per cent) whose degrees in computer applications were from AAAA institutions also worked in sole IT companies.

That Indian IT work was also open to those whose master's or undergraduate degrees did not have specific engineering content was a *third* pattern evident in Table 4.3. About half of the 13 who graduated with a master's degree from private-AAA+ colleges, worked in solely IT companies, with another quarter (23.1 per cent) in companies whose competencies were IT combined with ITES and BPO. Of the 27 Striver-AAAA graduates, a quarter each was employed by Solely IT (25.9 per cent) or IT/ITES/BPO or BPO+ITES companies (18.5 per cent).

Fourth, if a respondent had an undergraduate non-engineering degree from a Striver-AAAA institution (n = 30), he/she was most likely to be working in the sole IT sub-sector (36.7 per cent), followed by IT/ITES/BPO companies (23.3 per cent). On the other hand, the most common IT location for a private college graduate with a non-engineering degree

---

competencies were restricted to (solely) Programming, Infrastructure, and R&D; 22.8 per cent in companies that combined BPO (MNC customer service and Financial Back Office) and ITES; 10.1 per cent in either BPO/ITES combinations, and 7.4 per cent in sole ITES.

Table 4.3 Institution Type by IT Sub-Sector

Type of Degree† Completed	Tiers of Educational Institutions‡	IT Sectors*					
		Solely IT (6)	IT with Other Services (5)	Solely ITES (4)	3 = BPO with ITES	Solely BPO (2)	Other (1)
4 = MS/BE in Engineering/Tech	AAAAA (n = 7): Leaders	42.9%	28.6	14.3	–	–	14.3
	AAAA+ (n = 4): (Challengers)	50.0%	–		25.0	–	25.0
	AAAA (n = 72): Strivers	55.6%	19.4	9.7	6.9	2.8	5.6
	AAA+ (n = 82): Private Affiliated Colleges	47.6%	26.8	4.9	8.5	2.4	9.8
	IGNOU (n = 2)	50.0%	50.0	–	–	–	–
	Management Institutes	–	–	–	–	–	–
3 = Computer Apps (MA, BA, Diploma)	AAAAA (n = 1)	100.0%	–	–	–	–	–
	AAAA+ (n = 4)	50.0%	25.0	–	–	–	25.0

(Cont'd)

Table 4.3   (Cont'd)

Type of Degree† Completed	Tiers of Educational Institutions‡	IT Sectors*					
		Solely IT (6)	IT with Other Services (5)	Solely ITES (4)	3 = BPO with ITES	Solely BPO (2)	Other (1)
	AAAA (n = 40)	45.0%	27.5	–	12.5	2.5	12.5
	AAA+ (n = 91)	51.6%	22.0	9.9	7.7	4.4	4.4
	IGNOU (n = 53)	37.7%	34.0	–	28.3	–	–
	Management Institutes (n = 1)	100%	–	–	–	–	–
2 = MA-Not Engineering	AAAAA (n = 1)	100%	–	–	–	–	–
	AAAA+ (n = 4)	25.0%	25.0	–	–	–	50.0
	AAAA (n = 27)	25.9%	25.9	3.7	18.5	7.4	18.5
	AAA+ (n = 13)	53.8%	23.1	–	–	7.7	15.4
	IGNOU (n = 5)	40.0%	40.0	–	–	–	20.0
	Management Institutes (n = 14)	35.7%	14.3	7.1	7.1	–	35.7

	1 = UD-Not Engineering							
AAAAA (0)	–	–	–	–	–	–	–	–
AAAA+ (0)	–	–	–	–	–	–	–	–
AAAA (n = 30)	36.7%	23.3	–	6.7	–	13.3	13.3	6.7
AAA+ (n = 27)	11.1%	11.1	–	37.0	–	3.7	14.8	22.2
IGNOU (n = 11)	63.6%	9.1	–	9.1	–	–	9.1	9.1
Management Institutes (n = 1)	100%	–	–	–	–	–	–	–

Source: Author.

* IT Sectors: 1= Other; 2 = Solely BPO (MNC Customer Service and MNC Financial/Back Office); 3 = BPO with ITES; 4 = Solely ITES (E-Commerce and Engineering Service); 5 = IT with other services, 6 = Solely IT (Programming, Infrastructure, and R&D).

† Type of Degree completed: 1 = UD-NE = Undergraduate Degrees NOT Engineering; 2 = MA-NE = master's degrees NOT engineering; 3 = DG-Capp = master's, bachelor's, diploma in computer apps; 4 = EGD = MS or BE in engineering.

‡ Tier of HE Institutions: AAAAA (Leaders); AAAA+ (Challengers); AAAA (Strivers); AAA+ (Private Affiliated Colleges); IGNOU Open University); Management Institutes.

was companies who did only ITES (37 per cent out of 27) or solely BPO (14.8 per cent); another 11 per cent each were employed by Solely IT and IT/ITES/BPO companies.

And *fifth*, IGNOU and management institute graduates too found employment in the IT sector. A third (35.7 per cent) of the 14 IGNOU management post-graduates, two-thirds (63.6 per cent) of the 11 IGNOU undergraduates, and one management undergraduate worked in solely IT companies.

Engineering Content of Higher Education

Irrespective of sector in which the survey respondents worked, they had at least a college degree, if not a master's degree in IT with a mean ($\bar{X}$) 19 to 20 years of education (Table 4A.1). Again, not surprisingly, those who had completed their degree in computer applications (master's, bachelor's, or diploma) or a degree in engineering or technology (MS or BE) were more likely than not to be working in either a solely IT sector (50 per cent with engineering degree and 47 per cent with computer applications) or in an IT sector that also has BPO and ITES components. And the engineering content (last column) of education was much higher for IT professionals who worked in the sub-sector that was solely IT ($\bar{X} = 61.08$). Sub-sectors with a combination of BPO and ITES ($\bar{X} = 58.7$) or IT with ITES and BPO ($\bar{X} = 59.69$) had employees with slightly lower engineering content in their education.

Summary of the Market Potential of IT Education Credentials

The typical rank-and-file IT professional who participated in the web survey had either a bachelor's degree (in engineering, computer science, information systems) or MCA (master's degree in computer applications). They were more likely than not to have graduated from AAA+ (Private Affiliated Colleges) or AAAA (Striver institutions). But, irrespective of their alma mater's ranking, those who had a degree in engineering or technology, whether a BE or ME, or a degree in computer applications were more likely than not to find employment in IT companies whose core competencies were solely hardware, software, or R&D. And the engineering content of their education was significantly higher for professionals who worked in the solely IT corporations than companies with a combination of BPO and ITES, or IT with ITES and BPO.

Credentials Quality as Constructed by Indian IT Professionals

Another way to understand the caste-merit tensions in technical educational quality was how credential quality was defined and constructed by IT employees. For this purpose, the rank-and-file IT professionals who responded to the web survey were asked to distinguish between the characteristics of good quality, for example, the Indian premier or 'Ivy League' educational institutions versus the not so good ones.[24] The common wisdom in the Indian higher education circles about premier or good institutions and the quality of their credentials were ratified by the web survey respondents. They also identified specific markers of what they meant by the 'quality' education credentials that elite, good technology institutions offer their students. In addition to *ratifying 'pure merit'* they also spoke to *job networks* (Lin's 1999 network resources and Granovetter's 1973 *weak and bridging ties*) that are critical for success in the educational and labour market. Underlying the search for potential employees with quality credentials is the *recognition of quality* (Baron 2006) by employers, with *its potential for caste-class social reproduction in IT* (application of Kanter's homo-social reproduction 1977a, 1977b).

At one level, a 'quality education' is one that was provided by the 'best' public or publicly funded technology education institutions in India.[25]

---

[24] Q17. Of all the different colleges that offer technical degrees and diplomas, name three colleges that you think are good. Why do you think so? (see Appendix 1A.1).

[25] As listed by the survey respondents, they were the IITs, followed by NITs (National Institutes of Technology, the former RECs or Regional Engineering Colleges), NIITs (National Institutes of Information of Technology), IIMs, Indian Institute of Science, BITS Pilani, and Autonomous Universities. Ranking them, one professional noted, 'Almost all colleges are same except the IITs. Most of the time the brand IIT helps a lot'. Irrespective of caste hierarchies of IT professionals who provided their caste names, the established Technology Institutions were ranked at the top, with one exception. Professionals who identified as SC also listed Christian themed colleges for their economic diversity and social justice focus.

A set of rubrics or specific attributes, emerged in the comments of IT professionals when they listed their top three institutions, that in their opinion, provided quality credentials. *Merit quality* was defined by 'great infrastructure and ample opportunities for students', 'established, world level recognition, research facilities', 'quality staff and knowledge base', 'high admission standards', 'quality of placement and preparation for global companies', 'focus on students', and 'holistic education'.

Alluding generally to the *high (pure) merit quality* of education available through these premier institutions were sample comments like these: 'all have a class of education that is unmatched'; they provide 'good conceptual level education, training, the practical exposure, good campus recruitment'. To another, 'Good reputation, Good faculty' made for a good institution. Or, that premier institutions 'have very "Good" reputation'. Commenting specifically on the infrastructure and ample practical opportunities that premier institutions offered their students was this professional who wrote: The IITs, NITs (previously RECs), and Autonomous Universities are premier 'because of the research facilities they provide and the practical exposure'.

Others added 'stringent admission criteria' to their rubric. After naming a few that 'have a class of education that is unmatched ... they also have specific selection criteria that let real good students to enter in'. Or 'All of the three listed colleges are of premium value and hence in great demand, both, by the students and employers alike'. Another offered, 'getting into those colleges are not easy. You need to be in top 100 in order to get into them. The standard of education is high in those colleges and the opportunities are ample for the students'. In a similar vein, one noted, 'Getting seat in these universities itself is very difficult, only candidates who has good background in school education can get the seat of this university'. To another, elite institutions 'filter diamonds thru screening exams and polish them further'.

In other words, the best institutions of Technical Higher education 'are preferred by students who get high ranks in entrance exams', because these institutions 'take the most brilliant students' and can select from 'the best and very well qualified pool of students' or 'intelligent students'. Others used the quality of an 'institution's alum' as a measurement rubric. A college is considered 'good', 'because of the quality of the passing out students' and 'the passed out students are performing well after basic training period'.

Some tied the quality/merit of the teaching to the 'educational infra-structure', 'excellent funding to run a higher education centre' with 'good educational facilities', 'knowledge base, and staff'. Referring to the IITs, one wrote 'The place is full of knowledgeable professors and the environment scores a lot of space to learn and research on subjects'. Another wrote, 'the good institutions have experienced professors and well settled facilities which in turn develop well qualified professionals'. In a similar vein were these comments: 'Staff members are seniors and they have done a lot of research ... software developments in engineering discipline'. To others, 'Retaining the Teaching Staff is helping these colleges to concentrate on the student career' because 'College doesn't matter but teacher matters'.

To yet others, it was the 'quality of placements' (referring to 'networks in resources and weak/bridging bonds') made available to students and the preparation for employment in global companies that set merit wor-thy institutions apart from the rest of the pack. Premier institutions 'are rated as the best, due to well-structured program, which is best suited to meet the current job challenges'. Another said that institutions are good 'because they equip students with real knowledge. Compared to many bogus colleges, those who graduate from elite engineering colleges in India are real winners in life'. Another who listed the IITs and RECs as examples of premier institutions wrote, 'I can think of only these two- pri-marily for the fact that the courses covered in technical degrees are good enough to help a person start off in organizations such as Intel, NetApp, Google, Microsoft, Yahoo! etc.' Or 'having a degree from a standard col-lege will open doors for good networking'. Another important dimension was 'global preparation' as in 'the potential of institution's management to attract multinational companies for campus placement programs is so sig-nificant. Delivering high quality education is not the only quality factor, that is inevitable in many other colleges. If the wide area networks among different countries can contribute to campus placement programs, then it is highly admirable'. Also emphasizing the importance of job placements as a marker of a premier quality institutions were these respondents who made the connection to future employment as follows: 'good placements while studying to get a IT job', or that premier institutions have 'a very good placements', or 'They are rated as the best, due to well-structured program, which is best suited to meet the current Job challenges'.

Some professionals, rather than ranking all institutions by uniform standards, chose to commend institutions for their unique characteristics.

Some institutions offered a 'Good environment' for education, others were 'good in training', others offered 'good campus recruitment' and 'world level recognition', and 'groom students with vision and knowledge'. To yet another, 'economic diversity', 'discipline and spirituality', and grooming 'to learn and not to study'.

Soft skills, offered as an additional rubric, extended the boundaries of pure merit to make it more holistic. 'Programming skills can always be learnt. Communication skills cannot be measured based on the college largely. In that case only urban colleges will qualify in that category'. Or that premier institutions 'will train students not only subject but also communication skills'. Another said, qualities like 'technical and a well-rounded education, whole person development, and soft skills' are what makes these institutions stand out.

Extending the boundaries of IT education beyond technical skills were also those who addressed the importance of 'value-based education'. Distinguishing between public versus Christian/religious themed institutions, the latter were commended for their 'holistic focus' in the education they offered. Illustrating s holistic emphasis as an important rubric of 'quality' education were these comments: premier colleges 'impart knowledge as well as necessary skills, in addition to personality development programs and value-based education'. Others noted that religiously themed institutions 'gave much importance in coaching and discipline' and 'education is taught along with many other skills'. One wrote that religious themed premier institutions placed 'more importance to values than education'. A few commented on the philosophical versus the practical aspects of technical education such that 'I strongly believe that a college brand can only help in entry level, and it requires different skills to grow with in the company' and only 'some colleges provide healthy environment which supports them to focus on career development'.

Other aspects of *holistic focus* of best technology education institutions were: 'the graduates come out with an ability to think logically', they 'impart education with real training', offer 'quality education integrated with working environment' so that they graduate students who are 'technically as well as practically strong'. More comments about the 'holistic development' rubric read as: 'they concentrate more on personality development', 'put emphasis on creativity as part of the curriculum'. They also focus on 'punctuality', 'discipline', and even 'more self-learning based on research', 'allowing students to think wider'. Another summarized the qualities as, 'specifically, technical and a well-rounded education, whole person development, and soft skills', that makes these institutions stand out.

'Socio-economic and cultural diversity' was another minor rubric of institutional quality. A good institution is one where 'Brilliant but low income group can get good education'. Good institutions offer their students exposure to the international world, 'get exposure to all communities, culture also education'; 'As for my knowledge, .. really provided to whom really need'. 'These colleges believe in social Justice and affirmative action by providing 49% reservation to the oppressed classes'.

But, there were some professionals who struck an 'anti-institutional tone', discounting the notion of quality educational institutions and placing the onus on the individual student. Some sample comments: 'Whatever might be the college, is what I get or take from there'; or 'I don't believe some colleges are good and some are (not) good. I believe every institution/college is important for a student'; or 'Name is not important whereas education & ability & capability is most important'; 'I think individual calibre is more important than college pedigree'. Or that quality 'Depends on one's own interest and involvement. College plays only a small role here'. Another wished to pass on responding to the question about good institutions because, 'I have seen engineers working in Microsoft from normal and very normal engineering collages. Are they better software professionals than person from best known IITs?' And out of respect for educators was one who felt 'No need to specify specific colleges because all teachers should be respected'.

'On balance', when IT professionals constructed the social space of good technical institutions, they connected *quality with pure merit credentials* offered by these institutes, universities, and colleges. Among the rubrics for judging quality of credentials were 'quality infrastructure' and 'teaching, high admission standards, and quality post-graduation placements' reflecting the *resources in bridging networks* that scholars have identified as critical to job success. Adding *socioeconomic diversity, holistic approaches, and soft skills* to the merit rubric, while representing attempts to extend the boundaries of the culture making project beyond IT skills, pointed to the caste loopholes present in merit construction. There was recognition that one institution cannot meet all the quality parameters as IT rank-and-file professionals disaggregated the institutions by their specific strengths.

Glimpses into the Caste Underbelly of the Competitive 'Blood Sport' of Technical Education

'Another perfect storm'[26] of events has transformed the merit culture making project in the technical educational enterprise in India into the 'blood sport' it has become. As noted earlier, *IT* related education and jobs have become, in the eyes of many, the 'surest and fastest route to upward mobility'. And in response to the growing demand, there has been a move towards expansion of IT educational options both through 'government resourced technical institutions' and 'privatized options for technical credentials'. Yet, the limited *'unreserved seats'* in quality institutions of higher learning, the prohibitive costs of private technical education and the *symbolic nature of pure and holistic merit education* have turned technical education not only into a *competitive blood sport* but also a conduit for *introduction and reproduction caste inequalities* into the Indian IT sector.

More specifically, the *demand for seats* in technological institutions continues to *outstrip* availability, partly driven also by the sheer growth in college-aged population. On the supply side, the scarcity is rendered more acute by the *legal mandates to reserve* up to 50 per cent of seats (for SCs, STs, and OBCs) in state resourced educational institutions (like state and central universities, as well as the prestigious IITs and IIMs). A related contentious issue was the 93rd amendment to the Indian constitution that extended the quota provisions to the elite autonomous, government funded, educational institutions like IITs and IIMs, dubbed by some as the last bastion of upper caste privilege. A 2008 Supreme Court ruling required the 13 existing IIMs to maintain the reserved quotas for OBCs while holding constant the absolute number of general category of students.

The intense competition for the remaining 'open' seats has generated resentment among the rejected open seat candidates who feel that they are displaced by 'less qualified' reserved candidates. The presumption of questionable qualifications, because the admitted reserved candidates have reduced entrance examination scores, is seen as *muddying, or even assaulting, the merit* appropriate difference that has been assiduously

---

[26] The first perfect storm led to the explosion of the IT sector. And the 'blood sport' imagery applies to the intense preparations and competition for entrance into medical and even engineering schools.

created by the constructors of the merit culture project. Added to this contentious mix is that privatization has made the scarce technical education options *very expensive*. Test-specific tutoring in preparation for the stringent entrance criteria in technical institutions of higher learning, particularly for the remaining 'open' seats, have exacerbated the 'overall cost of education'; most tutoring centres are privately operated.

In the final analyses, the constraints in unassigned seats in quality institutions of higher learning, coupled with the prohibitive costs of private technical education, have made higher education access in India into a *metaphorically competitive 'blood sport'* and have exposed the underlying caste tensions in technical education. Competition for technical education has turned into one between the marginalized versus the dominant castes. Caste politics in education and internationalization have added more fuel to the competitive mix. These tensions are layered on to the entrenched caste inequalities in Indian education that start early in the educational career and continue into higher education.

Politics of Rapid Expansion and Questions about Quality

While the government has expanded options in technical education, to meet the growing demands, concerns have been raised about 'delinking quality from credentials' and the eventual dilution of merit. The expansion plans for the elite IITs, NITs, and IIMs during 2007 and 2011 are cases in point. Currently, there are 16 IITs in different stages of maturity and development; they provide BTech (most common), as well as M-Tech and few PhDs. Eight of the sixteen IITs added during between 2007 and 2011, came under the congress led UPA-I and UPA-II governments whose stated goal was to have an IIT in each state. Five more IITs were proposed, in the 2014 central government budget, for the following states, Jammu, Chhattisgarh, Goa, AP, and Kerala, to keep BJP-led NDA government's election promises in 2014.

With the rapid expansion have come expected wrinkles, which unless managed appropriately, will compromise, say scholars and opinion leaders, the quality educational credentials offered by IIT and other bastions of technical education in India. Despite the liberal resources from the central government, autonomous curricular and governance structure, apolitical leadership, elite faculty, and world class education, there is concern that the very qualities that made for a world-class education in the original IITs, might not be reproducible in the later ones. Questions have been raised about whether India needs high quality technical education for larger numbers. Will the new IITs hurt and dilute the IIT brand? Or should the country focus on improving existing ones? Or if new ones are set up, should they be called by another name than IIT? The new IITs, for example in Jodhpur, Udaipur, and Patna, are still in their infancy. While permanent campuses being built in Jodhpur and Udaipur were slated to open in 2016, delays in environmental clearance and in other sanctions from the union government, have forced these IITs to be housed in temporary campuses. These structural impediments, along with the difficulties in hiring/retaining new faculty, and recruiting/ retaining qualified students, end up leaving many faculty positions and student seats vacant; IIT Jodhpur is a case in point. The end result, detractors fear, would be diluting the coveted IIT brand and making it less exclusive.

Similar concerns about compromised quality have also been raised in the 'rapid expansion of other feeders' to the Indian IT occupational sector, the IIMs, the NITs, and the IISERs. Seven new IIMs were added during 2007–11, with 5 more proposed in the 2014 budget. And the capacities of 13 existing IIMs were doubled to accommodate the Supreme Court ruling to expand the reserved quotas for OBCs while holding constant the absolute number of general category of students. While reasonable modifications, such as spreading out the start of new IITs and other central institutes over 1–2 years or expanding the existing IITs, have been voiced, there is palpable concern that political duels will scuttle attempts to protect quality. Newer government colleges were rated by some IT professionals as 'weak when they are run by politicians'.

Privatization of Technical Credentials

Aside from IGNOU, much of the expansion in technical education seats has been in the private sector.[27] Deshpande's review of growth in colleges by institution types underscored the privatization trend in Indian higher

[27] To recapitulate, three major categories of higher education institution in India are: State-run colleges, private aided, and private unaided. Private aided institutions of higher education are often private in terms of origin (say Christian colleges) but are similar to state-sponsored institutions in educational mission and quality; their financial links with the government requires that they have to follow all state regulations, including reservations and quotas.

education. While the share of state-run and even private aided colleges declined between 2001 and 2006, share of private unaided institutions (for-profit) increased from 25.0 per cent to 43.4 per cent.[28] For-profit institutions have overshadowed not-for-profits, reported Jandhyala Tilak (cited in Deshpande 2012).

Small scale private institutes in technical education, as opposed to traditional university or colleges, have also mushroomed. For example, there has been a proliferation of government sponsored small vocation institutes (VOCAD or Vocational Academy) as well as private industrial training institutes and polytechnics. Their students, who receive certificates, typically leave school after the 10th or 12th standards or grades. A small institute like Sevasadan Training Institute (sevasadanorphanage. com) is a case in point. Primarily a mechanical (carpentry, welding, and masonry) training institute for destitute youth, Sevasadan added three basic 'computer' application courses in word processing, excel, and other software.

Privatization Challenges: Prohibitive Cost and Problematic Quality

Students in private colleges, particularly those that do not receive government aid, often directly bear the full cost of their education. The price tag can be quite hefty, when the required donations are added. Private options, like self-financed programs in professional or technical fields and even privatized public institutions, are prohibitively expensive and have priced out the average Indian student. And the questionable quality of private technical education, along with the *caste tensions*, has added to the volatile mix in the IT merit construction project.

Prohibitive Cost of Government-Unaided Private Sector Education

Annual fees for BTech program at elite private technical institutions is often more than double that of an IIT education.[29] For example, at SRM[30] in Tamil Nadu, in addition to tuition fees of Rs 1.85 lakhs there are book

---

[28] The enrollment share of private unaided colleges has shown similar growth.

[29] Data on fees were from the respective institution's websites.

[30] Sri Ramaswamy Memorial is a deemed, stand-alone university.

fees of Rs 15,000 and annual career development fee of Rs 15,000. At the VIT, affiliated with Anna University in Tamil Nadu, the annual fees are about Rs 3.5 lakhs. In addition, there is one time donation fees for management seats that could range from Rs 10 lakhs to 20 lakhs. In Kerala, (currentkerala.com), a BTech from a self-financed, but affiliated with state universities, would cost Rs 65,000 to a BTech student admitted under the 35 per cent management quota. Each seat (of the 15 per cent) reserved for non-resident Indians (NRI) students costs Rs 1 lakh + Rs 1.25 lakhs refundable deposit. Kerala Catholic Engineering Colleges are similarly expensive: Rs 75,000 per annum plus interest-free refundable deposit of Rs 1 lakh. Other charges include: caution deposit, university fee, PTA fee, and so on. The fees at BITS Hyderabad was Rs 1.40 lakhs per year or Rs 1.08 lakhs at Chaitanya Bharathi Institute of Technology, Hyderabad.

In contrast, a degree from a Kerala state government or a government-aided institution would be Rs 6,200 (per annum). Tuition fees range from Rs 80,000 at IIT Madras to Rs 1.7 lakhs at IIT Delhi. At the NITs (former regional engineering colleges till 2002) tuition fees are under Rs 50,000.

Questionable Credential Quality

Added to the prohibitive costs are questions about the quality of technical education offered by the newly expanded options. As one scholar wrote, many private institutions, despite government rules to the contrary, 'admit the students by charging exorbitant amount as capitation fee and ignore standard admission procedures like entrance test, merit list, interviews etc.'[31] The recent moves toward autonomy and deregulation, of private colleges that are affiliated with public universities, have left quality control largely in the hands of the private institutions' management. Despite the regulatory mechanisms that the UGC has in place, the explosive growth makes adequate regulation nearly impossible.

The challenges to merit quality were underscored by many a rank-and-file professionals when they evaluated weak or poor quality technical

---

[31] 'Impact of Privatization on Higher Education' by Harishchandra J. Sharma. Available at: http://www.academia.edu/2587032/_Impact_of_Privatization_on_Higher_Education. Retrieved on 22 June 2015.

education.[32] Some tied 'for-profit privatization' to 'weakening quality'. Using the strong technical institutions as a yardstick, they underscored the *delinking of merit credentials from quality* occasioned by the 'rapid expansion' and 'privatization' of technical education. To them, such delinking is rooted in the explosive expansion educational institutions through the profit motive of private institutions. The narrow mission, inexperienced faculty, weak curriculum, inadequate facilities and infrastructure, and non-existent post-graduation placements were the most common criticisms. In the words of two respondents, 'there are a number of colleges in India ... which are very bad in everything starting from infrastructure to teaching facilities, except for collecting donations'; to another, weak colleges 'do not have any education standards. They are not up to the mark in all directions'.

Profit trumps educational quality, alleged many IT professionals as well as news opinion makers. 'Education to a larger extent is a business in India', wrote one IT professional. Sounding a pessimistic tone was this respondent: 'Right now no college provides good technical degrees. They all look for money'. To another, weak institutions are 'Colleges that are not accredited, who do not have a recognized syllabus and curriculum. Such colleges are purely business oriented and are not for the career and skill of their students'. Others tied the profit motive of non-accredited private institutions to the corruption that is endemic to the society. One said, 'In the market now we have a college in every street and a student who get a rank by paying 1 lakh also is getting into engineering. Now we have a situation where we need to pick which are good colleges out of the lot rather than which are not good'. Another, 'It's tough to feed and retain the names of bad colleges in memory as many come up every year and wither out'; 'There are countless such colleges in every big city' or even 'Too many to name'. As another tellingly commented, 'there are many, people just start them and they are unable to cope up the technology'.

Regional newspapers in Karnataka, regularly publish news items about institutes inviting applications for admission not only for technical education but also for degrees in painting, graphics, art history, and commercial arts. Other stories have been of tutorials closing after admitting students, with the officials absconding. Tutorials, like many others, doubled up as an

---

[32] Q18. Name three colleges that you think are not that good? Why do you think so? (see Appendix 1A.1).

engineering college. Even though all tutorials register with the Directorate of Technical Education (DTE), their quality is questionable because the registration is only for holding or collecting tuition and not for running colleges, leaving the quality questionable. Besides, there are complaints that the DTE inspects tutorials only when these outfits seek renewals on a yearly basis, even when there are complaints. Students also come from North India, Nepal, and other neighboring countries to study at these tutorials and do not have the resources to take these institutions to task for failing to live up to the promises. These accusations were levelled particularly against the private colleges that are self-financed through donations for their management quota seats, political connections, and/or offer degrees for money. The proliferation or democratization or opening up of education beyond government and other long-standing private institutions of higher education have resulted in weakening of educational quality. In the public opinion articulated in newspapers, the newly mushrooming technology institutions are often profit oriented and weak; they did not provide the needed educational infrastructure for student learning.

Other dimension of questionable credential quality of technical education was the 'narrow educational missions' of weak private institutions. That their graduates are not well informed or up-to date with the latest technological developments were found in these comments:'Most mediocre engineering colleges ... not only that they don't teach well but they are simply out of touch with modern R&D initiatives taking place in good colleges. They only intend to graduate their students, somehow, without making them competent for job market'. Another complained that 'Few autonomous colleges and schools concentrate only on the academic subjects and they expect students to just memorize the theories and other technologies. I feel that students will not understand the subject to the core and hence may not implement them in real life scenarios'. Listing private, unaided by government engineering colleges in the category of weak institutions, this respondent wrote, 'These institutions are mostly concerned with churning out graduates, but not necessarily with quality education'. Narrow 'focus on theory, without much practical experience and old technologies' were additional complaints about technical degrees from Arts colleges; they rely on 'the same methodology and teaching style as they do to teach arts and humanities'.

'Weak faculty and infrastructure' (like labs) were another parameter of poor quality educational institutions. Complaints ranged from 'No proper Faculty', 'inexperienced faculty', 'temporary lecturers', or 'no proper staff for each department', to 'Faculty lack depth in subjects', that 'they are not adequately staffed', or that 'staff is not committed. They don't know the new changes in technology'. Granted that new institutions are bound to face infrastructure challenges, some IT professionals nonetheless held them responsible for the poor quality of education. 'Many newly opened colleges don't have sufficient infrastructure to educate people', 'don't even have proper shelters'. Others elaborated, 'Most of the newly mushroomed private engineering colleges are lacking basic amenities like labs'.

Others cited the ironic 'lack of resources or lack of willingness' to hire experienced faculty, despite soaring fees charged by private institutions, as contributing to poor quality education. Sample comments: 'The colleges which run in rural areas has no resources', or 'Distance education' while 'Good in Name have no Experienced faculty'. Private institutions are 'Not interested to spend money to get good/experienced faculty', and 'they have poor management and no commitment and consequently do not have the facilities and committed staff'.

'Weak curriculum' was a related complaint about private institutions. 'Not having a proper schedule of regular classes or curriculum, or discipline and punctuality not being updated', or that 'Those colleges/centers are not disciplined to provide quality education' or as this respondent wrote, '98% are not good. Because their syllabus is outdated, approximately 30 years. Even a BSc computer science graduate don't know how to change desktop background. This is the average report'.

Unlike the good or elite institutions, weak private institutions, in the IT professionals' judgement, did not have reasonable 'post-graduation placements'. Sample voices: 'No good placements'; 'Not providing campus interviews'; or 'Poor Success rate and placement options'; 'The colleges which don't arrange Campus interview for students and which doesn't have basic requirements must be immediately scrapped. So there are many like these :('. To another, 'Several colleges which have been opened up would not provide campus placements or good faculty support' or 'no campus interviews'.

'Weak student quality in admission criteria', due to the management quotas in private institutions, was another theme in the characterization of weak institutions. Students admitted under the management quota, more often than not, did not score anywhere near the high marks required for admission under the open or general category into the elite or good colleges; the required minimum is 50 per cent for management candidates as per *Indian Express* 30 July 2014. Consequently, complained the survey respondents, 'They do not have a good quality of students', or student are 'not ready to learn and improve knowledge without anyone help; always waiting for somebody instruction or command'. Others said, 'Peer group is not great. So, even with facilities, with poor faculty and poor peer group, the learning is restricted'.

A few criticized weak private institutions for not offering a '*holistic education*'. Two sample comments: 'I think there are many in this including my college of my hometowns. There they are following old rules for giving education & not concentrating on personality development, market strategies, management skills & many more which is required in this competitive world'. Another felt that weak institutions lacked 'programs for student development'.

In short, the 'profit motive in the new privatization' movement has weakened educational quality, lamented many IT professionals. 'Private colleges or part-time colleges run by politicians worry only about money' said one. Another, 'They run the college as a business enterprise'. Even 'Deemed' universities (see definition earlier in the chapter), 'select students on the basis of money'. The profit motive that guides many new private institutions has resulted in out of date curriculum, lab facilities, and hiring of inexperienced teaching staff. Limited infrastructure (labs, qualified teachers, buildings, and up-to-date curriculum) were also reported in 'private self-financed engineering colleges', or in 'money oriented colleges', or in 'engineering colleges which offer payment seats' or in 'colleges that just offer degrees for money', or in 'colleges that admit students on donation—They are only interested in money'. 'Privately owned institutes, publicize their courses heavily, very expensive but are not recognized by major government organizations or corporations'. Their 'only motive is to make money and not to provide quality education to Indians', alleged another. To summarize in the words of one more IT professional, 'There are many weak colleges to mention, not just one. Education to a larger extent is a business in India'.

Despite their many complaints, some IT professionals offered clues to potential pathways to upgrade quality of for-profit private institutions. 'Accreditation and not just recognition is needed', said one, to ensure quality. For example, many of these weak colleges 'have acquired the approval to open an engineering college, but do not have the right staff to handle it'. Another advised prospective students, 'You cannot name colleges that are not good. But make sure you study in a recognized college/university'.

Caste Politics in Privatization

Scholars, rank-and-file IT professionals, and newspaper columnists have spoken to the caste politics and tensions embedded in the recent privatization trends in technical higher education. According to researchers in the Hasan and Nussbaum (2012) volume, and social activists—privatization and expansion of IT education have been disadvantageous to the economically poor, including the marginalized castes, leading to worsening caste inequalities. Media reports[33] have concurred that private colleges run by members of a particular caste or religion run the risk of discrimination, in admission and syllabi content, against those from lower castes. For example, since autonomous colleges have latitude in setting tuition fees, the steep costs of education bar poor and SC/ST students from enrolling. Rural students, and particularly rural SC students, are at an even greater disadvantage. For the prospective SC and ST students who tend to be poor, higher education, and technical and professional education in particular, has become unaffordable. Some rank-and-file survey IT professionals illustrated weak technical institutions by citing the *caste and class tensions* and *discrimination* in private IT educational institutions.

Explicitly citing casteism were these comments about weak institutions by IT professionals. 'There is caste and race discrimination internally shown between students from other states and local students by the staff and management'. Institutions 'run by Hindutva groups have casteist teachers. They are ruthlessly casteist' bemoaned another. Linking the for-profit motive of private colleges to caste inequalities, another said, 'Maximum (98%) colleges don't provide proper education. So, they exist only to make money for upper caste industrialists and politicians. Good 2% colleges are extremely costly. Seats run in crores. High caste people can afford it easily and they have discount too. They study just to capture position and loot money'. Even the select few good private institutions 'are very expensive ("runs in crores") and can be afforded only by the dominant castes'.

---

[33] *Deccan Herald*, 27 July 2014 section titled, 'New, IITs, IIMs: Boon or Bane?'

Privatization is also viewed, by some scholars, *as a response to caste reservations.* At first glance, opening of private educational opportunities has eased crowding in state-sponsored technical colleges. Those that do not secure admissions in the public sector colleges can pay, if they have economic and social capital resources, to secure their technical credentials from private-unaided-by-government colleges. Unlike in government colleges, all private sector seats are theoretically 'open' to all castes because the mandate to reserve any seats for the historically marginalized caste groups does not apply to them. However, the caste politics in Indian Higher Education has intensified the fierce 'blood sport' of combative competition for coveted seats in higher education. On the one hand, 'qualified' marginalized students who are priced out of the private education market or do not fully meet the stringent admission standards in public institutions, primarily because of legacies of casteism and/or poverty, have to rely on the 'reserved' seats in the public universities and institutes. But, the dominant castes who have to compete for the 'open' seats that are not reserved for SCs, STs, and OBCs, have alleged 'reverse casteism' and added to the combativeness of the blood sport rhetoric. That the Indian courts have consistently ruled in favour of using caste community identity, and not the intersections between caste and class, as the sole marker of the reservation program in public higher education, has added more bitterness to the fight.[34]

In summary, despite complaints about faculty shortage, poor quality of education, and lower student quality (as in lower entrance standards for those admitted under the management quotas in private colleges) demand for seats continue to outstrip availability in technical colleges. But, notwithstanding the regulatory monitoring of Indian higher education, there are growing concerns in the policy, academic, and scholarly circles that the unfettered expansion through privatization of technical credentials might have come *at the expense of 'quality' of the IT merit.* At first glance, privatization and internationalization,[35] by broadening the

[34] Reservation programs are available to the 'creamy layer' or wealthy in the SC community, but not in the OBC communities.

[35] Internationalization in Indian technical education, has taken different forms. Ranging from students going abroad to Indian institutions developing ties with foreign institutions, and foreign institutions setting up franchises in India to recruit, establish exchange programs, or collaborative research, the goal of international connections is to improve candidate marketability in the globalized IT job market.

scope of higher education in India, are welcome trends to prepare the stakeholders, be they students or employers, to succeed in a globalized market. But, serious concerns remain about the impacts on the quality of credentials among education scholars in India. There is worry that 'growing privatization' of higher education in professional and technical fields is more 'a reflection of the pent up excess demand' in the credentials market, without serious attention to ensuring quality. This tension between quality education and credentials per se are fuelled by families and institutions alike. As Deshpande (2012) opined, for many families, the 'motto is credentials first, quality can be acquired later', since some families have enough resources to protect their children from the later adverse effects of incompetence. At the institutional level, private professional colleges that offer professional programs have become *a market for credentials, irrespective of quality*. In a society where corruption is rampant, even accrediting agencies, like the NBA, AICTE, and NAAC, have little to no teeth to enforce sanctions.

Caste Inequalities in Education Start Early and Continue

It has long been known that caste-class inequalities in education start early. Despite education in India being universal, it is a privilege, particularly starting at the secondary school levels. Under the various Articles of the Indian Constitution and the Right of Children to Free and Compulsory Education Act of 2009, elementary education, from 6 to age 14, is expected to be a fundamental right and free. Elementary education is offered primarily by the government (80 per cent), even if the quality might be dubious. Secondary education, that serves as a bridge between elementary and higher education, is expected to prepare young persons between the age group of 14–18 for entry into higher education or into work situations. However, in 2007–08, the age specific attendance ratios in the general population serially declined as the children got older: 6–10 years: 88 per cent; 11–13 years: 86 per cent; 14–17 years: 64 per cent; and 18–24 years: 18 per cent.[36]

---

[36] All India Education Survey (AISES), MHRD (available at: http://aises.nic.in/home); Education Statistics at a Glance_2014 (available at: http://www.oecd.org/publications/highlights-from-education-at-a-glance-2076264x.htm); State of Urban Youth in India, 2012 (available at: https://issuu.com/unhabitatyouthunit/docs/a201341118517_19). All retrieved on 29 May 2015.

A similar story is played out in declines in the gross enrolment ratios[37] as Indian youth move from higher secondary school ages (grades IX–XII) into higher education (18–23 age group). For example, in 2012–13 the GER in higher education (ages 18–23) dropped to 21.2 from a high of 56.3 in grades IX–XII. The GERs for SC men and women showed similar, but steeper, declines; from a 58.2 GER in IX–XII grades to a low of 15.1 GER in the higher education stage. Also noteworthy is that while there was fair gender parity in GER (for all castes and for SCs) in grades IX–XII,[38] the caste and gender gaps widened and reversed by the time they matured into higher education stages. The GERs for young men of all caste groups was 22.3, higher than that of the 19.8 GER for women. The corresponding rates for SC men and women were 16.0 and 14.2 respectively. Gender parity and disparity issues in the Indian IT sector will be explored further in Chapter 5.

Accumulated lifetime disparities, in insecure/distressed educational and cultural capital of Dalits vis-à-vis the forward castes was detailed in Chapter 3 (Tables 3A.1–3A.3). To recapitulate, data from the 2005 India Human Development Survey (IHDS) revealed deep caste disparities in education and access to cultural resources. SCs were least educated, followed by OBCs; the forward/upper caste members were the most educated. SCs also had the lowest literacy levels, followed by OBCs with forwards castes who the highest literacy levels (2005–06 NFHS3). And it is not surprising that SCs had the least access to news sources like news,newspaper, radio, and TV (SC $\bar{X}$ = 1.06). FCs had the most access ($\bar{X}$ = 1.44) followed by the OBCs ($\bar{X}$ = 1.29).[39]

When lifetime accumulation of education was disaggregated by age groups in the three caste communities, some generational improvements in educational achievements of SC/STs, OBCs, and FCs were visible. But, the marginalized communities continued to lag behind the FCs Table 4A.2). For example, younger SC cohorts (in the IHDS 2005

[37] GER: total student enrolment in a given level of education, regardless of age, expressed as percentage of the corresponding eligible official age group population in a given school year. Source: Education Statistics at a Glance 2014.

[38] GER 56.5 for boys and 56.1 for girls; 58 for SC boys and 58.4 for SC girls aged 14–17 years.

[39] Table 3A.3: Access to Newspaper + radio + TV = (access: 0-not at all; 1 = LT once a week; 2 = at least once a week; 3 = almost every day)/3.

survey) had completed three more years of education than the oldest age groups; 21–30 year old SCs $\bar{X}$ = 5.66 of education in contrast to only 3 years in the 36+ age group. The corresponding numbers for the forward communities were almost doubly higher, particularly in the older generations: $\bar{X}$ = 5.7 for the oldest and $\bar{X}$ = 8.4 for the youngest age group. The OBC communities fell in between.

It is not surprising that, in a social environment of entrenched hierarchies with its lingering pernicious effects on the marginalized castes, SC disadvantages show up in the higher education stages, despite government interventions. Even though primary/elementary and secondary education (provided through the public and private sectors) is quasi mandatory in India, there are many caste and class based obstacles as the young move through the educational system. To recapitulate, while university education in India that is controlled by the Union or the State governments is relatively inexpensive, private college education is prohibitively expensive. Scholars in the Hasan and Nussbaum collection of (2012) essays identified a variety of social sources of caste inequalities along the educational pipeline. SC/ST caste members are typically first generation school goers, if they even make it into the elementary educational system. Also, the almost 'essential' reliance on private out-of-the classroom tutoring starting early in a child's basic elementary education, puts the socioeconomically disadvantaged at a competitive disadvantage. The ubiquitous reliance on private tutoring is more a consequence of the heavy ambitious primary-secondary curriculum and poor teacher performance than of student ability. The educational disadvantage for the economically struggling SC/STs is even more acute. Subtle forms of discouragement and ostracism of SC/STs in grade schools (Nambissan 2010) and net inequalities in the mastery of reading and arithmetic (Desai, Adams, and Dubey 2010) add to the educational burdens of SC students.

Another dimension in the disparities is the limited access to higher education in rural areas. Nearly half of the institutions of higher learning are concentrated in five states (mainly southern) and professional courses in another five states (Government of India 2009; Viswanath 2009), adding a rural axis to the limited access of SCs to higher education. Taken together, these factors might explain the low rates of education in the SC/ST communities (Amartya Sen's Op-Ed in the *Hindu*, 19 December 2009).

Caste Disparities Continued into the Technical Education Rink

The practice of using expensive private coaching centres to prepare students for higher education entrance exams, a continuation of the tutoring pedagogies in elementary and secondary schools, has, perhaps become another conduit for continuing early caste-based class disparities into technical higher education. Of particular import for technology education is the high bar for entrance into the premier technical institutions like the IITs. It stands to reason that the entrance criteria is significantly stringent for the 15 IITs, the premier technology institutions in the country with 9,000 seats per year, or other professional and technical institutions. Consequently, there is a proliferation of coaching centres for the competitive entrance tests like the JEE tests for admission to the IITs, the premier technology institutions and feeders for IT occupations. Other top colleges (like BITS-Pilani) also have their own separate test requirements such as All India Engineering Entrance Examination (AIEEE), Common Entrance Tests (CET). Because the syllabi for entrance examinations are much tougher than the regular Class XII curriculum, in the final year of high school, parents who can afford the extra tuition shell out anywhere between Rs 40,000 and Rs 1.2 lakhs or Rs 1.2 lakhs[40] on their children's behalf (Sangeetha 2009).

Even after SC/ST students secure admission (often based on reservations or earmarks) to the prestigious IITs, the academic and social practices of these institutions have been documented to be less than conducive to the success of minority students. On the academic front, Parthasarathy (2012), using interviews with key informants and analyses of email and fora comments, documented educational practices that did not help, even hindered, the success of minority students. Parthasarathy's IIT faculty were more interested in research (than in teaching), in using standardized tests rather than projects or essays for evaluation, and allowing exams only in English and not also in Hindi; these alternative pedagogies are expected to help minority students. On the social interactional front, there have been news accounts (see Chapter 3 for more details) of caste bias, harassment, and unfavourable treatment in some of the IITs and AIIMs. In 2012, the UGC ruled that egregious actions like announcing the names of the students in derogatory manner, passing derogatory remarks,

[40] About US$1,000 to US$3,000 in 2009 US dollars.

segregating students in common facilities like hostels or residence halls, targeting them through ragging (bullying), or financial extortion, and differential treatment in sports/academic infrastructure run counter to the educational goals of these premier institutions. Defining caste bias in higher education as education malpractice, the UGC put in place a set of progressive measures, like suspending grants or canceling recognition, to reduce caste bias in colleges and universities.

Private auxiliary services, like residential hostels, organized for students from dominant caste exemplify the caste boundaries drawn between students from the dominant and SC/ST communities. Various newspaper ads inviting applications from backward classes, minorities, SCs, and STs for hostels in Bangalore are illustrative. In one ad, the target clients for the hostels, run by 'Trusts', were students from 'backward classes and Uppar community' (Uppar is a dominant Kshatriya community in southern India) who were studying PUC, degree, medical, technical, and other degrees. Another ad invited only applicants from 'poor merit girls from Veerashaiva community' (another dominant community) studying in medical, engineering, agricultural, and other post-graduate courses for free hostel in Bangalore. Scholarships only for 'poor Brahmins' students aspiring to higher education are another example of boundaries between dominant caste and SC/ST students.

Given these institutional biases in higher education against the marginalized, it is not surprising that caste inequalities in education favour the upper caste communities. For example, in Deshpande's (2012) figures from the 2004–05 National Sample Survey Organisation,[41] half (51.1 per cent) of the 18 and over Indians who had completed more than higher secondary school education (included degrees, diplomas, and certificates) were upper caste Hindus. Comparable OBC percentages were 28.4 per cent, SCs, at 8.1 per cent, and STs at 2.7 per cent, were far behind. Upper caste Hindus, Christians, and Sikhs, 18–23 year old, also had the highest graduate school enrollment rates while SC members, irrespective of religion, were least likely to be enrolled; upper castes dominated in the greater than 150 per cent of national average while SCs ranked below, even under 50 per cent of the national GERs.

Of greater import to the Indian IT occupational sector are the caste disparities in technical education. Deshpande's analyses of the 2004–5

---

[41] NSSO falls under the Ministry of Statistics of the Government of India.

NSSO revealed a mismatch between the shares of different caste groups in the urban population and in the population of those with some technical degree and with an engineering degree. An illustrative example: While upper caste Hindus comprised 32.9 per cent of the urban population, their corresponding proportions with some technical degree (62.3 per cent) or an engineering degree (62.2 per cent) were double. The SC percentages represented a stark contrast. Their 6.2 per cent share in engineering degrees and 4.1 per cent with some technical degree is much smaller than their 15 per cent share of the urban population. The scope of these deficits simply cannot be attributed solely to variations in human ability and interest. Since the system of higher education in India has increasingly become less favourable to SCs and other marginalized communities, much of the blame for these disparities has to be located in systemic casteism, say Deshpande and other scholars.

Deconstructing the Caste Foundations in the Merit Culture Education Project: A Play-by-Play Summary of Merit vs. Caste Debate in the IT Education Social Habitus

The multifaceted nature of the caste vs. merit blood sport in the Indian higher education was evident in the many arguments and counter arguments reviewed in this chapter. The workplace marketability of education credentials, evident in the educational backgrounds of the rank-and-file IT professionals who completed the web survey, showed that the merit-caste sport is not just in rhetoric, but has real life consequences for expanding. Yet, it offers options for loopholes to embed caste inequalities into the merit culture preparations in technical education.

Complaints about reservations programs for SC/STs and OBCs,[42] in public educational institutions, particularly in the elite IITs and AIIMs, and their never ending shelf-life, represented the first jab in the First Round of the culture making blood sport pitting the Merit versus Caste Camps. However, the Indian Supreme Court and the UGC have countered that, given the long history of casteism in India, continued preferences for SCs and poor segments of the OBC communities in higher education is essential in the interest of equality, justice, and social progress. Besides, the

---

[42] Higher caste women in Shenoy-Packer (2014) also complained about being discriminated against because of the reservation programs.

enduring presence of casteism in the social, and even in the educational environments has bolstered the Caste Camp's arguments. For example, the institutional biases in higher education favour the upper caste communities against the marginalized. And in a system of higher learning in India, that has increasingly become less favourable to SCs and to other marginalized communities, much of the blame for these disparities has to be located in systemic casteism, say scholars in the Caste Camp.

The growth of lucrative information technology jobs in India has opened up another frontier, a Second Round, in the intense merit-caste debate about the construction of the culture making project. According to the IT professionals, technical education of meritorious quality (human and cultural capital) was provided by the well-known established institutions like the IITs and other public sector or aided universities and colleges in contrast to the new private sector institutions. Institutions that offered merit-worthy education had world level recognition, excellent infrastructure (research facilities and quality staff), high admission standards, and were student focused with ample opportunities for quality job placements and preparation for work in global companies. But, caste-based reservation policies, said the Merit Camp, left only half the seats available for open or general competition among the dominant caste students who scored well on the merit entrance tests and wish to study at the very public institutions that provide the quality credentials that is a sure ticket into the coveted IT job market. Besides, open seat candidates are rejected for admission, says the Merit Camp, only because they are displaced by 'less qualified' or less merit worthy reserved candidates who are admitted despite receiving lower scores on entrance examinations. To these lines of arguments, the Caste Camp countered that equating 'merit' solely with entrance test scores in the IT culture making project ignores the lingering pernicious effects of entrenched caste hierarchies on the social advancement chances of disadvantaged groups; for example, the SC candidates are first generation school-goers who have limited cultural and social capital and network resources. That one's ability to do well in tests or the very construction of tests that are biased in favour of dominant caste's lived experiences is another constraint. In addition, doing well in tests is heavily dependent on expensive test-specific tutoring only advantages the already privileged. Besides, the Caste Camp continued: the economically dominant caste students, unlike their poor SC counterparts, have the option of accruing the needed technical capital by studying at the private, albeit expensive, technical institutions. And not getting their credentials (technical capital) from the elite public institutions might be a necessary hardship that dominant castes have to endure in the interest of redressing centuries-long casteism and promoting a just and equal society. For systemic reasons, even after more than 50 years of social redress policies, the SC community does not have the requisite social and cultural capital that make for smoother transition from elementary to secondary and to colleges and universities.

Private institutions of technical education that have emerged in response to demand far outstripping available institutions have opened up a Third Round in the Merit-Caste debate. Rather than soothing the caste tensions by easing the tight demand for technical education, the steep price tag of private institutions has only intensified the competitive 'blood sport'. For one, economically better off dominant castes resent having to incur such steep costs for a private seat in lieu of seats in a public institution they contend would have been theirs, if not for the reservation or earmark programs. To this, the Caste Camp countered, SCs who are typically economically poor cannot afford the costs of a private technical education or even the private tutoring that is almost mandatory if one is to succeed in the stringent entrance examinations to quality higher education. The only reasonable option available to these marginalized groups is the relatively cheaper public sector education. Recent supreme court rulings in favour of continuing reservation policies, earmarking up to 49.5 per cent seats, even in the elite IITs and IIMs has restored the numerical, at least in a proportionate way, caste representation in elite public institutions of technical education.

The high tech boom in India has opened up the Fourth Round in the technical education 'blood sport'. In the frenzied demand for an education that opens doors into the lucrative information technology job market, the growth of the private sector market in higher education has diluted the merit boundaries of technical education by delinking credentials from the quality of education. That profit motive trumps merit and quality in many private educational institutions was a common refrain in the survey respondents' assessment of weak higher education institutions. The ironies in the 'pure merit' in the caste-merit blood sport have not been lost on thoughtful commentators and scholars in the Caste Camp. To paraphrase Deshpande (2012: 229), while the Merit Camp has long accused caste reservation or earmark system of diluting merit (see Chapter

3), they seldom accuse private, government unaided management institutions of weakening merit when they admit students who can pay the steep donations and fees under the management quotas.

In the end, Indian higher education has become another social habitus in which multiple rounds of the 'blood sport' of merit culture making project are played out. The intensity of the sport is fuelled partly by the growing popularity of technology jobs but in equal part by the caste undertones in access to education. The publicly funded Indian technical education system, with its elite quality technical credentials, offers a sharp contrast to the weaker, but pricier, private institutions. Yet, the caste dimensions in the competitive blood sport of technical education still favour the dominant castes. The SCs and poorer segments of OBCs who are priced out of the private education market have access only to the seats reserved for them in public institutions. It is this public nature of technical institutions that have made them a primary site where the Merit-Caste blood sport is overtly waged. But, *the private technical institutions are yet another site where the foundations for caste infusion and transfer into the IT occupational sector*, are laid. In the final analyses, just as both public and private institutions of technical higher education are the sites where merit is culturally constructed, they also become ideal sites for deconstructing the merit culture making project and revealing the project's caste foundations.

Appendix: Table 4A.1   Educational Background of IT Employees by Sub-Sector

IT Sectors[‡]	Years of Education Means[¥] $\bar{X}$/D (n)	Engineering Related Highest Education Degree[*]				Engineering Content Years of Education[†] Means $\bar{X}$/D (n)
		UD-NE	MA-NE	DG-Capp	EGD	
1 = Other	20.1/1.96 (51)	14.3%	24.6%	5.3%	8.8%	51.73/21.61 (51)
2 = Solely BPO	19.32/1.89 (22)	12.9	4.6	2.6	2.9	44.59/25.02 (22)***
3 = BPO with ITES)	20.06/1.41 (51)	7.1	9.2	14.2	7.6	58.71/16.56 (51)
4 = Solely ITES	19.54/1.85 (37)	18.6	3.1	4.7	7.6	50.92/26.12 (37)
5 = IT (with 2-4)	19.89/1.6 (115)	15.7	23.1	26.3	22.9	59.69/17.68 (115)
6 = Solely IT	19.91/1.6 (219)	31.4	35.4	46.8	50.0	61.08/18.05 (219)
Overall	19.88/1.67 (495)	(70)	(65)	(190)	(170)	58.05/19.7 (495)

Source: Author.

* Engineering related Highest Education Degree: 1 = UD-NE = Undergraduate Degrees NOT engineering; 2 = MA-NE = master's degrees NOT engineering; 3 = DG-Capp = master's, bachelor's, diploma in computer apps; 4 = EGD = MS or BE in engineering.

† Engineering Content = Number of years of education completed * Engineering related highest education degree.

‡ IT Sectors: 1 = Other; 2 = Solely BPO (MNC Customer Service and MNC Financial/Back Office), 3 = BPO with ITES; 4 = Solely ITES (E-commerce and engineering service), 5 = IT (1-3) with other services, 6 = Solely IT (programming, infrastructure, and R&D).

¥ $\bar{X}$(SD): Mean and standard deviation.

*** Differences among sectors are statistically significant at the *** $p <= .001$.

Appendix: Table 4A.2 Completed Years of Education, IHDS 2005

Age of Respondent		$\bar{X}$ (Mean) (Standard Deviation)[*]
21–30	FC (Brahmin, HC, Religion (n = 14,368)	8.4 (4.9)
	OBC (n = 12,809)	7.1 (4.8)
	SC and ST (n = 10,331)	5.7 (4.9)
	Total (n = 37,508)	7.2 (5.0)
31–35	FC (Brahmin, HC, Religion (n = 5,779)	7.4 (5.1)
	OBC(n = 5,293)	5.9 (5.0)
	3 = SC and ST (n = 4,168	4.3 (4.7)
	Total(n = 15,240)	6.0 (5.1)
36 and older	FC (Brahmin, HC, Religion (n = 26,124)	5.7 (5.2)
	OBC (n = 22,442)	3.9 (4.6)
	SC and ST (n = 16,910)	2.6 (4.0)
	Total (n = 65,476)	4.3 (4.9)

Source: Author.

[*] Range 0–15 years of completed education.

5 Merit and Gender Diversity

Lessons about Caste Diversity in Indian IT

What does gender have to do with caste? On the face of it, an examination of gender diversity and inclusivity in Indian IT seems disconnected from caste diversity. However, it was important to include an assessment of gender diversity progress in Indian IT, both as a contrast point to the resistance to caste diversity (documented, for example, in Chapters 4 and 3) as well potential lessons for addressing caste diversity. *Streamlined pure merit*, of the non-reservation kind, is the entry point for women into IT; women who have the necessary *gender-neutral pure merit* skills have found a place in Indian IT. However, qualified IT women have faced the proverbial glass ceiling, perhaps because of their *limited weak network ties* (Granovetter 1973), *'resources-in-IT networks'* (Coleman 1988; Lin 1999, 2001), and *gendered pattern recognition* (Kanter 1977a, 1977b) by management with their *symbolic, hidden sources* (Bourdieu 1977, 1984) *of gendered merit*. Even more to the point of this monograph is the *intersectionality of caste and gender* and their *strong (family) ties* (Granovetter 1973) to IT men in their dominant caste backgrounds that has rendered qualified women to be more acceptable in Indian IT than Dalit men and women alike.

The focus of diversity in the Indian IT sector, to date, has been on gender, or more specifically gender parity. The NASSCOM-Mercer (joint research company) documented the growing share of women in the Indian IT industry, from around 20 per cent in 2004 to 30 per cent in 2014. But, how open is the Indian IT sector to integrating (inclusive) women into their merit habitus, assuming there is a large pool of qualified women engineers? Are they more open to women than to SC women and men in their habitus? What roles have women played in the IT merit culture making project? Is the merit culture metrics gender neutral or has it been broadened to be more gender inclusive? To what extent have women broken through the management glass ceiling where they might transform the IT merit culture to be more gender inclusive? And what lessons might be gleaned about the future of caste diversity and inclusiveness in Indian IT? These are some of the questions explored in this chapter.

Diversity, in much of the scholarly literature, is broadly defined in its multidimensionality to include not only gender, but also social class, race/ethnicity, and other social vectors like caste in India. Businesses across the globe are also taking note of the strategic values of diverse workforces. Access to a wider diverse talent pool, improved workplace climate, employee satisfaction, and limited turnover has been shown to sharpen competitive business advantages.[1] However, if the gender diversity progress in the Indian IT sector is contingent on *pure merit* and if even *holistic merit* (soft, communication skills, team work, and so on) is confined to the workplace and not broadened to account for the changing life cycle responsibilities, there are limits to the future of gender diversity and inclusivity.

There is also an important distinction to be made between *gender (or caste) diversity/parity* and *inclusivity*. While definitely related, they are far from identical goals. For example, to many IT companies and their professionals, the process of gender diversifying their work force is to bring in more women who qualify on *gender-neutral IT 'merit'* criteria. That is, women are more than welcome if, and because, they have the right gender

---

[1] Cox (1993); Ely and Thomas (2001); Goyal and Shrivastava (2012–13).

neutral merit qualifications. But, a gender diverse environment is not by definition also inclusive, although gender diversity in hiring and retention of women is a necessary condition for inclusivity. An inclusive workplace is one where the unique contributions women bring to the workplace habitat are appreciated and incorporated into IT values and work practices. It is only by transforming the gender diverse climate into a more inclusive one, that IT companies can tap into the unique gendered contributions that women bring to their organizations.

To their credit, NASSCOM has, starting in 2009, recognized Indian IT companies with Gender Inclusivity Awards. The awards, in principle, showcase and promote model programs that foster gender diversity and inclusion of women in ways that have improved organizational effectiveness through gender sensitive policies and procedures. Concerted attempts have been made by some IT companies to transform their workplace habitat into more secure and flexible environments in ways that have made IT a favoured workplace for women (Rao and Bagali 2014b). Some examples of gender inclusive benefits added to the lucrative IT salaries were free pick-up and drop-off facilities to their homes, part-time and flexible times, and extended maternity leaves and career policies to accommodate changing family life cycles in women's childbearing years. Companies honoured with NASSCOM's gender inclusive awards have implemented both hard human resource management approaches (changes in organizational structures, policies, and practices) and soft approaches (fostering pro-women consciousness, values, and commitment) to capitalize on the assets and competencies that a gender diverse set of employees bring to a company (Meena and Vanka [2013]).

Status of Gender Diversity in IT and their Education Pipeline

It is widely accepted in both scholarly and policy circles that diversifying the workplace habitat, while by no means easy in a patriarchal culture like India, is much easier than making it gender inclusive. In the absence of gender counts in the Indian IT labour force, IT professionals' educational accomplishments, the valorized educational merit credentials, contrasted with their male counterparts and the average Indian woman, can be used to evaluate gender parity progress in IT. Gender differentials in IT credentials, such as bachelor's or master's degrees in engineering, in the different ranks and in sub-sectors can also reveal constraints to gender parity in Indian IT.

Much of the progress in gender parity in Indian IT can be linked to the unique structural diversity of the Indian IT sector and women's gains in education.[2] Work in the IT sector, unlike in most professional sectors like medical, legal, or teaching, does not require all its members to have completed a technical degree. The new IT sector is open to those from a wide variety of educational backgrounds (*soft pure merit*), ranging from high school certificate, diplomas, and certificates to undergraduate and graduate degrees. For example, BPOs, which provide back office customer support operations, might hire someone with only two years of college education. Jobs in computer applications are open to those who have either a diploma in computer applications, DCA, or a master's degree. On the other hand, IT software development jobs require at least an undergraduate engineering degree. Even though women lag behind men in the core engineering sub-sectors, they have closed the gender gap in education needed in the non-core engineering sub-sectors of Indian IT such as computer applications.

Gender Differences in IT Merit Education[3]

Differences, between male and women IT professionals, in the engineering content of their IT education and in the institutional sources of their credentials provide a useful glimpse into the gender parity outcomes in the sector. The disparities reflected gendered differences in *educational and social (network) capital* that end with the proverbial glass ceiling barriers that women face. These disparities also pointed to *male patterned evaluation* of women's promotion opportunities and ultimately to the limits of gender parity outcomes.

Gender Disparities in Education in the IT sector

If engineering degrees are the hallmarks of *pure merit* in the IT sector, *IT women still lag behind their male counterparts*. Male IT professionals had significantly higher core engineering content ($\bar{X} = 59.1$) in their education

---

[2] See Chapter 2 for more details about the IT sector jobs.

[3] The education data presented in this section was drawn from the web survey of rank-and-file IT professionals.

than women (55.9 in Table 5.1). No doubt, the modal educational degree for males and females was a BE (bachelor's degree) in engineering, computer science, IT, or data base applications (DBA). But, slightly more male professionals reported having completed a BE (engineering 30.8 per cent) than females (27.2 per cent). And albeit by small percentage points, male IT professionals (6.3 per cent) outdid women (1.9 per cent) in having a master's degree in engineering (ME).

Of course, Indian IT has opened its doors to women in positions that do not require engineering credentials or hard pure merit. Women IT

Table 5.1 Gender Differences in Education Completed (Web Survey)

Highest Degree Completed	Male (n = 333)	Female n = 162)
MS or master of science degree (engineering, IT, CS, IS, DBA):	6.3%	1.9%***
BS or bachelor's degree (engineering, IT, computer science, IS, DBA):	30.8	27.2
MCA (master's in computer apps):	28.1	28.4
BCA (bachelor's in computer apps):	7.2	7.4
Diploma (DIT, DCT):	2.7	3.1
Other advanced degrees (PhD, CA, FCA, MPhil, MAEd, LLB):	2.4	3.7
MBA:	6.9	8.6
MA, MSC NOT in engineering or technology (communication, arts, pub-admin, commerce):	1.8	4.9
BA/BSc/PUC/BCom NOT engineering or technology	13.5	14.8
HSC:	0.3	0.0
Number of Years of Education: $\bar{X}$(SD)*	19.9 (1.6)	19.9 (1.7)
Min-Max	12.0–25.0	14.0–25.0
Engineering Content of Education†: $\bar{X}$(SD)	59.1 (19.8)	55.9 (19.4)***
Min-Max	12.0–84.0	19.0–84.0

Source: Author.

* $\bar{X}$(SD): Mean and standard deviation.

† Engineering Content = Number of years of education completed × Engineering related highest education degree.

*** Differences between males and females are statistically significant at the *** p <= .001.

professionals were equal to men in the second most sought after degree, a MCA or masters in computer applications; men 28.1 per cent and women 28.4 per cent. Similar percentages of males (7.2 per cent) and females (7.4 per cent) had an undergraduate degree in computer applications (BCA). Women also slightly outnumbered men in the non-engineering degree categories. There were more women working in the Indian IT sector with a MBA (8.6 per cent female versus 6.9 per cent male) or a MA/MSc (4.9 versus 1.8 per cent men) or a BA/BSC degree (14.8 per cent women vs. 13.5 per cent).

Where did these IT professionals get their credentials? Given that there is a wide variety in the quality of IT-related educational institutions in India (see Chapter 4), it is useful to ask: did men and women in the Indian IT sector attend similar quality institutions and have access to *similar IT network options* (Table 5.2)? Women were equal to men (albeit only a few attended, under 5 per cent), in having attended two of the top tiers institutions (AAAAA the Leaders and AAAA+ the Challengers). But, gendered differences in favour

Table 5.2 Gender Differences in Higher Education Institutions Attended

	Male	Female
Type of Institution-Ranking by Career Builder* AAAAA (The Leaders)	1.8%	1.9%
AAAA+ (The Challengers)	2.4	2.5
AAAA (The Strivers)	37.9	27.2
AAA+ Private Affiliated Colleges (The Soldier Ants)	41.5	47.5
Management Institutes (AIIMS, XLRI))	3.3	3.1
IGNOU (Indira Gandhi National Open University)	13.0	17.9
(n)	(333)	(162)

Source: Author.

* As per Career Builder.com, the top rating was AAAAA, 'the Leaders', included the five established IITs—Bombay, Delhi, Kanpur, Kharagpur, and Madras; the second tier was labeled AAAA+, 'the Challengers' (only 28 engineering colleges) in the country mix of public and private colleges in Tamil Nadu, Andhra Pradesh, and Karnataka and is dominated by the newer IITs, Tier-1 NITs, a few IIITs, MIT and VIT; The third group AAAA (372 'the Strivers'), admit students in the 99th percentile but have nascent research productivity; Fourth is The AAA+, 'the Soldier Ants', have over 100 high-quality affiliated fine teaching colleges.

of men were prominent in rungs below the top of the educational hierarchy. IT men (37.9 per cent) were more likely to have attended Striver institutions (AAAA) than women (27.2 per cent). On the other hand, women (47.5 per cent) were more likely to have finished their degrees from the privately affiliated colleges (AAA+) than men (41.5 per cent).

Gendered differences were also evident when the institutional alma-mater (another source of *resources-in-IT networks*) of IT professionals were disaggregated by the degrees completed (Table 5.3).

Table 5.3 Gender Differences in Institutions by Types of Degree and Institution (Web Survey)

Type of Degree	Ranking by Career Builder	Male	Female
MS: Engineering, IT, CS, IS, DBA:	AAA+ Private Affiliated Colleges	19.0%	0.0%***
	AAAA (**Strivers**)	**52.4**	33.3
	AAAA+ (**Challengers**)	9.5	0.0
	AAAAA (Leaders)	19.0	**66.7**
	(n)	(21)	(3)
BS: Engineering, IT, CS, IS, DBA:	IGNOU	1.0%	2.3%***
	AAA+ Private Affiliated Colleges	**52.0**	59.1
	AAAA (**Strivers**)	44.0	36.4
	AAAA+ (**Challengers**)	1.0	2.3
	AAAAA (Leaders)	2.0	0.0
	(n)	(100)	(44)
MCA	IGNOU	24.7%	23.9%***
	AAA+ Private Affiliated Colleges	**45.2**	58.7
	AAAA (**Strivers**)	**24.7**	17.4
	AAAA+ (**Challengers**)	4.3	0.0
	Management Institutes	1.1	0.0
	(n)	(93)	(46)
BCA	IGNOU	50.0%	50.0***
	AAA+ Private Affiliated Colleges	**45.8**	**41.7**
	AAAA (**Strivers**)	**4.2**	8.3
	(n)	(24)	(12)

(Cont'd)

Table 5.3 (*Cont'd*)

Type of Degree	Ranking by Career Builder	Male	Female
Diploma (DIT, DCT):	IGNOU	11.1%	0.0%***
	AAA+ Private Affiliated Colleges	44.4	40.0
	AAAA (**Strivers**)	44.4	60.0
	(n)	(9)	(5)
Other advanced degrees—PhD, CA, FCA, MPhil, MAEd, LLB:	IGNOU	12.5%	16.7%***
	AAA+ Private Affiliated Colleges	25.0	16.7
	AAAA (**Strivers**)	12.5	33.3
	AAAA+ (**Challengers**)	12.5	16.7
	Management Institutes	37.5	16.7
	(n)	(8)	(6)
MBA	IGNOU	4.3%	7.7%***
	AAA+ Private Affiliated Colleges	**21.7**	**38.5**
	AAAA (**Strivers**)	**47.8**	**23.1**
	AAAA+ (**Challengers**)	0.0	7.7
	Management Institutes	26.1	23.1
	(n)	(23)	(13)
MA, MSC Not in Engineering/ technology (Comm, Arts, PubAdmin, Commerce):	IGNOU	16.7%	0.0%***
	AAAA (**Strivers**)	**83.3**	**62.5**
	AAAA+ (**Challengers**)	0.0	12.5
	AAAAA (Leaders)	0.0	12.5
	Management Institutes	0.0	12.5
	(n)	(6)	(8)
BA/BSc/PUC/ BCom in (Comm, Pub Admin: NOT Engineering or Technology:	IGNOU	6.8%	33.3%***
	AAA+ Private Affiliated Colleges	36.4	45.8
	AAAA (**Strivers**)	54.5	20.8
	Management Institutes	2.3	0.0
	(n)	(44)	(24)

Source: Author.

*** Differences between males and females in Institution Type within each type of degree are statistically significant at the *** p <= .001.

IT degrees were more likely to be from higher ranked institutions for men than women. More women than men tended to have completed their BS, MCA, or BCA degrees from private affiliated colleges; 59 per cent of women with BS degrees (vs. 52 per cent men), 58.7 per cent women MCA (vs. 45.2 men). The exceptions were the 2 out of 3 women with MS degrees from the Leader AAAAA institutions.

On the other hand, AAAA Striver institutions were more often the choice of male IT professionals; 44 per cent for their BS and 24.7 per cent for MCA. Similar patterns were found even with non-engineering degree holders; women chose to get their MBAs from private colleges (38.5 per cent) more than men (21.7 per cent). Male MBA and MA/MSC degree holders, on the other hand, went to Striver AAAA institutions (MBA: 47.8 per cent men vs. 23.1 per cent women; MA/MSC 83.3 per cent men vs. 62.8 per cent women). On balance, women tended to graduate from private affiliated colleges while men from AAAA Striver institutions.

IT Women Have Also Yet to Break Through the IT Glass Ceiling

Reflecting possible *gendered pattern recognition*, *men led women* in all positions that have some element of managerial or leadership responsibilities (Table 5.4). For example, male IT professionals outranked women in mid-level management positions (17 per cent vs. 10.1 per cent female), as IT Leads (male 13.4 per cent vs. female 7.2 per cent), and a bit in upper management positions (4.2 per cent male vs. 3.5 per cent female). The most common job title of women IT professionals was engineers (44.6 per cent female vs. 32 per cent male).

Another way *glass ceiling challenges* and associated *gendered pattern recognition* operate in IT is when men are better able than women to parlay their education, particularly the engineering content of their education into jobs in different IT sectors (Table 5.5). Again, women in Indian IT were as educated as men (both have $\bar{X} = 20$ total years of education). But, men were better able to make use of the engineering education content to find jobs in most IT sub-sectors, be they BPOs, Core IT, or their combinations. For example, men in sectors like the BPO or BOP/ITES had a 17-point advantage (49.9 men vs. 33.2 women) in the engineering content of their education. While the gap narrowed in the IT sector, men still had an advantage ($\bar{X} = 63.1$) over women ($\bar{X} = 57.9$). It was only when the BPO sector was

Table 5.4 Gender Differences in IT Job Positions (Web Survey)

Position in Indian IT Companies[*]	Male	Female
Upper Management	4.2%	3.6%[***]
Managers-Mid Level	17.0	10.1
IT Leads but not managers	13.4	7.2
Senior, but not managers nor Leads-Individual contributors	18.3	13.7
Engineers; all levels	32.0	44.6
IT Support staff	4.6	11.5
Consultants	4.2	2.2
Trainees	5.9	4.3
Non-IT	0.3	2.9
(n)	(306)	(139)

Source: Author.

[*] See Table 2.A.3 for descriptions of each position.

[***] Differences between males and females in IT job positions are statistically significant at the $p \leq .001$.

Table 5.5 Gender Differences in Education and Engineering Content by IT Sector

IT Sector		Statistics	Male	Female
Pure BPO (MNC Customer Service and MNC Financial/Back Office)	Number of Years of Education	$\bar{X}$(SD)[*]	19.3 (2.3)	19.3 (0.8)
		Min-Max	12.0–21.0	19.0–21.0
	Engineering Content of Education[†]	$\bar{X}$(SD)	49.9 (26.4)	33.2 (18.3)
		Min-Max	12.0–84.0	19.0–57.0
		(n)	(15)	(7)
BPO with ITES	Number of Years of Education	$\bar{X}$(SD)	19.9 (1.3)	20.3 (1.6)
		Min-Max	19.0–25.0	19.0–25.0
	Engineering Content of Education[†]	$\bar{X}$(SD)	56.9 (18.9)	63.1 (7.7)
		Min-Max	19.0–84.0	50.0–76.0
		(n)	(36)	(15)

(*Cont'd*)

Table 5.5 (*Cont'd*)

IT Sector		Statistics	Male	Female
Pure ITES (E-Commerce and Engineering Service)	Number of Years of Education	$\bar{X}$(SD) Min-Max	**19.1** (1.7) 14.0–21.0	**20.8** (1.8) 19.0–25.0
	Engineering Content of Education[†]	$\bar{X}$(SD) Min-Max (n)	**51.0** (27.5) 19.0–84.0 (27)	50.6 (23.3) 19.0–84.0 (10)
IT with BPO and ITES services	Number of Years of Education	$\bar{X}$(SD) Min-Max	**19.7** (1.5) 14.0–25.0	**20.6** (1.8) 19.0–25.0
	Engineering Content of Education[†]	$\bar{X}$(SD) Min-Max (n)	**58.8** (18.6) 19.0–84.0 (93)	**63.5** (12.6) 42.0–84.0 (22)
Pure IT (Programming, Infrastructure, and R&D)	Number of Years of Education	$\bar{X}$(SD) Min-Max	**20.0** (1.5) 14.0–25.0	**19.7** (1.8) 14.0–25.0
	Engineering Content of Education[†]	$\bar{X}$(SD) Min-Max (n)	**63.1** (17.2) 19.0–84.0 (133)	**57.9** (19.0) 19.0–76.0 (86)

Source: Author.

* $\bar{X}$(SD): Mean and standard deviation.

[†] Engineering Content = Number of years of education completed × Engineering related Highest Education Degree.

combined with ITES and the ITES-BPO-IT sectors that the advantage was reversed in women's favour (BPO-ITES: women $\bar{X}$ = 63.1 vs. men $\bar{X}$ = 56.9; ITES-BPO_IT: women $\bar{X}$ = 63.5 to men $\bar{X}$ = 58.8).

Mixed IT Gender Diversity Outcome Report Card[4]

On balance, the Indian IT sector, at least in the experiences of the rank-and-file IT professionals who participated in the web survey, has made

---

[4] Also see Parikh and Sukhatme (2004).

progress in gender diversity. Indian IT women professionals were *equal to men on the streamlined pure merit metrics*. But, significant hurdles exist in transforming the IT workspace into a gender inclusive one. Men were more successful than women in parlaying their education, particularly the engineering content of their education, into jobs in different IT sectors. And, women had not broken through the proverbial glass ceiling; they were mostly located in the non-managerial levels of jobs in the IT sector. Narrative comments offered by women IT professionals (reviewed below) pointed to the boundary limits of *holistic merit* that stopped within the workplace and were not extended into women's family social habitat and their life cycle changes. Glass ceiling challenges faced by qualified women also pointed to the limits of gender diversity in Indian IT. It is clear that the Indian IT sector has more work to do in making the work habitat, not only gender diverse but also more inclusive. *Gendered pattern recognition metrics* will have to re-calibrated to adjust for family life cycle responsibilities of female professionals, if the sector is to stem the gender leakage and become more gender inclusive.

IT Professionals Welcome Gender Diversity/Parity

Most rank-and-file IT professionals recognized IT women's merit worthiness.[5] It was not surprising that supporters of gender parity outnumbered the critics. Typical comments on gender equality in merit in Indian IT went like this: 'They are equally qualified and capable' and 'That is why they are able to get that job'. Professionals also affirmed that there were

[5] Two specific set of questions about women's place in IT were posed in the survey to gauge how gender diversity and gender inclusivity were experienced by IT professionals. The first question was about the opportunities in Indian IT for women and read, 'How open are employment opportunities in Information Technology to women? Why do you think that?' (Q19). The second asked about the IT merit-worthiness of women; 'Do you think the women who work in Information Technology jobs these days are as qualified as the men? Please explain why you think so' (Q20). To capture the hermeneutic gendered dynamics in the Indian IT workplace, the responses were disaggregated by male and female survey respondent. 73 per cent (258 of the 355) male respondents and 76 per cent of the 164 female respondents, who identified their sex, answered Q19. Similarly 80 per cent (267) of the 335 male respondents and 82 per cent (135) of the /164 female respondents responded to Q20 (see Appendix 1A.1).

'equal opportunities available to women in Indian IT' for those women who 'have equal qualification/skills'. However, that work opportunities are equally open to qualified women in IT, while laudable in its own right, suggested that their *merit was of the streamlined gender neutral* kind. For example, resistance to women's presence in IT was attributed to the mismatch between work and gendered life-cycle commitments as well as other social pressures against women. Even when holistic merit criteria were invoked, it was limited to the workplace and not extended to their home lives. It is these perceived discrepancies between the cultural and work expectations that need to be reconciled if the Indian IT work is to become *gender inclusive*.

Gender Neutral Merit → Pathway to Gender Parity and Diversity

When asked to reflect on whether women who currently work in Information Technology jobs are as qualified as the men, both male and female IT professionals were laudatory about the IT merit-worthiness of Indian women (82 per cent of 267 males and 81 per cent of 164 women). They uniformly 'affirmed gender parity' in Indian IT. They spoke to 'women being equally qualified' as men on a 'gender neutral merit rubric' and having the necessary technical skills to compete with men. They also noted the 'equal opportunities available to women and men' in Indian IT and often attributed the growing presence of women in Indian IT to 'non-discriminatory hiring' practices, mainly in response to 'external pressures'. That very few expressed reservations about women's qualifications to work in IT (18 per cent males and 19 per cent women) reflected the general acceptance of gender parity in Indian IT.

Narrative comments about gender diversity offered by IT professionals ranged from a simple 'Yes'[6] to a majority who offered substantive explanations for their positive gender diversity assertions. All in all, male IT professionals agreed that 'Yes, women are qualified for IT work' or that they are 'equally qualified', they 'fit the job most of the time'. and 'of course, else they may not be selected'. IT women agreed, 'Yes, we are equal'

[6] A quarter of male (76/267) and female (42/164) IT professionals offered declarative assertions about *gender equality in merit* in Indian IT.

in qualifications and opportunities are 'very open', 'good' or 'very good'. A woman engineer declared, 'Yes, I am an example :)', of gender parity in IT.

Numerical representation of women in IT jobs was one strand among the different types of evidence offered by rank-and-file IT professionals to bolster their gender parity claims. Numerical evidence, offered mainly by male professionals, read as follows: 'Equal to men, because percentage of women will speak itself' and 'I don't think this is a question anymore. We see equal number of women in our company'. More specifically, IT is 'very much open as per the current scenario, about 30 to 40 percent of the work pool in IT industry is women'. Others used proportions ranging from 'around 40% are women', or '50.0% women in IT jobs', to demonstrate that women 'are competitive to men'. Women IT professionals added, 'Now women have so many opportunities… in IT field 50% employees are women' and that 'employment opportunities in information technologies are really available to women', and IT 'is 100% open' to women.

It was *gender parity in IT education*, said many IT professionals, that have led to the growing presence of women in IT. In the words of some male professionals, IT women 'have the same opportunity as men in getting into any accredited college', 'earn the same degree and undergo the same training', 'go through the same college education', attend 'same colleges, listen to same professors, take the same exams, get screened by the same panel, so no difference at all'. In fact, 'they are equally qualified as men because now a days equal opportunities for women on the education front and absolutely no restriction. Women from conservative families should come forward, break the social barrier'. In short, women's 'access to education has been improving especially in urban areas from where students are recruited into IT companies'. To these IT professionals, women have made progress on the IT education merit metrics.

But, when the IT professionals explained their reasoning for their gender equality assertions, they talked about 'talent being gender neutral'. Isolating IT skills from gender were these male respondents: 'It's an individual's ability and character and not the gender', that matters. Another said, 'It's got nothing to do with the gender, it's all about one individual and the talent they bring in everyday to work'. Further, 'IT requires more of mental effort than physical and I don't think that a woman's mental ability is any way inferior to a man's'. Besides, 'Skills are not gender specific'. Again, 'gender doesn't come into picture for employment. It is skills' and 'technical and communication skills' that matter.

Female IT professionals concurred that women in IT have the skills and qualifications, even if of the gender-neutral variety, to compete and be hired for jobs that have opened up in the Indian IT sector. Many said 'women are as qualified as the men', or 'surely there is no difference in gender'. Some female respondents even thought that 'Nowadays women are more qualified than men' because otherwise 'they would never be recruited. Government reservations do not hold good in private organizations'. Others spoke more specifically to the *equality of merit in technical education*. Some sample comments. 'Gender was never been the hindrance in acquiring technical knowledge and skill'; or 'Both men and women are equally qualified, as they have completed the same degree of education'; or 'the pool of fresh graduates that are hired into the job comprises of both men and women'; or that 'they go through similar education and selection process'. Women, one noted, 'are not only considered important but also are second to none' or 'qualification is not restricted to men alone', and that 'Talent and skill predominate gender'. In short, 'Gender has no value. Valuable people are valued'. 'Whether you are man or women if you have knowledge you get the job' because 'IT is open for all who have skill', 'good skills in the IT sector' and there is 'No difference in standards applied to them' particularly 'if the people have skill to get a job'. Others elaborated, IT is 'Very open' to women, because 'most of the companies would hire the best available candidate talent to stay competitive'. IT female professionals who agreed with the *gender neutral definition of work* said, 'whether you are men or women doesn't matter; only work matters' or 'It is the work and qualification that defines this' and that 'I'm a real example; I have seen in my experience' that 'there is no differentiation for women and men in the selection criteria for an IT job. So the selected personnel will be qualified irrespective of sex'.

Of course, parity in technical skills only goes so far as the opportunities available to women in technical education and in the workplace. Over two-thirds (69 per cent of 258) of male IT professionals attributed *the equal opportunities* available to qualified women in Indian IT to the structural changes in the industry. 'IT gives opportunities to women. Like if they are capable they are placed into many positions', said a male professional. To others, 'we won't find any walk'n interview calls of any IT company with sex mentioned in them'. In short, 'There are lot of opportunities for women when it comes to IT field. There is no gender discrepancy at all in IT'. And because there is 'No bar on sex' in IT, there is 'Huge opening for women'. Alluding to recent openness in IT to women, a few noted: 'These days women are also getting equal opportunity as male employees in IT field'.

Female IT professionals, once again, agreed that, in addition to gender equality in merit, there are 'equal opportunities for women and men in Indian IT'. They said, 'Many, many, and very good opportunities', because 'skills come first and not the gender', or that 'women not only are considered important but also are second to none'. Opportunities for women are, 'Equal to men', and that 'there are plenty of opportunities for women in IT' that are 'the same as in the case of men'. 'Employment opportunities in information technologies are really available to women', because 'women are also competent', and 'are equally employed based on their skills'. And because IT is 'widely open for women too ... in IT companies the percentage of women is more or less same as the men', and 'now a days both men and women have equal rights given' and are 'equally wanted'. 'Only talent is the main criteria, not gender', because in IT 'there is no physical work, only brain work is involved'.

Some women paired the education and skills women have acquired with the work opportunities for women in Indian IT with comments like these: 'Based on education, technical skill, and communication, opportunities are given to women because they are capable to do all things'; 'The jobs are given to well qualified women in IT. They do well the job better than men', 'It is just how well you know about your job' that matters. There are 'a lot of chances for the women folk ... todays women are more career oriented', and if women 'have real talent, they will give job'. IT identifies 'the right proportion of talent from women for the jobs', because 'if a person is good it does not matter if the person is he or she?' asked one and that 'Qualification & experience matters a lot- rest of the things depends how he or she clear the interview'. To sum up, 'IT gives same opportunities to male and female, if they have talent', because 'gender is not a factor to work in IT fields', and 'opportunities are open to women provided that they possess the required skills'.

IT professionals also talked about 'gender parity in effort and productivity' once women are hired. Not only are women equally qualified, said male IT professionals, 'they get equal work distribution', 'put same efforts' and that there is 'no difference as far as performance at work is considered. It's an age old mindset that lets few to specifically look into and differentiate women from us'. Women 'take equal responsibility' and are 'equally billed for their skill'. In other words, women 'have to deliver to the same set of metrics as men'. In fact, 'Project Managers also ensuring that each project will have at least 20% of women in team' because women have 'the skill level delivery and zeal to learn'. Female IT professionals confirmed women's 'work ethic'. Women are as qualified as men, they said, because 'the effort & commitment they put in the IT jobs is same as Men', or women 'can also be a good team player', and that 'they work at Sr. level like men too and handle senior responsibility'. In general, 'both are qualified well and shine according to their interest and dedication'. Women 'are very competitive' because they are 'definitely qualified and have similar attitudes to reach the top as men'. Women are 'equivalent to men, in both technical aspects and also hardworking' and 'have shown very good results in every field and determined to their goals despite the social limits'. They 'show the same dedication, some times more than men, and same kind of enthusiasm as men in delivering in a project. They don't even have any reservations in working in night shifts', or '24/7', and 'are interested to contribute back to society doing work home as well at the Office'. On balance, 'women can be as poorly qualified as men, or as fairly qualified as men' and IT women are 'meeting up the challenges thrown to them'.

In addition to gender parity in education, in opportunities, and in their work ethic, male and female IT professionals used the *language of non-discrimination* in hiring to explain the growing presence of women in Indian IT: 'There is no discrimination based on gender in IT. Everyone who has right technical skills with right attitude has the opportunity waiting for him at his or her door'. 'No Bias', said another male respondent, 'I don't think there is any biased opinion against women in IT. They have proved in many fields that they can be really good'. Women have equal chances in IT sector, because 'There is no discrimination of any sort'. In short, 'Information technology companies do not discriminate against women. I can cite personal reasons for thinking that - my wife used to work in the IT area, two of my cousins (women) work in the IT area'. Female IT professionals used gender neutral merit to bolster their claim of *no-gender-discrimination*. 'I have never faced a gender bias' because 'IT is a merit based industry and there is no gender discrimination, and women are given equal opportunities' and has 'heard of very little cases of discrimination personally' or 'no partiality or gender allocation'. Male IT professionals reinforced the *gender neutral hiring practices in IT*. Some sample comments: 'Companies are hiring based on qualification and skills match'; 'Most IT companies only look for talents'. IT companies 'pick the candidates based on eligibility criteria and there is no preference given to any gender. So whoever gets into IT is always equal to men at least in terms of educational qualification'. Women in IT are as qualified as men, 'Because IT is all about applying brain that knows no gender'.

Another reason cited for gender parity in IT was 'external structural pressures'. Some sample commentaries, irrespective of gender of IT professionals: 'MNCs prefer to have a correct balance among gender, race, origin, nationality etc.' Others referred to 'recent changes in the government policies' and 'effort of the non-profit social welfare organisations' for gender parity progress. IT companies, they said, 'are very transparent … recruiting around 40% women candidates' and many companies have 'special recruitment drives for women'. Along the same lines were these male professionals who noted that IT is 'equally open as it is open to men. I didn't come across any IT job advertisement mentioning only MALES APPLY :)' and that 'IT is probably one of the few areas where discrimination is at its least or unheard of. I have conducted lot of interviews in my 10 years of IT career and never have I been pressurized (sic) or asked to be biased towards male candidates'. Women professionals also referred to specific structural make-up of the company. They said, gender parity 'depends (on) the environment', 'on the company and its policies', and that while 'equal to men, may be promotions may be less if you get a manager who likes to control women; so depends upon your manager'.

Some IT professionals also used the 'success of women in IT to make a case for gender merit parity'. Yes, they said, women in IT are equally meritorious to men because: 'In my past experience I have worked with women in different roles as peers, boss and subordinates. I don't think there is a bias and feel that the system is open'. Others noted, 'if they were not qualified, they won't be still working in those companies. Since the companies require only qualified people', or that they need to be qualified 'to survive in IT', and 'if not they can't sustain'. Because, IT work 'is more related to programming and ability to deliver and work in teams. Women are equally good. And we see lots of female Project Managers in current industry' and in the 'managerial stream too'. Women also added examples of *women breaking the glass ceiling* in Indian IT. 'Women have equal opportunities as men. In fact, there are many women who hold higher positions in the industry' and there are a 'lot of options ... now days women are geared up for all kind of senior and responsible roles'. To one female respondent, 'Opportunities are really open for women, only depends on how women accept it. There are a lot of onsite offers and management positions given to them'.

Challenges to Gender Parity in Indian IT

Amidst these claims extolling gender parity and equality in Indian IT were *the scattering of* male and female IT professionals who were more circumspect in their evaluation of current state of gender parity. Indian IT is not quite open to women, they said, but it is getting better. Women's opportunities in Indian IT are 'Not like men, but it's good sign women are in IT' or 'the ratio is getting better now and many company's give good benefits for diversity'. To another, women's options are 'below normal compared to men', because 'we still see male domination in IT'.

On the other hand, a few complained about 'positive discrimination', as in women being preferred over men: 'Girls are given more importance than boys at present world' and that there is 'even better opportunity for women' because 'companies are working towards positive discrimination'. IT women 'have it much easier compared to men', and have 'more employments opportunities in IT'. And as might be expected in a gendered society, there were those few (14 per cent of 267) male IT professionals who categorically *denied the validity of the gender merit parity* argument. Women and men are 'not similar in qualifications', they said, or 'they might be qualified, but they are not as capable as men', or that they are 'hired in IT because they get affirmative/preferential treatment' were some refrains. Examples of female deficits in IT ranged from women 'lacking technical skills' to 'they are technically just behind as men', or 'Yes, they qualified, but not capable as men', or that women don't handle 'pressure' as well as men and 'do not excel in all areas'. To quote another, women are not equal to men in IT merit 'because IT information technology is a really challenging field', and even though women's 'communication skills are good, they are technically not good'. Added to the mix were the tongue in cheek comments from a few male professionals. 'They are equal even in drinking in POP club.' 'Many of them are in IT, because that is their only guarantee of going past the men, in a gender-biased society.'

Summary Assessment of Gender-Neutral Merit: IT Male and Female Voices

Despite these scattered negative assessments, IT professionals, overall, had 'a positive take on the state of gender parity' in Indian IT. Not only do women qualify on the *gender neutral criteria*, there are also more opportunities for them in IT. To quote a male IT professional, 'In Information technology employment opportunities are equally for men and women. Integrating gender concerns into employment promotion can contribute to more effective boosting of productivity and economic growth'. Aside from parity on gender neutral IT merit, 'work opportunities' have opened for women in the Indian IT sector, at least at the entry and mid-level level positions, they said. Of course there were the realists: 'OK. Need to improve'; Or 'Just opening up'; 'Not bad, but still has to improve'; Opportunities 'are not that good'; 'It is biased to some extent'. And that 'women have less opportunities; especially in development, where they do not do well'. Or that women are equal 'till they marry' or have 'family commitments' spoke volumes to the gender inclusive challenges that IT faces.

Nonetheless, the *relative openness to gender parity was in sharp contrast to the vehement resistance against being asked to reflect on caste minority diversity*, of SCs and STs, in discussions of merit in the IT culture. They were substantially more open about articulating women's place in the merit culture of Indian IT than that of SCs.

Gendered 'Leakage' in Engineering and General Education Pipelines

In order to appreciate the educational progress that IT women have made in acquiring their merit qualifications, albeit gender neutral, it is helpful to view them in the context of the average Indian woman. 'Gender disparities in education start early'. It is widely understood that the average Indian woman lags behind men, particularly as they transition into higher education ages. Education starts to become a privilege particularly starting after the X grade, even though education in India is universal (Table 5A.1). While the GERs (gross enrolment ratios) for boys and girls were even at the elementary school (I–VIII), secondary school (IX–X), and even senior secondary school (XI–XII) levels, women's enrolment in higher education (19.8), where IT related education is acquired, drops lower than that of men (22.3).

Gendered educational disparities also run the gamut along the many social and occupational dimensions of stratification. Social minorities, whether they are women, SCs, STs, or rural residents lag behind their more privileged counterparts in the educational opportunities available to them as well as in their achievements. Cumulative female deficits in education, in an intersectional caste-gender manner, can be seen over their life course and across different caste groups (Table 5A.2). Irrespective of age and caste group, males were more educated than females. And in the same age group, SC men had a 2.3 year advantage over SC women. No doubt, the caste education gap was somewhat bigger among older men and women. But, the gender deficits gaps were even higher in the SC than in the FC communities. For example, among the 21–30 year olds, FC males had a 1.5 year educational advantage over women; the deficit for SC women was 2.3 years compared to men.

On balance, Indian women, were less educated than men. But, the inter-sectionality of gender and caste were evident in the educational hierarchy. Irrespective of age group, FC males were the most privileged, followed by FC females. SC males and females, in that order, were the least educated. Even literacy rates, which have improved in the 10 year period starting in 2001 for men and women in India, *showed gendered and caste gaps* (Table 5A.3). For example, among Indians 15 years and older, there was a 5.4 per cent increase in literacy rates for men (73.4 per cent in 2001 to 78.8 per cent in 2011) and 11.5 percentage point increase for women (from 47.8 in 2001 to 59.3 in 2011). However, despite comparable improvements for SC males and women, they still lag behind the general population. Literacy rates for SC males improved from 59.3 per cent in 2001 to 71.6 per cent in 2011 (a 12 point increase) and for SC female from 28.5 in 2001 to 48.6 in 2011 (20 point improvement).

In addition to gender leakage in the general education pipeline, there is also gender leakage in technical education. It is axiomatic that gender diversity and inclusiveness in IT assume that qualified women are available to and interested in working in the IT sector. Globally, including in India, women are not well represented in the pipeline for IT jobs, engineering programs. Scholars have identified cultural and structural (within the educational system) barriers that women face in entering and leaving the engineering education system. In response, concerted efforts have been made, ranging from STEM programs in the US[7] to reduced fees/grace points in entrance exams in India (Aspiring Minds 2016), to encourage more women to study engineering. And there has been a concomitant growing interest among females in engineering. According to Aspiring Minds, the number of female students in India taking the IIT entrance exam has grown significantly from 29,291 in 2005 to approximately 1.5 lakh in 2012. In the USA, effective STEM related interventions that have focused on increasing women's choice of engineering in college are credited with around 18 per cent enrollment (2002–11)[8] and a stable 20 per cent rate (over 20 years) of women engineering graduates (Fouad et al. 2011: 11).

The leakage for women starts at the entry level into, and continues into graduation from, engineering colleges. For example, Aspiring Minds scholars documented a male-female ratio at initial acceptance into Indian IITs to be in the range of 14:1 compared to 10:1, and 8:1 into the next two rungs of institutions like NITs and other top state run colleges. One primary reason posited for these uneven gender ratios are self-selection by Indian women, namely women opting out because of weak self-perception of ability and weak test preparedness (Hill, Corbett, and St. Rose 2010). The narrow selection criteria in India's top engineering colleges, namely sole reliance on test scores, also disadvantaged Indian women; for every eight to fourteen men at IIT, NIT, and other top state-run engineering institutes in India, there was just one woman who made the cut. US colleges, in contrast, use a more holistic application process that included a portfolio of previous work, statement of purpose, and interviews. However, once admitted to Indian engineering programs, Aspiring Minds found no evidence of leakage for Indian females in their education and career path. US female engineering students, on the other hand, did experience a 'chilly climate' in engineering colleges; the isolation, psychological intimidation, and loss of confidence that women students faced led to high American female dropout rates during college. Gendered leakage continues into the employment level in the USA.[9] While women comprise more than 20

---

[7] Also see 'Increasing Interest of Young Women in Engineering' by Hinterlong, Lawrence, and DeVol (2014).

[8] http://www.nsf.gov/statistics/2015/nsf15311/tables/pdf/tab2-10.pdf; http://www.nsf.gov/statistics/2015/nsf15311/tables/pdf/tab2-9.pdf.

[9] Fouad et al. (2011) national longitudinal survey of 3,700 US women engineers' experiences in technical workplaces found that the majority (57 per cent)

per cent of US engineering school graduates, they are only 11 per cent of practicing engineers, despite decades of academic, federal, and employer interventions to address this gender gap. In the words of Mills, '… it is essential that the culture of the engineering profession changes to make it more accessible and user-friendly for women' (2011: 143).

Gender and Caste Inclusivity Indian IT: Promises and Challenges

Despite the declared openness to gender diversity by the rank-and-file IT professionals and progress in women's education, IT companies and their professionals are still *ways off from a gender inclusive work environment.* As IT professionals reflected on women's place in IT, the promise and limits to gender inclusivity sometimes became clear. *Family-work conflicts, gendered glass ceiling, and systemic and personal obstacles* were noted as standing in the way of inclusive environment. Yet, there were glimpses of promise in transforming the IT habitus into a more gender inclusive workplace.

Challenges of Gender Inclusivity: Male and Female Voices

Conflicts between family responsibilities and work, the most commonly cited impediments that prevented women from fully participating in the

----

were practicing engineers; but 20 per cent started an engineering career and left the field more than five years before the survey or (8 per cent) within 5 years; yet others (15 per cent) never entered the engineering workforce. Common reasons cited for leaving were work conditions related (about 50 per cent said too much travel, low salary, or lack of advancement; another third unpleasant workplace climate, boss, or culture; and a quarter to spend more time with family). Women who did not work as engineers feared that the engineering workplace would not be hospitable to them; some had lost interest in engineering and were using the knowledge in other more personally rewarding fields. On the other hand, it was a combination of positive work climate (mentors and companies that were gender inclusive) that were the major reasons for retention. When 2003 and 2011 US exit rate for women engineers were compared to men, female exit rate was primarily due to dissatisfaction over pay and promotion opportunities and significantly less so due to family reasons (Hunt 2016).

Indian IT sector, was one gender inclusive challenges faced by IT companies. Referring to family-work conflicts, while simultaneously affirming
progress to date, were these women: 'It's difficult for married women'; 'I
think it is equal. But the distinction at work is noticeable. For the reason
that - Women are considered to be family oriented and not work committed - Women cannot go out of their way to socialize, build relationship
like men do - Women are considered to be not physically and mentally
strong'. Even though conditions have improved, 'growth can be limited if
you are a woman'. Another voice, 'IT is not very suited to women. The
IT field requires highly concentrated work environment. Women find it
difficult to cope with it as well as family commitment since most of the
Indian women have a double role to play-in the career and in the family'.
Working in night shifts 'is one of the major concerns for women, specially
married women; this reduces their employment opportunities compared
to men'. Concerns that 'women are not as committed/will not be willing
to work long hours', drive some companies 'to prefer gents because it is
difficult for women to work in overnights'. Another reported that while
opportunities for women are very open, 'I don't know if women are able to
sustain themselves as they go up the career rungs because of the pressures
of work and the challenge to balance personal constraints' and 'women
suffer a huge amount of mental trauma at workplaces'.

When women spoke to the *gendered glass ceiling in Indian IT*, they
were alluding to the challenges in *transforming the IT habitat into a gender
inclusive environment*. These responses were illustrative: Women are equal
to men only at the 'Entry level positions' or 'in lower exec posts'. While
'the opportunities for female are almost 65% open', or 'as a fresher there is
no partiality', as women 'grow, there is some hesitation to go with women
employees; this is mainly due to womens' time constraints and flexibility
in working hours'.

Male IT professionals too attributed the glass ceiling constraints faced
by women in Indian IT to 'challenges at work', 'in social obstacles', 'and in
their personal lives'. The following responses illustrated *gendered work constraints:* 'In IT they have equal opportunity, but the women coming to the
field may be less due to constraints in working time (night shifts)'. Women
have same opportunities as men, except for 'networking difficulties', or
'work pressure and timing', and 'the working conditions being tough,
social and orthodox environmental conditions often serve as a barrier to
career progress'. Another said, '60%-70% positions are open to women in

the IT market but ... they cannot work in many onsite positions (Arab Countries)', are 'unable to relocate with in the country due to family constraints' and cannot 'meet 24*7 working schedules'. Besides, 'very few women are chosen for the development (software), most are in testing, technical writing'. All in all, women 'have good qualification. They are also valuable to the project and company. Only difference is some women cannot spend extra efforts if needed in project'; consequently, while women's opportunities are '50% open, filling only up to 30%'.

Some examples of *socially gendered social constraints* to gender parity and inclusivity read as follows: 'There are opportunities in IT to women, but with the fact that they have to face exploitation and violence here in India, coz these events make headline of most daily newspapers very frequent now'. Opportunities 'are equally open but are bound by several limitations laid by manu (Hindu)'.

Women's family responsibilities, an example of gendered social capital deficits, loomed large in other IT male comments about the constraints women face. Some samples: 'Very open. Less physical effort required and only brain effort. However, it might not be too suited to a woman putting a lot of stress on family'; or 'If women have skill and they wish to work well opportunities are not less. But most of them are getting married and don't wish to go for work'; or 'Employment opportunity are equal for both men and women and no discrimination in that. I feel due to some social setup many women can't be so committed to their job'. In a similar vein, 'both men and women are equal ... But still some think that women might not be suitable for long term onsite since they need to spend more time to take care of family', and 'when they come back after long medical leaves; also women find it difficult to put in long hours after a family'. One professional summarized the gender challenges women faced, as: 'Like any industry the chances still remain 85% male dominated, 15% woman, especially in a country like India where career objectives become a less or null priority for women post marriage'. Or 'I believe they are equally qualified. Most of the serviced based companies offer good opportunities but I think women are under-represented in high-tech jobs, especially in product companies', because while women are 'in fact very good in academics ... behind men in practical experience'.

A few other explanations from male IT professionals for women's presence in IT were, at best, 'compliments that were sexist, almost misogynist, or back handed' (n = 10). Some sample *sexist* comments: 'Now a days, women are preferred more than guys because of their communication and looks'; 'Presently women also have good opportunities in the IT sector because they are much manageable, 'are able to sit in a place a lot of times', 'very obedient and sincere and finish the task in the right time'. But other comments sounded like *back-handed compliments*. 'There is no major difference in IT but women might be preferred in some cases because of their patience level'. Another, while acknowledging that men are equally good as women, opined that 'I think women are more preferred by companies these days. The reason could be that they can be more focused on a job demanding mental attention'. And 'comparatively women are preferred, bcz their mobility is restricted and hence do not switch jobs frequently. Companies look for people who stay with them for longer time'. Or 'female candidates are appropriate for certain types of IT jobs, office work'.

Promise of Gender Inclusivity

It was when IT females, and some males, linked *women's personal capital or strengths* to opportunities in IT, that one began to see the promise of a gender inclusive climate in Indian IT. Focusing on personal gendered strengths that make women a good match, if not better, than men, for work in IT were these observations: '80% opportunities are opened to women because women are more responsible', they 'work with more concentration', are 'more patient, responsible, trustworthy than men'. In the modern world, women 'are preferred ... because of their skills'.

Other *hopeful glimpses of gender inclusivity* were also seen in the responses, although not that many, from both male and female IT professionals who opined that 'IT jobs and women make a good match'. As seen in these sample comments, some IT males were genuinely appreciative of women's talents and work habits that appeal to IT companies: women have ample opportunities in IT they said, because 'they are more dedicated and sincere towards their work', 'will work hard without any time frame', 'they stay in a single company longer than men'. Or 'In IT, women have more opportunities than they have in other fields, because IT does not have much physical hazards', like jobs in 'manufacturing or other services'. They have 'low turnover', 'are more focused on completing a task well'. And women excel in 'QA, Testing & Development'.

But, those who felt that Indian IT has more work to do, particularly when it comes to becoming gender inclusive had this to say: 'Women face a variety of obstacles when entering a high tech and competitive industry. It is just key to remember that whether the problem is sexual harassment, lack of respect, or trouble breaking into the "boys club" that the benefits far outweigh the cost. High salaries and respect are a pay off that come from a job in Information Technology, a far cry from the days of a woman's duty to be a secretary or receptionist. Having self-confidence enough in one's own abilities and finding the balance of respect and understanding can avoid all three of these taboo issues'. And the prospects for gender inclusivity are hopeful because, 'The major Technology Institutes in India are open to women'.

On balance, the overwhelming majority of IT professionals opined affirmatively that women in Indian IT are as meritorious as men. There was of course some male griping about positive discrimination in favour of women or that women are not suited for IT work even though they might have the IT training. But, to the gender merit equality camp, the merit metric was their gender neutral skills and talent. Ironically, those who pointed to women's educational achievements, and even work styles and ethic that render women as, if not more, suitable to work in the Indian IT sector offered examples of what a gender-inclusive, rather than a gender-neutral, definition of merit in the IT sector might look like. But, the typical gender stereotypes that a few of the male respondents held against women, such as the challenges of balancing between family and work life and the affirmative efforts of companies to promote gender parity in Indian IT, were challenges to be countered.

Concluding Comments on Inclusive IT Merit-Gender and Caste Considerations

Progress in gender parity in Indian IT, the hallmark of diversity in the IT work habitus, has been achieved through *gender neutralizing* the yardstick of the sector, IT merit. *Gender inclusiveness* was not quite on the radar of the rank-and-file IT professionals. Besides, the sector was much more open to discussing the merits of gender diversity than caste diversity. At this time in history, *caste diversity continues to be a bridge too high or far to cross.*

Gender Parity through Gender Neutral Merit

Women have definitely made inroads into breaking down some of the gender barriers in IT, at least at the entry and mid-level level positions in

IT companies. IT has become *more gender diverse*. IT men and women alike talked about the structural opportunities available to women in the IT sector, primarily because women have become fuller participants, like their male counterparts, in the solely-skill based streamlined IT merit project. For the most part, these IT professionals, both men and women, felt employment opportunities were quite open (indicating gender diversity) to women and women are recruited for IT jobs because they are skilled and merit-worthy like their male IT counterparts.

However, gender diversity progress in the IT sector has been achieved using *gender neutrality* in the conceptualization and application of merit. Rank-and-file IT professionals, both male and female, were quite uniform in their positive assessments of women's incorporation (based on qualifications, expertise, and success) in IT. But, gender diversity, while laudable, has been achieved through gender neutral cultural streamlining (Radhakrishnan 2011: 48–52); merit has been stripped of any gender connotations and renders merit and skill sets as the primary and only set of criteria in the IT sector. In this gender neutral world, being an educated, merit worthy woman is not expected to add more, if anything at all, in the IT workplace.

Equally important is this fact: rank-and-file IT professionals comingled the terms *diversity* and *parity*. Diversity is a broader term that includes parity. Parity often means equal, if not proportional representation of men and women and quality. Diversity can also mean more women in a company in comparison to other sectors in a company, or globally, or even over time. Of more significance for business productivity and effectiveness is *gender inclusiveness*. An inclusive workplace is one where a gender inclusive merit culture, not neutral merit, infuses the entire organizational structure and ethos. More details about what a gender infused culture are offered below and in Chapter 6.

To the extent that women qualify only because of their gender neutral credits, the IT industry under-capitalizes its potential for gender inclusivity. Whether IT professionals were talking about the openness of employment opportunity structures to women or the merit worthiness of Indian women, merit was *more gender neutral than inclusive*. Besides, the resistance to women's presence in IT, attributed to the mismatch between work and gendered life cycle commitments as well as other social pressures against women, gives pause to claims of full gender equality in Indian IT. It is these perceived discrepancies that need to be reconciled if the Indian IT work is to become, not only diverse, but also more gender inclusive.

Building Gender Diversity Competence

What is the *prognosis* for a *gender inclusive IT* work habitus? The overwhelming accord on gender neutral merit criteria in hiring and promotion indicated that gender inclusiveness was not a major issue for the IT sector. Besides, the unmistakable *emphasis on gender parity than on gender inclusiveness* signalled continued opposition to transitioning from gender parity to inclusiveness. While Indian IT has taken important steps towards gender diversity and gender neutrality, they have many structural and social miles to go before it can claim to be a gender inclusive workplace. Inclusiveness will require more than simply neutralizing the unique contributions that women bring to the merit culture. IT companies will need to make concerted attempts to access a more gender diverse talent pool, be more gender inclusive and diversity competent, if they are to tap into the business benefits of a gender inclusive workforce, sharpen their competitive advantage, and sustain excellence.

Some Critical Components in Gender Inclusive Merit and Climate

It is in comments that spoke to the multiple ways that women outdo men that one saw *spaces open up for making merit more gender inclusive*. The few male and female professionals that noted women's work styles and ethic as being better suited to working in the IT sector than men's styles were hinting at a broader, more gender inclusive definition of merit. Even the few who disagreed with the gender parity statement did so mainly because of the gendered conflicts in balancing family and work that women face; a gender inclusive climate will need to include accommodations for gendered life experiences.

Gender inclusive merit will have to take into consideration *women's work styles and work ethic* that buttresses, rather than detracts from, women's skills. They 'work that much harder than men', are 'more dedicated and committed to work than men', 'they take lot of responsibilities', 'tend to take their work more seriously and do it also with more accuracy'. And while 'there is not much difference between men and women, women don't waste time with coffee, smoke'. In fact, one said, 'Yes … I have worked with them and learnt from them', they are equally technically skilled and soft skilled'.

The rationale offered by female IT professionals for adding work ethic and work style into gender inclusive merit looked like this: 'women are more qualified than men; I think so because women have become more "career conscious" these days'. Other comments were in a similar vein: 'Many times women are more productive than men'; or 'they are sincere, hard work and dedicated in their job more than men'; or 'they are as qualified, but are more dedicated and take fewer smoking breaks :-)'; or 'they are also much more sincere and dedicated in most cases'. The female edge in comparisons went on: 'In fact they are more adhered to process and policy than men'; or 'they are also better in managing & handling teams', or 'They are qualified both in the technology sectors as well as management sectors; they handle higher position than men only because they are qualified and experienced'.

Other women IT professionals added women's superior academic performance to the work ethic component of a broader gender inclusive IT merit. Women, they said, are equally, if not more 'meritorious', as men. Women 'are often better qualified or even over qualified', they 'are taking effort to get the knowledge from outside world'. Others said, 'In India women are backed by great academic performance' and 'women are studying better and "*working harder*" than men'. A few IT males had similar assessments that 'women were more broadly qualified than men'. Yes, they said, 'They are equally or even more qualified in some instances. They compete well in all areas of technologies'; 'They are qualified and have sufficient skills as men (sometimes even greater)', 'maybe even more than men. If you check the ratio of students who drop-out of colleges, men are more than women; meaning from the very first step in a career (a college degree) women are more qualified than men'. Women are more qualified than men, 'coz they study well and implement it in the right areas'. Women, others said, 'sometimes are more qualified' or 'Better qualified than men', because IT work needs 'more mental strength and I believe women are mentally more stronger than Men'. 'I have seen women', another said, 'who are more logical and intelligent than men in solving IT issues'. Others added, 'Women study better in college level. So they are better qualified'; 'They dominate men'; and 'of course, sometimes they work smarter than men'.

'Building diversity competence'[10] (both in parity and in inclusive climate) in organizations and reaping its organizational benefits is 'not a short term project and neither it is linear or uniform'. Findings structural solutions to address obstacles to gender inclusiveness will take time. For example, scholars have found that systemic solutions that address structural obstacles, although time intensive, to be far more effective in fostering acceptance of gender diversity competence, than simply instituting company diversity programs (Rao and Bagali 2014b). The structural obstacles that need to be tackled involve broadening the merit culture parameters and revisiting the gendered pattern recognition in hiring and promotion. Besides, the positive productivity benefits of diversity might only be reaped when there was a time lag of five years between diversity efforts and employee productivity (Ali, Kulik, and MetzKulik 2011). There might also be a tipping point for diversity benefits after organizational diversity has reached medium levels (also Kanter 1977b). Other mediating variables that make for smoother diversity transition, identified by Ranganathan and Alfaro (2011), were prior work ties among team members that enhanced performance in globally dispersed software development teams.

In short, translating workforce gender diversity in globalized Indian IT companies into gender inclusive social spaces that can become a valuable resource for organizational improvements is not automatic. A gender inclusive project involves, among other issues, the critical organizational challenge of managing the diverse expectations and experiences of men and women at all levels of the organization. Promoting qualified women into the management ranks, offering flexible work environments to women, and figuring out ways to foster the unique contributions of women, like say collaborative work models, will require leadership commitment to feminizing the masculine/patriarchal corporate culture.

Caste, Gender, and a Broader Diversity Vision

But, developing a diversity competent workplace *does not stop with gender inclusiveness*. Workplace diversity is multidimensional in nature. The globalized environment in which Indian IT companies operate and the

---

[10] Rajlakshmi Saikia (2012). Available at: http://www.peoplematters.in/article/2012/01/04/diversity/its-beyond-gender/1443.

associated shifts in the business environment, customer base, and changing demographics of the available talent pool (NASSCOM @ www.nasscom.com) have initiated a rethinking and broadening of hiring and work practices to cover diversity in its many dimensions. Aside from gender, NASSCOM has started to bring awareness to and encouraging action on other of the multiple dimensions of diversity including disability, sexual orientation, religion, and generations.[11] Much of the incentive has come from the increasing number of multinational corporations operating in India; these MNCs have prodded IT organizations to not only move towards becoming more diverse but also broadening their definitions of diversity and becoming more inclusive and diversity confident.

However, just as engaging gender diversity is not straight forward, doing diversity in its multidimensionality is neither linear nor simple. Being gender diverse does not automatically translate into diversity on sexual orientation, disability, religion, or caste. In fact, there is scholarly evidence to demonstrate that not all diversity is equal. Rao and Bagali (2014a) found that employees of Indian IT and ITES-BPO companies were more accepting of cultural diversity (not surprising considering the global working environments of Indian IT companies) than gender diversity because of gendered social values in male dominated corporate structures. NASSCOM's initial focus on gender diversity was driven partly by the growing number of women graduating with engineering and information technology degrees. But, they have broadened the definition of diversity to include PwDs (people with disability), LGBT communities, multiple generations, and nationalities. To leverage the diverse talent pool on their organization's behalf, companies have also to become more inclusive, by systematically nurturing awareness of and improving diversity competence in its organization, whether gender, disability, generational, language diversity, or other relevant diversity dimensions.

[11] Rajesh and Ekambaram (2014) identified four cohort or generations in the Indian workforce with very different world views and approaches to work and life in general drawn from their lived experiences during different time periods in the country's history. The Free-Gens (1945–1960 cohort), Gen X's (between 1961 and 1970), E-Gen's (1971–80), and Gen Y's (1981–1990). The 'Veterans' were born between 1920 and 1945 in pre-independence India. Managing and leveraging diversity to build a cohesive organizational culture would require companies to appreciate and harness the respective generational strengths and weaknesses in the interest of organizational goals.

The initial progress in diversity in the Indian IT sector, not withstanding, there are *two critical diversity dimension* that are largely absent in the Indian IT discourse. *One is 'caste' diversity.* It was quite telling that rank-and-file IT professionals, both male and female, were quite uniform in their positive assessments of women's incorporation (albeit based on gender neutral qualifications, expertise, and success) in IT than they were about SCs/OBCs. To the IT industry and its professionals, caste is not part of their diversity consideration. The *intersectionality of caste, family, and gender* (Fernandez 1997) in dominant caste women's *access to IT networks* through their *strong family ties*, has rendered gender inequality and equality more readily accessible and amenable for discussion, analyses, and redress than caste (in)equalities. In the intersecting Indian social hierarchies of family, gender, and caste, despite the gendered Indian society, women in one's family and caste are accorded, even if unconsciously, higher status than women of lower castes/families. Partly as a result of their ties, dominant caste women have made inroads into higher education and related occupations.[12] In the words of some IT professionals, 'the caste Brahmins refer their male and female relatives and friends, while the low caste have no reference in the IT sector. So IT companies are full of high caste Brahmins'; Another said, 'Women are gaining entry in IT but this is just an urban phenomenon. There are no opportunities for women from the oppressed classes (Backward, Scheduled Castes) in IT that is dominated by Upper Castes'. The issue of how to foster caste diversity and caste inclusiveness will be further addressed in Chapter 6, the concluding section.

A second important missing link in IT diversity work is diversity that is *intersectionally defined and accounted for.* A deeper set of obstacles to gender inclusiveness for all women lies in the intersectionality of gender and caste at work in the educational institutions. National education data (see Tables 5A.1–5A.3) demonstrated the deep rooted educational disadvantages to women of SC communities. In the educational hierarchy, FC

---

[12] See Shenoy-Packer (2014) for a discussion of women in upper- and middle-caste and income households benefitting from family economic support, paternal knowledge of career paths, and maternal emotional encouragement (social and cultural capital) as they pursue their studies and work. But, the higher caste women also felt discriminated on multiple fronts, by the protective legislative practices for lower castes as well as in their public and private lives.

males were cumulatively the most privileged, followed by FC females, SC males and females, in that order. And while women's literacy rates have improved, the gender gap in the general population and between FC and SC groups has continued. These deficits represent deeper challenges for gender diversity and inclusivity in the IT habitus. Recognizing the special needs and unique contributions that disabled women bring to the table compared to disabled men or LGBT women compared to straight women or SC women versus upper caste women or older men versus older disabled men is crucial to cultivate a more inclusive work habitat.

The ultimate diversity goal in any organization has to be to ensure a fair and equitable working environment for all its employees so that companies can promote organizational effectiveness and maintain competitive advantage. This involves moving beyond tolerance of diversity to acceptance (Rao and Bagali 2014a, 2014b) and incorporation of diversity in its multidimensional and intersectional forms. In a historically patriarchal and caste imbued Indian society, this is a tall order. But, if there is one institution that can find innovative ways to surmount these obstacles, it might be the *Information Technology sector* or at least its *knowledge sector*.

Appendix: Table 5A.1   Gross Enrollment Ratios (GER) by Grade Levels, 2014[*][†]

	Elementary Grades I–VIII	Secondary IX–X	Grades I–X	Senior Secondary XI–XII	Higher Education: College and Beyond
All Boys	93.3	73.5	89.4	49.1	22.3
All Girls	96.9	73.7	92.4	49.1	19.8
Scheduled Caste Boys	104.2	76.0	98.6	48.1	16.0
Scheduled Caste Girls	109.4	76.2	103.0	49.7	14.2
Scheduled Tribe Boys	102.5	67.5	95.9	35.5	12.4
Scheduled Tribe Girls	100.5	66.7	94.2	33.2	9.7

Source: Author.

[*] Education Statistics at a Glance 2014. Available at: http://mhrd.gov.in/sites/upload_files/mhrd/files/statistics/EAG2014.pdf. Retrieved on 10 July 2015.

[†] GER: total student enrolment in a given level of education, regardless of age, expressed as percentage of the corresponding eligible official age group population in a given school year; *Source*: Education Statistics at a Glance 2014.

Appendix: Table 5A.2   National Gender Differences in Completed Education[*], IHDS 2005

Age Groups	Statistics	Male			Female		
		FC	OBC	SC/ST	FC	OBC	SC/ST
15–20	$\bar{X}$(SD)[†]	8.3 (3.7)	8.1 (3.4)	6.9 (3.7)	7.7 (4.2)	7.1 (4.1)	5.7 (4.2)
	(n)	(5,265)	(4,660)	(4,168)	(5,232)	(4,525)	(4,121)
21–30	$\bar{X}$(SD)	9.1 (4.6)	8.2 (4.4)	6.8 (4.7)	7.6 (5.2)	5.1 (4.9)	4.5 (4.9)
	(n)	(7,176)	(6,376)	(5,209)	(7,192)	(6,320)	(5,122)
31–35	$\bar{X}$(SD)	8.5 (4.9)	7.5 (4.7)	5.8 (4.8)	6.2 (5.1)	5.5 (4.9)	2.8 (4.1)
	(n)	(2,943)	(2,681)	(2,077)	(2,836)	(2,665)	(2,091)
36 and older	$\bar{X}$(SD) Min-Max	7.3 (5.1) (13,206)	5.4 (4.7) (11,335)	3.8 (4.4) (8,579)	6.8 (5.3) (13,082)	2.4 (3.8) (11,107)	1.4 (3.0) (8,331)

Source: Author.

[*] Respondent's Education, Completed Years (HH17 10.5).

[†] $\bar{X}$ (SD) = Mean and standard deviation; Minimum and Maximum = 0 years to 15 years.

Appendix: Table 5A.3   Trends in Literacy Rates[*]

	2001	2011
Per cent Literate, ages 7+	64.8	73.0
Males	75.3	80.9
Females	53.7	64.6
Scheduled Caste (SC) Males	67.0	75.2
Scheduled Caste Females	42.0	56.5
Scheduled Tribes (ST) Males	59.0	68.5
ST Females	35.0	49.4
Per cent Literacy Rates, ages 15+	61.0	69.3
Males	73.4	78.8
Females	47.8	59.3
Scheduled Caste Males	59.3	71.6
Scheduled Caste Female	28.5	48.6
Scheduled Tribes Males	54.8	63.7
Scheduled Tribes Females	26.7	40.2

Source: Author.

[*] Available at: http://mhrd.gov.in/sites/upload_files/mhrd/files/statistics/EAG2014.pdf. Retrieved on 10 July 2015.

6 Indian Information Technology, the New Caste Frontier

Deconstructing Caste Reproduction

This research analyses were guided by three related sets of empirical, theoretical, and applied/practical goals. The implication for caste reproduction through caste isomorphic practices, implicit in the valorized merit culture making project in the putative caste neutral Indian IT occupational sector, were the empirical and theoretical issues investigated. Discussions of diversity strategies in the IT workforce, as a strategic business practice, were informed by empirical and theoretical considerations. Diversity practices need to be broadly defined to include caste along with gender and other social vectors. And diversity competence will have to be about parity and inclusiveness.

At the very start of this research journey, it became quite clear that hard data on the caste makeup of the Indian IT labour force would not be available to outside researchers and perhaps not maintained within the company. Equal employment hiring policies and fears of sullying their *merit* standards or political/legal backlash for entertaining caste discussions, were some of the reasons expressed for caste avoidance in hard fact, and in the IT workplace discourse. In the absence of hard evidence on the caste composition of the Indian IT workforce, this research pivoted to deconstructing the *merit culture* discourse widely prevalent at all levels of IT organizations. It is in the contrasts that were laid out between *merit vs. caste-based-reservation earmarks* in hiring and promotion, that the broad outlines of caste isomorphism and reproduction became deductively visible in the ostensibly caste neutral Indian IT sector. In the final analyses, overt/explicit discrimination against SCs, STs, and even OBCs in the Indian IT sector was neither proven nor disproven. Rather the potential disparate impact of avowed seemingly 'caste neutral' policies, as heard through the voices of Indian IT rank-and-file and key industry informants, was the main contribution of this work.

Empirical, Theoretical, and Applied Lessons: An Overview

Several theoretical lessons were gleaned from the lived experiences of IT professionals and key informants. *IT Skills* (individualized human capital) appeared central to the merit culture making project and seemed to out-shadow traditional Indian group vectors of caste/religion/communities (Chapter 2). Respondents, irrespective of whether they were in the *Merit or Caste Camps*, valorized 'merit' (Upadhya 2007a, 2007b) and streamlined/created appropriate differences (Radhakrishnan 2011) between the IT and non-IT economic habitus. They rationalized their laser focus on IT skills in the interests of efficiency and needs of western clients. However, to the Caste Camp, *subjective markers of merit* (such as English fluency, habits of the mind/intellect/and spirit [Bellah and Madsen 1996], and other 'soft' skills of communication) opened up spaces for introducing, sorting out, and stratifying the IT social world based on traditional social vectors of caste, community, and religion. In other words, *caste inequalities* through caste isomorphic processes, have entered into the IT habitat (Bourdieu 1995), transforming it into the new frontier of caste inequality. If *soft skills* are the prerogative of members of the upper castes, classes, and urbanites and if the logic and tools of *pattern recognition* (Baron 2006) in hiring and promotion are used in the IT sector, it stands to reason that caste-class hierarchies are reproduced in the new occupational sector, setting the stage for caste reproduction in the IT world.

It was when pointed questions about the role of caste, a diversity marker, in the Indian IT occupational sector were raised that the Merit-Caste debate turned contentious and into a metaphorical *blood sport* (Chapter 3). The Merit Camp vehemently rejected caste considerations and forcefully described their IT space as being *'caste-neutral, read "no caste reservations"'*. On the other hand, for all the reasons outlined above (*a holistic merit yardstick* that includes *soft skills* and *pattern recognition* in hiring), the Caste Camp was equally vocal about the explicit and hidden caste reproduction in the Indian IT sector.

In the experience of IT professionals and their industry leaders, the *blood sport* of merit culture making project starts earlier in the Indian *technical higher education* arena, if not even before (Chapter 4). The intensity of the debate in education is fuelled in part by the growing popularity of lucrative technology jobs but in equal part by the caste undertones in access to technical education. For example, the SCs and poorer segments of OBCs, who are priced out of the private technical education market, have access primarily to the seats *reserved* for them in the elite public institutions. On the other hand, the *heavy reliance on entrance tests and test-specific tutoring* for excellence in admission tests privilege the economically advantaged castes. Besides, as the Caste Camp distressingly argued, the economically dominant caste students, unlike their economically disadvantaged SC counterparts, have the option of studying at expensive private technical institutions, even if they are not of the same quality as the elite IITs. In short, to the Caste Camp, the *caste-class disparities that favour dominant castes are conduits for solidifying caste inequalities in technical higher education*. Interestingly, just as both public and private institutions of technical higher education are the sites where merit is culturally constructed, they also become ideal sites for deconstructing, revealing, and hopefully undoing the merit culture making project and the project's caste foundations.

Theoretically, it was also clear that not all diversity is equal in the Indian IT. For example, the intersectionality of caste, family, and gender (Fernandez 1997), has rendered *gender inequality and equality more readily accessible and amenable* for discussion, analyses, and redress in the Indian IT environment than caste (in)equalities (Chapter 5). Gendered cultural streamlining (Radhakrishnan 2011: 48–52) was illustrated in women's incorporation in the IT sector. Women, mainly dominant caste women, have made inroads into higher technical educational institutions and into related IT occupations, but only if they qualified on the gender-neutral merit yardstick. In the intersecting Indian social hierarchy of family, gender, and caste women in one's family and dominant caste, despite the gendered Indian society, were more welcome, even if unconsciously, in the IT workplace than women of lower castes.

From a practical standpoint, why is diversity, in its many dimensions, a *relevant business and strategic consideration* for Indian IT businesses? What strategic business impediments does the contentious Merit-Caste discourse present for Indian IT companies? Without a census of the state of diversity (in caste, religion, gender, linguistic regions, and other relevant social vectors) in the IT labour force, it might be argued that any further evaluations of the benefits of diversity are moot. However, given the contentiousness of the debate outlined in this manuscript, as well as the extant research on the benefits of workforce diversity for productivity and corporate bottom line, comparative assessments of the impacts of diverse versus monolithic workforces in Indian IT companies are economically warranted. There is no reason to assume (as Hasan and Nussbaum 2012 and Patnaik 2012 did) that the distribution of talent, or lack thereof, is approximately similar in all social groups. Consequently, not tapping into the wider hiring pool might not be a good business decision. Further, as Williams and O'Reilly (1998) argued, managing workforce diversity is one of the most pressing, even if difficult, challenges of modern organizations. They call diversity a hot-button issue in corporate, political, and legal circles, and capitalizing on workplace diversity is an important strategic imperative in the global business environment. Besides, the Indian IT sector operates in an international environment. American and European companies, who either have outsourced and/or offshored their operations to India, or have labour force arrangements through, for example, body shopping units, with Indian companies have paved the way for Indian businesses to diversify their workforce and operations.

To their credit, under the direction of NASSCOM, India's major trade body and the chamber of commerce of the IT-BPO industry in India, select companies have started work on promoting *gender diversity* in their workplace. For one, NASSCOM annually honours Indian IT companies for recognizing and implementing soft and hard management strategies, which enable them to capitalize on the assets and competencies that a gender diverse workforce brings to a company. Researchers have also found that IT companies that offer flexible and secure work environments

have become the favoured workplaces for IT women. And there is movement towards recognizing physical disability, sexual orientation, and age/
generational status as part of the Indian IT diversity paradigm, BUT
NOT CASTE.

The Merit Culture Making Project: The Conduit to the New Caste Frontier

To understand the resistance to caste diversity in Indian IT, it is necessary
to understand the merit culture, the fulcrum, around which the merit-caste
debates revolve. What are the contours of the Merit vs. Caste debates in
the Indian IT Occupational and Education sectors? How has the debate
played out in the theoretical and deductive analyses of opinions of IT
professionals and industry leaders? As the discursive debate raged past
each other, the *default debate winner was the Merit Camp*, if only because
there is no evidence to prove or disprove the Merit arguments. And the
'Merit' metric historically constructed to favour the dominant castes all
but ensured that the Merit Camp was the putative winner in the merit
vs. caste debate in the IT sector. However, the deconstructive, deductive
analysis overwhelmingly came down *in favour of the Caste Camp.*

Valorized caste neutral IT Skills appeared to be pre-eminent in the
qualification discourses of the IT professionals, out-shadowing traditional Indian social vectors of caste/religion/communities (Chapter 2).
Confirming extant scholarly thinking about the valorization of merit (for
example, Upadhya 2007a, 2007b), respondents rationalized the need for
caste-neutral-skills in the interests of organizational efficiency in a globalized IT environment. They did so by streamlining and creating appropriate difference between the IT and non-IT, mainly the government sector,
economic habitus (Radhakrishnan 2011).

It is against this backdrop of valorized IT merit that the merit-caste
debate has been waged. Several lines of arguments in the debate were
detailed in the preceding chapters. First, what is valorized IT Merit and is
it caste neutral? Second, what do the industry leaders and its professionals
mean when they claim that caste is not an issue in Indian IT? How do the
two camps explain the limited Dalit presence in Indian IT as they perceived it? In the final analysis, how does IT merit become discriminatory?
And finally what makes the Merit-Caste debate a 'blood sport'?

One cardinal tenet in the Indian IT sector was the value placed on merit, constructed as IT skill based and work habits (Chapter 2). Irrespective of their camps, Merit or Caste, and rank-and-file IT professionals and key industry informants were nearly uniform in their construction of merit. They prominently profiled individual *Human Capital*, particularly *technical skills and related work habits* of the intellect, mind, and spirit, ability to work well in a team, willingness to put in extra effort, individual initiative and meticulousness, leadership, and workplace social responsibility. These skills are often developed at least initially in the technical institutions of higher education that offer engineering degrees and diplomas. Yet, the respondents also confirmed the importance of *soft skills*—English language fluency and communication skills. *Social Capital*—non-workplace social skills, and *Social Background* were also noted, even if less prominently. On balance, merit in the Indian IT work sector was a *holistic package* of individualized skills and work-related values that are critical for success in a multinational work environment. It was noteworthy that most respondents did not bring up the issue of caste or gender or other group vectors, until directly prompted later in the survey to speak about caste/gender diversity issues.

However, it was when the issue of caste was raised that the two camps, Merit and Caste, diverged (Chapter 3). To the Merit Camp, *merit was caste neutral*. In contrast, to the Caste Camp, merit, by virtue of the way merit has been constructed and earned, had *caste foundations* with discriminatory outcomes for SC and ST. So, what does it mean for merit to be caste neutral? And how does merit become discriminatory? And why the blood-sport like vehemence in the arguments on both sides?

Caste Neutral Merit = No Reservations

The *Merit Camp* characterized the IT work and social space as *caste neutral* because IT companies *did not use the government's caste reservation metrics* in their hiring and promotion practices. Reserving positions in a company for certain groups, like SCs, was contradictory to the EEO principles and ideals of meritocracy and equality that Indian IT companies ostensibly practiced. Besides, assigning reserved quotas for SC candidates only weakened or lowered their IT merit standards,[1] they claimed. That is, the Merit Camp vehemently painted caste earmarks as antithetical to the merit principle. After all, group benefits weakened their stringent merit standards which are reserved exclusively for the individual and their personal accomplishments. In short, the only valued currency in IT sector was Skill based Merit, and definitely not Caste. And if there is a small Dalit (SCs) footprint in IT, if hard evidence can be found to disprove or validate this claim, it is only because Dalits do not meet the stringent individual merit criteria.

There was also an urgency in the Merit Camp, for functional reasons, to valorize merit and to delink the pure-merit IT standards from caste metrics. A caste-neutral merit standard was considered a functional prerequisite for the successful operations of IT corporations in a globalized economy. According to the Merit Camp, caste neutral merit ironically opens up the talent pool to all qualified candidates, irrespective of their particular (also known as reserved caste or communal) identities.

'But, IT Merit Is Discriminatory', said the Caste Camp

With equal fervour, the opposing Caste Camp debunked the caste-neutral Merit Camp arguments at many levels, starting with the spheres of technical higher education and continuing into workplace hiring and promotion practices. The roots of the IT merit culture making project emerge in the *caste impediments in access to education*, and technical higher education in particular (Chapter 4). Scheduled Caste minorities face caste inequalities in education starting early in their educational career. Scheduled Caste/ Scheduled Tribe caste members are typically first generation school goers. The almost 'essential' reliance on expensive private out-of-the classroom tutoring, subtle forms of discouragement and ostracism of SC/STs in schools, and limited educational resources in rural areas where most SCs live, compound their education burdens.

At the higher education level, the Caste Camp also rejected the practice of equating 'merit' solely with entrance test scores because it ignored the lingering, pernicious effects of entrenched caste hierarchies on the social advancement chances of disadvantaged groups. The caste dimensions in the competitive sport of technical education still favour the

---

[1] The reference is to the practice in government institutions to use reduced admission standards for those from historically marginalized communities.

dominant castes. For one, a student's ability to do well in tests required for admission or the very construction of tests are biased in favour of the lived experiences of dominant castes. In addition, doing well in tests is heavily dependent on expensive test specific tutoring which leaves the SCs at a disadvantage. Besides, they argued, the economically dominant caste students, unlike their disadvantaged SC counterparts, have the option of studying at expensive private technical institutions. These practices that favour dominant castes have become conduits for continued caste-based class disparities into technical higher education. In contrast, for the historically disadvantaged SCs and other minority communities, public higher education institutions are the only viable options. In fact, said the Caste Camp, dominant castes not securing the requisite credentials (technical capital) from the elite public institutions might be a necessary hardship that dominant castes have to endure in the social interest of redressing centuries-long casteism and promoting a just and equal society.

These caste educational disparities *continue into the IT labour market,* contended the Caste Camp. Despite the Merit Camp's reverence for streamlined merit, neutral in caste and even gender, the subjective markers of merit, as in *soft skills,* open up spaces for transferring into the IT world the caste-class stratification associated with the traditional social vectors of caste, community, and religion. English fluency; habits of the mind, intellect, and spirit; and other 'soft' skills of communication are often the prerogative of upper castes, classes, and urbanites. Besides, if the IT sector, consciously or sub-consciously, uses the logic and tools of *pattern recognition* (Baron 2006; Kanter 1977a) in hiring and promotion, caste-class hierarchies are more likely than not reproduced in the new IT occupational sector resulting in caste reproduction in the IT sector.

The Merit-Caste Debates in Indian IT

It is these competing, almost mutually exclusive, interpretations of merit, which render the educational and occupational arenas to be the sites where the Merit-Caste debate has played out. The debate, as outlined in this research, *starts in the education arena.* A technical degree particularly from the elite publicly funded Indian technical institutions is coveted because they offer the quality credentials that are a sure ticket into the lucrative IT job market. There is also intense competition for a seat in public institutions because they, such as the elite technical higher education systems like the IITs, are constitutionally mandated to reserve close to half their seats for SC and poor OBC youth. Consequently, complained the Merit camp, only half the pie of the coveted technical seats is available for open or general competition among the dominant caste students. These students and their families often feel, perhaps mistakenly, that they have been robbed of their legitimate right, based on their superior merit, to study at the elite institutions by the weaker, less qualified, or merit unworthy reservation candidates who are admitted despite receiving lower scores on entrance examinations.

To these Merit Camp arguments about limited elite educational opportunities for dominant caste students, the Caste Camp countered as follows. While the dominant castes complain about the weak quality of SC graduates, including those SC graduates from the elite higher education institutions, there is seldom an eyebrow raised about the educational quality of graduates from the newly mushrooming private technical institutes (Deshpande 2012). Besides, those in the forward/ dominant caste communities who were 'denied' a seat at the public institutions have the option of turning to private technical institutions. Unlike in government colleges, all private sector seats are technically 'open' to all castes because they are not legally mandated to reserve any seats for the historically marginalized caste groups. In fact, the private technical education arena has become a new site where caste privileges are transferred and reinforced, setting the foundation for caste inequality in the IT occupational sector.

In the *IT occupational sector*, IT Merit Skills were the hub around which the debate was waged. Again, the Merit Camp continued to emphasize their sacrosanct mantra about *pure skills* as the only criteria that mattered in IT hiring. If you have the right technical skills you have a place in Indian IT, was a common refrain. It is what the individual, not his or her community background, brings to the IT workplace that is the sole criteria that matters.

But, again, the Caste Camp pointed out the *caste loopholes in the skill-only policies*. Merit is not caste-neutral, they argued. They highlighted the obscured caste privileges of the dominant castes, the implicit caste filtering using perceived and/or real upper caste merit, Dalit social capital deficit, and resulting discriminatory outcomes to articulate their case. In fact, they pointed to the *recent reshuffling in caste hierarchies* in the resource intensive IT sector. For example, the wealthy dominant communities, often founders of new IT companies, have joined the Brahmin caste at the top of the IT caste hierarchy. The new Indian IT company founders, who hail from the traditional land and wealth owning caste communities like the Reddys or Kammas, used their inherited resources to help community members move up the social hierarchy. Of course, preferences are given to community members who have the right merit skills, they said. Brahmins still maintain their status in the top management ranks. However, even in this modified caste landscape, SC communities, if they even make it into the IT company, remain at the bottom, at best middle, rungs of the management hierarchy. One would be hard pressed to find an SC in the CEO or other top management ranks, let alone be a founding member, the Caste Camp argued.

On an operational level in Indian IT, *does, and if so, then how did 'merit' become discriminatory?* The Caste Camp disagreed with the Merit Camp position that the small Dalit footprint in Indian IT was due to their merit deficits. Rather merit practices become discriminatory when Dalits are not hired or promoted because they lack the needed *social connections* and *referrals* to gain entrance into, and to move up the career ladder, in the coveted IT sector. A Brahmin manager typically hires only Brahmins, they said. Others spoke to the founder effect to explain why hiring preferences were given to locals from the same community as the founder. When managers hail from the FCs, and even if not always Brahmin, *implicit caste filtering* made it highly unlikely that SC merit will be judged to be equal to others, leave alone as first among equals. In other words, if appropriate qualifications for success are operationally recognized based on the hiring managers', or team members', personal successes,[2] even the most caste/community-neutral hiring practices are bound to be heavily influenced by FC experiences.

In short, the ostensible SC deficits in the symbolically and socially constructed IT merit and education metrics, the Caste Camp argued, were not solely the product of individual talent but were mostly due to *historically distressed family wealth and privilege*. The small Dalit footprint at all levels of Indian IT, to them, was squarely the result of the enduring caste inequalities. It is the disparities in ownership of merit related wealth and societal prejudices that result in discriminatory practices in educational

---

[2] Baron's (2006) and Kanter's (1977a) homosocial reproduction of management.

preparations for, as well as in hiring into, the IT sector. When merit is valorized as caste-neutral, it is as if *'earned' merit is compartmentalized and separated from the very socially rooted privileges* that have largely enabled the dominant caste members to study at the best schools, be hired into high paying jobs, move up the occupational ladder in a company, or even be founders of companies.

How Did the Merit-Caste Debate Become a 'Blood Sport'?

Several factors have intensified the Merit-Caste debate raising it to the level of a *Blood Sport*. The growing popularity of lucrative technology jobs has made work in the IT sector, the *preferred choice in modern India*. Consequently, competition for an IT job in the private sector is quite intense. Skill-based merit, the primary gatekeeper to the competitive and exclusive IT sector, was *passionately protected*. For example, that the caste neutrality of IT skills was something to be fervently protected became clear when pointed questions about the role of caste in Indian IT were posed to IT professionals and industry key informants. Those that chose to respond to the caste questions offered a complicated and contentious narrative of the blood sport that has evolved (Chapter 3). *Fears of litigation* by the government on behalf of SCs and STs, if Pandora's Box of caste is opened up, were voiced by some leaders. On balance, though, the *vehement rejection of caste* (read government reservations/earmarks for SCs and STs) and the force with which the survey respondents described their IT space as being caste-neutral raised questions about the resonance of caste in the new occupational sector. And those who spoke of caste (read upper caste dominance) realities in IT were *equally vocal about the explicit and hidden caste isomorphism and casteism in the Indian IT sector*.

The intense and vehement Merit-Caste Blood Sport in the IT occupational sector was also evident in the grievances of dominant caste groups in the higher education arena (Chapter 4). That the *non-reservation castes have access to only half the pie* of the coveted technical education opportunities is part of the grievance by non-marginalized communities. Allegations (at least in a narrow test score sense) also abound that open or general seat candidates are rejected for admission only because they are *displaced* by 'less qualified' reserved candidates who are admitted with lower scores on entrance examinations. Begrudging awareness that the reservation social *redress policies have no shelf life*[3] has further deepened the resentment. They also point to the fact that despite more than half a century long government affirmative programs or quotas, SCs and STs *continue to lag* behind the dominant castes. And the *growing costs of private sector education*, an expensive alternative to public sector institutions, have added more fuel to the intense caste tensions in the IT sector.

Current Stalemate in the Merit-Caste Blood Sport in Indian IT

One way to describe the current state of the Merit vs. Caste discourse in the Indian IT world would be that it is at a stalemate. The Merit Camp passionately clung to the ideals of meritocracy and equality. The associations that the Merit Camp critically drew between caste reservations/earmarks and diluted, even lack of, merit, rendered *caste discussions to be non-negotiable*. With equal fervour the opposing Caste Camp *rejected outright the meritocratic equality narrative* of the Merit Camp. The point of truth to the Caste Camp is that the 'merit' culture and norms constructed by the privileged have *never been equal*. Rather, the merit culture is just another tool used to transfer caste privileges into Indian IT, leading to caste reproduction in the IT sector.

Unfortunately for students of the Indian IT sector, the absence of hard evidence makes it next to impossible to fully test the respective assertions of the two camps. As a consequence, theoretical and deductive analyses of the seemingly caste neutral arguments made by the Caste and Merit camps had to be used to shed light on the caste bias in the Indian IT sector. IT engineers, analysts, or knowledge professionals are *globally valued, authorized* (Reich 1991), and *treated with high regard* by the competitive global IT society within which the Indian IT companies operate. But, merit valorization, with its dominant-forward caste foundation, had echoes of Bourdieu's (1977, 1990) rendering of the *symbolic nature of human, social, and cultural capital resources*—be they education, income, urban location, language, or culture. In this Bourdieun framework, ownership of resources is symbolically 'natural and permanent', even though Bourdieu

---

[3] Despite being in existence for more than half a century, the constitutionally enshrined reservation system cannot be challenged legally and is difficult to reverse.

was quick to add that it is misguided. It is but natural, they say, that those who have the resources, as in the case of FCs, are also dominant in the IT industry. Those who do not have the 'natural' talent and skills, either do not have them (as in lower entrance scores of SCs who apply to higher educational institutions) or do not want them even though opportunities to acquire the skills are available to all who desire them (as in the case of lower castes who have become dependent on government assistance) or are not qualified enough (due to weak English fluency and other needed social skills). *In these unequal playing fields, if no special allowances (like SC reservations in the IT sector) are made for the marginalized castes, casteism is bound to be reproduced in the Indian IT sector.* Despite its caste-neutral principled stance, the Indian IT sector could easily become the new host to the dynamics of centuries-long casteism.

It then stands to reason that, as the Caste Camp asserted, *casteism has not disappeared* as the Indian IT sector has matured. Rather, societal casteism has been reproduced in the IT sector either in its original or modified forms. In the original representation of caste in Indian IT, the caste Brahmins were at the top of the ritual caste hierarchy with SCs at the bottom. In a modified form, the top caste tier of a resource intensive IT sector has been expanded to make room for other dominant caste communities. Again, in the absence of hard evidence to test the competing contentions and their respective outcomes, the only tenable conclusion to be drawn is that casteism has been reproduced in the IT sector. The much valorized caste-neutral 'merit' criteria, by virtue of its exclusion of SCs and other disadvantaged groups, is leading the Indian IT into becoming the new vector of caste inequality.

Interestingly, the IT sector is *not closed to all forms of diversity.* It is ironic that the Indian IT companies and their professionals were quite open to welcoming *merit-qualified women* into their midst, although the IT work habitat is far from being gender inclusive (Chapter 5). It was quite telling that, for the IT sector and IT professionals, gender inequality and equality were more readily accessible and amenable for discussion, analyses, and redress than was caste diversity. In a multidimensional social hierarchy, *gender trumps over caste* when it comes to evaluating merit. Upper caste male IT professionals, managers, a CEO, or even a company founder recognized women, handicapped, or gay/lesbians in their own communities. Women, particularly those that qualify on the IT Merit metric, more often than not, hail from similar upper caste/class family backgrounds as their male counterparts. In this intersectional worldview, it follows that SC status, whether male or female, has not been part of diversity considerations in Indian IT.

The new attention to gender diversity models in the Indian IT sector offered conceptual support and potential pathways for introducing caste diversity and inclusivity. Because of the intersectional (rather than additive[4]) ways in which caste, family, and gender dynamics operate, gender, along with sexual orientation, disabilities, and even generations, has started to become part of the diversity conversations in the IT sector. But, the value placed on gender-neutral IT merit, the glass ceiling faced by women, and the absence of an intersectional perspective on multiple diversity dimensions were symptomatic of the challenges that even women in the IT sector faced in transforming the IT work habitat into an inclusive space.

Breaking the Stalemate in the Indian IT Merit vs. Caste Debate

Considering the intensity of the merit-caste debate, *forceful resistance is to be expected* to any talk of opening up the merit fortressed walls of the IT sector even to considering 'qualified' disadvantaged castes. For the reasons that the 'Merit Camp' advocates detailed, the resistance is understandable, even if not morally defensible, when private IT companies consider their stakeholders to be not only their clients, but also the founder's community in which they are located. But, does Indian IT not have broader social responsibilities?

It is quite possible that the *Merit Camp will walk away* from the debate because they perceive the status quo to be beneficial to them. But, as an activist interviewee asked, *will it take their global multinational parent or partner corporations*, or the government, to pressure the Merit Camp back to the IT mat? For a sector that prides itself on being at the forefront of the technological innovation and revolution, being *proactive about initiatives to break the Merit-Caste stalemate* might be appealing. What would the contours of these proactive solutions will be?

---

[4] Unlike an additive hierarchical ranking of caste and gender, in the interactional ranking, upper caste women follow their caste men; lower caste men and women remain at the bottom.

For starters, the stalemate will not be broken and the 'blood sport' continued, *unless hard evidence on the outcomes of 'meritocratic equality' policies becomes available*. Even if Indian IT companies never incorporate group (caste) reservation or earmark policies into their hiring modalities, maintaining evidence on caste and community backgrounds along with education, sex, and other employment attributes, of employees, at all levels in IT companies would be a starting point. At the very least, information on caste composition of their workforces would offer empirical evidence to burnish their EEO claims. Understanding the caste composition of the company, while shedding light on the company founder effects, can also become the basis for *thinking outside the box* for ways to *improve organizational efficiency*. Perhaps there is a wider pool of valuable, but hidden, talent that can only be accessed by opening up the employee and management pool to the full range of castes and communities. Again, there will be intense resistance to these ideas, for all the reasons that the 'Merit Camp' advocates have passionately laid out. But, as an activist interviewee asked, 'Why are we afraid of asking an applicant about their caste and community?'

Sites and Models for Deconstructing Caste Neutrality in IT Merit

The analytic arguments presented in this monograph revealed, that both public and private institutions of technical higher education have become the *initial sites* where merit, with its caste underpinnings, is culturally constructed. No doubt, in the public higher education institution arenas, the government's public policy interventions, in the form of reserving seats for SCs and poor OBCs, have been used to protect the historically marginalized caste groups against continued discrimination as well as to empower and develop their human capital. But the redress options against casteism in public educational institutions have been saturated; for example, reservation of seats has reached almost 50 per cent (see for example, Deshpande 2012). Reservations in public occupational sectors have also reached similar saturation limits.

In this context, there is palpable and widespread social anxiety and fear, that the private institutions might be the next target of mandatory quotas. There have also been intense campaigns to protect the non-governmental occupational sector from government encroachment. Yet the on-going national dilemma is that it is in the private institutional arenas, including the IT occupational sector, where casteism seems to be reproduced. If the nation is to move on the path towards a caste free society, the private sector is the only remaining arena for restructuring the entrenched casteism. A good start to chipping away at these enduring caste hierarchies might be through non-governmental, privately designed, interventions in the IT corporate world whose primary goal would be to deconstruct the merit culture making project and to construct a caste inclusive workplace. However, it stands to good reason that even non-governmental private initiatives are certainly not going to be easy to introduce and sustain.

Why Deconstruct Caste Reproduction in the Private IT Sector?

Ironically, *the IT revolution had provided a rare opportunity* for the Indian society to start working towards breaking down caste barriers in the occupational sectors. But, the caste problem in Indian IT has remained hidden because the two sides talk past each other. As one IT professional remarked, 'Caste is the 800 pound gorilla in the IT office; it is there and yet not there'.

On the one hand, Dalits and Dalit activists confirmed that the *IT sector society seems to have failed to live up to their, perhaps idealistic, caste-free expectations*. Even when the new caste hierarchy in Indian IT is bounded at the top by community background of the company founder, and not by Brahmins, Dalits are still excluded from the system. On the other hand, FC Indians refuse to acknowledge the relevance of caste dominance in the private occupational sector. In an industry that purportedly does not have the traditional ritualistic occupational foundations, the FCs in their hyper-negative reactions to the term 'Caste', ardently tried to separate IT work from other non-IT work environment. That the term caste was uniformly heard as 'caste reservations', or caste earmarks, was mostly likely due to the upper caste backlash against over a half a century of reservations or set-asides in government institutions of higher education, jobs, and political institutions. To the FC groups, set-asides or quotas, originally designed to compensate for Dalit deficits due to centuries long casteism, has come to mean lowered entrance standards. In fact, they would like to abolish caste reservations even in the public/government sectors. There were many a Dalit or Dalit friends who reported experiences which went like this: 'when the forward caste members encounter someone in government institutions where reservations apply, they deduce the person is a Dalit, by the use first initial of family name that precedes one's given name, family background, region of origin, skin color, etc. The presumption is that they have been admitted or hired only because of the reserved quotas and ergo is less qualified. That is, a Dalit would not have the job, except for the reservations. Such backlash carries over even when the Dalit candidate is qualified'.

On balance, despite the vociferous avowal of a no-caste Indian IT, it was clear in the deductive analyses presented in previous chapters that *the sector has become a new site for caste reproduction*. No doubt, the state of Dalit education, after over 50 years of reservation policies, has been mixed. Indian Dalits have made progress, albeit not extraordinary (Chapter 4). Yet, writings in *Dalit Voice*, by Dalits and friends of Dalits and others, have pointed to caste, particularly Dalit caste status, continuing to be a discriminatory marker in the new IT-BPO sectors. However, (again) because the private IT sector does not officially gather caste information about their employees, there is no hard evidence, just empirically grounded deductive analysis and logic, to prove or disclaim the respective assertions of the Merit and Caste Camps. And so the stalemate continues.

Making this stalemate more toxic are legal concerns, perhaps legitimate, that FC members voiced when the issue of caste was raised. A primary apprehension, in opening up their company profiles to public scrutiny, was about potential litigations that might legally force the private sector to follow the government's reservation redress policies. For example, many IT professionals and some key informants feared backlash and law suits if companies kept records on the caste composition of their employees. Perhaps they fear that the extant caste profile will more likely than not be one of dominant castes and communities, even if only because of the privileged access that higher castes and other regional dominant castes have, to social and cultural capital, and economic wealth. If the public, be they government or the SC community, comes to know that the caste distribution in the IT companies, or even in the industry as a whole, favours the dominant castes or communities, law suits and litigated remedies are quite likely to follow, they lamented.

In this contentious context, it stands to reason that *when respondents vehemently cried out loud and clear that caste does not matter in Indian IT, they meant that the government's reservation policies*, with the often unfounded associations with poor quality, *did not apply* to and were not implemented in the private occupational sector. Private sector IT companies burnished their no-caste corporate persona by *staying clear of public association with knowledge of their employees' caste status*; for example, caste is not asked on a job application. Another tool used by the private IT companies to reify a no-caste corporate stance was, as many HR managers suggested, the *equal employment opportunity policies* that overtly ascertained only merit and individual initiative. That not having official information about the caste composition of IT companies can also offer protection against real or assumed allegations of discrimination, both positive and negative, was on the minds of many company leaders. As one CEO remarked, caste identity politics become so heated that even talking about Dalits might get them jailed. At one level, there was a shared belief in the private IT sector, like many of the survey respondents, that talking about caste only reified the caste system. At the other end, as another upper level manager feared, if the private companies started maintaining information on caste status, some form of mandated quota system might soon follow.

In the final analysis, private IT companies seemed to *follow EEO policies and practices as a safe way out*. Opening up any discussion of caste, they feared, might take them down the slippery path of being forced to follow the government's reservation policies. Unfortunately, for the Merit-Caste stalemate to be broken, and the 'blood sport' abated, private IT companies will have to take a hard internal evidentiary look at the unequal or equal, as the case may be, outcomes of their meritocratic equal employment policies. Does the social stratification in Indian IT look like a replica of the modern day Indian caste system where the only difference might be at the top of the traditional ritual hierarchies; the traditional hierarchy of Brahmin at the top with Kshatriyas, Vaishyas, Sudras, and Dalits following behind, have been realigned to incorporate the wealth and political power of middle-castes into dominant caste status. Or is IT Merit truly caste-neutral and open to qualified SC and ST individuals?

What is in it for the Private IT Sector?

At this point, the reader might legitimately ask: What is the need for the Indian IT sector and their dominant caste/community stakeholders to break and move beyond the Merit vs. Caste stalemate? Is it even necessary, and from whose vantage point, to resolve the contradictions between merit and caste (scheduled) status that currently pervade the Indian IT sector? Is caste inequality in Indian IT, a functional and public relations impediment? If structural inequalities make IT organizations less efficient or a public relations nightmare, what will it take to break the stalemate? Irrespective of the impetus for dismantling the lingering historical caste inequalities, if they are to be dismantled, *the appropriate sites for caste diversity programs will have to be at the company structural level and not limited to individual managers or employees* (Richardson 2012). Besides, the diversity inclusive programs will have to include anti-discriminatory as well as empowering and developmental components (Hasan and Nussbaum 2012: 5).

There is some good news. The idea that workforce diversity, both in values and practices, is a functional imperative for Indian IT corporations has already made inroads into corporate thinking. Extant IT diversity initiatives, based on gender, disability, sexual orientation, celebrated by NASSCOM, are cases in point. In their search for ways to improve organizational efficiency, these diversity initiatives help companies think outside the dominant, male, heterosexual, and able-bodied boxes. If we assume, as many scholars of diversity (Hasan and Nussbaum 2012; Patnaik 2012) have done, that the distribution of talent, or lack thereof, is approximately similar in all social groups, then not opening up the hiring pool to the marginalized is not in the long-term business interests of any company. Perhaps there is a wider pool of valuable, but hidden, talent waiting to be accessed by opening up the employee and management pool to the full spectrum of qualified members from all caste communities. Scholars and NASSCOM have already made this case in nudging Indian IT companies to broaden their hiring pools to IT merit qualified women. Similar bold steps along caste lines, opening up the competition to all those with the requisite IT Merit Skills, regardless of caste and community, will, perhaps, also weed out the less talented in the dominant groups. Widening diversity thinking to include SCs might also have the added benefit of easing legal allegations of caste discrimination down the road. Besides, western parent IT corporation companies, if not business partners of Indian IT companies, have made significant advances in gender, and even disability, diversity, and inclusiveness, although glass ceiling issues still remain for women and the disabled. No doubt, race/ethnicity, particularly African Americans and even Asian Americans, and sexual orientation are two diversity dimensions that continue to be works in progress in the USA and other developed countries.

From a public relations point of view, information on the caste composition of IT workforces can offer empirical evidence to burnish the EEO claims of Indian IT companies and perhaps even reduce future litigations. Do equality policies of Indian IT companies result in 'equality in fact' (Hasan and Nussbaum 2012)? On this front, maintaining evidence, at least for internal evaluations, on caste, community, and other background social characteristics like sex, disability, sexual orientation, religion, along with merit skills (education and other employment attributes), of IT employees at all levels in IT companies will be *an important first step.*

Despite the functional and public relations appeals in favour of broadening caste diversity in the Indian IT sector, it bears repeating, for all the reasons that the 'Merit Camp' advocates have voiced, that there will be *intense resistance* to getting the Indian IT sector to candidly look at its caste profile, even for internal use. But, to repeat a question, an activist interviewee asked, 'Why are we afraid of asking to which caste, which community' the other belongs? While honouring this resistance, NASSCOM and other innovative leaders of the Indian IT sector can help move the needle beyond the stalemate. For, as long as there are doubts about the true sources of 'merit', the quality of even the meritorious candidates will remain in question.

Learning from Extant Gender and Disability Diversity Approaches in Indian IT

How can companies tackle the 800 pound caste gorilla in their midst? First, it should be loudly made clear that *a call to caste diversity is by no means a call to incorporate caste reservations*, as in government's hiring and promotion policies. But, IT companies, or even sub-units like their *cutting-edge knowledge production divisions*, could take the lead. Broad contours of models for opening up the IT doors to qualified women and disabled already exist and can be modified appropriately to meet the unique needs of caste diversity. Meena and Vanka (2013), in their analysis of model gender diversity programs, that were honoured by NASSCOM, also pointed to the need for aligning diversity strategies, if they are to be successful, with corporate strategic values and goals, by making diversity integral to corporate values, structures, and operations.

A brief review of extant diversity gender initiatives in Indian IT offer useful guidelines for thinking about caste diversity. Drawing from the rich human resource management literature,[5] hard and soft practices in the diversity programs can be outlined with the goal of transforming the IT workplace into a more diverse and inclusive environment. The primary goal of *soft approaches* was to gain broad-based commitment through changing the 'hearts and minds of employees' (Meena and Vanka 2013: 46). Involvement in diversity workshops, on-going diversity competence training, mentoring, and support groups were designed with the goals of increasing knowledge about diverse talented individuals as well as creating a safe, welcoming, and accepting working environment for them. The *hard human resource practices* were based on a fundamental organizational principle that no amount of discussions and training will have a transformational impact until companies align and incorporate diversity principles into their organizational practices. Besides, for diversity work to be successful it will have to be integrated throughout the different layers of the organizational hierarchies, starting with the Board of Directors, senior, middle, and junior management levels, and down to the rank-and-file. Hard approaches could range from opening up human resource hiring and retention practices to capture and retain the best qualified people, regardless of caste, gender, age, ethnicity, and other individual social characteristics.

There is no general agreement in the management literature about *sequencing the soft and hard approaches to diversity*. Should companies work on changing the hearts and minds first and then introduce the hard diversity friendly practices? Or can both be done simultaneously? What would a set of robust caste diversity initiatives look like? Given the volatility around caste and the long-standing distrust of the merit quality, associated with caste reservations or earmarks, in the private IT sector and in the general public, *soft caste diversity approaches might have to come first*. Because the technical degrees of SC candidates, even from elite institutions, are considered to be of dubious quality, breaking down these stereotypes will have to be parts of the first step. There is also a case to be made for treating caste as a singular and separate dimension of diversity rather than in its intersectional forms (combined with gender, sexual orientation, and disability). Irrespective of the starting points, soft or hard strategies, understanding the caste (and other minority status)

[5] The following discussion of soft and hard diversity strategies are drawn from Meena and Vanka (2013).

composition of a company might be a critical foundational step in developing relevant programs to break down the extant caste barriers in Indian IT. Diversifying the recruitment and selection processes can follow. But retaining the diverse workforce will require additional changes in opportunities for equal performance and compensation and rewards systems.

Even with soft discussions about the functional and human relations benefits of caste diversity, the *expected critique* would be, as some IT professionals complained, that talking about caste will only make caste tensions worse. But, following Rajshekhar's '*caste identity theory*', a case can be made to use the soft diversity programs as a platform for mutual learning about the productive histories and challenges faced by all castes—Dalits and FCs alike. The ultimate goal will be to develop a mutual vision of disrupting casteism that can be beneficial to all. Following Bourdieu's 'symbolic struggles' in a context of upper 'social domination' (Whitley Jr. 1999), affirming one's caste identity can be a symbolic way of disrupting casteism, provided all participants do not view the disrupting process as a zero-sum game.

· *The extant gender, disability, and sexual orientation models in Indian IT companies offer helpful guidelines in thinking about specific caste diversity programs* in the Indian IT corporate world. The specific caste diversity initiatives outlined below draws heavily from Meena and Vanka's review of NASSCOM and other industry leaders' award winning diversity programs. The sequencing of hard and soft caste diversity strategies will certainly have to be company specific. But, as noted above, given the intensity of resistance to caste considerations, it is quite possible that soft approaches to caste diversity management will have to precede the more structural organizational transformations. No matter the sequence, caste diversity programs, in order to be successful, will have to be integrated into the organizations through their HR practices and evaluated periodically.

Some Options for Soft and Hard Caste Diversity Approaches[6]

To reiterate, the goals of 'soft diversity strategies' is to learn about each other's caste experiences so that a mutually respective climate can be created, while at the same time supporting the disadvantaged to thrive in an

---

[6] Both, soft and hard approaches, have been adapted mainly from IT company websites and Meena and Vanka (2013).

inclusive environment. It is in this spirit that the following suggestions are offered.

Training, learning, and sensitization workshops that acknowledge, talk about, and *celebrate all caste backgrounds* and *raise positive caste consciousness* in ways that begin to affirm that no caste is inferior or superior to any other castes. Equally important in effective diversity programs will be, the setting up an *Internal Ombudsperson(s)*. If IT companies make the decision to go down the caste diversity route, an Ombudsperson(s) process will be useful, if not mandatory, to referee the contentious competing claims that are bound to arise. In addition, workshops offered by scholars like Professor Kancha Ilaiah (2009) about the productive histories of Dalits and working with real-life scenarios to assist employees understand and learn from the experiences of both Dalits and dominant castes alike, are two examples. IBM has a generational (age) diversity program in this mould.

Other suggestions include the following: A *Caste Meter*, akin to the 'Culture Meter' launched by TCS, on the company intranet where cross-caste information and experiences are shared; *Value based team building training programs* for new hires and existing staff that might include cross-caste projects where people of different backgrounds, including caste, come together; *Formal mentoring programs, matching senior management with new lower caste recruits*; and *core employee resource groups of staff from similar* caste backgrounds where they can meet to discuss and learn strategies for balancing the demands of diversity work.

'Hard diversity' approaches to diversifying the workplace entail *aligning diversity practices within the existing organizational practices*. Hard organizational caste diversity initiatives might range from an internal caste diversity audit to enhancing the diversity content of, among other critical functions, the companies' recruitment and selection processes, career development opportunities, equal opportunity for performance, and compensation rewards structures.

As first steps, companies could start with *an internal audit* of the caste composition of their labour force. This audit will be *solely for internal assessment and programmatic planning purposes*. Structurally robust caste diversity/inclusive programs will have to cover recruitment, selection, and retention of caste diverse employees. To consciously *broaden recruitment pools*, companies can target public higher education institutions to access their SC/ST graduates. Meena and Vanka cited two illustrative programs: IBM India's partnership with an NGO, NOIDA Deaf Society, to target PwD candidates; and Pepsico India's linkup with IndiWo to target women re-entering the workforce after family and childrearing breaks. *Specific language* will be needed in job descriptions about caste, gender, disabilities, age, etc. not being a barrier and availability of reasonable accommodations. *Recruiting friends of caste diversity* or even qualified Dalits at the senior levels could boost these caste diversity efforts. *Rethinking the candidate selection processes* might include ensuring that the hiring and selection processes fully comport with the job description to give qualified SC IT professionals an equal chance.

Once diverse caste candidates are hired, concerted attention will have to be paid to their *retention* by offering *equal opportunities for performance and success*. Because minority employees, particularly SC employees, are often first-generation IT employees, they are likely to be unaware of career path options within the IT structures. Existing empowerment and development programs for women at Wipro and IBM, designed to enhance their professional, technical, and even personal development, offer useful guidelines in this regard. Also, if Dalits are found to have English language and other cultural deficits, reasonable supplementary programs might be needed to get them up to par with the rest of the workforce. Reasonable accommodations that, for example, IBM and Wipro have provided to the physically challenged employees offer broad guidelines.

An *accountability system* for caste diversity outcomes will also be critical to measure progress or lack thereof, on caste diversity and inclusivity. Adding caste diversity to the performance scorecard can be an evaluation tool to measure progress. Performance scorecards tied to compensation and rewards are additional suggestions. The Indian subsidiaries of many global corporations, such Microsoft, Accenture, IBM, and P&G have adopted these diversity accountability practices at least for their leadership teams (Meena and Vanka 2013).

Indian IT, the Innovator in Caste Diversity?

It bears repeating, once again, that as demonstrated in the responses of rank-and-file professionals and key industry and knowledge leaders, there will be intense resistance, primarily from the upper castes, to acknowledge prevailing caste inequalities in modern India, leave alone doing something to address the disparities. Many upper caste Indians, in the general population, have been vehemently opposed to formal mandatory caste consideration in the private sector, particularly in IT. In fact, there has already been considerable push-back from the private sector, and many in the general population, when the government attempted to mandate employee quotas based on minority caste status in the private sector. They are vehemently against the existing quota system in the government sector and certainly do not want to see that practice adopted (leave alone mandated) in the private sector.

But in an industry like the Indian IT, whose call to fame is innovation, is the time ripe for the sector and its allies to start assessing whether making the workplace more caste diverse and inclusive (in addition to gender, disability, and sexual orientation diversity) is good business practice? While private companies should *not be mandated* to initiate caste diversity programs, leave alone introduce caste-based reservations or earmarks, NASSCOM and *socially conscious companies might take bold leadership steps* in fostering caste identity of dominant castes and Dalits alike. Such caste consciousness raising work can become the foundation for making organizational practices in Indian IT more caste diverse and inclusive. Of course, these practices will have to be self-arbitrated (like with an internal ombudsmen) and accompanied by *reasonable and enforceable limits on caste-based litigation.* Evaluative evidence on the progress of caste diversity initiatives can certainly be used by companies to verify, with hard evidence, official claims of companies as equal employment opportunity employers. In the process, IT companies might also become more self-aware and start self-correcting their own caste exclusionary hiring and promotion practices. It might also be a mechanism for IT companies to lead the country in promoting positive caste consciousness and ultimately paving the way for moving the Indian society beyond the negative vestiges of the caste. Much as one might wish, not seriously engaging with the 800 pound caste gorilla in the office will not make it go away.

In the final analysis, Indian IT will remain a 'perceived' bastion of casteism unless they find meaningful ways of transforming the IT work and social habitats into an inclusive one where diversity, in its many and intersectional dimensions, is promoted, valued, and embraced, if at least because it is a *strategic business imperative.* The Indian IT has begun to take small steps in this direction in addressing gender parity. While expanding diversity work to reflect the caste and religious heterogeneity of the country are the next steps, the necessary shifts will be strongly resisted (as seen in the previous chapters), unless diversity inclusiveness can be seen as a *value added* strategy to improve competitiveness. The international corporations in the USA and Europe, critical partners of the Indian IT sector, offer models for diversity inclusivity, albeit they are still works in progress. Indian IT corporations, with their creative energy and talents should be able to develop strategies that capitalize on the complex diversity in India. Perhaps, NASSCOM, the country's lead trade association, will take the lead, once again, in *inviting their member corporations to showcase and recognize caste diversity in their inclusive organizational frameworks.* Taking cues from the gender diversity models that are celebrated and encouraged, a call should be made for corporate social responsibility to adopt caste inclusive human resource techniques to potentially disrupt caste isomorphism and reproduction in IT.

Adding caste inequality to the diversity metric will by no means be a simple or easy step in the bridge to diversifying the sector. And given that caste is such a high voltage topic, it might be a bridge too far or high. But *if that bridge is not crossed, the new IT sector might, in the eyes of the world, continue to be the new frontier of casteism.* On the other hand, if Indian IT is to deliver on its promise to bend the arc of inequality in India, sub-units in IT organizations, like their *cutting-edge R&D divisions, might need to take leadership* in leveraging the strategic business values of caste diversity and inclusiveness.

References

Acharya, Sanghmitra S. 2010. 'Caste and Patterns of Discrimination in Rural Public Health Care Services'. In *Blocked by Caste: Economic Discrimination in Modern India*, Sukhadeo Thorat and Katherine S. Newman (eds), pp. 208–29. New Delhi, India: Oxford University Press.

Akhileshwari, R. 2000. 'Moolah [Money] is Hauled in Through the IT Way'. *Deccan Herald*, 17 June. Bangalore. Available at: http://www.deccanherald.com/.

Ali, Muhammad, Carol T. Kulik, and Isabel MetzKulik. 2011. 'The Gender Diversity Performance Relationship In Services And Manufacturing Organizations'. *The International Journal of Human Resource Management* 22(7): 1464–85.

Annapoorna, S. and S. T. Bagalkoti. 2011. 'Development of IT sector in India: Analysis of Reasons and Challenges'. *Journal of Economics and Sustainable Development* 2(2). Available at: http://www.iiste.org/Journals/index.php/JEDS/article/view/132/12.

Appadurai, Arjun. 1996. *Modernity at Large: Cultural Dimensions of Globalization*. Minneapolis: Minnesota Press.

Appelrouth, Scott A. and Laura Desfor Edles. 2011. *Classical and Contemporary Sociological Theory: Text and Readings.* Thousand Oaks, California: Sage Publications.

AspiringMinds.com. 2016. 'Women in Engineering: A Comparative Study of Barriers Across Nations'. Available at: http://www.aspiringminds.com/research-articles/women-in-engineering-a-comparative-study-of-barriers-across-nations. Retrieved on 13 May 2016.

Banerjee, Abhijit, Marianne Bertrand, Saugato Datta, and Sendhil Mullainathan. 2008. 'Labor Market Discrimination in Delhi: Evidence from a Field Experiment'. Available at: http://hdl.handle.net/1721.1/52303.

Baron, Robert A. 2006. 'Opportunity Recognition as Pattern Recognition: How Entrepreneurs "Connect the Dots" to Identify New Business Opportunities'. *Academy of Management Perspectives* 20(1): 104–19.

Bellah, Robert N. and Richard Madsen. 1996. *Habits of the Heart: Individualism and Commitment in American Life.* Berkeley and Los Angeles: University of California Press.

Bhatt, M.S. and Asheref Illiyan (eds). 2009. *e Technology (IT) in the Indian Economy.* New Delhi, India: New Century Publications.

Biao, Xiang. 2007. *Global 'Body Shopping': An Indian Labor System in the Information Technology Industry.* Princeton, NJ: Princeton University Press.

Borooah, Vani K. 2010. 'Inequality in Health Outcomes in India: The Role of Caste and Religion'. In *Blocked by Caste: Economic Discrimination in Modern India,* Sukhadeo Thorat and Katherine S. Newman (eds), pp. 179–207. New Delhi, India: Oxford University Press.

Bourdieu, Pierre. 1977. *Reproduction in Education, Society, Culture.* Beverly Hills, CA: Sage Publications.

———. 1984. *Distinction: A Social Critique of the Judgment of Taste.* Cambridge, MA: Harvard University Press.

———. 1990. 'Social Space and Symbolic Power'. In *In Other Words: Essays Towards a Reflexive Sociology,* pp. 122–39. Stanford, CA: Stanford University Press.

———. 1995. 'Forms of Capital'. In *Handbook of Theory and Research for the Sociology of Education,* J.G. Richardson (ed.), pp. 241–58. New York: Greenwood Press.

Brooks, David. 2012. 'The Power of the Particular'. The Opinion Page, *The New York Times,* 25 June. Available at: http://www.nytimes.com/2012/06/26/opinion/brooks-the-power-of-the-particular.html. Retrieved on 28 July 2017.

Buvinic, Mayra. 2004. 'Social Inclusion In Latin America' In *Social Exclusion and Economic Development in Latin America (Inter-American Development Bank),* Mayra Buvinic and Jacqueline Mazza (eds), pp. 3–32. Baltimore, MD: The Johns Hopkins University Press.

Channa, Karuna. 1993. 'Accessing Higher Education: The Dilemma of Schooling Women, Minorities, Scheduled Castes and Scheduled Tribes in Contemporary India'. *Higher Education* 26(1): 69–92.

Coleman, James S. 1988. 'Social Capital in the Creation of Human Capital'. *American Journal of Sociology* 94: S95–S120.

Cox, Taylor. 1993. *Cultural Diversity in Organizations: Theory, Research, and Practice*. San Francisco: Berrett-Koehler.

Currie, Wendy L. September 2012. 'Institutional Isomorphism and Change: The National Programme for IT—10 Years on'. *Journal of Information Technology* 27(3): 236–48. Available at: http://dx.doi.org/10.1057/iit.2012.18.

D'Costa, Anthony P. 2011. 'Geography, Uneven Development And Distributive Justice: The Political Economy Of IT Growth In India'. *Cambridge Journal of Regions, Economy and Society* 4(2): 237–51.

D'Cruz, Premilla and Ernesto Noronha. 2013. 'Ambivalence: Employee Responses to Depersonalized Bullying at Work'. *Economic and Industrial Democracy* 36(1): 23–45. DOI: 10.1177/0143831X13501001.

Desai, Sonalde, Reeve Vanneman, and National Council of Applied Economic Research, New Delhi. 2005. 'India Human Development Survey (IHDS)'. ICPSR22626-v8. Ann Arbor, MI: Inter-university Consortium for Political and Social Research [distributor], 16-02-2016. Available at: https://doi.org/10.3886/ICPSR22626.v11.

Desai, Sonalde, Cecily Darden Adams, and Amaresh Dubey. 2010. 'Segmented Schooling: Inequalities in Primary Education'. In *Blocked by Caste: Economic Discrimination in Modern India*, Sukhadeo Thorat and Katherine S. Newman (eds), pp. 230–53. New Delhi, India: Oxford University Press.

Deshpande, Ashwini and Katherine S. Newman. 2010. 'Where the Path Leads: The Role of Caste in Post-University Employment Expectations'. In *Blocked by Caste: Economic Discrimination in Modern India*, Sukhadeo Thorat and Katherine S. Newman (eds), pp. 88–122. New Delhi, India: Oxford University Press.

Deshpande, Satish. 2012. 'Social Justice and Higher Education in India Today: Markets, States, Ideologies, and Inequalities in a Fluid Context'. In *Equalizing Access: Affirmative Action in Higher Education in India, United States, and South Africa*, Zoya Hasan and Martha C. Nussbaum (ed), pp. 212–38. New Delhi: Oxford University Press.

Dika, Sandra L. and Kusum Singh. 2002. '"Applications of Social Capital in Educational Literature" A Critical Synthesis'. *Review of Educational Research* 72: 31–60.

DiMaggio, Paul J. and Walter W. Powell. 1983. 'The Iron Cage Revisited: Institutional Isomorphism and Collective Rationality in Organization Fields'. *American Sociological Review* 48(2): 147–60.

Dubey, Mohit and Aarti Garg. 2014. 'Contributions of Information Technology and Growth of Indian Economy'. *Voice of Research* 2(4): 49–53. March.

Ely, Robin J. and David A. Thomas. 2001. 'Cultural Diversity at Work: The Effects of Diversity Perspectives on Work Group Processes and Outcomes'. *Administrative Science Quarterly* 46(2): 229–73.

Engelhardt Barbara E. and Matthew Stephens M. 2010. 'Analysis of Population Structure: A Unifying Framework and Novel Methods Based on Sparse Factor Analysis'. *PLoS Genet* 6(9): e1001117. DOI:10.1371/journal.pgen.1001117.

Fouad, Nadya A., Romila Singh, Mary E. Fitzpatrick, and Jane P. Liu. 2011. 'Stemming the Tide: Why Women Leave Engineering'. Center for the Study of the Workplace at University of Wisonsin-Milwaukee. Available at: http://www.daweg.com/documents/resources/Stemming_the_Tide.pdf. Retrieved on 13 May 2016.

Fernandes, Leela and Patrick Heller. 2006. 'Hegemonic Aspirations: New Middle Class Politics and India's Democracy in Comparative Perspective'. *Critical Asian Studies* 38(4): 495–522.

Fernandez, Marilyn. 1997. 'Domestic Violence by Extended Family Members in India: Interplay of Gender and Generation'. *Journal of Interpersonal Violence* 12(3): 433–55.

Fernandez, Marilyn and Laura Nichols. 2002. 'Bridging and Bonding Capital: Pluralist Ethnic Relations in Silicon Valley'. *International Journal of Sociology and Social Policy* 22(9/10): 105–22.

Foster, Allan. 2007. 'Moving Up the Value Chain: Business Information Resources Survey 2007'. *Business Information Review* 24(1): 13–29. DOI: 10.1177/0266382107075903.

Friedman, Thomas L. 2005. *The World Is Flat: A Brief History of the Twenty-First Century*. New York: Farrar, Straus and Giroux.

Ghosh, Jayati. 2012. 'Towards a New Paradigm for Ensuring Universal Access to Quality Education'. In *Equalizing Access: Affirmative Action in Higher Education in India, United States, and South Africa*, Zoya Hasan and Martha C. Nussbaum (eds), pp. 202–11. New Delhi: Oxford University Press.

Government of India. 1950. *Constitution (Scheduled Castes) Order, 1950*. Retrieved on 27 April 2015.

———. 1950. *Constitution (Scheduled Tribes) Order, 1950*. Retrieved on 27 April 2015.

———. 1978. *Constitution (Sikkim) Scheduled Castes Order, 1978*. Retrieved on 27 April 2015.

———. 2009. *National Knowledge Commission Report 2006–2009*. Available at: http://www.knowledgecommission.gov.in/.

———. 2014. *The Constitution (Schedule Castes) Orders (Amendment Act) NO. 34 OF 2014*. Retrieved on 27 April 2015.

Goyal, Saumya and Sangya Shrivastava. October 2012–March 2013. 'Perception of Organizational Diversity Climate: A Study Of Indian IT Professionals'. *Cyber Times International Journal of Technology & Management* 6(1): 1–12. Retrieved on 30 June 2015.

———. March 2013. 'Role of Diversity Climate on Employee Satisfaction and Intent to Leave in Indian IT Personnel'. *International Journal of Management and Social Sciences Research (IJMSSR)* 2(3): 5–10. Retrieved on 30 June 2015.

Granovetter, Mark. 1973. 'The Strength of Weak Ties'. *American Journal of Sociology* 78: 1360–380.

Hamm, Steve. 2007. *Bangalore Tiger: How Indian Tech Upstart Wipro is Rewriting the Rules of Global Competition*. New York, NY: The McGraw-Hill Companies.

Hasan, Zoya and Martha C. Nussbaum (eds). 2012. *Equalizing Access: Affirmative Action in Higher Education in India, United States, and South Africa*. New Delhi: Oxford University Press.

Haub, Carl. 2011. 'The Caste Census: A Feudal Classification of Society in India'. Posted in *Population Basics, Race Ethnicity*. Washington, DC: Population Reference Bureau.

Hill, Catherine, Christianne Corbett, and Andresse St. Rose. 2010. 'Why So Few? Women in Science, Technology, Engineering, and Mathematics'. Washington, DC: American Association of University Women (AAUW). Available at: http://www.aauw.org/files/2013/02/Why-So-Few-Women-in-Science-Technology-Engineering-and-Mathematics.pdf.

Hinterlong, Diane, Branson Lawrence, and Purva DeVol. 2014. 'Increasing Interest of Young Women in Engineering'. *NCSSSMST Journal, National Consortium for Specialized Secondary Schools of Mathematics, Science & Technology* 20–25. Available at: http://files.eric.ed.gov/fulltext/EJ1045822.pdf.

Hunt, Jennifer. 2016. 'Why Do Women Leave Science And Engineering?'. *ILR Review* 69(1): 199–226.

Ilaiah, Kancha. 2009. *Post-Hindu India: A Discourse on Dalit-Bahujan, Socio-Spiritual and Scientific Revolution*. New Delhi: Sage Publications.

International Institute for Population Sciences (IIPS) and Macro International. 2007. *National Family Health Survey (NFHS-3), 2005–06*. India: IIPS.

Iyer, Lakshmi and Anandi Mani. 2012. 'Traveling Agents: Political Change and Bureaucratic Turnover in India'. *Review of Economics and Statistics* 94(3): 723–39. DOI: 10.1162/REST_a_00183.

Jayaraman, Anuja. 2013. 'A Demographic Overview'. In *State of the Urban Youth, India 2012*, UN HABITAT and IRIS Knowledge Foundation (ed.), pp. 7–14. Retrieved on 29 May 2015.

Jodhka, Surinder S. and Katherine S. Newman. 2010. 'In the Name of Globalization: Meritocracy, Productivity, and the Hidden Language of Caste'.

In *Blocked by Caste: Economic Discrimination in Modern India*, Sukhadeo Thorat and Katherine S. Newman (eds), pp. 53–87. New Delhi, India: Oxford University Press.

John, Sujit and Shilpa Phadnis. 2014. '6 Indian Cities Among Top Outsourcing Hubs'. *Times of India*. Gurgaon Haryana: Times Internet Limited, 23 January. Retrieved on 28 July 2017.

Joseph, K.J. 2009. 'IT Industry in India: Leading Software and Lagging Software'. In *Information Technology (IT) in The Indian Economy*, M.S. Bhatt and Asheref Illiyan (eds), pp. 3–21. New Delhi, India: New Century Publications.

Kaka, Noshir. 2009. 'Strengthening India's offshoring industry'. *McKinsey Quarterly*, August. Available at: https://www.mckinsey.com/business-functions/digital-mckinsey/our-insights/strengthening-indias-offshoring-industry. Retrieved on 25 October 2017.

Kaminsky, Arnold P. and Roger D. Long. 2011. *India Today: An Encyclopedia of Life in the Republic*. ABC-CLIO, pp. 403–404. Retrieved on 13 May 2015.

Kanter, Rosabeth Moss. 1977a. *Men and Women of the Corporation*. New York: Harper Collins.

———. 1977b. 'Some Effects of Proportions on Group Life: Skewed Sex Ratios and Responses to Token Women'. *The American Journal of Sociology* 82: 965–90.

Khanna, Anupam. 2013. 'India's IT/ITeS Industry: The Next Phase Non-Linear Growth & Broad-Based Innovation'. Knowledge-Based Capital Conference, OECD, Paris. 14 February. Available at: https://www.oecd.org/sti/ind/Khanna.pdf. Retrieved on 24 July 2015.

Krishna, Anirudh and Vijay Brihmadesam. 2006. 'What Does It Take to Become a Software Professional?' *Economic and Political Weekly* 41(30): 3307–14.

Laverty, Susann M. 2003. 'Hermeneutic Phenomenology and Phenomenology: A Comparison of Historical and Methodological Considerations'. *International Journal of Qualitative Methods* 2(3): 21–35.

Lin, Nan. 1999. 'Social Networks and Status Attainment'. *Annual Review of Sociology* 25: 467–87.

———. 2001. *Social Capital: A Theory of Social Structure and Action*. Cambridge, UK: Cambridge University Press.

Madheswaran, S. and Paul Attewell. 2010. 'Wage and Job Discrimination in the Indian Urban Labor Market'. In *Blocked by Caste: Economic Discrimination in Modern India*, Sukhadeo Thorat and Katherine S. Newman (eds), pp. 123–47. New Delhi, India: Oxford University Press.

Mahalingam, Ramaswami. 2003. 'Essentialism, Culture, and Power: Representations of Social Class'. *Journal of Social Issues* 59(4): 733–49.

Mandal Commission. 1980. *Report of the Backward Classes Commission*, Volumes I & II. New Delhi, India: Government of India.

Meena, Kavita and Sita Vanka. January 2013. 'Diversity Management and Human Resource Development—A Study of Indian Organizations'. *Pacific Business Review International* 5(7): 45–51. Retrieved on 30 June 2015.

Mills, J.E. 2011. 'Reflections on the Past, Present and Future of Women in Engineering'. Institution of Engineers Australia, *Australasian Journal of Engineering Education* 17(3): 139–46.

Mishra, Shiva. 2003. 'Funding by University Grants Commission'. Available at: http://ccs.in/internship_papers/2003/chap30.pdf. Retrieved on 1 June 2015.

Mohanty, Chandra. 2003. *Feminism without Borders: Decolonizing Theory, Practicing solidarity*. Durham, NC: Duke University Press.

Moorjani, Priya, Kumarasamy Thangaraj, Nick Patterson, Mark Lipson, Po-Ru Loh, Periyasamy Govindaraj, Bonnie Berger, David Reich, and Lalji Singh. 2013. 'Genetic Evidence for Recent Population Mixture in India'. *The American Journal of Human Genetics* 93(3): 422–38. September.

Nadeem, Shehzad. 2009. 'Macaulay's (Cyber) Children: The Cultural Implication of Offshoring to India'. *Cultural Sociology* 3(1): 102–22.

Nambissan, Geetha B. 2010. 'Exclusion and Discrimination in Schools: Experiences of Dalit Children'. In *Blocked by Caste: Economic Discrimination in Modern India*, Sukhadeo Thorat and Katherine S. Newman (eds), pp. 253–86. New Delhi, India: Oxford University Press.

NASSCOM. 2008. 'IT_Industry_Factsheet_May_2008'. Available at: http://www.nasscom.in/upload/5216/. Retrieved on 15 July 2008.

Parikh, P.P. and S.P. Sukhatme. 2004. 'Women Engineers in India'. *Economic and Political Weekly* 39(2): 193–201. 10–16 January.

Parthasarathy, D. 2012. 'After Reservations: Caste, Institutional Isomorphism, and Affirmative Action in the IITs'. In *Equalizing Access: Affirmative Action in Higher Education in India, United States, and South Africa*, Zoya Hasan and Martha C. Nussbaum (eds), pp. 256–71. New Delhi, India: Oxford University Press.

Patnaik, Prabhat. 2012. 'Affirmative Action and the "Efficiency Argument"'. In *Equalizing Access: Affirmative Action in Higher Education in India, United States, and South Africa*, Zoya Hasan and Martha C. Nussbaum (eds), pp. 89–99. New Delhi, India: Oxford University Press.

Powers, Charles H. 2010. *Making Sense of Social Theory: A Practical Introduction*. Second Edition. Plymouth, UK: Rowman & Littlefield Publishers, Inc.

Pratto, Felicia, Jim Sidanius, Lisa M Stallworth, and Bertram F. Malle. 1994. 'Social Dominance Orientation: A Personality Variable Predicting Social and Political Attitudes'. *Journal of Personality and Social Psychology* 67(4): 741–63. Available at: http://dx.doi.org/10.1037/0022-3514.67.4.741.

Radhakrishnan, Smitha. 2007. 'Rethinking Knowledge for Development: Transnational Knowledge Professionals and the "New" India'. *Theory and Society* 36(2): 141–59.

Radhakrishnan, Smitha. 2009. 'Professional Women, Good Families: Respectable Femininity and the Cultural Politics of a "New India"'. *Qualitative Sociology* 32(2): 195–212.

———. 2011. *Appropriately Indian: Gender and Culture in a New Transnational Class.* Durham, NC: Duke University Press.

Raghunath, Nilanjan. 2010. 'The Indian IT Industry and Meritocracy'. *ARI (Asia Research Institute) Working Paper Series.* No 140.

Rai, Sheela. 2002. 'Social and Conceptual Background to the Policy of Reservation'. *Economic and Political Weekly* 37(42): 4309–11, 4313–4318. 19–25 October.

Rajesh, Saundarya and Karthik Ekambaram. 2014. 'Generational Diversity in the Indian Workforce: An Exploratory Study'. *International Journal of Managerial Studies and Research (IJMSR)* 2(7): 54–64, August. Available at: *www.arcjournals.org.* Retrieved on 30 June 2015.

Rajashekar, V.T. 2002. *Caste: A Nation within the Nation.* Bangalore: Koshy Mathew for Books for Change (A unit of Action Aid Karnataka Projects).

Ranganathan, C. and Iván Alfaro. 2011. 'Project Performance in Global Software Development Teams: Do Prior Work Ties and Nationality Diversity Matter?' *European Conference on Information Systems.* Association for Information Systems AIS Electronic Library (AISeL), 10 June. Retrieved on 30 June 2015.

Rao, Shreelatha R. and M.M. Bagali. 2014a. 'A Comparative Study on Acceptance of Cultural Diversity and Gender Diversity among Employees in IT Industry, Bangalore'. *International Journal of Business and Administration Research Review* 1(2): 98–109. November–January. Retrieved on 30 June 2015.

———. 2014b. 'Workforce Diversity and Management: An Empirical Study on Relationship Between Diversity Management Practices, Obstacles and Acceptance of Gender Diversity among Employees in IT Industry; Bangalore'. *Journal of Business and Management* 16(2): 12–25. February.

Reich, Robert B. 1991. *The Work of Nations: Preparing Ourselves for 21st Century Capitalism.* New York: A.A. Knopf.

Remesh, Babu P. 2009. 'Economic Upgrading in India's IT/IT-Enabled and BPO Sectors'. In *Information Technology (IT) in The Indian Economy*, M.S. Bhatt and Asheref Illiyan (eds), pp. 22–44. New Delhi, India: New Century Publications.

Richardson, Henry S. 2012. 'On the Sites of Remedial Justice: Colleges, Clinics, and the State'. In *Equalizing Access: Affirmative Action in Higher Education in India, United States, and South Africa*, Zoya Hasan and Martha Nussbaum (eds), pp. 1–43. New Delhi: Oxford University Press.

Sachar, Rajindar. 2006. *Sachar Committee Report (2004-2005).* Government of India. Retrieved on 27 April 2015.

Sahoo, P. K. and Rajnandan Patnaik. 2009. 'Emergence and Growth of the Indian Software Industry: A Strategic Study'. *IUP Journal of Business Strategy the IUP Journal of Business Strategy* VI (3 & 4): 81–94. September and December.

Saikia, Rajlakshmi. 2012. 'Diversity & Inclusion is Beyond Gender'. *People Matters*. 4 January. Available at: https://www.peoplematters.in/article/employee-engagement/its-beyond-gender-1443.

Sangeetha, B.K. 2009. 'Students Favour National Unified Test'. *Deccan Herald*, 2 November.

Sassen, Saskia. 2000. 'Spatialities and Temporalities of the Global: Elements for a Theorization'. *Public Culture* 12(1): 215–32.

Sen, Amartya. 2000. 'Social Exclusion: Concept, Application, and Scrutiny'. *Social Development Papers No. 1. Office of Environment and Social Development Asian Development Bank.* June. Available at: http://www.adb.org/sites/default/files/publication/29778/social-exclusion.pdf. Retrieved on 27 July 2015.

———. 2009. 'Behind the Differential Reach of Primary Education'. *The Hindu.* 19 December. Available at: http://www.thehindu.com/opinion/op-ed/Behind-the-differential-reach-of-primary-education/article16854206.ece.

Sethi, Atul and A. Divya. 2010. 'A Gene Called Caste'. *Times of India*, 16 May.

Shenoy-Packer, Suchitra. 2014. *India's Working Women and Career Discourses: Society, Socialization and Agency.* London: Lexington Books.

Sinha, Vinita and K.S. Subramanian. 2013. 'Accreditation in India: Path of Achieving Educational Excellence'. *Business Education & Accreditation* 5(2): 107–16.

Srinivas, M.N. 1976. *The Remembered Village.* Berkeley: University of California Press.

Stiglitz, Joseph E. 2003. *Globalization and Its Discontents.* New York: W.W. Norton & Company.

———. 2007. *Making Globalization Work.* New York: W.W. Norton & Company.

Suriya, M. Dr, and R. Nagarajan. 2004. 'Gender Democracy in Digital Economy: An Indian Experience'. *IADIS International Conference e-Society 2004*, 71–78. Available at: http://unpan1.un.org/intradoc/groups/public/documents/apcity/unpan038255.pdf.

Thorat, Sukhadeo. 2008. 'Labour Market Discrimination: Concept, Forms, and Remedies in the Indian Situation'. *Indian Journal of Labour Economics* 51(1): 31–52. January–March.

Thorat, Sukhadeo and Joel Lee. 2010. 'Food Security Schemes and Caste Discrimination'. In *Blocked by Caste: Economic Discrimination in Modern India,* Sukhadeo Thorat and Katherine S. Newman (eds), pp. 287–307. New Delhi, India: Oxford University Press.

Thorat, Sukhadeo and Katherine S. Newman (eds). 2010a. *Blocked by Caste: Economic Discrimination in Modern India.* New Delhi, India: Oxford University Press.

Thorat, Sukhadeo and Katherine S. Newman. 2010b. 'Introduction: Economic Discrimination Concept, Consequences, and Remedies'. In *Blocked by Caste: Economic Discrimination in Modern India*, Sukhadeo Thorat and Katherine S. Newman (eds), pp. 1–31. New Delhi, India: Oxford University Press.

Thorat, Sukhadeo, M. Mahamallik, and Nidhi Sadana. 2010. 'Caste System and Patterns of Discrimination in Rural Market'. In *Blocked by Caste: Economic Discrimination in Modern India*, Sukhadeo Thorat and Katherine S. Newman (eds), pp. 148–76. New Delhi, India: Oxford University Press.

Thorat, Sukhadeo and Paul Attewell. 2010. 'The Legacy of Social Exclusion: A Correspondence Study of Job Discrimination in India's Urban Private Sector'. In *Blocked by Caste: Economic Discrimination in Modern India*, Sukhadeo Thorat and Katherine S. Newman (eds), pp. 35–51. New Delhi, India: Oxford University Press.

University Grants Commission. 2012. *HIGHER EDUCATION IN INDIA: Strategies and Schemes during Eleventh Plan Period (2007–2012) for Universities and Colleges*. New Delhi, India. Retrieved on 29 May 2015.

Upadhya, Carol. 2007a. 'Employment, Exclusion and "Merit" in the Indian IT Industry'. *Economic and Political Weekly* 42(20): 1863–68. 19–25 May.

———. 2007b. 'Management Culture and Managing Through Culture in the Indian Software Software Outsourcing Industry'. In *In an Outpost of the Global Economy: Work and Workers in India's Information Technology Industry*, Carol Upadhya and A.R. Vasavi (eds), pp. 101–135. New Delhi: Routledge Press.

Upadhya, Carol and A.R. Vasavi. 2006. 'Work, Culture and Sociality in the Indian Information Technology (IT) Industry: A Sociological Study' (Project Report). National Institute of Advanced Studies, Bangalore.

van Manen, M. 1997. *Researching Lived Experience: Human Science for an Action Sensitive Pedagogy* (2nd edition). London, Canada: The Althouse Press.

Viswanath, Subrahmanyan. 2009. '16 new rural BPO centres to dot Karnataka's districts'. *Deccan Herald*, 3 December. Available at: http://www.deccanherald.com/content/39318/16-rural-bpo-centres-dot.html. Retrieved on 27 October 2017.

Whitley Jr., Bernard E. 1999. 'Right-Wing Authoritarianism, Social Dominance Orientation, and Prejudice'. *Journal of Personality and Social Psychology* 77(1): 126–34. July. DOI: 10.1037/0022-3514.77.1.126.

Williams, K.Y. and C.A. O'Reilly. 1998. 'Demography and Diversity in Organizations'. In *Research in Organizational Behavior*, Vol. 20, B.M. Staw and R.M. Sutton (eds), pp. 77–140. Stanford, CT: JAI Press.

Index

About the Author

Marilyn Fernandez is professor of sociology at Santa Clara University, California, USA. Her research interests include diversity, inequality, and organizational change. Some of her books include *Modernity, Contraception, or Both? Determinants of Fertility in Kerala, India* (1985), *Altered Lives, Enduring Community: Japanese Americans Remember Their World War II Incarceration*, co-authored with Professor Stephen Fugita (2004), and *Restorative Justice for Domestic Violence Victims: An Integrated Approach to Their Hunger for Healing* (2010). Her works have also appeared in *Administration and Society, Sociological Inquiry, Sociological Perspectives, International Migration Review, Journal of Applied Sociology, Journal of Asian American Studies, Asian American Policy Review, Journal of Sociology & Social Welfare, Women & Criminal Justice*, and *Journal of Interpersonal Violence*. She teaches courses in survey research and statistical analyses, population studies, human services, and directs research capstone courses. She is a former vice-president of the Pacific Sociological Association and former co-editor (with Charles Powers) of the journal *Sociological Perspectives*. Marilyn loves teaching research methodology and writing about evidence-based transformations in organizations and communities.